SENSITIVITY TRAINING
AND THE LABORATORY APPROACH

Third Edition

F. E. PEACOCK PUBLISHERS, INC., ITASCA, ILLINOIS

Third Edition

sensitivity training and the laboratory approach

readings about concepts and applications

edited by
robert t. golembiewski University of Georgia
arthur blumberg Syracuse University

CONTENTS

PREFACE TO THE THIRD EDITION

The first edition of this volume was published at a time when the "group movement" was approaching a popular peak. It seemed as though everyone either had been in a sensitivity training group or was planning to go to one. By the time the second edition was published (mid-1973), much of the notoriety and some of the popularized mystique that attached to T-Groups appeared to have faded. This fading was indicated in the selections that appeared in the second edition, mostly through the addition of papers in the applications section.

The third edition reflects both the stabilization of the field and its continuing concern with theory development, applications and research. This volume, then, builds on the theme of the previous two: change within constancy. Over half of the selections are new, not simply for the sake of newness, we trust, but as an indication that the field is building on its own history—looking backward as it looks forward.

A final note is in order. As we reviewed the literature, we were struck by its increasing abundance and the fact that articles devoted to research and practice in laboratory education had appeared and continued to appear in a wide variety of professional journals. Judging from the literature, the laboratory approach to learning about individual, group and organizational behavior and change appears clearly to be established as a useful and respectable methodology in a wide variety of settings.

Arthur Blumberg   Robert T. Golembiewski
Syracuse University   *University of Georgia*

PREFACE TO THE FIRST EDITION

This collection of readings is one reflection of a collaboration that has extended over the years, and our fondest hope is that the reader will find the volume to be as fulfilling and rewarding at its own level as our collaboration has been to us at another level. We tether our exuberance in two senses. More realistically, we trust that this collection will at least prove useful to those interested in the more effective use of human resources. More specifically, we intend this book of readings for diverse readers, but hardly for all. College students should find the volume useful, for example, as should those undergoing a laboratory experience. The book also should be useful for a variety of other populations, such as managers in a business or government organization which is investing its resources in laboratory training.

The "laboratory approach" is a significant point of departure to improving the quality of human life, a conclusion suggested by the explosive growth of interest in it. But the research and instructional literatures have limped somewhat behind. These two facts motivate this volume, which is our way of providing some direction to an energetically developing area without setting rigid categories which accumulating experience may prove to be false or unwieldy. In a very real sense, then, this first edition is a book in-process. If there ever were such a thing as an organic book, consequently, this volume should be it. Developments in the laboratory approach have come thick and fast, and these must be channelled but not at the expense of prematurely closing significant options.

This book is a collaborative effort about a major approach to social collaboration. This collaboration is multifaceted at both the intellectual and interpersonal levels. Our deepest debts are to the authors and publishers of the works reprinted below. More specifically, we thank Mr. Jack Rabin for his research assistance. Mrs. Jackie Hall and Sigrid Sanders provided the critical typing and stenographic services.

INTRODUCTION

This volume has four major emphases which are identified in its title and deserve highlighting here. The title directs general attention to the laboratory approach, sensitivity training, concepts, and applications. Specifically, that is, this book attempts to describe and analyze

- A basic learning strategy, the "laboratory approach" or "sensitivity training";
- Various learning vehicles and designs that constitute the laboratory approach, such as the T-Group;
- Concepts that theoretically relate processes and outcomes that are induced by the laboratory approach; and
- The variety of ways in which the laboratory approach can be applied in the office, school, home, or wherever.

The "laboratory approach" constitutes the broad ball park of this effort, although the term "sensitivity training" is used below in much the same sense. We give immediate attention to the former notion, thereby also providing some content for the latter. There is no simple and direct way to comprehensively define the term, for the "laboratory approach" is a very complex something. While acknowledging the difficulties, it is still possible to stake out some boundaries for the notion. As Schein and Bennis see the "laboratory approach," for example, it is " . . . an educational strategy which is based primarily on the experiences generated in various social encounters *by the learners themselves,* and which aims to influence attitudes and develop competencies toward learning about human interactions. Essentially, therefore, laboratory training attempts to induce changes with regard to the learning process itself and to communicate a particular method of learning and inquiry. It has to do with 'learning how to learn.' "[1] Without stretching a point then, the laboratory approach amounts to nothing less (and nothing more) than a revolution in ways of looking at how people learn.

The laboratory approach uses a variety of ways and means of getting at experimental learning. The "T-Group" is the best-known vehicle in this repertoire. It involves a small group of people intent on exploring their own interpersonal and group relations with the help of a trainer. There are, however, diverse ways of inducing similar learning processes. For example, these other vehicles for experiential learning include "confrontation designs," "third-party interceptions," and a host of other spin-offs of the T-Group and its underlying processes. In a significant sense, the T-Group is a kind of ideal learning environment, then. Its properties can be diversely approximated but often cannot be, or need to be, duplicated in the world outside of the sensitivity training laboratory.

Describing what processes and outcomes the laboratory approach does induce is even more difficult than illustrating the diverse forms which its learning environments do take. For example, "feedback" is one of the basic processes that is induced in unusually direct form in the T-Group. Narrowly, feedback processes involve the ways in which people learn about the impact they are having on others. Broadly, but still validly, feedback processes touch the very heart of how people come to be what they are. Put otherwise, feedback processes are basic in human development and change.

The brief description above of feedback, and of its diverse human relevance and significance, in effect, drive home a significant point about the fullness of the laboratory approach. Let us make explicit what that description implies. Without gilding the lily, we know both practically and theoretically that feedback processes are significant. How feedback processes can be made more effective is one of the significant learnings to which the laboratory approach can contribute. Cognitive knowledge, as it were, can mother applied inventions. Perhaps of even greater significance, the laboratory approach can also demonstrate to people how much they depend on the quality and quantity of their feedback. In turn, such a personal insight reinforces the need to develop appropriate attitudes and better skills for giving and receiving feedback. These attitudes and skills are critical in determining the quality of one's interpersonal and group experiences; and their development is a difficult as well as a precious thing. This significance and difficulty both suggest the formidable nature of the task to which the laboratory approach seeks to contribute.

The sketch above of the approaches to feedback in the laboratory approach touches the vitals of this collection of readings. The illustrated

---

[1] Edgar H. Schein and Warren G. Bennis, *Personal and Organizational Change Through Group Methods: The Laboratory Approach* (New York: John Wiley & Sons, Inc., 1965), p. 4.

association of cognitive knowledge, personal insight based on experience, and the development of appropriate attitudes and behavioral skills appears prominently throughout this volume, in fact. That is, the title of this book might identify the following four emphases just as well as those introduced above: cognitive knowledge, personal insight, attitudes, and skills.

Finally, the "what" and the "how" of the laboratory approach must be applied "somewhere" to be of maximum value. Hence the concluding emphasis of this volume is on the variations of the laboratory approach that have been used to augment knowledge or increase insight about interpersonal and intergroup relations in the wide variety of situations in which people find themselves daily. Whatever the laboratory approach helps us to learn, that is, its ultimate payoff inheres in whether or not it improves the quality of life of the learner and of those inside his lifespace. Indeed, it is just such improvement in the quality of life in groups, large and small, to which this book is dedicated. To paraphrase Kurt Lewin, a scientifically good approach is one that helps us know what we can realistically aspire to and how we can achieve it.

I. WHAT IS A T-GROUP?

Descriptions and Reactions

INTRODUCTION

I. What Is a T-Group?
Descriptions and Reactions

1. Arthur Blumberg, "Laboratory Education and Sensitivity Training"
2. C. M. Hampden-Turner, "An Existential 'Learning Theory' and the Integration of T-Group Research"
3. Paul C. Buchanan and Jerome Reisel, "Differentiating Human Relations Training Laboratories"
4. Morton A. Lieberman, "Up the Right Mountain, Down the Wrong Path —Theory Development for People-Changing Groups"

This introductory chapter has a number of targets, which are best identified now, if only in general. First, some broad historical perspective will be given to the "T-Group movement." Second, several major characteristics of the T-Group will be described. And finally, attention will be directed at a number of things that do not characterize the T-Group, but which are nonetheless sometimes associated with it. These skeletal comments will provide an introductory orientation, and they also will serve to introduce four selections reprinted below which will provide help in answering the question: What is a T-Group?

HOW DID THE "T-GROUP MOVEMENT" DEVELOP? A MINI-HISTORY

Our brief history of the T-Groups begins with a global summary, and works backwards. As for the global summary, the learning experience known as sensitivity training is rather firmly implanted in mid-20th century American life. Testimony to this point can be obtained from a variety of sources.

Several thousand people each year, for example, take part in sensitivity training laboratories conducted by the NTL Institute for Applied Behavioral Science alone. Many companies and governmental agencies also incorporate T-Group training in their management development programs. Moreover, laboratory experiences for educational administrators and teachers, for community leaders coping with physical renewal or rapprochement between the races, or whatever, are becoming increasingly common at all levels. In addition, T-Group courses may be found in a growing number of college and university programs, and research dealing with sensitivity training is more and more finding its way into behavioral science journals.

Reasons for this expanded involvement with T-Groups by individuals and organizations from the entire spectrum of interests and professions are not all clear. Consider only the diverse motivations of those who take part. Some individuals go to a "lab" because they have heard that, by participating, a person can get "turned on." For others, it is a matter of learning more about one's own behavior, the behavior of others, and the dynamics of group interaction. Organizations invest their financial and personel resources because they see sensitivity training as a way of enhancing the personal development of their managers and, hopefully, establishing a base for developing better communications and greater problem-solving capabilities. And these only illustrate the diverse range of motivations for interest in T-Groups.

Despite this expanded interest and involvement, and even given the spate of articles about T-Groups that have appeared in the popular press, efforts to communicate in a clear conceptual way about the T-Group experience have not been particularly successful. Two factors are primarily responsible for this lack of success. First, though a T-Group experience is an educational one, it is unlike any previous encounter that most people have had in an educational setting. The teacher does not "teach" in any traditional sense of the word. Rather, he helps people learn by almost assuming a nonteacher role, which tends to be initially upsetting and confusing for many people. Second, the nature of the learning, deriving from the role of the teacher (trainer), has a heavy emotional loading. This emotionality, which is intended, makes it difficult for people to express in intellectual terms that which they have experienced. Typical responses of T-Group participants when queried about what happened to them reflect both significant impact and difficulty of defining it. These are sample descriptions:

- "It's hard to describe. You'll have to go yourself and find out."
- "I can't really tell you. But I sure learned a lot about myself."
- "The trainer just sat there. But it worked."
- "It was an unforgettable experience, but I can't talk too much about it."

Such reactions do not help much in reducing ambiguity. Quite the contrary, one of their prime consequences is the buildup of a certain mystique about the whole subject. It is a bit like a man trying to understand the pain and joy a woman says she experiences when giving birth to a baby. It is hard to understand without the experience, and perhaps even incredible.

This section seeks to clarify just what a T-Group is, then, with the hope that the reader will be able to communicate, on an intellectual level, about some of the concepts involved in the T-Group process. This goal is stated with a major reservation: Even if this presentation is clear and unambiguous, in the final analysis to really know T-Groups requires experiencing them.

A brief bit of history is needed here in order to make sense of major developmental features of the use of T-Groups in learning.[1] First, it is necessary to understand that the idea of creating something called a T-Group experience did not come about in a deliberate, planned way. The discovery of the potential of the T-Group as a learning vehicle was accidental—analogous, in a way, to the manner in which Goodyear discovered the process for vulcanizing rubber. As for the T-Group, the fortuitous discovery can be dated and located precisely: 1946 in Connecticut at an intergroup relations workshop. The workshop was staffed by social scientists. During one staff planning meeting, participants were invited to observe the staff group in operation and, at the end of the meeting, to feed back to the staff their observation about what had transpired, both on an individual and group level. The learning results of this small experience were stimulating and exciting. Some of the staff were thus motivated to develop theoretical reasons for what had occurred, as well as to begin planning how similar learning situations could be promoted for a wider audience. Out of this planning came the establishment of the National Training Laboratory for Group Development[2]—NTL[3]—which sponsored the first formal program in sensitivity training held in Bethel, Maine, during the summer of 1947.

The development of both NTL and the concept of sensitivity training since 1947 has been rapid. Today, with headquarters in Arlington, Va., NTL is a nonprofit organization with a central office staff numbering about 15 full-time professionals, most of whom have advanced degrees in one of the behavioral sciences. It conducts a year-round program of training and research. Perhaps its most unique organizational characteristic is its network of members. The network is comprised of about 150 professionals. They are based mostly in universities, and it is to these professionals that the central office looks to provide staff for the proliferating laboratory enterprises in

---

[1] For a more complete documentation, see Leland P. Bradford, Jack R. Gibb, and Kenneth Benne (eds.), *T-Group Theory and Laboratory Method: Innovation in Re-Education* (New York: John Wiley & Sons, Inc., 1964).

[2] It is important to note the "group development" emphasis. That is, early T-Group experiences were focused more on group processes and development than they were on individual behavior and sensitivity.

[3] NTL functioned at first, as a part of the Adult Education Division of the National Education Association. In 1966, its name was changed to the NTL Institute for Applied Behavioral Science.

which NTL is involved. In order to maintain and enhance the competencies of the network, membership is not easily achieved. Candidates are selected from social scientists, usually with a Ph.D., and participate in an internship program which lasts over a year.

The NTL Institute has no monopoly on conducting T-Group experiences. Indeed, a goodly number of organizations, some reputable and some not, have sprung up. They offer, in one fashion or another, programs that incorporate goals similar to those of NTL. This diversity is both a boon and a bane, and care is advised in selecting a program or a consultant for sensitivity training.

So much for history, and on to matters of substance. The remainder of this chapter will focus on a few key T-Group concepts, and on a few common misconceptions about the technique.

WHAT THE T-GROUP IS:
THREE DISTINGUISHING FEATURES

Let us make a start toward explicating what the T-Group is and what it does. The start involves distinguishing three features of the laboratory approach. The major distinguishing features of the T-Group are these: it is a learning laboratory; it focuses on learning how to learn; and it distinctively does so via a "here-and-now" emphasis on immediate ideas, feelings, and reactions.

A. The Concept of the T-Group as a Learning Laboratory

Central to the learning potential of the T-Group experience is the concept of its being a laboratory. But it is not a laboratory in the usual sense of the word. There are no test tubes, and even psychological measuring instruments are not usually used directly as part of the T-Group experience. Rather, the T-Group is a laboratory in a variety of other senses. Five deserve special emphasis.

- It is an experience in creating a miniature society.
- It is oriented toward working with processes that emphasize inquiry, exploration, and experimentation with behavior.
- It is oriented toward helping its members to learn.
- It is oriented toward developing a psychologically safe atmosphere that facilitates learning.
- What is to be learned is largely determined by its members, although a professional "trainer" is usually available to provide guidance.

The T-Group is a unique organization in many senses, then, but it is not "artificial." What happens in a T-Group really happens, although it happens under controlled conditions that may be very different from those normally encountered in life.

Arthur Blumberg provides elaboration of the skeletal description above in

"Laboratory Education and Sensitivity Training." Basically, he seeks to distinguish a genus from one of its species, the broader laboratory approach from one of its specific learning designs, sensitivity training or T-Grouping, Blumberg also emphasizes the conditions which the laboratory approach seeks to generate, as well as the values which guide its applications.

Conveniently, one facet of Blumberg's contribution can be developed here, by way of illustrating its thrust. One of the goals of sensitivity training is to help people examine their typical modes of behavior, in a psychologically safe atmosphere, to permit them to test whether their interaction with others is coming across as intended. One way in which this testing can take place is to experiment with one's behavior—to do and say things differently—and get feedback from other group members concerning its impact on them. For example, a person whose customary style is to be very active and talk a lot may choose to be quiet for awhile. He can observe the effects of his silence upon himself and others, get feedback from them concerning how his behavior affected them, and reflect on his own feelings about being quiet. Or, conversely, the typically quiet person can experiment with trying to be assertive and influential. In these various senses, then, the concept of learning laboratory is an apt description of a T-Group.

Regardless of the particular behavior tried, the point is the same. The laboratory for learning has great potential for providing what the real world denies. Most people pass through their day-to-day life being only dimly aware of their behavioral style and how it affects others. The world of work does not, as a rule, sanction discussion of such questions as: "How do you react to what I do?" The T-Group, on the other hand, because it is a behavioral laboratory, not only sanctions but encourages such discussion. And just such questions are nagging ones for many people.

Regardless of the kind of developmental history that specific T-Groups have, moreover, their prime goal is *not* making people change. Rather, the goal is to provide feedback and support for testing whether change will help the individual get more of what he wants in interpersonal and intergroup relations.

B. The Concept of Learning How To Learn

At first, the notion of "learning how to learn" seems nonsensical. After all, haven't we all been to school? And what else does one do in school except learn? Indeed, we do learn things in school. We also learn how to learn in a particular way. Primarily, for most of us, that way involves learning those things we have been told to learn from a lecture or a book. In far too many cases, it almost seems that learning was equated with memorizing.

"Learning how to learn" in the T-Group context has implications that extend far beyond those that are usually associated with education. Three ideas are central to this concept. First of all, T-Groups have an inductive orientation. This is at odds with much of our previous educational experience, particularly in higher education. Most T-Group participants have to learn that they can also really learn in a setting where the only real answers are provided by themselves and not the authority figure.

Second, what is to be learned in T-Groups is not at all clear, at least at the outset, for most group members. Though most participants have vague notions about increasing their sensitivity and awareness, they are seldom clear about the means by which these notions can lead to productive learning. Part of learning how to learn in a T-Group, then, is concerned with the development of a relatively high tolerance for ambiguity. For the situation *is* ambiguous, and particularly in its early stages. If a participant does not allow himself to be open to his experience he will cut off his opportunity to learn.

A third component of the "learning how to learn" concept involves the relationship of one's peers to one's own learning. Again, relating back to formal schooling, the teacher is the teacher is the teacher. In a T-Group, the teacher is any member of the group who can provide data for learning.

The multiple teachers in a T-Group expand the resources available to the learner, but they also create some real problems. For many people, for example, the idea of viewing one's peers as potential teachers is not an easy one to accept. It runs contrary to previous learning experiences which, in a way, have taught us to devalue the worth of our peers as far as their contribution to our learning is concerned. The attitude to be overcome in a sensitivity training experience is, "we are all equally ignorant, so how can he help me?" In contrast, "he" is the only expert about some matters that really count to others, "his" reactions and feelings toward "them." There are, of course, many areas in which "he" is not expert. These must also be recognized to exploit the real potential for learning available through others.

Arthur Blumberg provides broad perspective on how the T-Group variously helps its members to learn in the selection "Laboratory Education and Sensitivity Training." Blumberg relies upon Bennis, among others. Bennis explains that the specific way to learn that is unique to the T-Group has several major features. He notes that

- T-Groups work toward an expanded consciousness and a wider recognition of available choices.
- T-Groups embody a spirit of inquiry.
- T-Groups stress authenticity in interpersonal relations, of knowing what you are and how you feel, as a condition for being what you are and what you feel.
- T-Groups imply a collaborative concept of authority.

Contrary approaches to learning abound. The traditional authoritarian schoolroom, for example, negates each of these features of how T-Groups help one to learn how to learn. Sometimes such negations are useful. But they are probably much overused and, more significantly, the T-Group establishes that there are other ways to learn some things of real importance.

C. The Concept of the "Here-And-Now"

Basic to the notion of learning how to learn in a T-Group is that the information which is the grist for the learning mill is rooted in "here-and-now" phenomena and not in the "there-and-then." In other words, the basic focus is on what is happening at the moment, and not on something that happened a year or a decade ago. This focus frequently induces a good bit of frustration in the early stages of T-Group development. Again, it runs contrary to the previous learning experiences that most people have had. These previous learning experiences have usually been oriented toward what somebody else has said, done, or written outside of the immediate learning situation. The frustration tends to get verbalized in comments like, "How can we learn anything without referring to something else? Let's pick a problem, talk about it, and then analyze what we did."

Spencer Klaw[4] massively documented this fixation on here-and-now phenomena. Klaw observed the full life cycle of a group, and provided a richly detailed tapestry of how both trainer and members serve to channel comments in the direction of the unique expertise of each individual, what he is feeling and thinking, and how he is reacting. Klaw is no fervent advocate of T-Groups, and wisely advised being cautious about those who claim to have been "saved" by a T-Group experience. But Klaw saw serious-minded men being helped and helping each other, and he wrote about what he saw. And this fact cannot be overlooked.

Klaw's conclusions were mixed, then. They were melancholy while optimistic. People need authentic human relations, perhaps even hunger for them, and a T-Group can provide that experience. Hence his optimism. How sad, however, that a T-Group is necessary. Klaw's concern thus was not basically about what is taught in a T-Group, or how it is taught, but that it must be taught at all, and to adults. The T-Group's impact, from this perspective, is a sign of the massive failure of existing institutions of socialization and learning. This is a melancholy thought, indeed, especially since T-Group participants tend to be those for whom previous learning opportunities have been particularly rich. For example, typical T-Group experiences attract a very high percentage of professional and college-educated participants.

WHAT THE T-GROUP IS NOT:
SOME ISSUES COMMONLY ASSOCIATED WITH IT

Like any relatively new and still evolving approach, the laboratory method has to be as careful of its friends as of its enemies. And it should be more careful of its overenthusiastic true believers than of the serious skeptics.

---

[4]Spencer Klaw, "Two Weeks in a T-Group," *Fortune Magazine* (August 1961), pp. 114-116, 150-160.

At best, ambiguities about what the technique is and does will exist. The purpose here is to begin reducing the ambiguity by focusing on one specific issue and then, globally, on a related set of issues.

A. Training or Therapy?

One critical point in the here-and-now emphasis deserves special note. Members of a T-Group really share one thing from which, given the goals of sensitivity training, they can learn. This is the current group experience of which they are a part. Thus the emphasis on what is happening and on how people are feeling "here-and-now." It is *this* experience and *this* behavior that is immediately relevant to the members of the group, not what has transpired previously. T-Group learnings can be transferred to other situations, of course, either on the behavioral or emotional level. Chapter V deals with the major issues involved in transfer.

The issue of training versus therapy is related to the here-and-now versus there-and-then focus. That is, a common criticism directed at sensitivity training argues that it amounts to practicing medicine without a license. T-Group trainers are alleged to be really engaged in psychotherapy, in seeking to explore the genesis of ideas and feelings and behavior. If the T-Group trainer and especially its members are there-and-then oriented in a clinical sense, goes this line of criticism, they can get dangerously beyond their capabilities and training. The consequences of amateur and perhaps unwanted psychiatric exploration of this kind are seen as unprofitable if not genuinely dangerous.

It is not hard to understand the reasons behind the criticism. Both training and therapy are oriented toward providing help, for example. In many respects, moreover, the methodology and the role of the trainer bear similarities to the methodology and to the role of the therapist in group therapy. In addition, T-Group interaction does have a heavy emotional tone, and it is very much concerned with the development of insight and sensitivity about self and others. Sometimes, the criticism that T-Groups are pseudo-therapy rests on careless semantics. If one equates "therapy" with helping someone to grow or change, for example, then T-Groups trainers are practicing therapy. But so are mothers and so is almost everyone else.

There are major differences between training and therapy, however, and some of the differences are rather clear-cut. First of all, a basic assumption of sensitivity training is that the participants are normal people who are not "sick." For example, NTL literature makes quite explicit that its programs are not therapy, and that they should not be considered as a substitute for therapy.[5] Second, as we have indicated, the emphasis in T-Groups is on

---

[5]Parenthetically, experience suggests that in most of the small number of cases in which a person has "broken down" during T-Group training the individual had a previous psychiatric history and, not infrequently, had been sent to a laboratory to "get better."

here-and-now phenomena and *not* on matters that are psychodynamically oriented. For example, if member A in a T-Group is reacting negatively to what he perceives to be paternalistic behavior on the part of member B, he should be open with his feelings about the behavior of the other. The perception is not a platform to launch an autobiographical discussion about B's relationships with his father, or about the pathology these relationships may or may not have engendered. A judgment is always required in such cases, but the usual convention is clear. This latter discussion would typically be ruled out-of-bounds by the trainer, especially early in the history of a T-Group.

In a negative sense, the considerations above come to a distinct point which must be unequivocally made. There is a distinct qualitative difference between a T-Group and a therapy group. It is to the best interest of those involved in sensitivity training—both the professionals and the participants —that this difference be respected and maintained.

The differences between training and therapy can also be suggested in a positive way. C. M. Hampden-Turner's "An Existential 'Learning Theory' and the Integration of T-Group Research" provides such an approach. Hampden-Turner proposes a theory about learning in which the T-Group is seen as contributing to personal growth and development in three basic ways.

- The T-Group can improve an individual's *quality of cognition,* including his sensitivity to the needs of himself and others, his depth of understanding, and his capacity to develop alternative ways of gaining satisfaction.
- The T-Group can help a person *clarify his identity.*
- The T-Group can help a person increase his *self-esteem,* his acceptance of self and others.

Hampden-Turner includes these elements in a broader model, which he supports by a wide range of research. For our purposes, major significance is attached to such words above as "improve," "help clarify," and "increase" in descriptions of what T-Group training does. More extreme words would be appropriate to describe what therapy does, using the same three concepts above. "Establish his identity" or "get some notion of who he really is," for example, would be more appropriate therapeutic goals than "clarify his identity."

B. Some Related Misunderstandings About T-Groups

The recent development of the T-Group technology creates major problems in meaningfully describing it, as does the somewhat mystical quality which often surrounds the sensitivity training experience. Both factors, among others, encourage a number of misunderstandings about the goals and processes of the T-Group. Argyris[6] has noted a number of these

---

[6]Chris Argyris, "In Defense of Laboratory Education," *Training Directors Journal,* Vol. 17 (October, 1963), pp. 25-30.

misunderstandings. Their cataloguing here may help round out the frame of reference for the rest of this section, as well as for the entire book.

- Laboratory methods in general, and T-Groups in particular, are not a set of hidden, manipulative processes by which individuals can be "brainwashed" into thinking, believing, and feeling the way someone might want them to without realizing what is happening to them.
- A laboratory is not an educational process guided by a staff leader who is covertly in control and who by some magic hides this fact from the participants.
- The objective of laboratory education is not to suppress or induce conflict; and neither is it to get everyone to like one another, nor hate one another. Rather the focus is on understanding whatever does happen.
- Laboratory education does not attempt to teach people to be callous, disrespectful of society, and to dislike those who live a less open life. Rather the issue is how to make use of all group resources.
- Laboratory education is neither psychoanalysis nor intensive group therapy.
- Laboratory education does not have to be dangerous, but it must focus on feelings.
- The objective of laboratory education is to develop effective reality-centered leaders.
- Change is not guaranteed as a result of attending a T-Group.

The reader can make up his own mind about the validity of the list of conclusions above, as by complex cross-checking between sources provided in this volume. For example, Spencer Klaw's reactions, referred to earlier, must be weighed against critiques that will be introduced at various points below, critiques by both friendly observers and those who are overtly hostile. We have tried not to avoid the potentially embarrassing questions, although we had to be selective. We do want to encourage the reader to ask the hard questions about sensitivity training, for that is also our bias. We conclude that the benefits outweigh the costs, but costs there are.

Paul C. Buchanan and Jerome Reisel, in "Differentiating Human Relations Training Laboratories," provide an expanded perspective on the variety of laboratory education settings that have sprung from the early focus of learning about groups. Using the two dimensions of *participant mix* and *focus,* they describe six types of laboratories that are prevalent in the current scene. In addition, they point out the type of experience a participant is likely to encounter in one type of laboratory as opposed to another. For example, in a personal growth lab there will probably be continuing concern with fantasy experiences, whereas it is not likely that such concern will be evident in an organizational training lab. Thus, Buchanan and Reisel provide a service for the prospective laboratory participant by suggesting the variety of experiences that may be expected in one situation as different from another. In addition, their typology suggests criteria for laboratory evaluation studies of which the field is sorely in need, even though the volume of research in laboratory education has been increasing steadily.

The final selection in this chapter, "Up the Right Mountain, Down the Wrong Path—Theory Development for People-Changing Groups" by Morton

A. Lieberman, is a reflection of the increasingly fine tuning to which thought about T-Groups is being submitted. The article was written as a commentary on two proposals[7,8] to create a more scientific approach to the practice of laboratory education. While applauding the intent behind these proposals—one based on social learning theory and the second on psychotherapeutic theory—Lieberman concludes that they are both inadequate to the task of creating a practical theory of people-changing in groups. Such a theory must attend to certain focal questions that have been largely neglected. The focal questions, according to Lieberman, are concerned with to whom change is directed and for what purpose, what mechanisms apply to what person at what point in the group, what is the process of transferring learning from inside the group to the member's everyday life, and the limitations of leader influence on the group.

In concluding this introduction, we return to our earlier comment concerning the costs and benefits of sensitivity training. Our sense of the balance of benefits over costs can be sketched briefly.

When we talk about sensitivity training, we refer to a particular kind of educational experience that creates conditions that enable people to become more authentic as people—to be, perhaps, more honest with themselves and others, particularly in regard to their own sensitivity and awareness of the human environment in which they are interacting. The process is not manipulative, nor are its goals those of making everyone like or love everyone else. Because T-Groups deal, among other things, with the emotionality that attaches to behavior, situations do occur from time to time in a T-Group which are beyond a person's coping powers and during which he may suffer some kind of "break." But this is one of the risks of the situation, just as in many learning situations, and trainers are not unmindful of it. This puts the point too strongly for our tastes, in fact. If a T-Group situation is stressful enough to induce an individual to have a severe emotional disturbance, that individual's life space no doubt encompasses a large number of situations that would be equally stressful, or more so. And there are few better places to recognize the need for intensive therapy than in a well staffed sensitivity training laboratory. In our experience, indeed, it is the massive help and support available in the typical laboratory which allows some people to really recognize how aberrant their behavior is, or how distorted their perceptions are, and to actively seek therapy as a consequence. "I didn't believe the other executives when they talked about my gross misreadings of what they did and said," one T-Group alumnus noted, "because they were my competitors. But my T-Group buddies had no ax to grind. I was way off, they showed me."

---

[7]Michael Jay Diamond, "From Skinner to Satori? Toward a Social Learning Analysis of Encounter Group Behavior Change," *Journal of Applied Behavioral Science,* Vol. 10, No. 4 (1974), pp. 133-148.

[8]Richard L. Bednar, *et al.,* Empirical Guidelines for Group Therapy: Pretraining, Cohesion and Modeling," *Journal of Applied Behavioral Science,* Vol. 10, No. 4 (1974), pp. 148-165.

Sensitivity training is not the panacea for the ills of our time, then. It is, however, a powerful means of helping free individuals to become more of what and how they wish to be. In a more global sense, moreover, sensitivity training can help unshackle organizations from their stereotypic patterns of behavior, thereby contributing toward the search for more effective ways of interacting and solving problems.

Not everyone can learn in a T-Group, of course. Two issues are involved. The first is personality-oriented. Experience seems to indicate that those people whose needs for structure and authority are very high and rigid do not seem to find the experience of much worth.[9] It is simply too ambiguous for them, and too much at odds with their needs. This does not suggest that they are stupid or unworthy. It simply means that the barriers to their learning in a T-Group are too great. The second issue is one of voluntarism. People who are forced to go to a laboratory by their organization can be expected, in general, to have a less-productive experience. There is little need to elaborate on this point. People tend to learn best in situations to which they voluntarily expose themselves, and they tend to learn less when they resist the exposure.

This introduction to cost/benefit analysis with respect to the T-Group could be extended, but we trust our thrust is clear. Beyond this point, we encourage the reader to engage this volume in a dialogue about what the laboratory approach can do for him and for his specific life or work. The point of that dialogue is illustrated in an article by Donald Thomas and Thomas Smith, which is not reprinted here.[10] Thomas, a school superintendent, prepared a memorandum for his Board of Education in support of T-Group experiences for teachers and administrators. Smith, a school psychologist, reacted to the comments of Thomas. The critical issue he raised is: "What is the pay-off of such T-Grouping for boys and girls in a school?" It is toward helping frame and answer such critical questions that this book is directed.

---

[9]Roger Harrison, "Group Composition Models for Laboratory Design," *Journal of Applied Behavioral Science*, Vol. 1, No. 4 (1965), pp. 409-32.

[10]Donald Thomas and Thomas Smith, "T-Grouping: The White-Collar Hippie Movement," National Association of Secondary School Principals, *Bulletin* (February, 1968). pp. 1-9.

I. Laboratory Education and Sensitivity Training

ARTHUR BLUMBERG

The aim of this chapter will be to discuss and differentiate between the concepts of laboratory education and sensitivity training. As will be seen, the boundary lines between these concepts are not discreet. Frequently they are lumped together indiscriminately with the result, particularly for laymen, that adequate communication becomes difficult.

Laboratory education is the generic term. Essentially, laboratory education attempts to provide a learning environment centered upon personal, interpersonal, group, or organizational problems, in which the participants can learn and change through an inductive process based on experience. Thus the terminology "laboratory" derives from the notion that the learning environment is experimental to the extent that the participants are encouraged to experiment beyond their usual patterns of interacting with individuals and groups. In a very real sense then, the laboratory teaching-learning technology tends to be a polar opposite from that to which all of us have been exposed in our formal education. The critical learning issue in laboratory education is not the absorption and regurgitation of content, as is the case in most school and college classrooms. Quite the contrary, laboratory education puts the onus for learning on the individual to create through his own behavior and skills the kind of human situation from which he can learn what is meaningful for him.

This is not to say that laboratories are structureless, or that no skilled professional personnel are present as "teachers." In a way, there is a great deal of structure involved and the "teacher" is usually present. The difference is that the structure is very open and the role of the "teacher" (trainer) is at wide variance from our typical expectations about what a leader in a teacher-learning situation does. Instead of becoming a didactic conveyor of knowledge, the laboratory educator's role is to establish a collaborative helping relationship with the learners. It is through this relationship and that which develops among the group that the learner can acquire the understandings and skills appropriate to his interaction with other people, groups, and organizations.

Reprinted from Arthur Blumberg, *Sensitivity Training: Processes, Problems, and Applications* (Syracuse, N.Y.: Syracuse University Publications in Continuing Education, 1971), pp. 6-18.

The essential methodology of laboratory education is the creation, " . . . for the purposes of analysis and practice, (of) group situations where the same basic factors of individual and group relations are present as in the pressing problem situation of each person back home" (Bradford, 1953, p. 14). Thus, laboratory education presents the learner with an analogue of the interpersonal, group, or organizational system that he confronts in his daily life. The difference, of course, is that in a laboratory he is not "playing for keeps."

It can be seen from the foregoing that it is impossible to utilize the laboratory methodology for a variety of focused learning situations—and indeed this is the case. Laboratories are conducted which emphasize personal, interpersonal, group, and organizational life, the management of conflict, community development, labor negotiations, educational leadership, consultation skills, and so forth. It is important to note and reiterate that regardless of the focus of a laboratory, there is always continuous effort to deal with and analyze the process of what is going on as the substance is developing. Thus, a community development lab is apt to use itself as the developing community from which the participants can learn. Or, theory presentations in a conflict management lab are used as a basis from which the conflict present in *that* situation may be analyzed. Or, in a laboratory on consultation skills, where the participants may actually engage in live or role-played organizational consultation, the premium is on the learnings that come from the process more than the actual results—though these, too, are important.

Another and more detailed way to convey the underlying process orientation of laboratories is to consider a set of conditions for laboratory learning (*NTL Readings Book*) that it is important to meet in any of a variety of ways if training goals for participants are to be reached. These are:

Presentation of Self. Until the individual has an opportunity to reveal the way he sees things and does things, he has little basis for improvement and change.

Feedback. Individuals do not learn from their experiences. They learn from bringing out the essential patterns of purposes, motives, and behavior in a situation where they can receive back clear and accurate information about the relevancy and effectiveness of their behavior. They need a feedback system which continuously operates so that they can change and correct what is inappropriate.

Atmosphere. An atmosphere of trust and non-defensiveness is necessary for people both to be willing to expose their behavior and purposes, and to accept feedback.

Cognitive Map. Knowledge from research, theory, and experience is important to enable the individual both to understand his experiences and to generalize from them. But normally, information is most effective when it follows experience and feedback.

Experimentation. Unless there is opportunity to try out new patterns of thought and behavior, they never become a part of the individual. Without experimental efforts relevant change is difficult to make.

Practice. Equally important is the need to practice new approaches so that the individual gains security in being different.

Application. Unless learning and change can be applied to back-home situations, they are not likely to be effective or lasting. Attention needs to be given to helping individuals plan application.

Relearning How to Learn. Because much of our academic experience has led us to believe that we learn from listening to authorities, there is frequently need to learn from presentation-feedback-experimentation.

In essence, then, these conditions suggest that laboratory education involves the creation of a learning environment of an atypical variety. It is an environment in which the focus is not on subject matter per se but on the self as an interacting and perceiving organism. This is not to negate the importance of cognition but only to put it in perspective, this perspective being that in matters of behavioral change cognition becomes the ground and not the figure. Essential to the laboratory learning environment is the creation of an atmosphere of trust so that (1) individuals are free to give and receive behaviorally-oriented feedback, and (2) they can experiment with and practice new behaviors. Thus, for example, an individual whose prevailing pattern of group behavior is to dominate may, after receiving feedback about this by his co-learners, decide to experiment with and practice a new style which, if effective and satisfying to the individual, can be applied to back-home situations.

In some reiteration of points made in Chapter I [not reprinted here], then, —and as these conditions suggest—part of the learning environment is devoted to relearning how to learn. That is, if an individual is to engage in laboratory education he will find that the learning style which he has integrated into his being is typically inadequate for the situation. The focus is not on absorbing subject matter from an authority figure but on the reciprocal use of self and others for learning. Laboratory education moves away from the notion of truth resting in authority and toward the concept of colleagiality in learning and living. It involves the shift away from fear which immobilizes toward a condition of trust which frees (Gibb & Gibb, 1969, p. 43).

The points that have been discussed thus far can be considered as illustrative of the operational goals and processes of laboratory education. That is, the professional staff of a laboratory implicitly or explicitly takes, for example, the "Conditions for Laboratory Learning" into consideration as it plans and conducts a lab. Beyond these goals and processes, and underlying them, is a more abstract set of "meta-goals" serving to provide, in a sense, the philosophical rationale for the type of learning with which we are concerned. This set of meta-goals (Bennis, 1962), much like the nature of the learning that takes place in a laboratory, was not arrived at in a deductive fashion. That is, no one sat down and conceptualized them prior to the development of laboratory education and said, "These goals will guide and underpin what we do in a lab." Rather, they developed out of a sense of experience which seemed to repeat itself. These meta-goals, then, are seen as follows:

1. Expanded consciousness and recognition of choice
2. A spirit of inquiry
3. Authenticity in interpersonal relations
4. A collaborative conception of the authority relationship

Most of us live and work in situations where our perceptions of the environment, our awareness of what "is," and our recognition of our freedom to make choices are circumscribed, sometimes severely. These constraints emanate from a variety of circumstances such as organizational goals, communications patterns, the decision-making structure, personnel policies, norms pertaining to authority relations and the level of interpersonal intimacy, and so forth. The net effect of the forces deriving from this conglomerate of factors is to create a sort of "tunnel vision." That is, they induce limitations on our ability to perceive the total field, thus putting restraints on the range of choices we can consider when making decisions about ourselves, our relations with other people, or elements of organizational life. In short, formal or informal mechanisms often defeat the purpose for which they were designed: namely, to help an individual or an organization achieve self-awareness so that the most appropriate choices can be made. In a totally unplanned way, such mechanisms limit the sources and types of information we perceive to be at our disposal.

In a laboratory, regardless of its focus, the structure and processes tend to put a premium on the individual's awareness of the existential phenomena of the moment, thus encouraging him to consider a wider range of behavioral choices than he might ordinarily think about. The dynamics of this process to encourage recognition of a wider range of choices are complicated and fluid.

According to Bennis, the meta-goal concerned with making choices bears a close relationship to that of "a spirit of inquiry." (Bennis, 1962, p. 2). The essence of it all seems to be: Running throughout every laboratory experience is a continual theme of investigation and experimentalism. The central question raised over and over again is, "What is happening and why?" The "why" is a crucial point. What it suggests is that an ongoing investigation of the human condition is relevant and necessary; that the behavior of individuals, groups, and organizations is a legitimate subject for inquiry outside of the psychological laboratory or the therapist's office; and that the very act of inquiring can be freeing in and of itself.

As in the matter of choice, the development of a spirit of inquiry concerning behavior is in contradistinction to the overt and covert norms associated with the day-to-day life in which most people engage. One advances in life, so we have been taught, not by raising questions about the norms of an organization—or of a society, for that matter—but by accepting them. "My country, right or wrong" makes this quite explicit to the extent that those who disagree and turn their questions into action are characterized as non-patriotic or, in some cases, criminal and lacking a sense of moral duty. The point at issue, of course, is not that the meta-goal or inquiry is aimed at revolution, peaceful or violent. It is that to inquire and to broaden the areas about which one may inquire can make a person more whole, and holds the promise of inducing change on the basis of rational investigation rather than irrational assumption based on ritual and tradition.

An emphasis on the meta-goal of authenticity in interpersonal relationships is one that pervades all laboratory settings. "Authentic relationships are . . . those relationships in which an individual enhances his sense of self—and other awareness and acceptance in such a way that others can do the same." (Argyris, 1962, p. 21). The development of the skill enabling one person to establish authentic relationships with another is a difficult process. Primarily, what is involved is learning to be in touch with what one is experiencing at the moment, both on the cognitive and feeling level, and being able to communicate it to the other in a manner which encourages him to reciprocate. Thus, in laboratories there is a heavy emphasis on "How are you feeling?" It is not a game but an effort to help people experience openly the wholeness of themselves, not only as thinking and acting organisms, but as emotional ones, as well.

Once more, this meta-goal of laboratory education is one that is not congruent with the expectations of everyday life. Indeed, in some situations, they are polar opposites. One must keep one's feelings to oneself in order not to disrupt the organization. There certainly are situations in which it is inappropriate to express one's feelings at the moment. But, relating this goal to that of the previous one concerning a spirit of inquiry, it only seems reasonable to raise the issue in an investigatory manner rather than not to raise it at all in a coercive complying way. If a person is to experience himself as an integrated whole, laboratory education suggests that his wholeness includes his emotional processes as well as his cognitive and behavioral responses.

The fourth meta-goal of laboratory education, a collaborative concept of the authority relationship, carries with it substantially different implications for task-oriented interaction than the commonly accepted notions about authority connected with bureaucratic functioning—the pattern in most organizations. If we can think of authority relationships on a continuum with one pole representing power and coercive control and the other colleagiality and mutual influences, the problem can be presented in perspective. Laboratory authority relationships would be set toward the colleagial end of the scale; bureaucratic authority relationships would be the opposite.

The ethic of laboratory education does not take this position with regard to authority just to be different. Rather, it is consistent with the theme that has run all through this discussion of meta-goals. That is, the goals of laboratory education, above and beyond being concerned with developing a higher level of personal behavioral and diagnostic skill, are concerned with a humanistic and existential view of man and his relationships with others, regardless of the social context in which the relationships occur.

A summary point regarding meta-goals, then, might be this: In essence, laboratory education is directed toward change and how it is induced in human, group, and organizational relationships. The position taken is that more productive ways of helping people relate to each other, to groups, and organizations can be discovered; that all the evidence is not in by any stretch of the imagination; and that the quest for these more creative relationships is of primary importance to our present and our future.

SENSITIVITY TRAINING

The term sensitivity training is not a precise one and has been applied rather indiscriminately to the whole range of the laboratory education environment. This is understandable because, as has been indicated, laboratories, regardless of their focus, typically include a concern with matters of interaction, process, emotionality, and so forth. Nevertheless, it seems reasonable to try to differentiate between sensitivity training per se and other types of laboratory experiences, recognizing in the process that preciseness is hard to come by. Perhaps the best way to make the differences clear is to describe in some detail the activities of a typical two-week sensitivity training laboratory and compare it to one with a contrasting focus—the learning of consultation skills—in which the author was involved.

First, it is important to know that there is no standard form which laboratories of any kind must or do take. Each one is of a different design, and draws heavily on the experience and particular areas of expertise of the staff, which usually meets two or three days in advance to plan. Though the designs are all different, basic learning strategies and structures tend to be similar.

For the participants in a sensitivity training lab, this is usually the first time they have encountered laboratory education. They attend for a variety of reasons: out of interest, curiosity, professional and personal growth, and so on. The primary learning vehicle over the two-week period will be the

T-group (T for training, not therapy), in which they will spend upwards of 40 hours. There will be a professional trainer in each group, and the abiding concern of the group will be to establish valid communication among the participants through interactive and feedback processes. A variety of general sessions will be held in which the total laboratory community takes part. These sessions will take different forms. There may be lectures or role-playing exercises on various dimensions of human interaction processes—communications, feedback, leadership, conflict, group development, and the like. If one member of the staff is skilled in so-called non-verbal techniques, it is quite likely that one or more of the general sessions will be given over to this particular way of learning. It is an effort to enable the participants to sense and communicate with each other in a non-verbal way on the theory that a heightened awareness of the physicalness of self and others can lead to increased insight into one's emotions and behavior.

It is quite possible that the lab design will also include fairly large blocks of time (a day or more) devoted to an intergroup or organization exercise. In the former, the procedures typically involve the creation of a sense of competition between groups (usually, but not always, the T-groups), so that the participants will be able to examine and analyze their behavior and that of their group under the pressures induced by highly competitive circumstances. It is frequently a very revealing operation. An organization exercise also involves the total laboratory community, but it is not comparable to an intergroup. Instead of deliberately creating a competitive situation, for example, participants may be asked to develop an organization, of which they are a part, that will produce some product related to human relations training. Whatever the product is—a schedule of related learning activities in which the lab will engage, a plan for restructuring the T-groups for some specific goal, etc.—it is less relevant to the total laboratory experience than is an analysis of the process by which the organization was formed, the variety of new behaviors that emerged, the means by which people or groups were co-opted to work on projects, the formation of organizational subsystems, or any of a host of other situations which might develop.

What we have, then, in what might be called a typical sensitivity training session, is a human relations learning design revolving around a core known as a T-group experience. Other parts of the design usually draw on the developments in the T-groups or feed in to them. Sensitivity training labs are non-specific with regard to any particular skill or organization focus. Indeed, they are referred to as "General Human Relations Labs."

It is important to note that all sensitivity training is not conducted on a two-week basis. There are many one-week or week-end labs held. Time limitations, of course, put constraints on the variety of experiences that it is possible to create. Week-end labs, for example, tend to be almost totally devoted to T-group development.

The Consultation Skills laboratory, to which generalized sensitivity training will be compared, was a much different experience. First of all, this was conceived of as an advanced laboratory. All the participants had had previous sensitivity training. Some were involved in this one simply because they wanted to enhance their skills as consultants, while others saw it as a step in the direction of becoming laboratory education professionals.

The staff decided that though the major emphasis of the two weeks would focus on consultation theory and skills, it would be well to work into this phase via an abbreviated but intense classic T-group experience. Accordingly, it was announced at the orientation session that after a first day "Planning For Living" exercise, T-groups would be formed to run, in marathon fashion, the same evening and all through the next day and evening. After that the T-groups would be disbanded, not to meet again. It was felt that this activity would do two things: (1) meet the expectations of some participants for whom laboratory equaled T-group, and (2) help open up communications among the total laboratory community.

The remainder of the week and the first part of the following week are devoted to the development and operationalizing of consulting projects by participant teams. Members of the staff had previously contacted several organizations in the small New England town where the lab was being held to see if they would be willing to have participants consult with them in organizational problems. These organizations, which all gave their consent, included the municipal government, police and fire departments, and a state college. The lab participants split up into project teams, contacted their clients, and went about their tasks of data collection and problem diagnosis. Reports were fed back to the clients. General sessions were held throughout this process which dealt with intervention strategies, role problems in consultation, and personal style differences. At the end of the consultation projects, the team analyzed their experiences together. The total effort was on applying behavioral science technology to problems of an ongoing organization—and learning from the attempt.

The remainder of the second week was spent on two major events. First, the better part of two days was devoted to a presentation, discussion, and analysis by a visiting staff member of a particular model of organizational analysis and change strategy. The second event was the planning and execution of a lab-wide "Free University" during which time anyone, staff or participant, could offer his resources to the total community.

Though the foregoing description of these two laboratories can scarcely convey their real flavor, enough of a picture emerges to indicate that they were clearly different experiences, yet both were laboratories by our definition. In the prototype of the sensitivity training lab, the spotlight was sharply on the T-group setting, with a variety of other experiences contributing to and drawing from it. The consultation skills lab possessed a T-group component, but the focus tended to be on tasks to be done with a continual process analysis accompanying the tasks.

A final point or two remains to be made about sensitivity training laboratories: first, there is a wide range of human relations training activities which pass or are billed under the heading of sensitivity training. This range includes packaged programs of exercises, personal growth labs, the "far out" offerings of the Esalen Institute in California, week-end T-group marathons, and what has been described briefly above as a typical lab. *Caveat emptor* is a wise position for one who is thinking about participating in a lab. Make sure you will get what you bargain for. The field is a burgeoning one with many "institutes" and "centers" being formed around the country, some reputable and some not so. As Birnbaum points out, a serious threat to sensitivity training is posed by ". . . a host of newly hatched trainers, long on enthusiasm or entrepreneurial expertise, but short on professional experience, skill, and wisdom." (Birnbaum, 1969, p. 82.)

SENSITIVITY TRAINING OR GROUP THERAPY

A question continually raised about sensitivity training is whether or not such training really isn't group therapy in disguise. Further, the question goes, if it is therapy aren't those who engage in conducting "training" guilty of practicing medicine without a license or, at least, passing themselves off as healers?

In theory there are clear-cut answers to these questions; in practice the situation becomes somewhat fuzzy. NTL Institute promotional or descriptive literature about sensitivity training makes clear its programs are not intended to provide therapy for the individual, nor should they be considered as a substitute for therapy. This is a specific and unequivocal position and, as such, has general acceptance among the Institute Network members and other professionals. That is, sensitivity training is conceived as a learning technology which can help most people grow in both their understanding and capacity to relate to themselves, others, groups, and organizations. It is not seen as a vehicle for overcoming serious characterological deficiencies or as a way of dealing with mental illness.

Operationally, of course, the problem is not as clear-cut as the above paragraph might suggest. Despite positions taken and pronouncements made, there seem to be fairly widespread perceptions that sensitivity training is therapy under a different name. Two major reasons why this state of affairs exists are as follows:

1. The experiences that many people have in sensitivity training *do* possess, or so it seems, a quasi-therapeutic quality. But it is of a particular character that is different than what one might expect from a psychotherapy group. For example, if gaining insight and understanding into oneself is equated with therapy, then certainly much of this transpires in sensitivity

training. But there is a crucial difference in that the kind of insight which tends to develop is most typically related to the existential situation of the moment—"the here and now"—and is not of the intrapsychic variety associated with therapy. Thus, if I as a person have fed back to me the reaction that my joking style makes some people not take me seriously on the level of task performance, I have achieved an insight into the effects of my behavior of which I have been previously unaware. But it is at this point that sensitivity training departs from therapy. That is, the aims of therapy would then be served by my engaging in an analysis of how I got that way. This process would probably be autobiographical, with the assistance of symbolic interpretation on the part of the therapist. The idea would be that if I could understand the derivations of the behavior pattern I would (a) be more of a whole person, (b) be potentially freer of any neurotic anxieties giving rise to it, and (c) be better able to alter my behavior.

In the sensitivity training situation, the autobiographical tactic would tend to be discouraged, as would references to or concerns with unconscious motivation. The issue would be, given this insight about the effects of my behavior, what might be some alternative ways of dealing with myself so that if I wanted to joke I could do so and not "turn people off" to me. Or, I might discover that others have found me using humor to protect myself from close relationships with people, or to cover up my hostility—and this very discovery might help me deal with myself better.

It can be seen from these brief descriptions that the boundary lines between the goals and strategies of therapy and sensitivity training are not as clean and discreet as one might desire—but they are there.

A second reason for the existence of the training—therapy problem is historical. Those people who were responsible for the early development of sensitivity training as a social learning technology came primarily from the fields of social psychology and adult education. Their concerns focused on group dynamics and behavioral skill development, the potential personal sensitivity impact of the training experience notwithstanding. However, as the sensitivity training approach achieved wider recognition, it attracted professional personnel whose background was either clinical psychology or psychiatry. Quite naturally, these people had interests leading them to create training interventions which were more personal than group-oriented. The groups they led tended to have more of a therapeutic flavor than an existential behavioral one.

This influence of clinically-oriented people on sensitivity training should not be taken as unfortunate or bad. Indeed, they have contributed much to our understanding of the dynamics of individual behavior in group settings. And, in some sort of exchange, learning more about group phenomena and potential has influenced some therapists to alter their therapeutic focus and style. The training-therapy issue, however, remains, at least in the eyes of many beholders. It is, perhaps, a cross that sensitivity training will have to bear for some time to come.

REFERENCES

1. Argyris, C., *Intrapersonal Competence and Organizational Effectiveness* (Homewood, Illinois: Dorsey Press Inc. 1962).
2. Bennis, W., "Goals and Meta-goals of Laboratory Education" *Human Relations Training News,* Volume 6, No. 3 (Fall 1962).
3. Birnbaum, M., "Sense About Sensitivity Training" *Saturday Review,* Nov. 15, 1969.
4. Bradford, L., *Exploration in Human Relations Training* (Washington, D.C.: NTL Institute for Applied Behavioral Science, 1953).
5. Gibb, J., and Gibb, L., "Role Freedom in a Tori Group" in Burton, A. (ed.), *Encounter* (San Francisco: Jossey-Bass Inc., 1969).
6. NTL Readings Book (Washington, D.C.: NTL Institute for Applied Behavioral Science).

2. An Existential "Learning Theory" and the Integration of T-Group Research
C. M. HAMPDEN-TURNER

The purpose of this paper is twofold. First, I aim to integrate the perspectives of several T-Group theorists within a single model of human learning and personality development. Second, I hope to show that three follow-up studies which have evaluated the effectiveness of T-Groups have revealed behavior changes fully consistent with my model. Moreover, the proposed model is one on which a very wide variety of data from many fields of inquiry can be integrated.

THE CYCLE OF HUMAN EXPERIENCE

This existential "learning theory" takes the form of a self-perpetuating cycle of accumulating human experience. The cycle, in a relatively "mature" stage of development, reads as follows.

Reproduced by special permission from *The Journal of Applied Behavioral Science,* Vol. 2, No. 4, "An Existential 'Learning Theory' and the Integration of T-Group Research," C. M. Hampden-Turner, pp. 367-386, 1966, NTL Institute for Applied Behavioral Science.

According to

(a) the quality of his cognition
(b) the clarity of his identity
(c) the extent of his self-esteem —

(j) The investor will attempt to integrate the feedback from this exchange into a mental map whose breadth and complexity are a measure of investing success.

(i) According to the enhancement (or reduction) experienced by the Other, the latter will reinvest (or avoid) in a manner which moves toward synergy (or conflict).

(h) and seek self-confirmation through the impact of his invested competence upon the Other.

(d) all three of which he orders into a purposeful synthesis of his experienced and anticipated competence —

(e) the subject invests with a degree of autonomy in his human environment

(f) by periodically "letting go" and risking a portion of his experienced competence.

(g) He will thus try to "bridge the distance" between himself and the Other

It should be obvious that the integrated feedback from one successful investment will become part of the experienced competence which is invested anew. In this way, a series of successful investments (and the fearless comprehension of some unsuccessful investments) will cause *every segment of the cycle to enhance itself.* Cognition (a) will become even more powerful, more competence (d) will be experienced, greater self-confirmation (h) achieved, along with integrative complexity (j), and so on.

To illustrate the operation of the cycle, let us take a simple two-person interaction: John kisses Mary. If we were to investigate this with the use of our model, we might arrive at the following description.

Because John perceives (cognition) that Mary would like a kiss, and because of his image of himself as a virile man and a romantic lover (identity), and because he thinks highly of himself in these roles (self-esteem), he decides that he will approach her with the purpose of enhancing and confirming all these experiences. He can do this by organizing these experiences into a purpose which aims to deepen their relationship, express the experience, and satisfy sexual needs. He therefore kisses her more ardently and adventurously than she expected (invests autonomously) and risks her displeasure by exposing himself to rejection (letting go). In the act of so risking he hopes that she will come to understand him better as well as the extent of his feelings toward her, and that this will bring them closer (bridge the distance). When she reacts pleasurably to his ardor, he realizes that his ambitious view of their relationship has been confirmed. He has actually *created* new competence for them both. She, for her part, is now likely to express her affection so as to enhance him and in a manner synergic with his own purposes. He takes this pleasurable experience of exchange and integrates it into his mind, and thus adds to his store of accumulated skills and understandings.

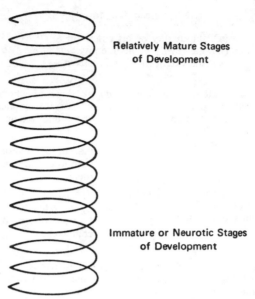

Relatively Mature Stages
of Development

Immature or Neurotic Stages
of Development

The maturing subject is conceived as developing up the spiral. The
illustration is grossly simplified. There would be literally
millions of "coils."

Figure 1.1. The Development Spiral

Certain observations need to be made concerning the philosophical assumptions behind this model, as contrasted with behaviorism. The language of this cycle is *pro*-active rather than reactive. It assumes the basic phenomena of "growth" and investing (or existing) to gain competent relations with the environment. Such existence precedes the essence of things. Our perspective is from the "inside" view of the actor, who sees objects as related to and cognitively organized by his purposes. The values and assumptions of the actor are regarded as part of his cognitive structures and hence essential determinants of his behavior. The cycle itself is an "organismic whole," from which the different segments *cannot* be severed or isolated without breaking the human mold. "Reality" is not seen as an objective universe, preordained. Rather Investing Man creates part of this reality. He is bound by the human condition of the investing cycle, yet is free "within the law" of his development. It therefore becomes my purpose to try to illuminate the process and preconditions for such development, as fostered by T- (Training) Groups.

If, as I have argued, the cycle develops, so that one successful cycle helps to generate the experience and motivation for a further successful cycle, then we may think of the developmental process as an "upward spiral." This is illustrated in Figure 1.1. We may think of the higher reachers of this spiral as representing more mature levels of interpersonal functioning. We may think of the bottom of the spiral as representing either temporary neurotic breakdowns or longer-standing levels of immaturity. Neurosis may be regarded as a kind of immaturity wherein anxiety is uncontrollable or controllable only by behavior which is regarded as deviant and "sick" by significant others in the patient's environment. A major weakness or stress within any segment of the cycle may cause it to become "stuck" or to regress downward. If the cycle breaks down at point (g), so that the subject cannot "bridge the distance" to significant others, he is likely to be diagnosed psychotic. Breakdowns in other segments of the cycle have other diagnostic labels, e.g., "delusional system," "rigidity," "amnesia," among others.

I now intend to demonstrate:

1. That the enhancement of every segment of the cycle has been observed by at least one of the more prominent T-Group theorists to be an outcome of the training experience.
2. That the enhancement of every segment of the cycle has been found among three recent research evaluations which followed up the effects of T-Group training upon the behavior of participants when again they were back in their natural surroundings.

Unless otherwise stated, theoretical discussions of T-Group training are quoted from *T-Group Theory and Laboratory Method: Innovation in Reeducation* (Bradford, Gibb, & Benne, 1964). Research results come from Bunker (1965), who evaluated a number of "educational conferences" at National Training Laboratories, and Valiquet (1964), who studied an in-company training program based on modified T-Group principles and organized by Warren Bennis. Bunker and Valiquet used identical methodologies, thereby largely replicating a pilot study by Miles (Schein & Bennis, 1965, pp. 244–254). Questionnaires were sent to associates and friends of each participant who were asked to report changes in the participant's everyday behavior. All three studies used a control group for comparison. All reported improvements were greater than those in the control group. A fourth study, which will be discussed here, is by Greiner (1965), a summary of which has been published by Blake, Mouton, Barnes, and Greiner (1964). The last-named two persons evaluated a modified T-Group designed by Blake and Mouton, called a "Managerial Grid Seminar." The participants were followed up a year after the training period began, and their performance was compared with the pretraining period. The idea of a cycle and of cyclical development is not new to T-Group theory. Bradford (Bradford, *et al.,* 1964) states:

One way of looking at the T-Group is to see it as a cyclic process in which learning recurs in increasing depth (p. 205).

As learning increases . . . so a cycle of growth continues (p. 200).

We shall now proceed around the investment cycle from parts (a) to (j), and show how each segment has been observed to develop, both by clinicians and researchers.

(A) The Quality of His Cognition

T-Group theorists have recognized several facets of cognition, including sensitivity to the needs of others, breadth of understanding, and the capacity to construct alternate means to gaining satisfaction. Gibb comments (Bradford, *et al.*, 1964):

Most observers agree that one significant change from T-Group experience is a widening and deepening of the sensitivities of the learner (p. 182).

Such cognition is regarded as closely related to others aspects of the cycle. Without it, the subject "fails to recognize and so to achieve, the development of his full potential as an individual." Gibb also describes "the illuminative function" of T-Groups, whereby the participant takes "a larger vantage point, a broader frame of reference. . . ."

In his research evaluation, Bunker found that T-Group participants showed significantly increased improvement in "sensitivity to others' feelings." Valiquet also found an increase, but it narrowly missed significance.

Greiner found a 12 per cent increase in the number of subordinates rating their bosses as "aware of others." There was an increase of 17 per cent in the number of subordinates who felt informed by their bosses. Fifty-five per cent of the participants in the training group felt that they had gained clearer understanding of other people's point of view.

(B) The Clarity of His Identity

A subject's cognition of others is always *in relation to* the way he sees himself, however "detached" he may pretend to be. This has not been lost on T-Group theorists, who have distinguished several facets of identity: identity as self-awareness, as the capacity to play roles, and as the process of increasing self-differentiation. Bradford puts it this way (Bradford, *et al.*, 1964):

People gain identity partly in relationship to other people, in differentiation from them, and in relationship to position and function in the social organization (p. 196).

The T-Group process strengthens identity because it necessitates the playing of varied roles by group members who shift in "a more or less planned way among the roles of observer, diagnostician, evaluator, actor, and inquirer" (Bradford, *et al.*, 1964). A point of unanimity among theorists is the development of self-awareness.

A first purpose of the T-Group is to help individuals to learn from their continuing experiences in the areas of self-awareness . . . and understanding of the consequences of behavior—one's own and others' (Bradford, *et al.*, 1964, pp. 191-192).

Bunker found that participants in T-Groups had, on average, significantly increased their "awareness of their own behavior" and had more "insight into self and role." Valiquet replicated both these findings.

Greiner found an increase of 8.9 per cent in the number of subordinates who rated their boss "self-aware." Forty per cent of the participants described themselves as learning "a great deal about why I behave as I do."

(C) The Extent of His Self-Esteem

Gibb, who appears to have been influenced by Carl Rogers (1961), lays considerable stress upon self-acceptance which is close in meaning to self-esteem as I have used it here.

A person learns to grow through his increasing acceptance of himself and others. Serving as the primary block to such acceptance are the defensive feelings of fear and distrust . . . (Bradford, et al., 1964, p. 279).

Gibb regards the need for acceptance as a "primary modal concern." The T-Group participant learns how to create interpersonal situations, "which help him to accept himself and others—to grow and help others to grow."

Research findings on self-esteem are difficult to differentiate from overall competence which, I have argued, is the synthesis of cognition, identity, and self-esteem. We shall therefore discuss these findings under the next segment of our cycle.

(D) All Three of Which He Orders into a Purposeful Synthesis of His Experienced and Anticipated Competence

The notion of competence seeking as a universal mode of human motivation has been proposed by R. W. White (1959). The concept of interpersonal competence is well known in T-Group theory and research, especially in the work of Argyris (1964, 1965). Gibb speaks of "a greater feeling of personal adequacy," as the outcome of T-Group training, along with greater "ego strength," confidence, and the capacity for problem solving.

It is important to assure ourselves that interpersonal competence is transferable to situations *beyond* the laboratory. Otherwise the increasing competence of participants with the T-Group may signify nothing more than the filling of a social vacuum and the increase in data available to all members concerning one another. *If* the learning is transferable, then we could argue that the participants have learned something concerning the basic human condition and not just the rules of an in-group game.

We may consider the following research findings as bearing upon self-esteem, in addition to the overall experience of competence.

Bunker and Valiquet each found increases in "self-confidence greater than those in the control groups. Although T-Group/control group differences just failed to reach significance at the .05 level, Bunker did find a significant reduction in manifest anxiety, which is the reverse of experienced competence.

Greiner found a 5.9 per cent increase in the number of subordinates describing their bosses as "self-confident," and an additional 4.8 per cent reported their bosses "at ease." Moreover, a year after training had started, 80 new task groups had been set up. This was a remarkable increase. Managers began an active search for tough problems to solve.

The gains in experienced competence are less clear-cut than in other segments of the cycle. A reason could be the higher level of risk taking, with anticipation of success at much the same level as before.

(E) The Subject Invests With a Degree of Autonomy in His Human Environment

We have now come to the crux of our whole cycle. It is the act of investment, the act of offering our self-related meanings to others, for acceptance or rejection, which is decisive for the achievement of growth. Investment must have the quality of autonomous creativity, of intensity, of authenticity, and of anguish (or risk). We shall now discuss the first three qualities of investment and consider anguish under segment (f) of the cycle.

Creative autonomy means that the subject invests a meaning which is novel to the particular relationship he has formed. The meaning may be "creative" in the more usual sense of being novel to the culture as a whole. However, such a definition is too restrictive for our purposes. By creative investment, I mean an addition to the social reality of the group or dyad. T-Group theorists have spoken of "the struggle to create a productive and viable organization, a miniature society." Bradford explains:

Experience in social creativity provided by the T-Group has learning values difficult to secure elsewhere. Seldom in life does one share in the creation of a segment of society (Bradford, et al., 1964, p. 190).

There is some agreement among theorists that investments of group members become increasingly creative, bizarre, and full of imagery as training processes. Intensity of investment refers to the amount of competence which is invested and placed at risk. Where nothing is ventured, nothing can be won. Bradford describes the scene:

Anyone who has observed or participated in a T-Group has been struck by the amount of emotional involvement and energy expenditure. After a two-hour session, people frequently feel drained . . . (Bradford, et al., 1964, p. 195).

Close in meaning to intensity is the *authenticity* of investment. There can be no genuine investment or experience where the subject does not "own," value, or take responsibility for the meanings he has invested. Carl Rogers (1961) has referred to "congruence," which is a similar conception. Authenticity or congruence is what binds the cycle together. No subject can integrate into his mental "map" the impacts of himself upon others if these invest-ments are not the true products of his experience. Integrity has come to mean authenticity as well as wholeness. The two meanings are interdependent. Schein and Bennis (1965) have linked authenticity with autonomy.

Another meta-goal in laboratory training concerns authenticity in interpersonal relations. Implied is a relationship that enables each party to feel free to be him-self . . . a line from *King Lear* sums up this particular meta-goal: "Speak what we feel, not what we ought to say . . ." (p. 33).

Let us now turn to research findings on each of these qualities of invest-ment. On autonomy, Valiquet found highly significant increases in a measure of "putting ideas across." Greiner found a shift in top management values toward initiating new ideas upon the external environment. Fifty per cent of the managers agreed that their training had helped them to "experi-ment with different behaviors" back on their jobs. There was also an increase in rewarding the *potentiality* within employees rather than just their results. Such an attitude assumes that management can help to nurture and create the excellence of others.

Intensity showed substantial increases also. Valiquet's measure of "ex-pression of feelings" increased significantly. Bunker's findings were in the same direction. Greiner found that those managers who were rated "most improved" overall had greater commitment to their careers. There was a 24 per cent increase in the number of supervisors who described their work groups as high in effort.

Authenticity was not measured by Bunker or Valiquet but improved markedly in Greiner's study. The number of subordinates describing their managers as "leveling with group members" jumped from 45.9 per cent before training to 67.7 per cent at follow-up. There was a similar increase of 22 per cent in the number of managers reporting that members of their work groups "laid their cards on the table."

(F) By Periodically "Letting Go" and Risking a Portion of His Experienced Competence

The concept of "letting go" means that the subject risks the discon-firmation of his invested competence and "opens himself up" to feedback which could entail the rejection or modification of self-related meanings. I discover that I am valuable and meaningful to the Other only through risking that I am worthless and meaningless. Existentialists argue that the road to meaning and self-confirmation is along the edge of the abyss. Benne has quoted Kenneth Burke, to the effect that "men build their cultures by huddling together, nervously loquacious, at the edge of an abyss" (Bradford, *et al.*, 1964, p. 241).

This is why existential philosophers are so insistent on the fact of death. Man must "let go" *for something*. Montaigne said, "A living man must die a thousand times." Christ told his followers, "But he that shall lose his life, shall save it."

"Letting go" and risking involve the anguish which signals our commitment and deepens our awareness by burning the experience of life into our minds. T-Group theorists are explicit on the need for pain:

Equally, when pain is not felt, there is little dissatisfaction. The provision of situations in which people may discover pain is also an avenue to learning (Bradford, et al., 1964, p. 36).

It was Otto Rank (1929) who saw his patients as caught between two fears, the "life-fear" of going forward, investing, trusting and risking, and the "death-fear" of *not* investing, atrophying, and losing individuality in a sea of humanity. It takes existential courage to go forward and endure the anguish.

Robert Blake (Blake & Mouton, 1965) has emphasized that "peace on earth" is not harmony or equilibrium but resolute problem solving in the heat of the fire. T. S. Eliot (1943) has communicated a vision of the "peaceful dove" as ringed with fire:

> The dove descending breaks the air
> With flame of incandescent terror
> Of which the tongues declare
> The one discharge from sin and error
> The only hope, or else despair,
> Lies in choice of pyre or pyre,
> To be redeemed from fire by fire (p. 37).[1]

While many maturing men voluntarily "let go" in order to reintegrate afresh, others may be helped by *involuntary* "unfreezing," whereby the subject's existing assumptions are pried from his grasp by the shock of disconfirmation or situational ambiguity. Schein and Bennis (1965) explain:

Unfreezing is a graceless term that implies that a period of *un*learning or "being shook up" . . . must take place before learning can be initiated (p. 43).

Theorists generally agree that the social vacuum created by bringing together a group of strangers without a formal purpose is a source of anguish and unfreezing. Every attempted investment is *perforce* creative and autonomous where no conventional wisdoms or social rituals exist. In vain do members turn to the trainer for help. God is dead. Or as Tillich has put it, "God is the ground of our being." In investing our own values and creating our own assumptions we bear witness to His creative force within us. Like

---

[1]From "Little Gidding" in *Four Quartets,* copyright, 1943, by T. S. Eliot. Reprinted by permission of Harcourt, Brace & World Inc.

Victor Frankl in the concentration camp and Sartre beneath the heels of the Nazis, T-Group members see only mindless chaos outside themselves and experience themselves as the source of invested values.

As a T-Group develops, trainers have observed increasing spontaneity and mutual trust. Only by "letting go" and risking can such trust be learned.

In the follow-up evaluations, Valiquet found a marked increase in "risk-taking" behavior. Bunker's results were in the same direction but narrowly missed significance. Also, Bunker found a reduction in "dogmatism" (a rough measure of the disinclination to "let go" or resynthesize). Valiquet found significant increases in "functional flexibility."

Greiner reported that nearly twice the number of supervisors were describing group discussions as "lively." This suggests increased spontaneity and intensity. There was a substantial shift in top management's values toward the open and authentic expression of disagreement, along with the acceptance of such tension as was necessary to solve problems. There was also a strong vindication of the "unfreezing" process (Blake structures his groups, or Grid Seminars, so that the feedback-disconfirmation-unfreezing process is made deliberate and explicit. Each manager rates himself on the "grid instrument" and compares his self-ratings with those ascribed to him by group members.) It was found that there was a curvilinear relationship between the severity of disconfirmation and improvement at follow-up. The moderately disconfirmed managers improved the most, on average; then came the severely disconfirmed; and finally, the "rewarded managers" improved the least.

(G) He Will Thus Try to "Bridge The Distance" Between Himself and The Other

The idea of "psychological distance" between the perspectives of different people will be familiar to the students of Piaget (1937) and Kurt Lewin (1951). Only the capacity to "bridge the distance" between one's own differentiated self and the Other can reconcile the conflict between autonomy and need for confirmation. Where ethnocentric men are obliged to conform to a unidimensional yardstick of virtue, their relative virtues will "compete" and eclipse one another. In this sense we can appreciate Karen Horney's (1937) concept of "neurotic competition." Only if I can allow the Other to be different and span his "distance" from myself can we then exchange perspectives that will enrich us both.

We see in color prejudice, anti-Semitism, and much of anti-communism the frantic search to avoid investing in persons whose "distance" from the bigot threatens to disconfirm the bigot's investments. Where interaction is inevitable, the belief in the basic inferiority of the "distant" person will sanction the bigot to invest *downward* in the Negro "boy," for example, so that the very style of investment can protect the frail sense of competence.

A basic principle of T-Groups is to induce confrontation among strangers. The purposes for which the movement was founded include the aim of synthesizing and integrating cross-disciplinary approaches to learning. As a group develops, the capacity to bridge the distance is enhanced. According to Benne, the process—

... involves some of the deepest dilemmas of personal and social life, the dilemma of self and society . . . of conservation and change. It involves the odyssey of human loneliness and of apartness partially overcome in an association which, while firm and security-giving, yet enhances and affirms rather than eclipses and derogates individual variation and difference (Bradford, *et al.,* 1964, pp. 235-236).

Is there any research evidence that T-Group training develops a capacity to "bridge the distance"? Bunker found substantial increases in "tolerance for new information." Valiquet's reported increase barely missed significance. This measure suggests an acceptance of the novel investments of the Other.

Greiner discovered that a number of "distances" in the plant had been successfully bridged. The distance between hierarchical levels was one of these. Among the "50 most highly rated managers" 14 per cent came from the lower levels, compared with 2 per cent the year before. An increasing percentage of middle-level managers received praise and attention also. The clique at the top was turning outwards. Fifty-three per cent of participants felt that they had learned "the importance of combining the interests of people." Among subordinates, 93.5 per cent agreed that their supervisor's behavior had improved.

There was an interesting switch in top management attitudes toward Negroes in this Southern plant. In 1962, 67 per cent believed in segregation even if it limited the Negro's right to advancement. A year later, 53 per cent declared that Negro rights were more important. On their private initiative some managers set up scholarships for Negro children. Several managers moved into prominent positions in the town council and urged the implementation of the Civil Rights Act.

A similar change has taken place in union-management relations. So impressed were union officers by the new understanding they were receiving from management that they volunteered to undergo Grid training. At about the same time they disaffiliated themselves from the International Union which provided the security they no longer needed but not the local autonomy which was now desired. So productive are the new relations between union and management that the latter is attempting to strengthen the union, while safeguarding its independence. The plant as a whole also improved its relationships with corporate headquarters, other plants, and the local community.

(H) And Seek Self-Confirmation Through the Impact of His Invested Competence upon the Other

I have borrowed this segment of the cycle from Martin Buber (1957):

The basis of man's life is twofold, and it is one—the wish of every man to be confirmed as to what he is, even as what he can become, by men; and the innate capacity in man to confirm his fellow men in this way (p. 101).

T-Group theorists use such words as "reinforcement," "reality testing," and the "achievement of behavioral effectiveness" to convey this idea. Bradford says of group members, "each discovers part of his own identity as he relates to others" (Bradford, *et al.*, 1964, p. 193).

Only by the successful impact of his own assumptions upon the social reality around him can a man experience himself as a creative process, who "becomes human in the moment of decision." He discovers immortality as his competence is transferred from its mortal container to expand the consciousness of others. It may be said of several creative leaders, "He came that we might have life, and might have it more abundantly."

The research studies show that, on average, T-Group participants make substantially improved impacts upon their friends in the outside world. Both Bunker and Valiquet found significant gains in "relational facility." Subjects were described as more tactful, better to negotiate and easier to deal with.

Greiner found that managers who were "most improved" as the result of training had the closest congruence between their own experience of competence and the impacts which their invested competence made on others. Failure to improve was most strongly related to the degree to which assumptions and impacts remained discrepant. There was substantial evidence that subordinates felt more confirmed. The number who reported that their bosses inspired them to high goals rose by 11.4 per cent. Those reporting that their suggestions were encouraged rose by 11.6 per cent; and that their bosses "listened carefully" to them, by 10.7 per cent. The clarity of communication appears to have risen, with an additonal 11.1 per cent of subordinates reporting that their boss "states his views clearly."

We must not forget that a manager's identity is confirmed by managing successfully. Productivity per employee jumped from an index figure of 103.9 prior to training to 131.3 a year later. Controllable costs fell from 94.1 to 86.2, a reduction which increased profits by at least $60 million. Both indexes had remained almost steady the previous year.

(I) According to the Enhancement (or Reduction) Experienced by the Other, the Latter Will Reinvest (or Avoid) in a Manner Which Moves Toward Synergy (or Conflict)

I have borrowed the concept of "synergy" from Maslow (1954, 1965) who, in turn, acknowledges Ruth Benedict. Synergy involves the resolution of the selfish/unselfish dichotomy by making the enhancement of the Other the precondition or result of personal enhancement. The achievement of synergy is, in part, the consequence of effective functioning in those segments of the cycle already discussed. For instance, an aspect of strong cognition (a) is the capacity to construct alternative ways of achieving personal goals, so that others' needs are included. To perceive what will enhance the Other permits one to synergise the growth forces of both parties, so that the impact of investment is immensely potent. Self-awareness (b) will permit the subject to recognize his needs beneath the "moral aims" he pursues in public life. Several T-Group observers have argued that "hidden agendas" and unadmitted needs can drastically block the search for synergic solutions. Murray Horwitz explains it thus (Bradford, *et al.*, 1964):

> On the other hand, if needs could be stated, it would appear that not a single goal, but a range of goals would be potentially satisfying to a member[s] . . . [who] would be able to design activities to yield more widespread satisfaction . . . (p. 372).

If self-understanding is essential for synergy, so is "letting go" (f) and reintegrating (j), so that one's own needs can be synthesized with those of others. T-Group theorists have used several terms approximating synergy. Warren Bennis sees consensual validation as growing out of the group process. This combines synergy with the idea of self-confirmation (h). "Interdependence" is another term commonly used. Benne speaks of the group moving from "polarization to paradox." Blake refers to problem solving and conflict resolution. His "Managerial Grid" is specifically designed to illustrate and measure the extent to which "concern with people" can be synergised with "concern for production." He deliberately contrasts compromise between these two with their capacity to enhance each other and optimize the whole. The integrated personality can, by definition, integrate and synergise many of the relationships in which he lives.

In the research studies, both Bunker and Valiquet found substantial gains in "interdependence," a measure which included "encourages participation, involves others, gives greater leeway to subordinates." Indeed Valiquet's reported increase was the biggest gain found in any of the measures. Another measure which showed significant increase was "consideration for individual differences."

Greiner's study gives strong support to the notion that the developing cycles of individuals synergise to enhance one another. "Most improved" managers back on the job enjoyed a ratio of 2.24 to .5 between "most" and "least improved" companions. The "least improved" managers lived in a ratio of 1.31 to 1.32.

Further evidence for synergy came from the supervisors' reports on their work groups. There was a substantial increase in groups which reached decisions by mutual agreement and in reports that "differences in opinion are directly confronted and discussed to productive solutions."

(J) The Subject Integrates the Differentiated Feedback From This Exchange into a Mental Map Whose Breadth and Complexity Reflects an Accumulation of Successful Investments Given and Received

In a scientific culture, where reductive analysis and professional encapsulation are breaking down our world into a myriad of dead pieces, men need more than ever a mental apparatus capable of integrating and organizing their experience. The playwright, Arthur Miller, has recently observed:

What is needed are people who, quite simply, know how to think, who know how to synthesize knowledge and find connections between distantly related phenomena, who seek constantly to relate rather than isolate experience.[2]

It is clear from the cycle as described so far that a man who cannot "bridge the distance" (g) and share the perspective of the Other will be unable to integrate such perspectives. A man without a stable identity cannot risk "letting go" and therefore lacks a sense of self around which to organize his experience. His experience, lacking anguish or intensity, is probably too shallow to integrate or to recall.

Schein and Bennis (1965) have argued that a meta-goal of T-Groups is an expanded consciousness. A founding principle of T-Groups is that of integration.

Another objective is the development of concepts and theoretical insights which will serve as tools in linking personal values, goals, and intentions to action consistent with these inner factors and with the requirements of the situation (p. 17).

Neither Bunker nor Valiquet attempted to measure the degree of cognitive complexity or the personality integration among participants. However, there was evidence suggesting more acceptance of feedback which is essential for integration. Bunker found marked increases in "sensitivity to group behavior." Valiquet found improvement in the same direction but not reaching significance. We have already seen that "tolerance for new information" increased in both samples, as did "acceptance of people and individual differences."

Greiner found evidence for increased attention to feedback and increased integration of norms and values. There was an increase of 30.5 per cent in the number of managers who reported that their groups were highly conscious of profit and loss. This attention was not confined to "impersonal" data. We

---

[2]Quoted by Penelope Gilliat, *Sunday Observer,* London, Jan. 30, 1966.

have already seen that awareness of others and the capacity to listen improved.

The overcoming of polarities and the integration of varying points of view are principal focuses of the "Managerial Grid." Strong gains were made in measures of "integrated values," including, of course, "concern with people" and "concern with production." There was an increase of 11.4 per cent in the number of subordinates who set their goals jointly with their managers. Managers were given a card-sort of three kinds of norms—"polarized" on the assumption of win-lose conflict, "compromised" on the assumption of splitting the difference, and "integrated" on the assumption of synergy and optimization. Between 1958 and 1963, the number of "integrated" norms rose from 14 per cent to 40 per cent. Over the same period, "polarized" and "compromised" norms fell. We must not assume that it is easy to integrate the values and perspectives of ourselves and others. Nor is it possible to have integrative norms where synergy has not been achieved. How long will it be before we learn to achieve synergic relations with the Chinese or North Vietnamese? The current political norms regard those who even attempt to implement such relations as cowards or traitors. It is as hard to solve problems and gain peace as it is to mature, for all these capacities are interrelated.

This concludes my summary of the three evaluation studies on the effectiveness of T-Groups. It should not be thought that the existential cycle will integrate only T-Group phenomena. Currently in preparation are integrative studies of psychotherapy, political affiliation, organizational development, and change-agent intervention. It is even possible to predict the stability of democracy in a nation by sampling the opinions of inhabitants which relate to the operation of the cycle.

In this study we have seen that the researched outcomes of T-Group training reveal increasing development in each and every segment of the existential cycle, so that it "spirals upward." The cycle is proposed as an "existential learning theory" which will enable workers in this area to consolidate and compare their viewpoints.

REFERENCES

Argyris, C. T-Groups for organizational effectiveness. *Harvard Business Review,* March–April, 1964, *42* (2), 60–74.

Argyris, C. Explorations in interpersonal competence—I. *Journal of Applied Behavioral Science,* 1965, *I* (1), 58–83.

Blake, R. R., & Mouton, J. S. *Managing intergroup conflict in industry.* Houston: Gulf, 1965.

Blake, R. R., Mouton, J. S., Barnes, L. B., & Greiner, L. E. Breakthrough in organization development. *Harvard Business Review,* Nov.-Dec., 1964, *42* (6), 133–155.

Bradford, L. P., Gibb, J. R. & Benne, K. D. (Eds.) *T-group theory and laboratory method: Innovation in re-education.* New York: Wiley, 1964.

Buber, M. Distance and relation. *Psychiatry,* May 1957, *XX* (2).

Bunker, D. R. Individual applications of laboratory training. *Journal of Applied Behavioral Science,* 1965, *1* (2), 131–147.

Eliot, T. S. Little Gidding. In *Four quartets.* New York: Harcourt, Brace & World, 1943.

Greiner, L. E. Organization change and development. Unpublished doctoral dissertation, Harvard University, 1965.

Horney, K. *The neurotic personality of our time.* New York: Norton, 1937.

Lewin, K. *Field theory in social science.* New York: Harper, 1951.

Maslow, A. H. *Motivation and personality.* New York: Harper, 1954.

Maslow, A. H. *Eupsychian management.* Homewood, Ill.: Richard D. Irwin, 1965. P. 88.

Piaget, J. *La construction du réel chez l'enfant.* Neuchâtel: Delachaux, 1937.

Rank, O. *The trauma of birth.* New York: Harcourt, Brace & World, 1929.

Rogers, C. R. *On becoming a person.* Boston: Houghton Mifflin, 1961.

Schein, E. H., & Bennis, W. G. (Eds.) *Personal and organizational change through group methods: The laboratory approach.* New York: Wiley, 1965.

Valiquet, M. I. Contribution to the evaluation of a management training program. Unpublished doctoral dissertation, Massachusetts Institute of Technology, 1964.

White, R. W. Motivation reconsidered: The concept of competence. *Psychological Review,* 1969, *66,* 297–333.

3. Differentiating Human Relations Training Laboratories

PAUL C. BUCHANAN and JEROME REISEL

Laboratory training originally focused on learning about groups. As interest in this form of training has grown, clients have been offered an ever increasing array of laboratories, such as "Laboratory for Organizational Effectiveness," or "Laboratory in Consultation Skills," or a specially designed laboratory in supervisory skills.

Reprinted from *Social Change,* Vol. 2, No. 2, 1972, pp. 1-3.

For the participant, this variety raises questions like *"How do I determine which lab best meets my needs and interests?"* or *"How do I avoid duplication if I want to attend another laboratory?"* For staffs, *"How do we make sure that the laboratory we design and conduct is in relevant ways different from (or the same as) other available labs?"* For researchers, the question *"How do I identify criteria that help me assess the extent to which a given lab attained its intended objectives?"* remains. And for all: *"Do labs purporting to have special objectives really differ in their outcomes?"*

A SCHEME FOR CLASSIFYING TYPES OF LABORATORIES

Group composition offers one basis for differentiating current laboratory designs. Some laboratories are open to the general public without previous experience. Some are intended for people from one type of vocation. Some are designed for people from one specific organization. And some require previous laboratory experience.

Several years ago, the Midwest Group in Human Relations distinguished between human relations laboratories according to their specific focus. Using these two dimensions, *participant mix* and *focus,* we can derive six categories of laboratories:

Emphasis on personal development
Emphasis on group development
Emphasis on inter-group phenomena
Vocational laboratory
Organizational laboratory
Advanced specialized laboratory.

KEY DIMENSIONS IN THE DESIGN OF LABORATORIES

We identify seven dimensions of importance in the design and conduct of any laboratory in which learning about human relations is central. Some are more crucial than others, as we shall see.

Focus

Laboratory training deals primarily with relationships, such as the relationships between Self and Self, Self and Other, Self and Group, Self and Organization, and Self and Vocation. The direction of flow in each set can be in either way. Reciprocal relationships can become the focus, for instance, by examining the influence of the Self on the Group and the influence of the Group on the Self.

A laboratory with a Self-Self focus deals with the relation of a person to himself, or intrapersonal phenomena. Participants in this kind of laboratory seek data about themselves. By looking at their thoughts, feelings, and overt actions, they are afforded opportunities to acquire learnings relevant to personal growth and development.

Laboratories with a Self-Other focus aim at learning in the sphere of interpersonal relations. They help participants become more conscious of their impact upon others and their response to the behavior of others. One set of expected consequences is increased understanding of the role of power, trust, openness, affection, and choice in the quality of interpersonal relations. The development of skills in listening, resolving conflict, establishing interdependence and communication also follows from such a focus.

A laboratory with a Self-Group focus helps participants increase their awareness of how they function in a group, their knowledge of factors that facilitate or inhibit effective group behavior, and their skills in performing as a leader and member of a group.

A Self-Organization laboratory focuses on the interaction between the individual and the organization. A participant seeks knowledge about his relationships with the unit of which he is a part and about factors influencing the relations between this group and others within the organization. Questions of inter-group cooperation and conflict, the role of norms, tasks, and structures are explored; skills of leadership and membership in two or more interdependent groups are developed.

A Self-Vocation laboratory concentrates on the participant's feelings and views about his occupational role and their relation to his effectiveness, his career, and the sense of meaning he achieves from his particular type of work.

Table 1.1 provides an estimate of the importance of each focus in the typology described above.

TABLE 1.1
THE PRIMARY FOCUS OF DIFFERENT TYPES OF LABORATORIES

	Type of Laboratory				
Focus	Personal Growth HR	Group Basic HR	Inter- Group HR	Organiza- tional*	Voca- tional**
Self—Self	Primary	Secondary	Tertiary	Tertiary	Secondary
Self—Other	Primary	Secondary	Secondary	Secondary	Primary
Self—Group	Secondary	Primary	Secondary	Secondary	Primary
Self—Organization	Tertiary	Secondary	Primary	Primary	Primary
Self—Vocation	Tertiary	Tertiary	Tertiary	Primary	Primary

* This category includes laboratories conducted for specific organizations, such as a corporation or a school district.

** This category includes laboratories for such groups as educators, or business managers who are not from the same company.

Goals

Bennis (1962) has suggested that at one level the goal of all laboratory training is the expansion of (1) awareness and recognition of choice, (2) authenticity, (3) an attitude of inquiry or curiosity, and (4) a collaborative view of authority relations.

Inasmuch as these "metagoals" are fundamental to the concept of laboratory training, they cannot distinguish types of laboratories: they provide a "container dimension" within which a wide variety of designs can be placed. Yet each of these four types of learning can be applied to different specific content, or to what we referred to as the emphasis or focus of learning. Thus a laboratory focused on personal development is likely to have as its goals the development of a participant's authenticity, spirit of inquiry, etc., in regard to himself and his relations with others. A laboratory with an inter-group focus is likely to aim at the development of the participant's authenticity, spirit of inquiry, etc., as a member of one group in its relations with another. Thus in establishing *focus* as a basic dimension we obviate the need to include goals as a separate dimension.

Modalities

If one conceives of a laboratory as a means of creating dilemmas, the resolutions of which lead to significant learning, then the type of issues involved in the dilemmas is important in the design of a laboratory. When we speak of modalities we refer to technologies that provide dilemmas. Such dilemmas, which often disconfirm a previously accepted state of affairs, generate behavioral data relevant to the focus of the particular laboratory. Table 1.2 is a summary of the more frequently used modalities and our

TABLE 1.2
MODALITIES CHARACTERISTIC OF DIFFERENT TYPES OF LABS

	Type of Laboratory				
Modality	Personal Growth HR	Group Basic HR	Inter- Group HR	Organiza- tional	Voca- tional
General Non-Verbal	Continuing	Optional	Optional*	Optional*	Optional*
Graphic Arts	Continuing	Optional	Optional*	Optional*	Optional*
Body Awareness	Continuing	Optional	Optional*	Optional*	Optional*
Fantasy	Continuing	Optional	Not likely	Not likely	Not likely
Improvisation (Theatrical)	Continuing	Optional	Optional*	Optional*	Optional*
T-Group	Primary	Primary	Primary	Optional*	Primary**
Other Structures (pair)	Optional	Secondary	Optional	Optional	Optional
Group Activities	Optional	Primary	Secondary	Secondary	Primary***
Organization Exercises	Optional	Optional	Primary	Secondary	Primary***
Organization Problems	Optional	Optional	Optional	Primary	Primary***

  * This option is generally seen as a demonstration feature of the lab, designed for one-shot purpose.
  ** If the T-group is a primary focus in the vocational lab, group and organizational exercises become secondary.
  *** If problems of the organization are given primary focus, the T-group becomes secondary.

estimate of the pertinence of each for a given type of laboratory. Examination of the table indicates considerable overlap in the use of certain modalities. This broad usage of modalities on an optional basis blurs some of the possible differences between laboratories; yet many modalities can be used in ways that are organic and contextual for a laboratory, without shifting its primary focus. Particular learnings from a given activity flow both from the *experience* and from the *way the experience is processed.* For instance, a non-verbal activity, such as two people approaching one another, can be processed in terms of what the experience tells the participant about himself (the Self-Self focus) or in terms of how it fits the norms of behavior in the participant's work setting (a Self-Organization focus).

Participant Population

We have already emphasized the importance of this dimension by using it as a basis for making our original typology.

Duration

Laboratories currently conducted for a specific organization, such as a corporation or school district, tend to be shorter than those offered to the general public. This is surprising since the institutional laboratories usually have a greater number of primary foci than do general human relations laboratories. The rationale for determining the duration of a given type of laboratory apparently needs further explication. For the present, we conclude that duration is not a dimension of importance in distinguishing laboratories.

Location

Laboratories are residential (participants work and live in a conference or retreat-like setting), non-residential (meetings are held in the work setting), or mixed (meetings are held away from the work setting but participants reside at home). In certain instances the modality used may be restricted by site selection, but location does not appear to be important in differentiating types of laboratories.

Staffing

This dimension of design refers to both the style of the individual trainers and the compositon of the staff of a given laboratory. Although little systematic research about the significance of differences in staff styles and the dimensions of such style has been conducted (Reisel, 1961; Bolman, 1968; Culbert, 1968), experience suggests that it is an important issue. Most trainers will agree that staff composition is a highly relevant issue. The two prime considerations are that staff members be skilled in the modalities to be used and able to collaborate with one another.

Conclusions and Implications

The three major dimensions in which laboratories differ are *focus*, *modality*, and *participant-mix*. When these dimensions are related to each other, as in Table 1.2, the resulting typology takes on meaning for decisions about design, for describing the laboratory to potential participants, and for selecting criteria for evaluation studies.

Whether learning outcomes from laboratories of a specified type are similar and whether outcomes from laboratories of different types are different in expected ways, are empirical questions on which there are few data. Laboratories are seldom designed to meet fully the specification of any one type. Important issues regarding dimensions of design are not reported in the literature, thus making comparisons of findings from different studies difficult (Buchanan, 1969).

REFERENCES

Bennis, Warren G. Goals and meta-goals of laboratory training. *Human Relations Training News*, 1962, *6* (3), 1-4.

Bolman, Lee. The effects of variation in educator behavior on the learning process in laboratory human relations education. Unpublished doctoral dissertation, Yale University, 1968.

Buchanan, Paul C. Laboratory training and organization development. *Administration Science Quarterly*, 1969, *14* (3), 466-480.

Culbert, Samuel A. Trainer self-disclosure and member growth in two t groups. *Journal of Applied Behavioral Science*, 1968, *4* (1), 47-73.

Reisel, Jerome. Observations on the trainer role, a case study. In R. Tannenbaum, I. Weschler & F. Massarik, *Leadership and Organization*. New York: McGraw-Hill, 1961.

4. Up the Right Mountain, Down the Wrong Path—Theory Development for People-Changing Groups

MORTON A. LIEBERMAN

Diamond and Bednar[1] issue the same call: to convert the group people-changing business from an art to a science. Their objective calls forth in most of us reflexive, positive response—right on! Although the authors share a common goal, their suggestions on how to reach it differ. Diamond wants us to incorporate an analytic framework borrowed from social learning theory as a way of systematizing what it is that is done in encounter groups. In contrast, Bednar and his colleagues suggest a pragmatic approach, which they support with findings from the group psychotherapy literature on processes affecting outcome. Both approaches, in the view of this reviewer, suffer some inherent problems and contradictions.

THE ADAPTATION OF SOCIAL LEARNING THEORY TO PEOPLE-CHANGING GROUPS

It is perhaps helpful to place Diamond's suggestion in a historical perspective. Therapeutics in groups, whether they fall under the rubric of formal group psychotherapy or activities associated with the Human Potential Movement (in contrast to the educational goals of the T-Group movement), have had extensive experience in adapting models of dyadic relationships to the multipersonal relationships of a group. Almost every known dyadic therapeutic theory has its counterpart in group-based people-changing endeavors. More often than not, these translations of dyadically based theories to groups have suffered a common negative fate. Perhaps one example will suffice to illustrate the problem. Evidence that the particular conditions of the relationship between a therapist and patient constitute a central facilitative mechanism leading to positive outcomes has accrued over the past ten years and is now widely accepted in individual psychotherapy. The work of Truax[2] and his colleagues on the three therapist-induced

Reproduced by special permission from *The Journal of Applied Behavioral Science*, Vol. 10, No. 2, "Up the Right Mountain, Down the Wrong Path—Theory Development for People-Changing Groups," Morton A. Lieberman, pp. 166-174, 1974, NTL Institute for Applied Behavioral Science.

[1]See footnotes 7 and 8, page 12 of this volume.
[2]See, for example, Truax, C. and Corkhuff, R., *Toward Effective Counseling and Psychotherapy: Training and Practice*, Chicago: Aldine Publishing Co., 1967.

conditions is perhaps the clearest illustration of this finding. Yet, when similar behaviors—genuineness, positive regard, and empathy—of group leaders were assessed by Truax, they did not have the same facilitative characteristics. The reason seems rather obvious but often ignored: By placing several individuals in a group setting for change induction, we construct a social system that has a number of important properties that do not characterize dyads and alter the relationship between a central person and members in ways that mere technical adaptations by the therapist or leader will not overcome. Thus my initial reaction to Diamond's suggestion was one of *déjà vu*. It's a tale often told, one that unfortunately has in the past provided more conversation than illumination.

It might be argued that there is a considerable difference between applying dyadic psychotherapeutic systems and applying a model of change based primarily on experimental psychology to groups. Let us, however, examine some of the implicit as well as explicit issues that social learning theory raises. For me, the most important is the implicit but inherent notion that the group leader is in precise control of the situation, and thus has the power to shape, to desensitize, to model, and so forth, all the behavior that is required. I believe too much is known about the limitations of leader influence and the conditions necessary for its emergence to take such a simple view of such a complex situation. Power and influence are considerably more diffused issues in a multi-person relationship than they are in a dyadic one. The sources of power and the ability to wield it are not simple issues. The nature of the reward-punishment system in groups as compared to dyads is different: for example, ultimate "punishment" in a dyad is withdrawal of love; in a group it is exclusion, a punishment more under the control of the group than the leader. Thus, the various mechanisms proposed under social learning theory (arousal enhancement and reduction, vicarious learning, cognitive restructuring, and so forth), most of which necessitate that the leader reinforce or punish (elicit, arouse, model, and so on), is just not adequately developed by Diamond with respect to how those behaviors are or are not muted in the group context, where influence is a function of how the group social system takes shape.

Even more sketchy under the social learning theory is the role of others. General statements like, "The members will reinforce, will model, will vicariously learn," are commonplace in that approach. It is as if the author assumes that group members will do just the right thing at the right time, so they will be facilitative, and this can be explained on the basis of social learning theory. To take but one example, what behaviors become reinforced by the group can perhaps be best explained in terms of group norms—those shared agreements among members about what constitutes appropriate or inappropriate behavior. Diamond seems implicitly to assume that the norms of the particular learning environment will be harmonious with the intention of the central person. Recent studies, however (Lieberman, Yalom, & Miles, 1973; Beismier, 1974), suggest strongly that group norms are not necessarily or primarily functions of leader behaviors or desires.

Another fundamental problem I perceive in the adaptation of social learning theory to the group is that it tells us very little about what behaviors should be reinforced or aroused or restructured. Diamond uses terms like "risk taking," "feeling orientation," "genuineness," and "self-disclosure" as if they were fundamental truths about the critical events or experiences of people changing. Nonsense. Take self-disclosure, for example. There really is no empirical evidence that the amount or kind of self-disclosure in groups relates to positive outcomes (Lieberman, Yalom, & Miles, 1973). It is for these reasons, then, that I consider social learning theory, as portrayed by Diamond, to be a model of limited usefulness in reaching the goal he so devoutly desires—turning the encounter group art into science.

Does this mean that there is no value in following the pathway that Diamond suggests, which I take to be a systematic application of social learning theory concepts to ongoing practices of encounter groups and their leaders? On this question I am more of a fence-straddler. Some aspects of social learning theory have now reached the stage where they are wittingly or unwittingly incorporated in a number of researchers' minds when they are investigating people-changing endeavors. Clearly, a call for their conscious rather than unwitting use in our examination of the learning context makes sense, but the misleading precision suggested by Diamond's article should be noted. Social learning theory can be a precise theoretical system, but many issues about the group context fall outside the realm of social learning theory at its present level of development. Those questions take precedence in this reviewer's mind, but will be raised in relation to both Diamond's and Bednar's formulae.

Bednar's answer to systematizing the group healing art departs radically from Diamond's. He asks us to read with care the current empirical findings with regard to group therapy and to construct our practice in light of those findings. I think such a message should not be ignored, although the history of psychotherapeutic practice is not marked by notable examples of the utilization of such information. Perhaps what is required more than deter-mining factors that influence therapeutics is research directed toward finding out methods for changing therapists' behavior on the basis of empirical findings. Most troublesome for me in Bednar's paper was understanding his criteria for selecting the particular change parameters surveyed. Pretherapy preparation, levels of group cohesiveness, and the influence process of therapist modeling are certainly three that would generally be considered important. Unfortunately, they are neither sufficiently exhaustive nor inte-grated to indicate directions for a theory of group-based people changing. They are not the foundations of an encompassing theory, but rather technical points—pragmatics for increasing therapeutic effectiveness. Why exclude others that have shown empirical support, such as patient selection or group composition, to name but two? Certainly, those two exist at somewhat the same level of primitive, but positive, empirical support as the three Bednar has identified. Bednar is telling us implicitly that the path to the summit is the generation of empirically grounded theories of people changing in groups. This message is clearly consonant with my own views on the pressing need for them. Unfortunately, I don't believe we can quickly cut through thickets on the road by working over findings currently available in the field. More studies need yet to be done.

REQUIREMENTS FOR A PRACTICAL THEORY OF PEOPLE CHANGING IN GROUPS

I have added the requirement "practical" to signify that strategies for research on people-changing groups must include steps which make such inquiry a basis for influencing practitioners. The first requirement for a practical theory is that it attend to the question of *to whom change induction is to be directed and for what.* Our whole system of providing such group healing services could be enormously improved if we were able to match change systems with the needs of the people entering such systems. One of the fundamental weaknesses of the Human Potential Movement has been its avoidance of this question and its unreflective attitude that its methods are good for all, for all need the same thing. To assume, for example, that "freeing up" (encouraging expressivity) is a basic need of the constricted white, middle class client and also of the black, ghetto-dwelling client, and to conclude that the same techniques are therefore operable for both, borders on being an unregulated, omnipotent fantasy. It is an equally gross error to assume that the techniques of confrontation, the "leveling" so characteristic of the Synanon model, have equivalent effects when used with addicts who live in a tightly bound residential treatment community as when used with addicts who live "on the street" and experience "the method" only in a once-a-week session. These are not new problems; they have been mentioned frequently in questioning the universal applicability of psychoanalytically oriented treatment modes developed from exclusive experience with middle class, cognitively oriented populations. Unfortunately, what was learned from attempts to take traditional treatment to the masses has not been remembered in structuring the theoretical premises of current people-changing ideologies. Almost any manipulation of human beings probably has helped someone. The enormous creative fertility of people-changers is reflected in the range of activities developed to induce or encourage change. All, no matter how outlandish, have helped some, although I know of none that have helped all. Being able to match technology with need and specify the technological conditions appropriate to the needs under review might enhance our understanding of what works, when, and why.

A second important practical as well as theoretical aid may inhere in asking *what mechanism to apply to which person at what point in the group.* For every Ramon and his fantasy trip, one can cite ten people for whom similar experiences were not useful (Lieberman, Yalom, & Miles, 1973). The experience and expression of intense emotion, self-disclosure, finding similarity, experiencing communion, developing insight, and so forth are all events that probably contribute to change, but to say this imprecisely identifies for whom and under what conditions such events are helpful. In order to explain adequately changes in behavior and to develop a pragmatic model, we need (1) a system for assessing the particular experiences or events that will be helpful to particular persons, and (2) a model which takes into account the social forces (the conditions of the system) which may affect the degree to which exposure to a particular experience may or may not be therapeutic. For example, in the encounter groups studied by the reviewer, self-disclosing behavior tended to be ineffective or even destructive in early stages of the group, but more beneficial at later points in the group history. The essence of this finding, relative to the question of practical utility, would seem to be that practitioners need the help of theory that precisely explains why specific techniques sometimes "boom" and at other times "bust."

TRANSFER OF LEARNING

The persuasiveness of groups has been so amply demonstrated in sociolocial and psychological literature that it needs no amplification here. Because the persuasive power of groups is so great, however, an illusion that individuals have changed is often created when in fact their alterations of behavior within the group context are perhaps only accommodations to a new referent group, to a different set of norms. The "change," therefore, is often ephemeral because it is more a response to specific group conditions and depends on the treatment group for maintenance.

A major unsolved conceptual problem in constructing a theory of people changing is how changes that occur in a group lead to changes in the member's life outside the group. That lasting change does occur with some frequency is not as important as that it does not occur as frequently as we would like; yet no reasonable conceptual system exists to explain the specific relationships between person and group which account for observed differences in maintenance of change or transfer of learning. How does generalization from the specific context of the treatment group take place? (After all, if the change group were identical with normal life, little change would probably occur.) Does the inherent persuasiveness of the group situation mean that more attention should be given to providing situations that teach strategies of change and maintenance in therapy itself? Too often, after participation in the group, the individual faces the external world little prepared to use what he has learned, to try out in real life the behavior that he has tried out in the group. Or, just as sad, some individuals emerge from the group ready to try their "new learnings" directly and overtly in situations where response is direct and swift ridicule, exclusion, or similar forms of punishment for nonconformity to the norms of the "outside" group. Treatment groups may be more like "real life" than dyadic therapeutic relationships, but they are certainly not identical with the outside world.

LEADERSHIP

Theories of personal change in groups, like theories of individual therapy, emphasize the central importance of the group leader or therapist. It is through his actions or abstinence from action that change processes are initiated, are set in the right (or the wrong) direction. The development of an adequate practical theory *requires not only a more precise delineation of particular leader modes of intervention and their consequences, but perhaps more importantly, an examination of the issue of the limitations of leader influence on the change process.* It is possible that the importance of the leader's behavior, personality, and skill level has taken on mythic proportions in explaining successful personal change in groups. Many forces within the field have lent credence to this notion—most theories of change have been developed by artful practitioners, and it would be understandable if such persons have overestimated their contribution to the curative process. The observation that complex, convoluted, supercharged feelings focus on the person of the leader (transference) does not of necessity demonstrate that the leader is central to the curative process. Other factors, such as professionalization, have also served to support a possible mythology about the importance of the leader in the change process.

Counteracting this trend are disturbing research reports which suggest that highly skilled leaders may not do better than unskilled personnel or leaderless groups or groups conducted by tape recorders. Studies of curative factors in groups, suggesting that certain experiences (such as the ability of a person to identify with the experience of another without directly participating in it or the experience of finding similarity between oneself and other human beings) are powerful mechanisms of change, also call into question the contribution of leaders. Such mechanisms exist more because of the intrinsic characteristics of intensive peer group experience than because of the behavior of the leader. The previously cited findings about the relatively low influence of leaders on group norms also suggest the priority of questions pertaining to the limits as well as the potentials of leader inputs.

These, then, are some issues to be explored in developing a practical theory for group-based people changing. Most readers will readily think of others. How, then, shall we proceed? Our track record has been less than stellar. Practitioners have contributed most of our ideas about how to change people in groups and have attempted to distill theoretical principles from an examination of aspects of their own expertise. Such distillations, however, impose the limitation that the leader as theoretician may not be in the best position to understand the active ingredients of changes occurring under his nose. The potential for experimental manipulation in group action situations is limited, and the use of experimental groups is dogged by the problem of determining the degree of continuity with real groups. Clinical studies of the kind reported by Bednar have certainly played a role in upgrading practice, but are limited in assessing possibly critical processes because of their inherent lack of access to comparative conditions. Clinical studies may, for example, discover replicable relationships between particular leader interventions and outcome but nevertheless fail to demonstrate the degree to which the leader intervention itself contributed to the change process. The ecological conditions in clinical research do not possess sufficient variation of input to test such broad questions. It is this reviewer's belief that reliable data for an empirically grounded theory of group people changing can be best generated by comparative analyses of a wide range of methods and settings for groups engaged in change. The contemporary scene offers many natural experiments in the use of groups to produce growth, change, personal learning, or therapy. Differences in populations, methods, and settings in the various types of groups (psychotherapy, self-help, encounter, consciousness-raising) offer the power of large variations in input parameters in action setting. Questions such as the exact characteristics of useful leader behavior and the degree to which the leader makes a difference and what it is that makes a difference can really be tested only in situations in which there is a sufficient variation in leader behavior (a potential not easily available in most traditional therapy systems, where therapists generally employ similar behaviors). Research on the wide variety of methods currently extant in our society seems requisite before we can begin to formulate systematic statements regarding critical variables in the induction of personal change.

Ultimately, a practical theory for people changing in groups means also the careful consideration of how to put empirically derived principles into a format that practitioners can use. The despair of many practitioners and their dissatisfaction with current aids need to be taken into account. The frequency with which professionals attend workshops on this or that set of techniques or "new theory" suggests that they wish to be aided and influenced. Whether research on people-changing groups is conducted along the lines suggested by Diamond, Bednar, or the more comparative approach suggested here, it is imperative that the findings of such research be packaged for influence. What is being suggested is that the research be so designed that its results eventually lead to the development of a *fully integrated set of principles* for how to do it. It is only in this way that the needs expressed by practitioners can be met. The wide swings in current practice and the almost faddish adaptations suggest that a well-packaged system with clearly developed training methods could hold sway. Unless researchers take this additional step, their findings on the people-changing processes in groups, no matter how statistically significant, may fail to meet the desired goal of systematizing practice.

REFERENCES

Beismier, P. Unpublished doctoral dissertation. Chicago: Department of Psychology, University of Chicago, 1974.

Lieberman, M. A., Yalom, I. D., & Miles, M. B. *Encounter Groups: First Facts.* New York: Basic Books, 1973, Chapters 8, 12, and 15.

II. WHAT HAPPENS IN A T-GROUP?

Perspectives on Processes and Outcomes

INTRODUCTION

II. What Happens in a T-Group?
Perspectives on Processes and Outcomes

5. Walter R. Mead, "Feedback: A 'How to' Primer for T-Group Participants"
6. David Nason, "Disclosure in Learning Groups"
7. Roger Harrison, "Defenses and the Need to Know"
8. William Underwood, "Roles that Facilitate and Inhibit Group Development"
9. A. Paul Hare, "Theories of Group Development and Categories for Interaction Analysis"

Providing perspective about what goes on in a T-Group is no simple matter,
and handling this complexity will require an early and somewhat arbitrary
factoring of these editorial comments into two parts. First, certain common
dynamics underlying T-Groups will be stressed, largely in this editorial essay.
Second, a variety of specific perspectives on these common dynamics will be
provided by five selections from the literature. This essay will introduce these
methods of looking at and interpreting what happens in a T-Group, with the
detailed exposition being left to the selections reprinted below.

At a general level, what happens in a T-Group is clear enough. Thus
individuals produce a variety of data about how they relate to others, and
how and when they go about:

- Attempting to control others;
- Seeking support from others;
- Punishing others or themselves;
- Withdrawing or involving themselves or just waiting;

- Listening to people, or turning them off;
- Accepting people for what they are, or forcing them to be what others wish them to be;
- Emotionally reacting to the situation, the people in it, and their behavior, or being detached from them;
- Scrutinizing what goes on within and between group members, or being largely unaware.

At a general level, again, what happens in a T-Group involves the basic distinction between "content" and "process." Roughly, the terms distinguish what people ostensibly are dealing with and what they are alluding to or gently working around. Illustratively,

CONTENT	PROCESS
When T-Group members talk about how many bad meetings they have attended	They may be signalling how bad they perceive their T-Group experience to be, and perhaps they are testing whether it is legitimate to air their perceptions

Individuals need not be aware of the process meaning of their content. But their communicative efficiency will be the worse for it.

In its essentials, the need to distinguish process from content implies that we are all like Plato's Cave of Addulam. That is, we project our real needs and concerns as variously distinct shadows on the facade or wall of the self that we expose to others. The "wall" or "facade" is what people are likely to see, at least at first, and what people have to get beyond in order to understand the essential self. "Process" in analogy is an important part of "more basic reality." "Content" is also real enough, but real only in the sense that the shadows flitting across Plato's Cave of Addulam are real.

What goes on in a T-Group, then, is a complex blend of the "real world" and the "laboratory." In part, what happens is just what happens in life. However, real-life phenomena may seem less intense, or more complicated by history or the job to be done, than in a T-Group. And real-life phenomena are far less likely to be analyzed as closely as in a T-Group. In such senses, the T-Group is a laboratory designed to permit intensive analysis of some behaviors at the expense of the broader reality that exists "out there."

These differences from the real world, whether in degree or in kind, are not accidental. The unstructured T-Group situation helps to induce such differences,[1] for example, as do laboratory norms which encourage a

---

[1] For example, such effects often are traced to the anxiety induced by the unstructured T-Group. All evidence suggests that this resultant anxiety is well within the tolerance of almost all participants. In one experiment, for example, the highest level of stress in a T-Group approximates that experienced by college students during exams. Bernard Lubin and Alice W. Lubin, "Laboratory Training Stress Compared with College Examination Stress," *Journal of Applied Behavioral Science*, Vol. 7 (July, 1971), pp. 502–507.

"loosening up" or "regression in the service of the ego."[2] Constraints are more prevalent in everyday life. Moreover, T-Group norms prescribe detailed analysis of behavior and reactions that normally escape conscious scrutiny in daily life. In addition, the T-Group climate encourages trust and interpersonal leveling that may be very different from the experiences of many participants in the outside world. The opportunity is to see ourselves as others see us, with unusual confidence that they are telling it the way it is, and with the intention of contributing to the mutual learning of all involved. T-Groups also provide an unusual opportunity to modify behaviors, and to have the changes reinforced and reacted to by fellow T-Group members who have a strong desire to be constructively helpful. The real world seldom permits such a luxury, let alone encourages it.

COMMON DYNAMICS UNDERLYING T-GROUPS

Explaining why T-Groups develop as they do can only be suggested here. Basically, the common dynamics underlying T-Groups inhere in a single observation: the behavior, attitudes and beliefs of individuals are rooted basically in interpersonal and intergroup relations. It is amazing how this root insight variously popped into prominence and out of it again. For Aristotle, for example, "social animal" was a tolerable definition of man, and man's very humanity rested in his group memberships and attainments. LeBon also was willing to acknowledge the power of the group, but largely as a medium for bringing out the worst in individual man. Whether for base purposes or noble, however, one generalization underlies even such disparate notions as Aristotle's and LeBon's: groups are a major source of influence over their members' behavior, attitudes, and beliefs.

In this elemental sense, the group is a *medium of control.* It is a major context in which people develop their concepts of who they are or, to say almost the same thing, of how they relate to others. Hence the compelling character of T-Group dynamics.

The T-Group effectively derives from two conceptual extensions of the basic observation that groups influence behavior.[3] One developmental notion was immediate. If the group influences or controls, then it is expedient to think of the group as a *target of change.* A variety of theoretical and applied work leaped at the challenge of gaining the leverage inherent in a group's influence over its members so as to change either individual or group

---

[2] Regression seems to influence T-Group dynamics, and a severe regression to childhood or infantile patterns of relating to others may explain the ego breakdowns occasionally seen in training groups. See Cyril R. Mill, "A Theory for the Group Dynamics Laboratory Milieu," *Adult Leadership,* Vol. 11 (November, 1962), pp. 133–34, 159–60.

[3] The following argument is based on Dorwin Cartwright, "Achieving Change in People: Some Applications of Group Dynamics Theory," *Human Relations,* Vol. 4 (1951), pp. 381–92.

behavior.[4] A number of useful principles derived from such work, and they may be noted briefly.

- The greater the attractiveness of a group for its members, the greater the influence it can exert over its members, and the more widely shared are a group's norms by its members.
- The greater the attractiveness of a group for its members, the greater the resistance to changes in behavior, attitudes, or beliefs which deviate from group norms.
- The greater the prestige of an individual among group members, the greater the influence he can exert.

There is one particular weak link in attempts to apply such principles, especially in industrial or administrative situations. Encouraging the development of groups does make available an enormous potential for the control of behavior, but there is no guarantee that groups will "do the right thing" as far as formal authorities are concerned. For example, if workers view a group as attractive on social grounds, that group will not necessarily be a useful medium for changing attitudes about output levels in the way that management desires. The group might only therefore be able to better mobilize its resources to resist management. Other principles of group dynamics, that is, are necessary to help predict the ways in which a group's influence will be applied in specific cases. Some significant "other principles" illustrate the broader field.

- The greater the sense of belonging to a common group that is shared by those people who are exerting influence for a change and those who are to be changed, the more probable is acceptance of the influence.
- The more relevant are specific behaviors, attitudes, or values to the bases for attraction of members to a group, the greater the influence a group can exert over those behaviors, attitudes, or values.

The T-Group avoids much of the resistance inherent in the concept of the group as a target of change by using the group as the *agent of change* as well as the target of change. The T-Group trainer does represent and model a set of values prescribing how its members should interact and, in extreme cases, he might be very active in requiring adherence to these guidelines. But these guidelines are usually accepted with minimum conflict. More commonly, the trainer may become a central figure because he is perceived as a manipulator. But such concern about the trainer is likely to be a passing thing. Group members early "begin to focus upon their relationship to each other, the problems of intimacy and closeness," one observer notes, "and learn from this emphasis on peer relationships about their characteristic modes of inter-

---

[4]Robert T. Golembiewski, *The Small Group* (Chicago: University of Chicago Press, 1962), esp. pp. 8–33.

action."[5] Within very wide limits, then, the T-Group can determine its own destiny as a temporary social system.

The great scope for self-determination in a T-Group enhances the probability of undiluted group influence. Crudely, the group needs to apply fewer of its resources to resisting outside authority, which resources it can thus apply to the learning process. Specifically, the T-Group respects several other principles of group dynamics.

- The greater the shared perception by group members of the need for a change, the more the pressure for change that will originate within the group and the greater the influence that will be exerted over members.
- The more widely shared among group members of information about plans for change and about their consequences, the greater is member commitment to the change and its implementation.
- The strains deriving from change in one sector of a group will produce systemic strains in other sectors, which can be reduced by negating the change or by re-adjusting the several sectors of a group.

The power of the T-Group, then, lies in the degree to which the group itself is used as the agent of change. This makes available the considerable power of the group to influence the behavior, attitudes, and beliefs of its members, and in an unusually undiluted degree. The point can be viewed from another perspective. Employing the T-Group as an agent of change avoids many of the manipulative pitfalls inherent in conceiving the group as a target of change to be acted upon by some external agent. Being acted upon of course, tends to encourage resistance. Group forces need not be applied nearly as much to resistance against authority when the group itself is the agent of change or influence, however. Consequently, group influence over member behavior should be quite direct in a T-Group.

SPECIFIC PERSPECTIVES ON COMMON DYNAMICS UNDERLYING T-GROUPS

Providing more specific perspectives on what happens in a T-Group can be approached in various ways, and the strategy here is to build from the simple and direct toward the complex and subtle. The Johari Window[6] will provide our takeoff platform. Usefully, the Window divides a person's life-awareness into four areas, utilizing the dimensions "known to self" and "known to others" to characterize knowledge about what a person is and how he appears to others. The sketch below presents the essentials of the Johari Window. Examples to fit the four areas are easy to develop. For example,

[5]Leonard Horwitz, "Transference in Training Groups and Therapy Groups," *The International Journal of Group Psychotherapy*, Vol. 14 (1964), p. 208.

[6]Joseph Luft, *Group Processes: An Introduction to Group Dynamics* (Palo Alto, Calif.: National Press, 1963), pp. 10–15. The Johari Window is named for its two originators, Joseph Luft and Harry Ingram.

individual A has a habit about which he was unaware, but that is very annoying to others. This habit lies in the Blind Area. Feedback from others concerning his impact on them would be necessary to enlarge A's Public Area in this case, as is depicted by the broken-line extension above into the Blind Area. The reader is encouraged to generate other examples.

T-Groups essentially focus on enlarging the Public Area, the "how" and the "why" of which enlarging can be explained briefly. First, concerning the "how," enlarging the Public Area can be accomplished by two basic interpersonal processes. The individual can come to know more of himself by receiving "feedback" from others who tell him how he is perceived by them. This reduces the Blind Area. Or the individual can make himself more known to others by "disclosure," which will reduce the Hidden Area. The Unknown area also may be reduced by unexpected insights.

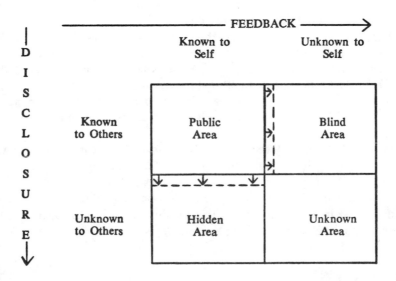

Second, the "why" for expanding the Public Area is a basic element of the *raison d'etre* of the T-Group. The enlargement of this area means that more data about an individual's attitudes and behaviors are made available, both to him and to the group. Thus, the potential for both individual and group problem-solving is raised to a new level.

Directly related to the enlargement of the Public Area is the issue of how group members deal with "unfinished business." Unfinished business may be illustrated briefly. Consider the case in which A becomes aware of a feeling or thought about himself or others *and* does not disclose this information. This enlarges the Hidden Area, and accumulates what is called "unfinished business." That business acts as an unresolved tension system that interferes with the individual's ability to operate effectively and congruently in relation to others. By the same token, if A's behavior hinders B—blocks him from behaving congruently with his feelings, for example—B develops unfinished business with A and increases the Blind Area until he openly deals with A's unawareness.

In general, there are four modalities for dealing with unfinished business. These are fight, flight, pairing, and confronting. Fight, flight, and pairing are substitutes for confronting. That is, if for one reason or another an individual does not deal overtly with his unfinished business, he may engage the other in conflict, he may avoid the issue, or he may join with the other in a supportive maneuver. Whichever of these three strategies a person chooses, the problem is taken care of only for the moment. And the Public Area remains constricted unless the issue is confronted through the processes of feedback and self-disclosure. Fight, flight, and pairing may be necessary from time to time, but their effect is generally to increase rather than decrease the amount of unfinished business.

The following selections also highlight various aspects of the rationale for expanding the Public Area in the Johari Window. By way of overview, as a person's Public Area is constricted, so also is he likely to feel restricted and ineffective in his dealings with others. Expanding the Public Area, at its core, is oriented toward testing the ways in which a person can be more fully himself while he is also increasingly effective by being more available to others and to himself.

Walter R. Mead's "Feedback: A 'How to' Primer for T-Group Participants" provides detail on one basic process for enlarging the Public Area of the Johari Window. Basically, Mead specifies a number of guidelines that will increase the likelihood of effective feedback, guidelines for both giver and receiver in a mutual helping relationship. That is, his concept of feedback can be sketched as a complex two-way street:[7]

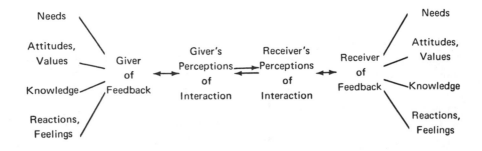

[7]"Feedback and the Helping Relationship," *NTL Institute: Reading Book* (Washington, D.C.: NTL Institute for Applied Behavioral Science, 1967), pp. 44–47. Mimeo.

The quality of the feedback, then, is a blend of: Who Giver and Receiver are in terms of specific needs, values, knowledge, and reactions or feeling; how they interact; and how they individually perceive their interaction. Mead also sketches the characteristics of specific feedback, or helping, situations that increase the probability that help will be offered and will be accepted as such. The helping relationship of feedback, in short, is at least subtle, and in some respects has an Alice in Wonderland quality. For example, the receiver of help is in the supremely influential position of determining whether or not he will accept the help in the sense that some change will take place. That is, the helper vitally depends on the help of the person needing the help. And so the subtleties of giving effective feedback go.

The quality of feedback can be critical in determining the outcome of a helping relationship, for feedback constitutes a corrective mechanism through which the receiver of help can learn how his behavior is perceived and reacted to by others. Giving feedback is not the only way to help, of course. For those situations in which feedback is appropriate, however—and this covers an incredible range—this first selection provides a detailed list of the criteria for increasing the effectiveness of feedback processes. T-Groups are, in an important sense, arenas for practicing feedback skills and for learning how to elicit feedback from others. This is another way of saying that T-Groups deal with the vitals of social life.

The primacy of feedback in T-Group development is reflected by James V. Clark.[8] He suggests a cyclical dyadic process that commences with a persistent pattern of incongruous behavior on the part of a group member—a pattern of which that person is unaware. As that incongruity is fed back to the person by others whom he or she perceives as authentic and caring, and to the extent that the incongruity is at variance with the person's self-concept, there is a predisposition to change. As the change occurs, it creates a problem for the other members who have encouraged it. That is, as the first person behaves more congruently, other group members are confronted with their own incongruence. The stage is thus set for the cycle to repeat itself, including more people each time the sequence recurs, and leading to more authentic group behavior.

The Public Area in the Johari Window also can be enlarged by "self-disclosure" by the individual making more of himself known to others. Self-disclosure plays yin to the yang of feedback. That is, feedback is often directed only at persons who are willing to disclose data about themselves. Relatedly, appropriate feedback often will elicit self-disclosure. As in most of life, you have to give in order to get.

"Disclosure in Learning Groups" by David Nason summarizes some

---

[8]James V. Clark, "Authentic Interaction and Personal Growth in Sensitivity Training Groups," *Journal of Humanistic Psychology*, Vol. 3, No. 1 (Spring, 1963), pp. 1–13.

current thinking concerning group and interpersonal forces that encourage low disclosure, as well as suggesting some ideas by which self-disclosing behavior can be made more effective. In addition, Nason makes a telling point: that it is possible for one person to use self-disclosing behavior in a punishing way under the guise of "true" openness. We recall, for example, in the first session of one T-Group when one man said to another, in the name of openness, "I've got funny feelings about you. Are you a homosexual?" The result was paralysis of the person addressed and of the group, a paralysis from which neither really ever recuperated.

Patently, then, some kinds of disclosure can terminate or severely complicate an interpersonal relationship, rather than deepen it. Similarly, too much self-disclosure can be as destructive to interpersonal relationships as too little. The former overwhelms the other persons, while the latter starves the relationship. Effective self-disclosure, then, may be characterized as being appropriately uninhibited. The specific situation defines what that means, and sensitivity to who is ready for what self-disclosure in which form at one time is an important product of T-Grouping.

The centrality of feedback and self-disclosure in a T-Group is easier established than capitalized upon, for there are substantial elements of skill involved in both that must be practiced rather than talked about, and practiced in environments that provide real challenges. Two inputs provide insight concerning the difficulties of doing what needs to be done in a T-Group. In the following editorial comments, we stress the defensiveness that characterizes much communication, even when major efforts are made to train professionals in communicating so as to reduce defensiveness. Subsequent comments introduce a selection reprinted below which broadly stresses the use and pathology of psychological defenses. Together, our editorial comments and the reprinted article clearly sketch the massive obstacles that inhibit feedback and self-disclosure.

The defensiveness characteristic of much communication can be illustrated by relying on Jack R. Gibb's "Defensive Communication."[9] That article emphasizes a people process rather than a language process, and stresses that fundamental improvements in communication consequently require improvements in interpersonal relationships. Gibb's approach to improving such relationships is to reduce the degree of defensiveness that commonly characterizes them. Gibb relates defensiveness to perceived threat or anticipated threat. The challenge of improving communication thus becomes one of behaving in ways that reduce threat. This in turn implies the building of suitable socio-emotional climates.

Based on his study of recordings of numerous discussions, Gibb isolated two contrasting climates and six categories of behavior that are characteristic

---

[9]Jack R. Gibb, "Defensive Communication," *The Journal of Communication,* Vol. II (September, 1961), pp. 141–42.

of each of them. The contrasting nature of these two climates can be suggested economically, although reference to the original piece is necessary to provide details. Defensive climates are characterized by evaluation, for example; and supportive climates emphasize description. Moreover, controlling behaviors are numerous in the former climates, while a problem-solving orientation characterizes the latter, and so on. Gibb stresses the tendency of these two categories of behaviors to increase and reduce defensiveness, respectively, with individual reactions specifically depending on the level of personal defensiveness and the climate of interpersonal or group relations within which the behaviors occur.

Defensive Climates Tend to Be Induced By	Supportive Climates Tend to Be Induced By
1. Evaluation	1. Description
2. Control	2. Problem orientation
3. Strategy	3. Spontaneity
4. Neutrality	4. Empathy
5. Superiority	5. Equality
6. Certainty	6. Provisionalism

T-Groups, in a major sense, are vehicles for experimenting with attitudes and skills necessary for inducing the two climates, as well as for observing their effects on others. Both foci are vital, for they establish the significance of climate to communication, as well as demonstrate the difficulty of inducing the appropriate climate. As for significance to communication, reduced defensiveness permits receivers, in Gibb's words, to "become better able to concentrate upon the structure, the content, and the cognitive meanings of the message." The significance of climate can be established from another perspective. Not only do defensive communicators send off multiple value, motive, and affect cues, but defensive recipients also distort what they perceive, Gibb explains.

The difficulty of developing attitudes and skills required to induce supportive climates is also easy to establish. Gibb emphasizes the difficulties of shifting behaviors from (for example) evaluation to description, and hence the problems of building supportive as opposed to defensive climates. "Anyone who has attempted to train professionals to use information-seeking speech with neutral affect," Gibb explains, "appreciates how difficult it is to say even the simple 'who did that?' without being seen as accusing." The T-Group increases the chances of effectively learning the difficult, as via feedback to a learner about the effects of his behavior on others.

Roger Harrison's "Defenses and the Need to Know" takes a broad look at the issue with which Gibb dealt. He describes a neat battleground, in effect.

"The study of defenses . . . ," Harrison explains, "is the study of the processes that protect the [individual's] organization of conceptual systems in the face of information and experiences which, if accurately perceived, would tend to break down or change the relationships among concepts in the system." Defenses are a major tool of man in adapting to a changing world and, indeed, everyone of us vitally depends on defenses to make some order of life. Consequently, defenses take on value as objects to be protected. But a real tension exists, for defenses not only help us in life, but they also may prevent us from capitalizing on learning situations. And humans tend to have a strong need to know, to gain knowledge, and to extend their competence.

The T-Group is one of the arenas in which the tension between defenses and the need to know becomes manifest. If an individual's defenses have great adaptive value for him, for example, he may prefer not to have others look at them too closely in a T-Group. His tendency will be to opt against self-disclosure and to inhibit or not hear feedback directed to him, all things being equal. But all other things are not equal. The individual also has a need to know how he is being perceived by others, if only to learn if his defenses really are as effective as he believes them to be. Getting the feedback he requires may expose his defenses to scrutiny, however. Essentially, all T-Group members must continually decide the complex mix of tradeoffs that are acceptable to them.

Out of this dynamic tension of defenses and the need to know, learning may occur or it may not. If an individual decides his need to know is greater than his need to protect his defenses from scrutiny, he has effectively made the major step toward meaningful learning about himself. More or less, at least at superficial levels, most participants in a T-Group make such a choice. They may learn what effects their defenses have on others, whether particular defenses are as necessary as they seem, or whether new defenses might be developed that have less undesirable fallout as the learner judges the situation. If the inviolability of a person's defenses is paramount, oppositely, learning in a T-Group is not likely beyond the point of demonstrating how desperately the individual needs his present defenses, or of highlighting how behaviorally frozen he is. And that just might be enough learning for some people, at least the first time around. Or the individual might get confirmation that his defenses serve his own purposes well while they are only minimally off-putting to others.

Enlarging the Public Area of the Johari Window also requires massive attention to the full-blown diversity of what goes on in a T-Group. T-Groups, in short, are not all feedback and disclosure. They encompass a complex arena of behavior, attitudes, and feelings. Initially, the trainer is a crucial resource in directing attention to this full range of phenomena, but members become more active in this area as their T-Group matures. William Underwood's "Roles That Facilitate and Inhibit Group Development" highlights some of the phenomena to which both trainer and members must give attention.

"Roles That Facilitate and Inhibit Group Development" stresses the importance of distinguishing the purposes or functions that specific behaviors seem to serve. The selection stresses two kinds of role-behaviors that are useful for interpreting what goes on in groups: behavior that contributes directly to the performance of a task; and behavior that serves a maintenance function, as by preparing a good climate for work or by repairing relationships that have been somehow impaired in the course of getting a task done. These two functions or purposes can be distinguished from self-oriented behavior, a third kind of set of behaviors or functional role.

The three functions or roles can enrich observation and interpretation of what goes on in a T-Group in a variety of ways. These functions help to characterize stages in the development of a T-Group, for example. Early in a T-Group's development, self-oriented behavior will tend to be common. T-Group members will not be listening to one another; their contributions will tend to be nonadditive; and members will tend to feel that they "are going nowhere as a group." Not uncommonly, T-Group members soon will discover the value of maintenance behaviors, perhaps induced by an early crisis such as managing a member's dissatisfaction with the lack of progress. A very pleasant honeymoon period of high cohesiveness may follow. Sooner or later, some members may tire of the "tea party" or mutual admiration society," asking if that is the only purpose for their being together. Members of a T-Group then may begin to look closely at their impact on one another. In the process of such work, a mature group will be sensitive to the points at which major attention to group maintenance is necessary, so as to consolidate a plateau of learning on which additional learning can be based. This sketch of group phases is grievously simplified, but it should suggest the value of seeing apparently disparate behaviors in terms of the common functions which they serve.

A. Paul Hare, in "Theories of Group Development and Categories for Interaction Analysis," presents a most comprehensive discussion of the development of theory concerned with the processes of group change and growth. The service he performs in this article is a profound one, as it enables the reader to receive both an historical and up-to-date view of theoretical thinking relative to patterns of group development. It would be a disservice to the article and to Hare's thinking to attempt a brief summary here. Suffice it to say that one is impressed by the interrelatedness of thought concerning developmental processes in a group that is evinced by a variety of researchers who approach their problem from different perspectives. Perhaps most intriguing is the potential, suggested by Hare, for the analysis of all types of social systems that has derived from the study of small groups. The point is that the microsociety of the T-Group contains within it not only a vehicle for personal learning, but for testing of hypotheses that may help us learn more about the social world in which we exist.

5. Feedback: A "How to" Primer for T-Group Participants

WALTER R. MEAD

A major purpose of Sensitivity Training is to provide an opportunity for the participant to learn how others see him and react to him. This process is called feedback.

Early in the life of a T-Group, participants are often cautious about giving feedback. "If I tell him what I really think, will he collapse in a pool of tears or will he fly into an uncontrolled rage?" Uncertainty about how the feedback will be received and consequent fantasies of disaster inhibit the giving of feedback.

This paper describes and illustrates how feedback can be given and received in ways that are most helpful, as well as ways that minimize the chances of hurting people or precipitating defensive retaliation.

GUIDELINES FOR GIVING FEEDBACK

1. *Feedback is most likely to be understood when it is given immediately after the behavior has been observed.* "I don't think you're aware that you just interrupted me. I guess I have a hang-up about that but it annoys hell out of me."

The receiver of this bit of feedback might not like what he heard but he's much more likely to understand it than if the feedback were delayed or generalized. For example, "John, I've noticed over the past two days that you sometimes interrupt people."

2. *Feedback is more likely to be understood and accepted when it describes specific observed behavior.* "When Al made that remark to Pete

---

Written expressly for this volume.

you seemed to come immediately to Pete's defense. That irritated me because I think Pete can take care of himself." This would be more helpful than, "You always protect everyone." It's more likely that there would be many exceptions to the generality. The exceptions provide ammunition for an argument and enable the receiver to avoid learning about himself.

Feedback which characterizes the whole person instead of describing specific observed behavior is not very useful. "You're a very kind person." "You're a nice guy." "You're stupid." While these statements imply the impact of the other person's behavior, they give no hint as to the action which prompted the conclusions.

Speculation about others' motives for behavior is not useful. "You're trying to dominate the group." "You want everyone to like you." These kinds of statements indicate that the speaker knows *why* others behave as they do. It's rarely true or relevant. What *is* important is the behavior itself and the effects it produces in others.[1]

3. *Useful feedback reveals one's emotional reaction to another's behavior without making moral or ethical judgments about the behavior.* Words such as *relieved, angry, sad, excited, confused, afraid* describe emotional reactions. Words such as *right, wrong, mature, immature, good, bad, should,* and *shouldn't* express moral or ethical judgments.

The distinction between judgments and emotional reactions is very important. Value judgments about another's behavior often stimulate intellectual debates, polarize adversaries into win-lose postures and raise defenses. Revealing emotional reaction makes others aware of reality. One can speak with complete authority about his own feelings but he is not likely to be accepted as an authority on values.

Feedback is more useful when it conveys a flavor of "maybe this is my hang-up." "This may be your fault or it may be mine." "Perhaps this says more about me that it does about you." If one participant is offended by another's use of four letter words, that's simply a fact. It does *not* necessarily follow that the person who swears is bad or the person offended is a prude.[2]

4. *Feedback is more meaningful when it comes from several people, not just one.* One person's perceptions and reactions may be typical for the group or they may be unique. Therefore it's helpful to solicit other views. "I wonder

---

[1] An essential difference between T-Groups and Group Therapy is the focus on motivation for behavior. In Group Therapy patients are presumed to exhibit significant self-defeating behavior motivated by irrational fears. Participants are encouraged to examine events from their childhood in an effort to discover the cause of their problems. T-Group participants are not presumed to be "sick"; they *are* presumed to be unaware of some aspects of their behavior and their effects on others.

[2] T-Groups have been criticized for encouraging "moral anarchy." If this means that T-Group advocates believe that no person has the right to force his values on another adult, the criticism is valid.

if others saw that as I did or felt the same way." Thus the *giver* of feedback also has an opportunity to learn to what extent his perceptions and reactions are shared by others.

Throwing the question to the group also avoids the problem of the receiver of feedback believing, inaccurately, that one person's views represent a consensus.

GUIDELINES FOR RECEIVING FEEDBACK

1. *Feedback is more likely to be understood if the receiver listens attentively.* A typical reaction to hearing negative feedback is to stop listening and start preparing a rebuttal. Unfortunately, this prevents the receiver from hearing the whole message.

2. *Communication can be assured by the receiver paraphrasing the feedback.* If the receiver can restate the message in his own words to the satisfaction of the sender both know whether the message got through. If one listens to feedback with the intention of paraphrasing it later, he disciplines himself to listen more attentively and keeps himself from "tuning out" to prepare his "rebuttal."

3. *The receiver can learn whether the feedback represents only one person's opinion or a consensus by checking with others in the group.* In most cases there are subtle or substantial differences in participants' perceptions and reactions.

4. *Feedback does not require that the receiver change his behavior.* T-Group participants often sense a strong pressure to conform to group standards. This has been called "the tyranny of the group."

The "standards" imply criteria for membership in the group. Some restrictive standards might be:

a) "Everyone must do what the Trainer suggests."
b) "Everyone must confess some weakness, past 'sin' or 'hang-up.'"
c) "Everyone must cry."
d) "Everyone must participate equally."

A participant is free to modify his behavior to please others but is equally free to continue behavior that displeases others. If the group standards seem to require certain behavior or forbid others, the standards should be examined. How were they set? By whom? How are they to be enforced?

5. *The best way to get feedback is to give it.* Some T-Group participants become concerned because they haven't received feedback. They solicit it but get only vague or general responses. In most cases, the person who isn't getting much feedback hasn't given much. If he is unwilling to risk giving others feedback, others will be unlikely to risk giving him feedback.

SUMMARY

Chart 2.1 distinguishes between effective and ineffective feedback.

Effective	Ineffective
Immediate	Delayed
Specific observed behavior	Conclusions about behavior Characterizations of the whole person Diagnosis of other's motivations
Emotional reactions	Value judgments
Several peoples' perceptions and reactions	One person's perceptions and reactions

Chart 2.2 distinguishes between effective and ineffective modes of receiving feedback.

Effective	Ineffective
Listen	Prepare rebuttal
Paraphrase message	Assume understanding
Check for consensus	Assume uniqueness or consensus
Retain autonomy	Submit to group pressure
Demonstrate willingness to give and receive feedback	Solicit feedback while withholding own perception and reactions

Our fantasies about the "dire" consequences of hearing how others see us or telling others how they affect us, keep us from experiencing open, honest relationships. The ego-building effect of the T-Group experience comes largely from replacing fantasy with reality.

6. Disclosure in Learning Groups

DAVID NASON

One way to conceive of what happens in a T-Group is to see it as a process of continually broadening and deepening the group-sanctioned boundaries of interpersonal communication. The mechanisms through which these boundary lines become widened are the complementary ones of feedback and self-disclosure. The usage of feedback about behavior, group, and organizational processes has wide acceptance. In many circles, for example, it is "good" to give feedback. Self-disclosure, on the other hand, particularly about the way one is feeling at a moment in time, is not necessarily viewed as a "good" thing. We are taught to keep our feelings to ourselves. This is so despite the fact that, as people persist in keeping both their feelings and ideas hidden, they may: (1) well build up an unpleasant psychological burden within themselves, (2) prevent themselves from engaging in meaningful interpersonal contacts, and (3) inhibit the group members from learning about themselves.

A considerable body of literature has developed in recent years concerning the subject of personal and interpersonal self-disclosure. The literature ranges from theory and research (Jourard, 1964; Cozby, 1973) to philosophical speculation on the "I—Thou" relationship (Buber, 1937). With few exceptions, self-disclosure has not been studied within the context of a group experience, but has been conceptualized as a personality trait of individuals (Cozby, 1973), or as a linear communication process involving only two people. While it is probably true that individuals differ in the things they would disclose to different people in dyadic situations, studies of those differences provide little assistance in the understanding of self-disclosure as a communication process in groups.

Pearce and Sharp (1973), writing on self-disclosing communication, reject the personality trait studies on methodological and conceptual bases. To include these studies in the analysis of communication processes, they suggest, "would commit the fallacy of treating communication as a thing 'suis generis' "; that is, treating self-disclosure as if it could stand alone, disconnected from any communicative phenomena. The usefulness of the psychodynamic literature for their purposes (and ours) is reduced further by "the fact that the findings of studies based on this orientation [psychodynamic] are contradictory", due in part to the "quite different conceptualizations of self-disclosure and some questionable methodologies" (p. 411)

Written expressly for this volume.

employed by the researchers. For Pearce and Sharp, "self-disclosure must be described in terms of a more adequate understanding of communication".

The comments about disclosure discussed here are made within the context of experiential group learning situations as presented by Luft (1970) under a communication theory model. Within that model, self-disclosing behavior can be analysed as a function of the quality of the interaction system, rather than as a function of the personalities of the participants. Analysis of self-disclosing behavior can be made by looking at the forces pushing against disclosure and the forces pushing towards disclosure.

FORCES ENCOURAGING LOW DISCLOSURE

In his analysis of the basic causes of low disclosure in organizations (we make the transfer to T-Groups), Steele (1975) suggests that there are several threats or risks that confront the would-be discloser and which thus may be inhibitors of this behavior. First is "the threat that the discloser will be evaluated negatively as a result of the disclosure" (p. 9). An act of disclosure, for example, may violate group norms, thus bringing down sanctions of the group or the authority figure on the person involved. The second area of threat is to the investment the individual may have in maintaining a particular relationship. The risk is the potential loss of social contact or satisfying relationships if the other persons(s) is alienated or angered by the disclosure. Third, there is the threat of loss of control or the ability to influence a situation. That is, as a person discloses, that very act contains the potential for opening up the situation even further in a fashion that is unpredictable, implying a loss of control.

Steele further suggests that the very nature of the disclosing situation may have some risks attached to it. Those risks are concerned with: (1) the nature of the content of the disclosure, (2) the sender's perception of the group, its tasks, and his or her relationship to the group, and (3) the social climate in which the sender and receiver are operating.

The Nature of the Content

Topics that are of a private nature about one's self imply more risk than disclosing topics that are public. Jourard (1964) found that people more readily disclosed information on attitudes, tastes, and work (or studies) than the more intimate information on money, personality, and body. Typically, disclosures that include the sender's feelings are felt as more risky than those that disclose only ideas. The reason this is so is that such disclosures generally are not supported by social norms. Also, feelings originate within the sender, implying ownership, whereas ideas can be attributed widely to other sources. Present tense disclosures imply higher risks as they generally involve "here-and-now" relationships and control patterns.

Self-disclosures that carry an implicit or explicit evaluation of oneself or other's abilities, competence, or general worth as a person are more risky than statements that are neutral. Another area of high risk content, noted by Culbert (1973), is disclosure to correct previous impressions that were allowed to go uncorrected. Risk of rejection can stem from either the new data or from the basis that one knowingly allowed a lie to be continued, thus permitting the group to proceed on inadequate or incorrect data.

The Perceptions of the Sender

The discloser's perception of the group, its tasks, and his or her relationship to the group relate to the perceived risk of disclosure. If the discloser sees the group as hostile, disclosure will seem riskier to personal self-security. Disclosure increases one's vulnerability. When the group is seen as a battleground for power struggles, the sharing of information is riskier as the information may be used in retaliation. Thus when power is at stake, disclosure becomes guarded, occurring when one feels it will not bring hurt and/or will help to defend and build one's own power in the situation. On the other hand, when the group is seen as a vehicle for growth and change or as a problem-solving situation, the sharing of information is a more natural and necessary part of the process.

The discloser's perception of the level of commitment in the group, both on the part of the discloser to the group and the group to the discloser, makes for differences in the level of risk. If the group tends to have a high evaluative orientation (Gibb, 1961), the risk involved in making disclosures is high. High risk exists if the group is seen as not listening and unresponsive. If the relationship is weak, new information increases the risk of a break in the relationship.

Climate

When the social norms of the group support disclosure and do not punish openness, the risk of disclosing is lower. Such norms tend to be built up over a period of time. A history of positive experiences with disclosure make disclosure in the present less risky. A high level of trust, a predictability of the other's behavior when one is vulnerable, also makes for lower levels of risk. A climate of psychological safety allows individuals to be more congruent in their feelings, behavior, and communications.

Theories to Justify Low Disclosure

Steele offers several "tongue-in-cheek" theories people use to justify low disclosure, two of which seem appropriate here. The "satellite theory of communication" states the common belief that it is better to communicate something indirectly than directly. This theory is often invoked by persons who wish to be seen as sensitive to the other person, especially in the case of conveying negative communications. Take, for example, the group member who felt he was not ready to receive direct feedback from people in the group. He makes a comment to the group on "how some people take a long time to develop a readiness to deal with feedback." Then, a short while later, another group member gives him some direct negative feedback. The first member becomes angry because the other person had not listened to him say he was not ready for direct feedback. The second member's defense is, "I thought you were making a general comment; I did not realize you were talking about yourself!"

A second theory is the "one-shot assumption", which has its origins in the belief that image formation, impressions, and evaluation are based on a single act. Thus, if one shares some negative data about oneself, that person will be condemned regardless of any other information that may exist.

EFFECTIVE SELF-DISCLOSURE

In sensitivity training one's decisions to self-disclose relate directly to how one is using one's self in the experience. We can use ourselves in a destructive and hurtful manner or we can choose to use ourselves in ways that facilitate the growth of the group and ourselves. Culbert (1973) lists several characteristics of effective disclosure. They are adapted here to relate to the effective use of ourselves through self-disclosure in laboratory groups.

First, effective self-disclosure is appropriate to the context and structure where it occurs. Self-disclosure of strong negative reactions too early in the life of a group, before support and trust have been built, can contribute to a history within the group that does not support disclosure. At other phases in the group, the same disclosures can be helpful and supportive of group norms for openness and leveling. Self-disclosures that are unrelated to current themes or topics, that seem to come from "out of the blue," can cut off discussions and move the group on before topics are completed, leaving some group members hanging. If the sender of the disclosure is bored or just wants to talk about something else, it probably would be more appropriate to state those feelings and see if the group is ready to change. Otherwise, this person makes a unilateral decision to change the topics which discounts the feelings and needs of the other group members. Such a decision can undermine the support and trust that has been built in the group.

In some cases disclosures that violate the norms of the group are appropriate. Culbert notes, "the most positive experiences emerge as a result of persons taking risks" (p. 114) that go beyond the expectation of the group. This does not mean the group will respond positively to the disclosure. The discloser should be cognizant of the potential consequences of such acts. Even with the risks involved, such disclosures expand the public area of topics the group can explore. An alternative to the direct violation of a group norm is to openly question the norm itself and assess the impact of the norm on the group and on the feelings of participants. This gives the group opportunities to make decisions about its own functioning and can lower the risk level associated with violating taboos.

Other issues related to the effectiveness of self-disclosure are the reasons, needs, or motivations that prompted the disclosure. This dimension is revealed most through what Chelune (1975) called the "affective manner of presentation" of the disclosure. If group members perceive a lack of congruence between the sender's stated motivations and the way the sender actually behaves, they will have a guarded reaction and probably develop defensive measures to protect themselves. For example, consider the different reactions group members might have to someone who in a soft voice, with a smile, says, "I'm really angry with the group" versus someone who is red in the face and says loudly, "I AM REALLY ANGRY WITH THE GROUP!"

In the first case the person may not be believed and group members may question the motives behind the statement. The disclosure will not be accepted at face value and will be viewed with suspicion. In the second case the person's anger will probably be taken more seriously by the group and the issues surrounding the anger can more easily be explored. Self-disclosures that are consistent with one's current state of awareness and experience, then, lead to a more receptive climate for the disclosure. However, a cautionary note is offered by Dyer (1972). He suggests that congruence is a personal value and that behaviors that are "congruent at the moment" could violate other values, such as values regarding the rights of others. He sees congruency, not as a license for behavior, but as encouragement to "express his feelings without necessarily acting them out" (p. 13).

Disclosures about the past can reduce one's effectiveness in learning groups. Past-tense disclosures are useful to shock, distract, or disinterest the listener. Egan (1970) states that past-tense disclosure can often be labeled as history. He notes of history:

It is actuarial and analytic, and usually has a strong "there and then" flavor. It clicks off the facts of experiences and even interpretations of this experience, but leaves the person of the revealer relatively untouched; he is accounted for and analysed, but unrevealed. The person relates many facts about himself, but the person within still remains unknown. History is often a long account. It is long and often steady because it fears interruption. Interruption might mean involvement, and a person engages in history to avoid, rather than invite, involvement (pp. 234-235).

We tend to be more effective in the use of ourselves in sensitivity training when our self-disclosures are in the present tense. Present-tense disclosures share with our listeners our current experience. Culbert (1973) emphasizes the key status given to present-tense disclosure in sensitivity training:

. . . such disclosures typically have the highest interpersonal relevance, generate the greatest amount of feedback, and make for the greatest receptivity to the feedback of others. Hence present tense disclosures, other things being equal, are believed to possess the highest potential for increased self awareness and personal growth. (p. 115)

DISCLOSURE AND FEEDBACK

In a sense, every time one person gives feedback to another or to a group, that person is engaging in a disclosure activity. What is at issue is the type of disclosure that accompanies the feedback or is withheld from it. An example may help clarify. Picture the following situation:

In the early stages of a T-group one person is dominating the group interaction by insisting on the development of a task and blocking attempts to analyse the process. The effect of this behavior on another member of the group is as follows: the member is uncomfortable, angry at the dominator, feeling put-down and inconsequential, angry at self for not being able to deal more effectively with the situation, angry at the group for letting all this happen, and angry at the trainer for not intervening to change the situation. In this case one can conceive of a number of feedback options that will at the same time disclose different things to the group and to the other person involved. For example, the member may:

- lash out at the dominator, engage in a fight—thus disclosing utter frustration and the member's way of dealing with frustration;
- lash out at the group for being so impotent—disclosing, perhaps, feelings of wanting to punish in the process;
- lash out at the trainer for not doing something, disclosing feelings of anger at the person and disappointment with the trainer;
- talk *about* feelings of discomfort and anger at what is occurring;
- talk *about* feelings of helplessness in the face of the power of the dominator;
- talk about how it feels to the member to feel helpless, engaging in disclosure on a more interpersonal level.

This list does not exhaust all the options. It is sufficient, though, to reinforce the idea that as a person engages in feedback certain elements of self-disclosure are typically involved. As we engage with others in an interpersonal context we usually communicate something about ourselves as well as the subject about which we are talking.

USELESS DISCLOSURE

In learning groups, all acts of self-disclosure are not of equal value. In some cases disclosure may be useless and under some conditions detrimental. Egan (1970) sees uselessness as the probable outcome of disclosure to the degree that the disclosure is:

- exhibitionistic rather than oriented toward establishing or deepening a relationship;
- not responded to with support and acceptance by listeners;
- history (in the sense earlier noted);
- first promised by someone who then reneges on the promise;
- incomplete in a situation where completeness is required.

NONVOLUNTARY DISCLOSURE

Most definitions of self-disclosure, as a positively valued behavior, state the information is *voluntarily* shared by the sender. In learning groups the norms that develop around the issue of self-disclosure and openness can go beyond being supportive of disclosure to demanding self-disclosure. Self-disclosure becomes part of the dues for psychological membership in the group. As such, disclosure becomes an end in itself rather than a means to an end. For instance, silent members of the group may be put "on the spot" by other group members by demands for feedback, or forced to defend why they have remained silent. History and other "useless" varieties of disclosure are usually not acceptable to the persons demanding the disclosure and such perfunctory attempts to satisfy their demands may further alienate the individual from the other group members. In some cases the group may want the individual to express anger, cry, or engage in a specific behavior that the other group members have gone through. The individual on the spot can attempt to assuage their demands or can engage in effective self-disclosure of the present feelings that surround being put on the spot and being subject to group harassment.

DISCLOSURE TO PUNISH

Earlier the destructive use of self-disclosing behavior was mentioned. While self-disclosure offers much potential for growth and interpersonal learning, it can also be used to hurt, punish, or put down other group members. In the literature this aspect of self-disclosing behavior is often defined as something apart from true self-disclosure. The differing position taken here is that self-disclosure is a behavior; its use and value depend upon the situation and context in which the disclosure is made. Furthermore, in the case of self-disclosure to punish, the motives of the sender are directly relevant. The concern here is not the disclosures that accidentally hurt others due to the ineptness of the sender in timing or wording. The concern is for self-disclosures made as a response to one's own anger or desire to gain revenge on another group member. The sender's behavior and affect may be congruent, but there often are attempts to disguise the punishment in the cloak of helpful disclosure that may accompany feedback. For example, a group member has received negative feedback from another member of the group, which has made her angry with this other person. At a later point in the groups she turns to the second member and says, "Yesterday, when you were talking about your feelings toward the trainer, I thought you were really being stupid. I was angry with you for wasting the group's time." Other group members may come to the defense of the second person and begin to attack the sender for being malicious. She responds, "I was just telling him how I felt. Isn't it OK to give feedback in this group?" If the recipient of the "feedback" had experienced difficulty in discussing his feeling about the trainer, the feedback could be detrimental and cut off future disclosures. It cannot really be known if the first group member was trying to be helpful and not trying to hurt the other person. Motives can only be inferred. The only person who truly knows is the sender. The sender should be aware of what is prompting the disclosure, and if it is being prompted to anger and revenge, the person might do well to follow Dyer's suggestion to talk about feelings without necessarily acting them out.

CONCLUSION

Early in the life of learning groups, participants are faced with decisions on the nature and amount of information about themselves they will share with other group members. At first, they may only share their names. Throughout the life of the group, acts of self-disclosure continue to provide the group with information on the participants and the processes of the group. Self-disclosure is necessary for interpersonal feedback to take place. Self-disclosure holds no *a priori* value as a behavior. Its value rests in how one chooses to use it, in the context of one's experience. Information about self can be shared with the intent of securing power and to punish and alienate others. Or one can choose to use acts of self-disclosure as an invitation to others to share in personal experience and to allow others to know that person as he or she is. When choosing to use self in the latter manner, one can more fully utilize personal experience and the experience of others in the process of growth and change.

REFERENCES

Buber, M. *I and Thou.* New York: Scribner, 1937.

Chelune, G. Self-disclosure: An Elaboration of its Basic Dimensions. *Psychological Reports,* (1975) 36, pp. 79–85.

Cozby, P. Self-disclosure: A Literature Review. *Psychological Bulletin* (1973) 79, pp. 73–91.

Culbert, S. A. The Interpersonal Process of Self-Disclosure: It Takes Two to See One. In Golembiewski, R. T. and A. Blumberg (eds.), *Sensitivity Training and the Laboratory Approach* (second edition), Itasca, Ill.: F. E. Peacock Publishers, Inc., 1973, p. 73.

Dyer, W. *The Sensitive Manipulator: The Change Agent Who Builds with Others.* Provo, Utah: Brigham Young University Press, 1972.

Egan, G. *Encounter: Group Processes for Interpersonal Growth.* Belmont, Ca.: Wadsworth Publishing Co., 1970.

Gibb, J. Defensive Communication. *Journal of Communication,* 11, 1961.

Golembiewski, R. *Renewing Organizations: The Laboratory Approach to Planned Change.* Itasca, Ill.: F. E. Peacock Publishers, Inc., 1972.

Jourard, S. *The Transparent Self.* Princeton, N.J.: Von Nostrand, 1964.

Luft, J. *Group Processes: An Introduction to Group Dynamics.* Palo Alto, Ca.: National Press Books, 1970.

Pearce, W., and Sharp, S. Self-disclosing Communication. *The Journal of Communication,* 1973, 23, pp. 409–425.

Steele, F. *The Open Organization: The Impact of Secrecy and Disclosure on People and Organizations.* Reading, Ma.: Addison-Wesley Publishing Co., 1975.

7. Defenses and the Need to Know

ROGER HARRISON

The purpose of this paper is to discuss the ways we have of protecting our views of ourselves and others. Specifically, it is intended to rescue the concept of "defensive behavior" from the ostracism in which it is usually held, to restore it to its rightful place as a major tool of man in adapting to a changing world, and to consider how defenses may help and hinder us in profiting from a learning situation.

Let us consider how we understand the world we live in, and particularly those parts of it concerning ourselves and our relations with other people. First of all, we organize the world according to *concepts,* or categories. We say that things are warm or cold; good or bad; simple or complex. Each of these concepts may be considered a dimension along which we can place events in the world—some closer to one end of the dimension, some closer to the other.

Actually, we can't really think without using these categories or dimensions to organize our thoughts. Any time we consider the qualities of ourselves, other persons, or events in the inanimate world, we have to use categories to do it. We are dependent for our understanding of the world on the concepts and categories we have for organizing our experiences. If we lack a concept for something which occurs in the world, we either have to invent one or we cannot respond to the event in an organized fashion. How, for example, would a person explain his own and others' behavior without the concept of

Reproduced by special permission from *NTL Human Relations Training News,* Vol. 6, No. 4, "Defenses and the Need to Know," Roger Harrison, pp. 1–4, NTL Institute for Applied Behavioral Science.

This paper was inspired by a theory session by Harry Ingham and a paper by Abraham Maslow.

love and hate? Think how much behavior would simply puzzle or confuse him or, perhaps, just go on by without really being perceived at all, for lack of this one dimension.

Concepts do not exist in isolation; they are connected to one another by a network of relationships. Taken all together, the concepts we use to understand a situation, plus the relationships among the concepts, are called a *conceptual system*. For example, we may say, "People who are warm and friendly are usually trusting, and hence, they are often deceived by others." Here we have a conceptual system linking the concepts of *friendly warmth, trust in others,* and *ease of deception.* Because concepts are linked one to another, the location of an event on one concept usually implies something about where the event is located on each of a whole network of concepts. It is thus almost impossible to take in a small bit of information about a characteristic of a person or event without its having a whole host of implications about other characteristics.

Images and stereotypes operate this way: when we discover that a person is a Negro, or a PTA president, a social scientist, or a wife, the information on these concepts immediately calls up a whole network of expectations about other characteristics of the person. In the case of stereotypes, these expectations may even be so strong that we do not check to find out whether our conceptual system worked accurately this time, but may even go to the other extreme of ignoring or distorting information which doesn't fit the conceptual system, so that the system may remain quite unaffected by disconfirming experiences.

The study of defenses, like the study of stereotypes, is the study of the processes that protect the organization of conceptual systems in the face of information and experiences which, if accurately perceived, would tend to break down or change the relationships among concepts in the system.

Why should conceptual systems be resistant to change? Actually, if they were simply intellectual exercises, they probably would not. In real life, conceptual systems come to have *value* attached to them. The values seem to be of two kinds: one kind I will call *competence value.* By the competence value of a conceptual system I mean its value for helping us to be effective in the world. After all, the conceptual systems we have were developed because we needed some way of making sense of the world; of predicting what kinds of results would follow from what kinds of causes; of planning what kinds of actions we needed to take in order to accomplish some desired result.

People have the conceptual systems they have because in some important situations the systems proved *adaptive* for them; by seeing the world in just this way they were able to get along better, to be more effective, to prepare better for what was coming next. For human beings conceptual systems are, in a very real sense, very nearly the most important survival equipment we have. Animals have instinctual patterns of response: complex systems of behavior that are set off without thinking in response to fairly fixed patterns of stimulation. Human beings have to do it the hard way, by developing systems of concepts that make sense of the world and then using these systems to make decisions as to what to do in each situation. Those conceptual systems that pay off over and over again tend to become parts of our permanent equipment for understanding the world and for deciding what to do in it. If we were to lose these systems we would become like ships without rudders; we would have lost our control systems and, with them, our chances of acting in an organized, intelligent fashion to meet our needs. This is what I mean by the *competence value* of conceptual systems.

Unfortunately, no conceptual system fits the world perfectly. In the interests of economy we simplify and leave things out as being unimportant: for example, we act as though relationships which are *statistical* (they are only true most of the time) are *necessary,* and hence true all of the time. On the rare occasions when the relationships don't hold, we tend to overlook it, rather than trying to understand why things didn't go as expected. We may, for example, conceptualize the qualities of warmth, lovingness, and femininity as incompatible with a ready ability to express anger. This conceptual system may not change even in the face of strong anger on the part of a woman about whose warmth and femininity we have ample evidence in the past. We simply pass it off as, "She's not herself," or "She's not really that mad," or even, "Deep down inside she isn't so warm and feminine as she appears to be." We go through a lot of mental gymnastics to avoid seriously questioning a conceptual system which has proved useful in the past. So, frequently, the *last* alternative explanation we consider is, "It is perfectly possible for a woman to express deep anger readily and still be warm, loving, and feminine." Such an alternative would mean the significant alteration of a conceptual system.

The trouble is, you can't just alter one little conceptual system at will, and let it go at that. Concepts are too closely and complexly linked to change one or two relationships in isolation. One change leads to another, and pretty soon a major reorganization is going on. It may be, of course, that the reorganization may lead to substantial improvement in the person's understanding and effectiveness in the world, but in the meantime there may be considerable turmoil and confusion as the person questions relationships that once seemed solidly established and before new ways of seeing the world have been adequately tested and confirmed.

Of course, the more important the particular conceptual system in question is in making it possible for the person to meet his needs, the more strain and upset is involved in changing it. For example, one might believe that heavy objects fall more rapidly than light ones. The disconfirmation that would follow upon learning that all objects fall at the same rate would perhaps be uncomfortable, but only moderately so. Consider, on the other hand, the anxiety and stress which could be produced by the discovery that complying with another's demands does not always make the other like you and may, indeed, have the opposite effect. For a person who has put much reliance in his interpersonal relations on the techniques associated with such a conceptual system, its disconfirmation may have the dimensions of a major crisis in life.

So, much of the time we hang on to our not-so-accurate conceptual systems because they work for us most of the time, and to give them up would plunge us into mild or severe confusion without any real promise of eventually attaining a more accurate, effective reorganization. The picture does not look so good for improvement, and before I finish, it will look even bleaker.

There is another kind of valuing that goes on in placing events into conceptual systems, and I will call it *evaluation*. This is the well-known process of saying that some states of affairs are better and some are worse. For most conceptual systems, there is an element of evaluation: most concepts have a good end and a bad end, and we would rather see events come out on the good end than on the bad.

Again, it is less important to see events come.out well in some areas than in others. The closer we get to conceptual systems that are concerned with our self-perceptions and our important relationships with others, the more important evaluation becomes, and the more uncomfortably responsible we feel when events don't fall on the valued ends of the concepts. Thus, if we value love as against hate, and intelligence against stupidity, it becomes important to protect conceptual systems that organize the events so that we can see ourselves as brilliant and loving. People may desperately protect quite maladaptive, ineffective conceptual systems in order to maintain a favorable perception of self or others.

Sometimes *competence value* and *evaluation* compete for influence on the conceptual system. For example, some persons have led such difficult childhoods that it is only by seeing themselves as bad, worthless people that they can seem to make sense out of the awful things that people they trusted have done to them; at the same time, they have normal needs for self-esteem, and for seeing themselves at the valued ends of concepts. These people may experience considerable conflict between these two motivational influences on their conceptual systems.

These, then, are the "defenses." They serve to keep us from becoming confused, upset, and rudderless every time something happens contrary to our expectations. Frequently, they protect our liking for ourselves and others when we and they fail to live up to our ideals. Defenses give life as it is experienced more stability and continuity than could ever be justified by reference to the contingency and complexity of real events alone. Defenses keep our relations with others more pleasant and satisfying, protecting us from our own and others' anger, and helping us to go on loving people who are usually less than perfect and sometimes less than human.

At the same time, these same defenses block our learning, often dooming us to make the same mistakes over and over again. They make us blind to faults of our own we could correct, as well as those we can do nothing about. Sometimes they make us turn the other cheek when a good clout in the nose would clear the air and establish a new and firmer footing for an honest relationship. They can, in extreme cases, make so many kinds of information dangerous to our conceptual systems that we narrow and constrict our experiences, our feelings, and our thoughts, becoming virtual prisoners of our own protection.

I believe there is in each of us a kind of counterforce which operates in the service of learning. Let's call it a *need to know,* or a drive toward competence. We are used to thinking about physiological needs, and we recognize there are probably social needs, such as needs for love; but we often overlook the need for competence and knowledge. Yet it is in operation all around us. We see it in the baby when he begins to explore as soon as he can crawl; we see it again in the "battle of the spoon," where the child actually gives up the certainty of getting the food into his mouth for the less effective but exciting experiment of "doing it himself." We see this need again as the adolescent struggles to carve out for himself a life that is uniquely his own; and we see it reflected in continuing efforts to understand and master the world as adults. People who read history for pleasure, who have creative hobbies, or who attend sensitivity training laboratories are all manifesting this drive to competence and knowledge.

The need to know is the enemy of comfort, stability, and a placid existence. For its sake we may risk the discomfort of examining and revising our assumptions about groups and people; we may expose ourselves to the anxiety-provoking experience of "personal feedback," in which we often learn others do not see us quite as we see ourselves; we place ourselves in groups where we know in advance we will be confused, challenged, and occasionally scared. Some of us expose ourselves to such situations more than once; to me, there could be no more convincing proof that the need to know is frequently stronger than the desire to maintain the comfort and stability of accustomed conceptual systems.

The sensitivity training laboratory thus frequently becomes a battleground between our desires to increase our competence and understanding, and our defenses. In this battle, we tend to take the side of the need to know and, like partisans everywhere, we malign, attack, and propagandize against the other side. Sometimes we forget that both sides are parts of a person, and that if either side destroys the other the person loses a valuable part of himself. This is particularly true in the case of defenses. We know from clinical practice and, I think, from personal experience and logic, that when a person's first line of defense becomes untenable, he drops back to another one, a sort of "second string" defense. Unfortunately, since we usually put our best and most adaptive defenses out in front, the second string is apt to be even less effective and reality-oriented than the first. To put it strongly, the destruction of defenses does not serve learning; instead, it increases the anxiety of the person that he will lose the more or less effective conceptual systems he has with which to understand and relate to the world, and he drops back to an even more desperate and perhaps unrealistic defense than the one destroyed. Though it may seem paradoxical, we cannot increase learning by destroying the defenses which block it.

What we can do is to create situations where people will not need to stay behind their defenses all the time. We can make it safe to sally forth from behind the moat, so to speak, secure in the knowledge that while we are exploring the countryside no one will sneak in and burn the castle.

People need their defenses most when they are most under threat and pressure. To make a mistake or become confused or admit to oneself that the world, ourselves, and others are not quite what we thought they were means that while we are revising or building new conceptual systems we will not be able to cope so well as before with the "slings and arrows" of a difficult situation. If we need every bit of competence we possess, we simply can't afford to give up conceptual systems which are tried but not perfect, in favor of exciting new ways of looking at things that are untested.

It is for this reason that I believe we cannot really begin to learn deeply from one another in a training group until we create relationships of mutual support, respect, and trust.

When we know that others will not place us in situations where we need every bit of our competence to cope with what is going on; when we know they will respect our own personal rate of growth and learning; when we know we have friends to help if we get into difficulties exploring new relationships, understandings, and behavior—then we can begin to look hard at the inadequacies in our ways of making sense of the world. We can examine those "exceptions to the rule" that we've always half expected might prove the rule inadequate; we can afford to really explore why ways of behaving that used to work fine are for some reason not producing satisfactions for us the way they used to, or why they seem to work with some people but not others; and we can really listen to the things people say that indicate they don't see us quite the way we see ourselves.

Out of this kind of exploration can come new and more effective conceptual systems, new ways of behaving that go along with them, and the excitement and pride that accompany increases in competence and knowledge. And when the excitement is over, and the new ways have been tested and integrated and have become habitual ways of seeing and behaving, I hope we will not be surprised to find that under conditions of stress we defend them against new learning just as strongly as we did the old. For these two partners go hand in hand: the need to explore and learn and the need to defend against disconfirmation and confusion. The challenge is to know how we can create conditions under which we can suspend one to enhance the other.

8. Roles That Facilitate and Inhibit Group Development

WILLIAM UNDERWOOD

T-Groups are growing and developing social organisms much as any other type of problem-solving group or committee. In order for a group to attain its potential for productive work and learning, a balance, unique to itself, must be developed between two types of role-behaviors that are enacted by the members. These behaviors are (1) aimed at the task—at solving the problems that confront the group, and (2) focused on maintaining and improving the relationships that exist among the members of the group.[1] Frequently, some members are more skillful at engaging in task behaviors while others focus their attention on enacting maintenance behaviors. Group members also behave in nongroup-oriented ways. That is, they enact roles whose aim is the satisfaction of self-oriented needs which may, for the moment, take precedence over the task on which the group is working or over the needs of the group to maintain itself.

Regardless of the type of role in which a member may be engaging, it is important to note that the particular behavior—standing by itself—is neither constructive or destructive. That is, whether or not a particular role facilitates or inhibits the development of the group is dependent upon the needs of the group and its members at the time. Thus, for example, as the following scheme[2] indicates, though efforts to harmonize, to reconcile disagreements among group members are typically facilitative, there may be

This selection is written expressly for this volume.

[1]K. D. Benne and P. Sheats, "Functional Roles of Group Members," *The Journal of Social Issues,* Vol. 4, No. 2 (Spring, 1948), pp. 42–47.

[2]This particular way of conceptualizing the facilitative and inhibitive dimensions of member roles was developed by Dr. William Underwood, Personnel Training Section, Radio Corporation of America, New York, N.Y. and is used here with his permission.

TABLE 2.1
TASK-ORIENTED ROLES

Inhibitive	Facilitative	Inhibitive
	Initiating New Ideas	
Not initiating ideas when needed.	Suggesting or proposing new things to do or changes in doing something.	Initiating ideas or changes when not needed.
	Seeking Information	
Allowing issue to bog down when new information is needed.	Asking for clarification of additional facts.	Seeking information when enough is already present.
	Seeking Opinions	
Not asking others for opinions when they might be helpful.	Asking not for facts but for the opinions or values pertinent to issues.	Seeking opinions when facts are relevant.
	Giving Information	
Withholding information when it is needed.	Offering facts or generalizations about issues or relating own pertinent experience.	Clouding the issue by supplying more information than is needed.
	Elaborating	
Withholding sufficient elaboration.	Developing clearer or additional meaning or providing reasons or deductions.	Providing elaboration when issue is already clear.
	Coordinating	
Not providing coordination when needed.	Showing relationships between ideas and events. Pulling ideas, suggestions and activities together.	Forcing relationships between ideas or events.
	Orienting	
Failing to supply needed orientation.	Defining the position of a goal with respect to its start and goal. Showing deviation from appropriate direction.	Orienting that is overdeterminative and restrictive.
	Evaluating	
Too little or no evaluating.	Supplying standards of accomplishment and subjecting group progress to measure.	Too much or unrealistic evaluating.
	Stimulating	
Accepting lethargy or apathy.	Prodding the group to greater on-target action. Arousing greater or higher quality activity.	Overstimulation resulting in non-productive activity.

TABLE 2.2
MAINTENANCE-ORIENTED ROLES

Inhibitive	Facilitate	Inhibitive
	Encouraging	
Failing to encourage others, or deflating them.	Commending, complimenting, supporting the contributions of others. Indicating understanding, interests, and acceptance of others.	Shallow encouraging
	Harmonizing	
Not acting to reduce stifling conflict.	Mediating differences between *others*. Endeavoring to reconcile disagreements.	Preventing needed conflict from occurring or surfacing.
	Compromising	
Refusing to yield or give in.	Yielding own position, admitting error, or "coming half way" when involved in disagreement or conflict.	Yielding too soon or too far.
	Opening Communication	
Undertalking or not trying to encourage or control others.	Keeping channels open. Assuring that those who want to contribute feel comfortable to do so. Limiting over-talkative members, soliciting information from nontalkative members.	Overtalking or overcontrolling others.
	Evaluating Process	
Inattentiveness to or ignoring process problems.	Calling attention to group needs. Offering observation about group functioning problems. Encourages members to work on process needs.	Overfocusing on process, or creating pseudo issues.
	Accepting	
Too little accepting and interested listening.	Going along with group movement. Serving as interested audience.	Being too passive and not contributing.

TABLE 2.3
ROLES NORMALLY DESTRUCTIVE TO BOTH TASK ACCOMPLISHMENT
AND GROUP MAINTENANCE

Facilitative	*Inhibitive*	*Facilitative*
	Aggressing	
Withholding aggressive behavior.	Deflating others. Expressing disapproval of ideas, opinions, feelings of others. Degrading members or group.	Expressing aggression in a constructive way.
	Blocking	
Withholding blocking behavior.	Being negativistic, stubbornly resistant. Maintaining or returning issues which the group has rejected. Disagreeing or opposing beyond reason. Being caustic, cynical.	Admitting blocking tendencies and asking to help deal with these tendencies.
	Dominating	
Withholding dominating behavior.	Trying to exert authority in manipulating the group or certain members. Using flattery, directing, demanding.	Channeling dominating tendencies into constructive help for the group.
	Seeking Recognition	
Shifting recognition to others.	Maintaining a central position or the center of attention. Overtalking, being boastful, or seemingly humble.	Entering central position for specific purpose then leaving it.
	Playing	
Inhibiting low involvement behavior cues.	Maintaining and displaying lack of involvement. Using nonchalance, joking, raising off-target or mundane issues.	Using levity to relieve tension for constructive purposes.
	Pleading Special Interests	
Resisting pleading special interests when not constructive to the group.	Using the group to satisfy personal interests only. Standing on sterotypic principles to detriment of group.	Expressing only those personal interests which are helpful to the group.
	Sympathizing	
Withholding expression of self-pity.	Endeavoring to elicit sympathy responses from whole group or certain members. Depreciating self beyond reason. Self-pitying.	Honestly expressing feelings when useful to the group.

times in a group's life when conflict needs to surface and be dealt with. At such times, efforts to harmonize may prove to be inhibitive as far as group development is concerned.

What is needed, then, as T-Groups attempt to grow and develop, is an awareness on the part of group members of (1) the wide variety of role requirements that may be demanded by the group, and (2) a sensitivity to what role is most appropriate to the existential needs of the group and individual members at particular times in group life.

Tables 2.1 and 2.2 address themselves to these central issues involving role-behaviors that normally facilitate group development. Table 2.1 empha- sizes nine different kinds of behaviors whose performance can facilitate work on a task. The table also suggests how too much or too little of the same behaviors can inhibit group development. Table 2.2 does the same things for role-behaviors that are maintenance-oriented, that is, directed toward developing and sustaining effective work team processes.

Table 2.3 establishes a similar point from an opposite perspective. It focuses on role-behaviors that are normally viewed as destructive or inhibitive to group development. Again, depending upon the state of the group and its individual members, variations on either side (as it were) of these inhibitive behaviors also can facilitate work on task or group maintenance.

9. Theories of Group Development and Categories for Interaction Analysis

A. PAUL HARE

Although some interest in the stages of group development can be traced in the writings of behavioral scientists in the 1920s, 1930s, and 1940s (see Coyle, 1930), the first studies which caught the attention of a number of group observers, leaders, and therapists were the works of Bales (1950) and Bion in 1948-1951 (see Bion, 1961). Their work, along with that of about fifty others, was summarized by Tuckman (1965) in the first major review of studies of group development. He reviewed studies drawn from four somewhat distinct

Reprinted from *Small Group Behavior*, Vol. 4, No. 3, August 1973, pp. 259–303. © 1973 Sage Publications, Inc.

fields: therapy groups, training groups (i.e., educational groups conducted with a nondirective leader in group dynamics tradition), natural groups, and laboratory groups. From these various studies, he abstracted a theory of four stages of group development.

After Tuckman began his review, studies were published by Dunphy (1964), Mills (1964), Slater (1966), and Mann (1967). They used observations of a version of the training group developed at Harvard University (Social Relations 120) to generate theories of development which combined elements of Bales and Bion, as well as other themes.

The theories of group development of most of the major authors have been associated with category systems for the observation of interpersonal behavior which could be used to test or illustrate the theories. Over the same period of time that theories of development were being proposed, some of the same authors, as well as others, were making refinements in various category systems with the intention of discovering the smallest number of dimensions which would be necessary to describe most of the variance in interpersonal behavior. Prominent among these were Chapple and his associates (Matarazzo et al., 1957), Carter (1954), Leary (1957), Couch (1960), Borgatta (1963, 1962), and Bales (1970). Over the years, the number of dimensions

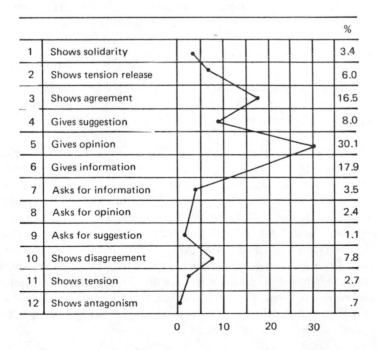

FIGURE 2.1. Interaction Profile for a Small Discussion Group (Bales, 1955)

thought to be necessary to predict behavior has increased from one (Chapple: talk versus not talk), to two (Leary: dominance versus submission and positive versus negative), to three (Bales: the previous two plus task-oriented and conforming versus rebellious and deviant). Presently, there is some evidence that it would be desirable to split the third dimension into two (task serious versus expressive and conforming versus nonconforming), thus differentiating at least four dimensions (Hare, 1969).

BALES' CATEGORY SYSTEM FOR INTERACTION PROCESS ANALYSIS

When Bales first began in 1946 to observe groups in the laboratory and in natural settings, he used a set of as many as 87 categories to describe the processes of interaction. Gradually, these were reduced to twelve categories, which were described in detail in Bales (1950).[1] These twelve categories include both "task" and "social-emotional" behavior (see Figure 2.1). However, the major emphasis is on rational problem-solving behavior.

Figure 2.1 gives the average percentages of the total number of acts for a single group meeting which fall into each of the twelve categories. The typical group meeting being observed was conducted by a group of college students, usually male, who had been brought together in a laboratory setting. Usually they did not know each other before the discussion began. They were given one or more human relations or construction problems to solve. No formal leader was appointed for a meeting which would last about forty minutes.

In Bales' system, the unit to be scored is bit of behavior (usually verbal) which can provide enough of a stimulus to elicit a meaningful response from another person. In practice, this is usually a sentence. Each sentence or comparable act is given only one score to indicate the element of task behavior or social-emotional behavior which appears to the observer to dominate the act.

The first three categories, "shows solidarity," "shows tension release," and "shows agreement," are *positive reactions* which, coupled with the three *negative reactions,* "shows disagreement," "shows tension," and "shows antagonism," constitute *social-emotional* behavior. The six categories describing *task* behavior are also grouped in sets of three. "Gives suggestion," "gives opinion," and "gives information" are *problem-solving attempts,* and "asks for information," "asks for opinion," and "asks for suggestion" are *questions.* Since the categories "shows agreement" and "shows disagreement" serve to help the group members reach solutions between members in the *social-emotional* area, the weight of the category system is on the task side. This is in contrast to the system proposed by Bion which gives more weight to the social-emotional categories.

---

1. An extensive revision of this system is given in Bales (1970) but the new version has not yet been used for the direct observation of groups.

The principal categories of activity in the sample of laboratory groups shown in Figure 2.1 are "gives opinion" and "gives information," which account for approximately 48% of the acts. The frequency with which the twelve process categories are used by group members varies with the task of the group and the roles of group members. Bales and Hare (1965) gives profiles for groups in 21 different settings. In an initial psychiatric interview, for example, 74% of the acts fell in the categories of giving opinion and information (Hare et al., 1960). Here the primary purpose of the interview was to encourage the patient to give information which could be evaluated by the psychiatrist.

The first type of sequence of behavior reported by Bales was a sequence of actions and reactions as group members went through the steps in problem solution (Bales, 1965, 1954, 1950). Again turning to Figure 2.1, we see that about half (65%) of the acts during a group session are problem-solving attempts, whereas the remaining 44% are distributed among positive reactions, negative reactions, and questions. In this two-sided process, the reactions act as a constant feedback on the acceptability of the problem-

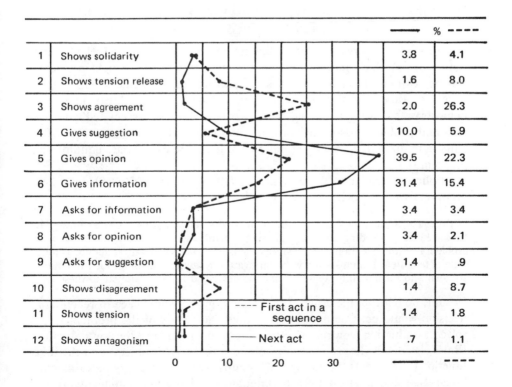

			%	
1	Shows solidarity		3.8	4.1
2	Shows tension release		1.6	8.0
3	Shows agreement		2.0	26.3
4	Gives suggestion		10.0	5.9
5	Gives opinion		39.5	22.3
6	Gives information		31.4	15.4
7	Asks for information		3.4	3.4
8	Asks for opinion		3.4	2.1
9	Asks for suggestion		1.4	.9
10	Shows disagreement		1.4	8.7
11	Shows tension	---- First act in a sequence	1.4	1.8
12	Shows antagonism	—— Next act	.7	1.1

0   10   20   30

FIGURE 2.2. A Comparison of a Speaker's First Act with His Following Act (Bales, 1955)

solving attempts. A typical interchange between two group members is illustrated by the following example:

Member 1: "I wonder if we have the same facts about the problem [asks for opinion]? Perhaps we should take some time at the beginning to find out [gives suggestion]." Member 2: "Yes [shows agreement]. We may be able to fill in some gaps in our information [gives opinion]. Let's go around the table and each tell what the report said in his case [gives suggestion]" (Bales, 1955).

As in this example, as speaker's first remark is likely to be a reaction, and if he continues speaking, the probability is very high that his second act will be a problem-solving attempt. Figure 2.2 sums up this finding statistically: about 50% of the time a member's first remark in a series is a reaction; if he continues, about 80% of the succeeding comments or other offerings are classified as attempts to solve the problem.

There are about twice as many positive as negative reactions. This indicates that members share a common definition of the situation and can make problem-solving attempts which will be in line with the group's goals most of the time.

PHASE MOVEMENT WITHIN A SINGLE MEETING AND MEETING TO MEETING TRENDS

From his observations of groups up to 1950, Bales already had some notion of the phase movements which would appear in a single problem-solving session and also in a series of meetings of the same group over a period of time. He also felt that a major source of regularity in group behavior was a swing back and forth between problems associated with the task and problems associated with maintaining group structure. The difficulty in maintaining the proper balance of forces he called the "equilibrium problem."

In phrases similar to those of Dewey (1933), Bales (1950: 49) described group activity as moving toward a goal:

With regard to time involvement, the total process of action as a system of acts is conceived as proceeding from a beginning toward an end, from a felt need or a problem toward a solution, from a state of tension toward tension reduction, from a state of heightened motivation toward motivation reduction, or in an instrumentally oriented and meaningful way which may be described in terms similar to these.

In sum, he felt that the order of problems a group would face in reaching a decision would be: Communication (about the nature of the problem to be solved), evaluation, control (of overt action), decision, and tension reduction (Bales, 1950: 60). The relationships between these five problems and the four functional problems faced by all groups (adaptation, goal-attainment, integration and latent pattern maintenance and tension management) are described briefly in this early work. The relationships were made much more explicit in work by Parsons and Shils (Parsons et al. 1953).

As a general trend over time, Bales (1950: 175–176) saw groups becoming more formal and less solidary.

[There is a] balance of conflicting tendencies, fluctuating according to more or less temporary changes in the relative urgency of functional problems of instrumentation, adaptation, integration, and emotional expression [which] probably shows a trend toward greater specificity of functional social roles, a greater differentiation of property rights, a greater formality of authority, a greater differentiation of strata, and a lesser overall solidarity.

These same trends would tend to appear as the group increased in size, added new members, or became more heterogeneous or complex.

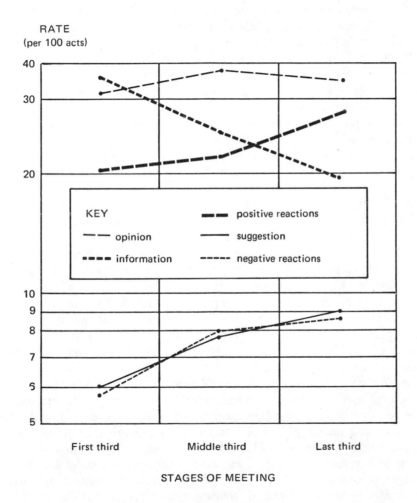

FIGURE 2.3. Phase Movements in Group Progress Toward a Decision (Bales, 1955)

The year after Bales published his category system, Bales and Strodtbeck published the first evidence of trends within a single meeting using this new system. The balance between task and social-emotional activity appears over the course of a whole meeting. However, when problem-solving discussion meetings are divided into three time-periods, the predominant type of activity shifts from one phase to another in a manner which reflects the stages in the group's progress toward a decision (Bales and Strodtbeck, 1951; Plank, 1951; Bales, 1952; Landsberger, 1955). These shifts are illustrated in Figure 2.3. The rate of acts of information decreases steadily from initial to final phase, while the rate of acts of suggestion rises. Acts of opinion increase in the middle phase and then fall off again. Both positive and negative reactions increase in rate from the initial to the final phase, with the positive reactions increasing more rapidly in the final phase. In phase one, the group members are collecting information; in phase two, evaluating the information; and in phase three, pressing for a decision with a concomitant increase in support of some members and rejection of others.

The increase in positive and negative reactions may be connected mainly with the social-emotional problems of the group process. Since the ratio of negative to positive reactions tends to be higher in response to suggestions than to factual statements, the *decision point* is the critical bottleneck in the process. Once the decision point has been passed, the rates of negative reaction usually fall off and the rates of positive reaction rise sharply. Joking and laughter, indicating solidarity and tension release, become more frequent. With the problems of the task settled for the time being by the decision, the group apparently turns its attention to the emotional states of the individuals and their social relationships.

Evidence that the nature and duration of the phases which may appear are directly related to the task of the group is found in a study of therapy groups in which the Bales categories for interaction process analysis were used (Talland, 1955). In these groups, the phases described above did not appear, nor was there any tendency to establish equilibrium, since the group did not have to reach a decision, and the therapist's job was to keep the level of emotional involvement sufficiently high so that the patients would talk about their problems.

In contrast to Talland, Psathas (1960) did find some evidence for phase movement and equilibrium tendencies within therapy groups. He did so, however, by combining the data for meetings at the beginning, middle, and end of a nine-month period of treatment. In the two therapy groups he observed that the movement of acts from beginning, through middle, to end of the nine months of therapy was similar to the pattern Bales and Strodtbeck reported for a single problem-solving session. He notes that Talland observed only the beginning of therapy and suggests that the "task" of therapy takes place over a longer period of time than the single 50-minute session.

Meeting-to-Meeting Trends

In addition to shifts or phase movements in activity within a single meeting, Bales found that patterns of activity in groups also change from meeting to meeting. In a series of four meetings, members of initially leaderless groups gradually spent less time in task behavior and more time in positive social-emotional behavior as the series progressed from the first to the last meeting. Negative social-emotional behavior rose briefly in the second meeting during the "status struggle" in which the hierarchy was established (Heinicke and Bales, 1953). In Table 2.4, these tendencies in ad hoc groups with *high* status consensus over four meetings are indicated by decreasing rates of activity in the task-oriented categories (giving information, opinion, and suggestion) and rising rates in the social-emotional categories. Negative reactions are low in the first meeting, show a sharp rise during the second, and then drop off again.

TABLE 2.4

MEAN PERCENTAGE OF GROUP INTERACTION IN VARIOUS CATEGORIES AND COMBINATIONS OF CATEGORIES IN SUCCESSIVE SESSIONS FOR GROUPS WITH HIGH STATUS CONSENSUS[a]

	Weekly Sessions				Level of Significance for Total
Categories	1	2	3	4	Trend
A. Positive reactions					
1 + 2 shows solidarity and tension release	6.1	7.4	15.2	18.4	c
3 shows agreement	17.7	16.4	14.7	12.6	
B. Attempted answers					
4 gives suggestion	9.0	10.2	9.1	9.0	
5 gives opinion	27.2	27.4	23.7	23.3	
6 gives information	16.8	12.1	13.8	12.6	
C. Questions					
7 + 8 + 9 asks for information, opinion, and suggestion	4.2	3.4	2.9	3.5	
D. Negative reactions					
10 shows disagreement	12.8	17.8	11.4	11.2	
11 shows tension	.18	.49	.45	.47	
12 shows antagonism	.06	.20	.01	.44	
Subtotals for four classes of categories					
A. Positive reactions	24.6	24.2 b	30.3	31.1	
B. Attempted answers	53.9	50.2	47.6	45.4	
C. Questions	4.2	3.4	2.9	3.5	
D. Negative reactions	13.3	18.7	11.9	12.6	
A–D (positive reactions minus negative reactions)	10.5 b	2.7 c	16.2	17.5	b

a. Heinicke & Bales, 1953. (Note: Volumes 1 through 18 of *Sociometry* were edited by J. L. Moreno and published by Beacon House, Inc.)
b. The difference between two numbers is significant at the .05 level.
c. The difference between two numbers is significant at the .01 level.

There are two different trends within the area of positive reactions. Overt showing of agreement shows a steady downward trend, which is counteracted by a sharp rise in showing solidarity and tension release through joking and laughing, especially in the final session. In other words, there is a marked shift from the more neutral and tentative task-oriented agreement to the more emotional positive reactions as the meetings progress.

Although groups with *low* consensus on the relative status of members go through a similar period of social-emotional conflict, in general the trends within each of the categories are not as sharply focused as they are in the high status consensus groups. As a result of their continued attention to "social-emotional" problems, the low status consensus groups tend to be less efficient and less satisfied with their group and with their group's solution to the problem. Phase movements similar to those in the high status consensus groups have also been noted in discussion groups over a longer series of meetings (Theodorson, 1953).

If the members of the group have the experience of taking part in a series of meetings, each with a different set of group members, then the effect is the same as if the group is meeting for the first time. Although the task and other aspects of the situation remain the same, the individuals must take time to get to know the other group members at the beginning of each meeting. Group structure is not given a chance to develop, and the status struggle usually reflected in the interaction pattern of the second meeting does not take place (Borgatta and Bales, 1953).

Phase Movement and Trends in Psychotherapy

A modification of the Bales categories was used in an analysis of communication between psychotherapists and their patients (Lennard et al., 1967). This study provides another example of phase movement within a session and trends between sessions. Tape recordings were made of eight therapies (four therapists with two patients each) for a period of eight months. One hundred twenty of the five hundred recorded sessions were then subjected to content analysis. Previous to and concurrent with the therapy, each patient and therapist responded to eight questionnaires and interviews. For the content analysis, six sets of categories were used covering type of content, grammatical form, affective content, interaction process, and role-system reference.

A major theme throughout the study was the analysis of the process through which the patient learns his role as patient with the possibility of later transferring what he has learned about role patterns in therapy to other significant role relationships. The "socialization" of the patient in his role appears to be more of a conscious effort at the beginning of the therapy. As therapy progresses, the amount of discussion about therapy itself and about the reciprocal therapist-patient roles tends to decrease. There is a similar decrease within each session. At the same time, there is an increase in the amount of communication about affect as the patient learns to put his thoughts and feelings into words. The therapist and patient establish rather stable "norms" for their interaction rate with the patient talking most of the time. However, in a given hour, if the patient talks less, the therapist will talk more. When patient and therapist differ initially in their expectations about the activity of the therapist, the therapist spends more time in the socialization process.

The Equilibrium Problem

One way of looking at the status struggle in laboratory groups that takes place in the second session is to note that, while group members are in this type of social-emotional activity, they have less time and energy available for the task. In industry, for example, the most productive teams were found to spend less time on "within"-team interaction (Horsfall and Arensberg, 1949). In another study, when carpenters and bricklayers who were accustomed to being assigned to work teams each day by their foremen were given a chance to choose the men they would prefer to work with, they showed marked differences in performance when compared with teams composed in the usual way (Van Zelst, 1952). In the groups of buddies, job satisfaction increased, labor and material costs dropped, and labor turnover decreased practically to zero. These effects presumably occurred because the "buddies" did not have to spend as much time in the solution of status problems.

This tendency of the group to swing back and forth between attempts to complete the task and attempts to maintain the group and to satisfy the needs of its members had been identified by Bales (1953) as the *equilibrium problem*. Pendulum-like swings in activity occur as members become more absorbed in the task and neglect individual member needs and then lose sight of the task as they turn their attention to group solidarity. In an extreme case, members of three-man groups who were drugged by an "anxiety-reducing medication" (a mixture of Seconal and Benzedrine) showed little anxiety, were elated, unassertive, and happy, but carried out little task-related behavior (Lanzetta et al., 1956).

BION'S CONCEPTS OF WORK AND EMOTIONALITY IN GROUPS

At about the same time that Bales began his systematic observations of groups in the United States, Bion was conducting group therapy with neurotic patients in England. As a result of his "experiences in groups," he wrote a set of discursive articles over the period 1948–1952 in which he described the ways in which the members of his groups reacted to his leadership and to each other. The articles were later collected and published as a book (Bion, 1961).

In the summer of 1951, after all but the final review article by Bion had appeared, Thelen and his colleagues decided to develop Bion's concepts into a systematic set of observation categories similar to those of Bales.[2] The first groups to be observed using the new system were training groups at the National Training Laboratory at Bethel, Maine. The results of this research are reported by Stock and Thelen (1958: 12-15).

In brief, Bion felt that the emotional aspects of group operation could be described in terms of three rather comprehensively defined emotional states which he called "cultures." These are dependency (when group members seem to be dependent on the leader or some external standard for direction), pairing (when group members turn to each other in pairs for more intimate emotional response), and fight-flight (when group members act as if their purpose is to avoid some threat by fighting or running away from it).

In addition, the group is continuously "at work" on some problem. At specific times, the particular emotional state associated with the work activity may be dependency, pairing, or fight-flight. The ongoing process of a group can be described in terms of successive shifts from one of these work-emotionality states or cultures to another.

Each individual in the group can be seen as having a "valency" for each emotional state. Individuals with high or low valencies on a particular emotional state will tend to combine with others in the group to develop, maintain, or move away from the various work-emotionality cultures.

In generating a set of observational categories from Bion's theory Thelen and his colleagues distinguished between four levels of work ranging from activity which was personally need-oriented and unrelated to group work which was highly creative, insightful, and integrative. They also separated "fight" from "flight" and added an "E" category for statements which had some emotion that was too confused or diffuse to be classified. In practice, they would distinguish between a lot of emotion in a statement (noted for example as "F" for strong fight) and a little emotion in a statement (noted for example as "f" for fight). In contrast to Bales, who gave only one score to each "act" for its dominant process category, Thelen et al. would score each act twice: once for the amount of work being performed and again for the amount and type of emotion represented. Their scoring system was as follows:

(a) The quality of work expressed: every statement receives one of the four work ratings:
    (1) Level work is personally need-oriented and unrelated to the group work;
    (2) level work is maintaining or routine in character, may involve attempting to

---

2. Thelen's colleagues were Saul Ben-Zeev, Paul Hare, Ida Heinz, William Hill, Joseph McPherson, Robert Rogers, and Dorothy Stock.

define a task, searching for methodology, clarifying already established plans, and the like;

(3) level work is group-focused work that introduces some new ingredient; active problem-solving;

(4) level work is highly creative, insightful, and integrative, often interprets what has been going on in the group and brings together in a meaningful way a series of experiences.

(b) The character of the emotionality expressed: a statement may contain no detectable affect. If it does, the affect is placed in one of the following emotional categories:

—Fight (F): expressions of hostility and aggression.

—Flight (FL): expressions of avoidance of the problem or withdrawal from participation.

—Pairing (P): expressions of warmth, intimacy, and supportiveness.

—Dependency (D): expressions of reliance on some person or thing external to the membership.

—E: This category is reserved for the relatively few statements in which some affect is clearly present but is too confused or diffuse to be placed in any one or any combination of the above categories (Stock and Thelen, 1958: 193).

Although this scoring system could be used with units of interaction as small as those used by Bales, Thelen et al. used larger units for some of their research. One procedure was to identify "natural units" of group interaction. This meant identifying points in the group discussion where a shift could be detected in the particular subgroup which was actively participating. This method was based on the theoretical assumption that, because of their individual valency patterns, different members "carry" different kinds of work-emotionality operations in a group. Consequently, when there was a definable shift in participation pattern, it was likely to reflect a shift in the amount of work and emotionality being expressed and in the character of the content. Using this scheme, protocols of group meetings would be divided into from four to twenty natural units of interaction ranging in length from three to eighteen minutes (Stock and Thelen, 1958: 194).

Although Stock and Thelen describe the ways in which several groups move through sequences of work and emotion over a period of time they did not see any one sequence of development which seemed to predominate. They hoped that eventually "it may be possible to identify a fairly limited number of developmental patterns" (Stock and Thelen, 1958: 206).

Bion also was more interested in the swing back and forth between the various emotional states in combination with work than he was in a specific theory of group development. However, Dunphy (1964) observed that Bion's scheme does contain a sequential analysis of group development. In the first stage, the group members are dependent on the leader. Next, they begin to attack him (fight) followed by scapegoating a rival leader (flight from the group leader). Next, they pass through the stage of pairing and finally develop into a work group with relatively little emotionality (Dunphy, 1964: 21–22).

BENNIS AND SHEPARD'S THEORY OF GROUP DEVELOPMENT

In 1956, Bennis and Shepard presented the first detailed theory of group development related to training groups (Bennis and Shepard, 1956). They based their theory on their own experience with training groups in workshops and educational settings and the theoretical insights of Freud (1949), Schutz (1955), and Bion (1961). Freud had stressed the ties each group member forms with the group leader, Schutz had noted two major orientations in groups, one toward authority and the other toward personal intimacy with other members, and Bion had also noted that groups combine these orientations in states of "dependency," "fight-flight," and "pairing."

The core of the theory of group development for Bennis and Shepard "is that the principal obstacles to development of valid communication are to be found in the orientations toward authority and intimacy that members bring to the group" (Bennis and Shepard, 1956: 417). As members joining a new group, they face two areas of internal uncertainty: they are concerned about dependence (how they will relate to authority) and interdependence (how they will work out the personal relations with their peers).

The development of a training group (in this case, one that meets for seventeen weeks) is seen as passing through two phases, each with three subphases. Each of the main types of activity for each phase and subphase is given in Tables 2.5 and 2.6. For each subphase, there is a brief description of the dominant (1) emotional modality, (2) content themes, (3) roles, (4) group structure, (5) group activity, (6) behavior which facilitates group movement, and (7) defenses. In the first phase, the members are concerned with dependence and power relations. In the first subphase, the members act as if they were in an ordinary discussion group and avoid the task of training by talking about outside issues. They seem dependent on the leader for direction. In the second subphase, the most assertive counter-dependent members attack the leader and search for an effective way of organizing the group. In the third subphase the members assert their independence of the leader, become very involved in the work of the group, and take over the leadership roles formerly perceived as held by the trainer.

In Phase II (Table 2.6), the members now deal with the problem of inter-dependence and their personal relations with one another. They begin subphase four in a period of enchantment. This is a high point of group morale, with much joking, laughing, and good fellowship. With such a good group, the members feel that no further analysis is required. Next, in subphase five, the members become disenchanted. They wonder how close or distant they should be. They wonder, as they did in subphase one, what the goals of the group are. Their disparagement of the group and its activities shows itself in tardiness and absenteeism. Finally, in subphase six, provided that the group has developed through the previous five subphases, group members deal with each other with understanding and acceptance. Members gradually with-

TABLE 2.5

PHASE I. DEPENDENCE—POWER RELATIONS[a]

	Subphase 1 Dependence-Submission	Subphase 2 Counterdependence	Subphase 3 Resolution
1. Emotional Modality	Dependence-flight	Counterdependence-fight. Off-target fighting among members. Distrust of staff member. Ambivalence.	Pairing. Intense involvement in group task.
2. Content Themes	Discussion of interpersonal problems external to training groups.	Discussion of group organization; i.e. what degree of structuring devices is needed for "effective" group behavior?	Discussion and definition of trainer role.
3. Dominant Roles (central persons)	Assertive, aggressive members with rich previous organizational or social science experience.	Most assertive counterdependent and dependent members. Withdrawal of less assertive independents and dependents.	Assertive independents.
4. Group Structure	Organized mainly into multi-subgroups based on members' past experiences.	Two tight subcliques consisting of leaders and members, of counterdependents and dependents.	Group unifies in pursuit of goal and develops internal authority system.
5. Group Activity	Self-oriented behavior reminiscent of most new social gatherings.	Search for consensus mechanism: Voting, setting up chairmen, search for "valid" content subjects.	Group members take over leadership roles formerly perceived as held by trainer.
6. Group Movement Facilitated By:	Staff member abnegation of traditional role of structuring situation, setting up rules of fair play, regulation of participation.	Disenthrallment with staff member coupled with absorption of uncertainty by most assertive counterdependent and dependent individuals. Subgroups form to ward off anxiety.	Revolt by assertive independents (catalysts) who fuse subgroups into unity by initiating and engineering trainer exit (barometric event).
7. Main Defenses	Projection Denigration of authority		Group moves into Phase II

[a]Course terminates at the end of 17 weeks. It is not uncommon for groups to remain throughout the course in this phase.

TABLE 2.6

PHASE II. INTERDEPENDENCE—PERSONAL RELATIONS

	Subphase 4 Enchantment	Subphase 5 Disenchantment	Subphase 6 Consensual Validation
Emotional Modality	Pairing-flight. Group becomes a respected icon beyond further analysis.	Fight-flight. Anxiety reactions. Distrust and suspicion of various group members.	Pairing, understanding, acceptance.
Content Themes	Discussion of "group history," and generally salutary aspects of course, group, and membership.	Revival of content themes used in Subphase I: What is a group? What are we doing here? What are the goals of the group? What do I have to give up—personally—to belong to this group? (How much intimacy and affection is required?) Invasion of privacy vs. "group giving". Setting up proper codes of social behavior.	Course grading system. Discussion and assessment of member roles.
Dominant Roles (central persons)	General distribution of participation for first time. Overpersonals have salience.	Most assertive counterpersonal and overpersonal individuals, with counterpersonals especially salient.	Assertive independents.
Group Structure	Solidarity, fusion. High degree of camaraderie and suggestibility. Le Bon's description of "group mind" would apply here.	Restructuring of membership into two competing predominant subgroups made up of individuals who share similar attitudes concerning degree of intimacy required in social interaction, i.e. the counterpersonal and overpersonal groups. The personal individuals remain uncommitted but act according to needs of situation.	Diminishing of ties based on personal orientation. Group structure now presumably appropriate to needs of situation based on predominantly substantive rather than emotional orientations. Consensus significantly easier on important issues.

TABLE 2.6 (Continued)

	Subphase 4 Enchantment	Subphase 5 Disenchantment	Subphase 6 Consensual Validation
Group Activity	Laughter, joking, humor. Planning out-of-class activities such as parties. The institutionalization of happiness to be accomplished by "fun" activities. High rate of interaction and participation.	Disparagement of group in a variety of ways: high rate of absenteeism, tardiness, balkiness in initiating total group interaction, frequent statements concerning worthlessness of group, denial of importance of group. Occasional member asking for individual help finally rejected by the group.	Communication to others of self-system of interpersonal relations; i.e. making conscious to self, and others aware of, conceptual system one uses to predict consequences of personal behavior. Acceptance of group on reality terms.
Group movement facilitated by:	Independence and achievement attained by trainer-rejection and its concomitant, deriving consensually some effective means for authority and control. (Subphase 3 rebellion bridges gap between Subphases 2 and 4.)	Disenchantment of group as a result of *fantasied expectations of group life.* The perceived threat to self-esteem that further group involvement signifies creates schism of group according to amount of affection and intimacy desired. The counterpersonal and overpersonal assertive individuals alleviate source of anxiety by disparaging or abnegating further group involvement. Subgroups form to ward off anxiety.	The external realities, group termination and the prescribed need for a course grading system, comprise the barometric event. Led by the personal individuals, the group tests reality and reduces autistic convictions concerning group involvement.
Main Defences	Denial, isolation, intellectualization, and alienation.		

draw their personal involvement in the group and sum up the progress of the group as the course ends.

In their summary of these phases of development, Bennis and Shepard observe that the evolution from Phase I to Phase II represents not only a change in emphasis from power to affection, but also from role to personality. Phase I activity generally centers on broad role distinctions such as class, ethnic background, and professional interests. Phase II activity involves a deeper concern with personality modalities, such as reaction to failure, warmth, retaliation, and anxiety. This presents an interesting contrast, for the *group* in Phase I emerged out of a heterogeneous collectivity of individuals, whereas the *individual* in Phase II emerges out of the group.

SCHUTZ'S THREE-DIMENSIONAL THEORY OF INTERPERSONAL BEHAVIOR

In his book on fundamental interpersonal relations orientation (FIRO for short), Schutz (1958) presents a number of postulates concerning interpersonal behavior together with evidence from his own research to support each of the postulates. The first of these is:

Postulate 1: The Postulate of Interpersonal Needs

(a) Every individual has three interpersonal needs; inclusion, control, and affection.
(b) Inclusion, control, and affection constitute a sufficient set of areas of interpersonal behavior for the prediction and explanation of interpersonal phenomena (Schutz, 1958: 13).

In brief, Schutz suggests that each individual has a need to be included and to include others in groups. This need may be found at any point along a continuum from wanting to be the focus of attention in the center of a group to wanting to be completely withdrawn and isolated. The individual also has a need in the area of control which can represent any combination of wanting to control others or to be controlled by them. Finally, each individual has a need for affection which can represent any combination of liking for other people and a desire to be liked in return.

Most of Schutz's book is devoted to showing how these needs can be measured and how they affect the interaction of individuals who find themselves working in groups composed of "compatible" or "incompatible" members. However, he also suggests a sequence of events in the development of groups which he sees as paralleling the sequence of events in the development of the child in the family. He acknowledges that the theory is strongly influenced by the Bennis and Shepard theory described above. The theory is set forward as a postulate:

Postulate 4: The Postulate of Group Development

The formation and development of two or more people into an interpersonal relation (that is, a group) always follows the same sequence.

—*Principle of group integration.* For the time period starting with the group's beginning until three intervals before the group's termination, the predominant area of
interaction begins with inclusion, is followed by control, and finally by affection.
This cycle may recur.

—*Principle of group resolution.* The last three intervals prior to a group's anticipated
termination follow the opposite sequence in that the predominant area of interpersonal behavior is first affection, then control, and finally inclusion (Schutz,
1958: 168).

The control and affection stages of Schutz are essentially the same as the
dependence and interdependence phases of Bennis and Shepard. They are
also related to the dependent and pairing modalities of Bion. The problems
of inclusion were not stressed by Bennis and Shepard, in part because the
determination of who is to be included or excluded from the group has
already taken place by the time the "training" begins.

Dunphy (1964), in his case study of two training groups, gives an example
of the impact that problems of inclusion can have on a group. In this case, so
many students had registered for the training group with the senior
instructor that on the first day of class he had to ask half of those present to
leave and take part in a group to be led by a less-experienced trainer. Since
no one volunteered to leave, he went around the room, pointing to each
person in turn saying "you stay" or "you go." Many times in the life of the
groups, this incident was referred to, with the ones who stayed calling
themselves the "chosen people."

Schutz's theory is different from those which precede it, in that he poses a
definite set of recurring cycles and also that he suggests a reversal of the
order of events as the group nears termination. First, group members break
their ties of affection, then they cease to control one another, and finally they
give up their attendance and sense of identity with the group.

TUCKMAN'S FOUR STAGES IN GROUP DEVELOPMENT

As we have indicated earlier, Tuckman's summary of the literature on
group development covers almost all the research on group development up
to the time his study was published, including the theories which have been
presented here in some detail, as well as many more, especially derived from
work with therapy groups, which have not been mentioned. His review can
therefore be taken as representative of the current state theory about group
development.

Tuckman first abstracted his theory from some 26 studies of development
in therapy groups. The task in these groups was to help individuals deal with
personal problems. The groups typically contained from five to fifteen
members and a therapist and existed for a period of three months or more.
The developmental data for groups of this type consist of the observations of
the therapist and those professional observers who may be present, usually as
trainees. The data are highly anecdotal in nature and reflect the clinical

biases of the observers. The accounts are usually formulated after the fact
and based on the observation of a single group. Tuckman then went on to
show how this same theory might be applied to training groups and later to
laboratory groups and those observed in natural settings.

Each of the four major stages in group development which Tuckman
describes are divided into two aspects: (1) *group structure*, where he
describes patterns of interpersonal relationships—that is, the way in which
members act and relate to one another as persons; and (2) *task behavior*,
where he describes the nature of the work being done by the group. This
distinction between task and social-emotional behavior had earlier been
proposed by Bales (1953) and others. The four stages in group structure are
briefly: testing and dependence, intragroup conflict, development of group
cohesion, and functional role-relatedness. The four stages of task activity
are: orientation and testing, emotional response to task demands, discussing
oneself and other group members, and emergence of insight. Each of these
stages as it applies to a therapy group will be summarized in outline form
below.

Stage 1

- *Group structure:* Testing and dependence. An attempt by group members to discover what behaviors are acceptable in the group, based on the reactions of the
  therapist. Members look to the therapist for guidance and support in this new and
  unstructured situation. (With anti-social individuals, there may be a prestige of
  resistance, silence, and hostility.)
- *Task activity:* Orientation and testing. At this stage, the group members make
  indirect attempts to discover the nature and boundaries of the task. These attempts
  are evident in the following kinds of activities: (a) discussion of irrelevant and
  partially relevant issues, (b) discussion of peripheral problems, (c) discussion of
  immediate behavior problems, (d) discussion of symptoms, (e) griping about the
  institutional environment, and (f) intellectualization. Also, the group members
  make more direct attempts at orientation toward the task as illustrated in: (a)
  search for the meaning of therapy, (b) attempts to define the situation, (c) attempts
  to establish a proper therapeutic relationship with the therapist through the development of rapport and confidence, (d) mutual exchange of information, and (e)
  suspicion of and fearlessness toward the new situation which must be overcome.

Stage 2

- *Group structure:* Intragroup conflict. Group members now become hostile toward
  one another and toward the therapist as a means of expressing their individuality
  and resisting the formation of group structure.
- *Task activity:* Emotional response to task demands. Emotionality is expressed by
  the group members as a form of resisting the techniques of therapy or of sensitivity
  training groups which require that they "expose" themselves. They also challenge
  the validity and usefulness of the training.

Stage 3

- *Group structure:* Development of group cohesion. Group members accept the group and accept the idiosyncracies of fellow members. Harmony is of the maximum importance, and task conflicts are avoided to ensure harmony.
- *Task activity:* Discussing oneself and other group members. The self and other personal characteristics are discussed. Information is acted on in such a way that alternative interpretations of the information can be made. The openness of members to each other is characteristic.

Stage 4

- *Group structure:* Functional role-relatedness. The group members work together on the task with a minimum of emotional interaction. This is made possible by the fact that the group as a social entity has developed to the point where it can support rather than hinder the task of processes through the use of function-oriented roles.
- *Task activity:* Emergence of insight. Group members show insight into their own problems, an understanding of their own abnormal behavior, and, in many cases, modifications of their behavior in desired directions.

Tuckman sees these stages in group development as parallel to those in individual development—namely, dependence, affection, and maturity. In his formulation, the stage of dependence precedes that of intermember conflict, whereas, in the Slater formulation (which will be discussed below), the stage of dependence follows the stage of intermember conflict.

In his summary of groups, Tuckman considers groups that have met for only a few meetings as well as those who have met for a longer period of time, although he recognizes that there could well be a difference between the phases over a single meeting and those of longer duration.

Certainly duration of group life would be expected to influence amount and rate of development. The laboratory groups, such as those run for a few hours by Bales and Strodtbeck (1951), followed essentially the same course of development as did therapy groups run for a period of a year. The relatively short life of the laboratory group imposes the requirement that the problem-solving stage be reached quickly, while no such imposition exists for the long-lived therapy group. Consequently, the former groups are forced to develop at a rapid rate. The possibility of such rapid development is aided by the impersonal and concrete nature of the laboratory task. Orientation is still required due to the newness of the task, but is minimized by task rules, players' manuals, and the like, that help to orient group members [Tuckman, 1965: 397].

Training Groups at Harvard

During the years 1964 through 1967, four major studies of group development were published, all based on observation and experience with a version of the training group which had been developed at Harvard University. These training groups were conducted as part of a course in the

Department of Social Relations (Social Relations 120). For a number of years, Bales had been the director of the course, and these authors had worked with him as trainers in sections of the course. The class format at this time was a combination of the "case analysis" approach, developed at the Harvard Business School, and discussions of the group's own process following the group dynamics tradition, developed at the National Training Laboratory at Bethel, Maine. Usually a class of about 25 students and an instructor would meet three times a week for one hour throughout the nine-month academic year around a circular table in a conference room. At one end of the room was a one-way mirror with a hidden observation booth. The group sessions were recorded on tape. Three of the authors used category systems for an analysis of the content and process of interaction in the groups, the other relied on anecdotal evidence taken from the group transcripts.

DUNPHY'S STUDY OF SOCIAL CHANGE

Dunphy's (1964) study of social change in self-analytic groups is based on an analysis of two of the Harvard Social Relations 120 groups. One with 23 students was led by Bales and the other with 26 students was led by Dunphy. Both groups met at the same hour, three times a week for a full academic year.

The data for the study consisted of weekly reports of group interaction written by the group members. Each report, approximately 250 words in length, was punched on IBM cards for analysis by computer using the *General Inquirer* system of content analysis (Stone et al., 1966). As the actual verbatim reports are read into the computer, the program removes certain regular word endings, and each word is looked up in a dictionary, which is stored in the computer. If a word is found in the dictionary, the defining tags which indicate its membership in one or more categories in the dictionary are automatically assigned to the sentence. Later, a "tag tally" program counts how many times each of the tags has been used. The observer then notes the differences in the frequencies with which certain of the tags have been used during the various phases of the group's development and uses this information as a basis for his theory of development. The tags consist of 55 first-order tags which are discrete, independent variables such as self, small-group, food, affection, and work, and 28 second-order tags which are not independent variables. Several of the second-order tags—such as academic, political, higher-status, and male-theme—could be used to define a single word (Dunphy, 1964: 83–98).

In his summary of the major shifts in themes in the two groups over the year, Dunphy notes that at first the individual member differentiates himself ("self"), the instructor, and other members who are able to gain the attention of the group ("leaders") from an undifferentiated collection of others ("people"). At this time, there is little coordination of group activity.

After a short period of trying to maintain traditional patterns for discussion groups, action takes on a strongly manipulative character. The men become particularly active with behavior directed toward the satisfaction of aggressive and sexual drives. Emotional involvement with the group is avoided as each person throws up a barrier around his ego for its protection.

In the first part of the second semester, there is a change in this pattern. Ego boundaries are undermined, and there is more involvement with the group. Students feel lost in the group. There is increased effort toward the realization of group goals with a primary concern with personal involvement with others and affection. Toward the end of the group, the group seems to develop its own human qualities. There is a sense of group identity as members develop a set of symbols for communication and a set of norms. "The earlier defense of non-involvement which found its active expression in aggression, gives way to the deeper defense of resistance and denial, actively expressed in avoidance" (Dunphy, 1964: 165). Then, as the group ends, there is a concern for the loss of the group and for its relative state of unity and achievement.

In addition to these general trends, Dunphy also reported some intergroup differences related to differences between the status and style of the leaders. However, his main analysis follows the pattern suggested by Tuckman, with more explicit emphasis on the problems the group faces at its termination. For a later comparison with a functional analysis of group development, we note that Dunphy, like Bennis and Shepard, gives evidence that the "group" under study is at first a collection of individuals and only becomes a "group" after the members have met together in interaction for a period of time.

MILLS' ANALYSIS OF GROUP TRANSFORMATION

Mills (1964) sums up some of the observations which he and others have made of the Social Relations 120 training groups at Harvard. He then presents his analysis of a training group he conducted, using a new system for group analysis called "Sign Process Analysis." His title, *Group Transformation,* is taken from the fact that, by taking a comparatively passive role in the group, the instructor forces the group members to work out their own method of learning, thus undergoing a "transformation." Mills felt that previous accounts of training groups had not sufficiently stressed three processes:

(1) The process of forming indigenous norms. To do this, members first have to give up their preconceived normative notions, create a state of normlessness, and then select new norms and refashion them through experience.
(2) The process of *partial* consumption of new knowledge about human behavior. Mills stresses the word "partial" since he feels that so little is actually known about human behavior that group members cannot help but be dissatisfied with the group's achievements.
(3) The process of group termination. The fact that anticipating the group death and

handling its reality is an important issue to those who commit themselves to the group (Mills, 1964: 67-69).

By adding these emphases to the type of analysis of group development represented by Tuckman, Mills proposes five principal periods in the life of a training group:

(1) The encounter (similar to Schutz's inclusion);
(2) testing boundaries and modeling roles (Tuckman's Stage 1);
(3) negotiating an indigenous normative system;
(4) production (Tuckman's Stage 4);
(5) separation (Schutz's final period of inclusion); (Mills, 1964: 70-80).

Mills builds his actual case analysis on his category system "sign process analysis" (SPA) which he proposed for the systematic collection of group process data. An observer, or in this case a person listening to a tape recording of the group, records the principal object and the secondary object in each simple sentence and whether the "sign" that links the two objects is positive, neutral, or negative. For example, the sentence "She greeted him warmly" links the principal object "she" with the secondary object "him" with a posit've valuation.

Mills suggests that objects be distinguished according to their locus (internal or external to the group), sociological status (superior or subordinate), sex, social versus nonsocial nature, and finally, individual versus collective nature. This gives 11 categories for each object. Since each type of principal object can be linked with each of the 11 categories of secondary objects, plus a separate category when the principal object appears alone, a matrix of 11-by-12 cells represents all possible relationships. Further, within each cell, valuations may be positive, neutral, or negative, yielding a grand total of 396 possibilities for classifying each assertion made in the group.

The principal difficulty is that an observer can seldom accumulate enough data from a single group to analyze who-to-whom interaction within a single meeting or trends through several meetings. In this case, Mills observed his group for 68 meetings over an 8-month period, recording over 34,000 statements. In summarizing his data, however, he found it necessary to combine several categories, leaving a matrix of 90 cells rather than 396. Even then, 6 cells are empty, and 24 contain fewer than 10 entries. About one-third of the entries fall into 2 of the neutral cells, leaving only about half the entries for the positive and negative indices on which Mills bases most of his analysis. Fortunately, his analysis of group development does not depend entirely on the usefulness of his category system.

SLATER'S MICROCOSM

Slater (1966) covers a wide range of material as he discusses parallels in the stages of the evolution of consciousness and its correlates at the psychological level, the social-psychological level, group level, and societal level. His principal thesis is that many of the concerns which societies and groups have dealt with over time are reenacted as new groups are formed and developed. His description of the processes in small training groups follows the same overall pattern that Tuckman describes. The first period includes the anxiety of members over their lack of differentiation from each other and their frustration with the passive leader. Next, members go on to attack the group leader. As they try to incorporate his mana, which represents his learning, they often have symbolic feasts. At the time of the revolt, the female group members experience almost no guilt, whereas the male members evidence a great deal (Slater, 1966: 119). Following the revolt, there is a period of high group morale as members come close to each other and feel a spirit of equalitarianism.

The underlying theme in development is a continuing increase of consciousness of self and differentiation from others. "Prior to the group revolt," Slater (1966: 146) suggests, "three entities are bound together: the person of the group leader, the group deity (i.e., the object of the worshipful attitude, the dependence needs, or whatever of the group members), and a set of abstract skills, qualities, or powers which are desired by the members."

"The symbolic ideas of communal killing and communal devouring express the fact that before a group can become united around a set of principals, it must (a) rid itself of the fantasy of a living omnipotent protector, (b) separate the valued principals from their living vehicle, and (c) make them available to all on an equal basis." (Slater, 1966: 147).

In a summary of his ideas, Slater indicates that there are really three different stages in the structural development of the member-member-leader triangle. In the first stage, as a result of normal social training, there is generalized inhibition of hostile sentiments. However, the group members have throughout their lives found that the expression of hostility toward their peers has been sanctioned less rigidly than manifest hostility toward authority, so that there is a certain amount of displacement from the authority to their peers. As the revolt builds, this process is increasingly reversed and, finally, a successful revolt depends on near unanimity of animosity toward the leader. Following the revolt, this demand for unanimity of feeling continues, and there is an intense taboo on intermember conflict. Gradually, however, this restriction is relaxed, and there is again a great deal of hostility expressed between individual members. This coincides with the more or less universal acceptance of the usual training group value on free and candid expression of feelings in interpersonal relationships (Slater, 1966: 150).

The major difference between Slater's and Tuckman's theories lies in the sequence of modalities described by Bion as fight-flight, dependency, and pairing. Tuckman describes the group as going through the dependency mode first, then fight-flight, and finally pairing, whereas Slater feels that fight-flight precedes dependency, although he agrees that the final stage is pairing.[3] He feels that the stages in this order reflect the major concern of the group members toward differentiation. When they first enter the group and find themselves essentially undifferentiated from each other, they attempt to fight or fly. Thus, by setting themselves off from each other, they gain some minimum of differentiation. This might be seen as comparable to the stage in the development of the child when he takes a negative stance toward his mother, who in this case is represented by the group. In the next stage, the group members begin their attack on the leader and first suggest that they are very dependent upon him. This gives them some feeling of differentiation by identifying with the leader. Presumably, this reflects a second stage in child development, where the child looks to the father who is at least different from the mother (group). Finally, having overthrown the leader and absorbed his mana, the group members become anxious about being too differentiated from each other and losing something of the group feeling. They therefore begin to establish subgroups and close interpersonalities through pairing.

MANN'S ANALYSIS OF MEMBER-LEADER RELATIONSHIPS

In developing his category system for the analysis of member-leader relationships in training groups, Mann (1967) combined categories from Bales, Bion, and others, but his final result comes closer to Bion's scheme. He is primarily concerned with the way the members of a training group relate to the leader. This can occur at four levels, ranging from a direct expression of feeling toward the leader to remarks in which the reference to the member may be disguised or symbolized although the reference to the leader may be direct. The first problem for the scorer using this system is to note the level at which the inference about content is being made. The four levels are as follows:

Level One: Both members and leader are referred to directly.
Level Two: Member referred to directly, but leader symbolized by equivalent within the group.
Level Three: Member referred to directly, but leader symbolized by equivalent outside group.
Level Four: Member symbolized by equivalent inside or outside the group, leader referred to either directly or symbolically (Mann, 1967: 40.)

3. In a personal communication, Slater qualifies my statement that fight-flight precedes dependency in his model, with the following observation: "This would only be true for a totally independent society. In a group which forms in the midst of a society like ours, the fight-flight stage is more a matter of fantasy than behavior. Empirically, open inter-member conflict is more likely to occur after the dependency stage, as a function less of the fight-flight modality than of the long-delayed confrontation of realistic differences. The problem is that the same behavior may mean different things. Fight-flight conflict is too abrupt, sporadic, and explosive to get defined as an empirical stage, partly because cultural defenses available to all members can be used as a substitute during the early life of the group."

TABLE 2.7

MANN'S MEMBER-TO-LEADER SCORING SYSTEM CATEGORIES

Area	Subarea	Category
Impulse	Hostility	1. Moving against 2. Resisting 3. Withdrawing 4. Guilt inducing
	Affection	5. Making reparation 6. Identifying 7. Accepting 8. Moving toward
Authority relations		9. Showing dependency 10. Showing independence 11. Showing counterdependency
Ego state	Anxiety	12. Expressing anxiety 13. Denying anxiety 14. Expressing self-esteem
	Depression	15. Expressing depression 16. Denying depression

Once the scorer has noted the level of inference, he selects the appropriate content category from the list given in Table 2.7. The content categories of the member-to-leader scoring system can be looked at as three separate systems which are used simultaneously. Eight of the sixteen categories describe the affective response a member may have to the leader; three of the categories describe feelings which are activated by the leader's status in the authority structure of the group; and five of the categories describe how the member feels about himself in relation to the leader. These three approaches to the member's feelings are referred to by Mann as areas of (1) impulse, (2) authority relations, and (3) ego state.

The impulse is divided in turn into two subareas—hostility and affection—and the ego state area divided into the subareas of anxiety and depression. The authority relations area is also considered one of the five subareas. These five areas are important in one of the scoring conventions which Mann proposes. Each act may be scored in as many subareas as seems appropriate, but no more than one category within a subarea may be used. Also, self-esteem is never double-scored with an anxiety or depression category. Thus "expressing self-esteem" is considered a category, but not a subarea within the ego state area. Examples of each of the sixteen categories are given in some detail in the text (Mann, 1967: 41–60). For some of the categories, Mann has been guided by definitions of similar categories used by Bales: for example, "moving against" for Mann is similar to "showing antagonism" for Bales, "resisting" similar to "disagrees," "accepting" similar to "agrees," and "moving toward" similar to "shows solidarity."

Mann's unit of analysis is more global than that of both Bales (1950) and Mills (1964) who used the simple sentence as the prototypic act in an effort to isolate the most rudimentary element of interaction. In contrast, Mann is attempting to infer the member's feelings from statements which range from the direct to the symbolic. In many cases, the scorer can only discern the latent, leader-relevant feelings by examining the recurrent shadings of many phrases and sentences. For this reason, he defines an *act* as a single speech or burst of sentences within which the expressed feelings are uniform. One of two events signals the end of an act: (1) the speaker is interrupted by another member or by the leader; or (2) the speaker shifts from expressing one set of feelings to expressing feelings which call for a different array of scored categories.

The length of an act in this scoring system can vary from a single word to a speech extending over almost a page of double-spaced typescript. Whereas Bales typically records around 1,000 acts per hour using the smallest unit which would be coherent, Mann's scoring system averages 200 acts per hour (Mann, 1967: 60–61). Mann's system could still result in a larger number of scored units than the Bion system as it was proposed by Stock and Thelen (1958: 194), who might include several different speakers in the same unit if the emotional content of the act remained the same.

The behavior of the leader is also scored using the sixteen categories, although the observer does not ask what feeling he is expressing toward the members. Instead, Mann records the leader's reflection of members' feelings back to the group.

TABLE 2.8

MANN'S FACTOR PATTERNS FOR MEMBER PERFORMANCES

Factor I: Relations with the leader as analyst (work)
    I+: Enactment
    I—: Dependent complaining

Factor II: Relations with the leader as authority figure (dependency)
    II+: Rebellion
    II—: Loyalty

Factor III: Relations with the leader as manipulator (fight-flight)
    III+: Counterdependent flight
    III—: Resistant complaining

Factor IV: Relations with the leader as audience (pairing)
    IV+: Relating to the leader as colleague
    IV—: Concern with inner distress

Factor V: The effect of the leader on the ego state of the member
    V+: Anxiety
    V—: Depression

Factor VI: Commitment to the member-leader relationship
    VI+: Emotional involvement
    VI—: Emotional neutrality

The sixteen categories and four levels of inference were applied to the interaction in four classroom groups conducted at the Harvard Summer School in the years 1961–1963. They were all sections of the "Social Relations 120" course. Before carrying out his analysis of the process of development in the four groups Mann subjected the twenty dimensions to the statistical method of factor analysis to see if a smaller number of underlying dimensions could be used to describe the behavior. That is, he wished to know if the various categories fell into a smaller number of clusters. For this purpose, he converted the amount of behavior in each category for each member of the groups in each session to percentages. This unit of one member for one session he called a *performance*. A performance was only included in the analysis if he had recorded at least twenty acts to the group member for that session. This gave him a sample of 430 performances. As a result of the factor analysis, Mann identified six basic factors.

These six factors, together with the behaviors which represent the positive and negative end of each factor, are given in Table 2.8. In parentheses next to each factor name is included the Bion category which seems to come closest to the predominant factor content (Mann, 1967: 68–70).

Before using these six factors in the description of group development, Mann added a description of the conceptual framework which emerged from his clinical study of the groups. He saw four themes which occurred with considerable regularity: nurturance, control, sexuality, and competence (Mann, 1967: 73). His theory of group development in its simplest form is that groups pass through phases of development in this same order. That is, group members begin in a dependent stage concerned with problems of nurturance, then move to a struggle with the leader as they work on problems of control, then to more concern with intermember relations and the problem of sexuality, and finally arrive at a stage of mature work which they do with competence. In general, these phases are similar to the four phases described by Tuckman (1965).

Using examples from the transcripts of group meetings and graphs showing the trends in activity on each of the six factors over the life of the four training groups, Mann goes on to show the relationships between the four themes, the six factors, and other theories of group development. In brief, the primary factor associated with the first theme of nurturance is Factor II: relations with the leader as an authority figure. The principal Bion category associated with the theme is "dependency." The second theme, control, is associated with Factor III: relations with the leader as manipulator and with Bion's category "fight-flight." The third theme, sexuality, is associated with Factor IV: relations with the leader as audience and Bion's category "pairing." Finally, the fourth theme, competence, is associated with Factor I: relations with the leader as analyst and Bion's category "work." Thus, after beginning with Bales' twelve categories and amplifying

TABLE 2.9

MANN'S SUBGROUP CHARACTERISTICS BY PHASE

Phase	Dominant Subgroups	Deviant Subgroups
Initial complaining	Dependent complaining Loyal compliance Counterdependent heroics Self-sufficiency	Enactment in the service of autonomy
Premature enactment	"The sensitive ones" Withdrawal and denial "The accepting enactors" "The heroic enactors"	Disappointment and resentment
Confrontation	Rebellion and complaining (including "the spokesmen") Independence Anxiety and withdrawal	"The heroes"
Internalization	Enactment and work	"The scapegoats"
Separation and terminal review	Depression and manic denial Personal involvement Complaining abdication of responsibility	

them with four more interpersonal categories and four levels of inference, Mann finds that four themes are sufficient to account for most of the process of group development. These themes are quite similar to those proposed by Bion. In his final analysis, Mann does add a fifth phase to emphasize a type of activity which he feels previous observers have overlooked. Just after the period of initial complaining and nurturance, group members appear to take over the group for a brief period of work at the task of group and case analysis. Since the group has not yet worked out its basic problems, this period of work cannot be sustained. For this reason, Mann calls this period one of "premature enactment." In his final presentation of a theory of group development (Table 2.9), Mann places the themes of control and sexuality in the middle phase of "confrontation" and, like Mills, stresses a final phase of "separation and terminal review."

A FUNCTIONAL ANALYSIS OF GROUP DEVELOPMENT

Mann's account of group development is not only the most recent of these analyses of group development but also the most comprehensive (Mann, 1967). However, Mann's theory can in turn be described in terms of a functional theory of groups developed primarily by Parsons (Parsons et al., 1953; Parsons, 1961). This approach begins with an analysis of the four basic problems which every social system must solve in order to survive. These problems are latent pattern-maintenance and tension management (L), adaptation (A), integration (I), and goal-attainment (G). For a whole society the solution to these problems is usually centered in four types of institutions:

L, the church, family, and educational institutions (which give the basic meaning to the society and bring new members into the system); A, the economic institutions which create materials to be used by the society; I, the law which defines the norms for the activities of the society; and G, the political institutions which coordinate the activities in the interest of goal-attainment.

A category system based on the AGIL scheme has been developed by Effrat and Hare (Hare, 1968; Hare and Effrat, 1969) which makes it possible to analyze the content of the activity of a social system to determine the functional nature of each unit of activity and to test hypotheses about the "typical" sequence of development of the system. This developmental sequence of L-A-I-G with a terminal stage of L is similar in many respects to the previous analyses of group development based on data from therapy groups, self-analytic groups, classroom groups, and work groups described earlier (Bennis and Shepard, 1956; Mann, 1967; Mills, 1964; Schutz, 1958; Tuckman, 1965).

When the AGIL categories are applied to the description of a learning group such as a classroom group, the forces at work seem to be as follows: the work of the group requires that the purpose of the group be defined (L), that new skills be acquired (A), that the group be reorganized so that the members can try out the new skills without being too dependent on the leader (I), and that the group's members work at the task (G). Finally, there is a terminal phase in which the group returns to L to redefine the relationships between the members and the group as the group is disbanded. The amount of time the group spends in each phase is determined by the activity of the leader (his direction or nondirection) and by the skills and emotional strengths of the members. Presumably, the leader is "ready" for each stage at the outset, since he has been through the stages before. However, members come to the group with different degrees of problem-solving skills or preferences for different emotional modalities (for example, a preference for fight-flight, pairing, or dependency: Bion, 1961). Subgroups tend to form on the basis of skills or emotional modalities. If the subgroup with the appropriate skills and emotional state for each stage is large enough, it can carry the whole group through that phase (Bennis and Shepard, 1956; Mann, 1967). If not enough members of the group are ready for a particular stage, more intervention by the leader may be necessary. Some groups may never progress beyond the early stages.

The assumption that the group moves from phase to phase when a subgroup or leader is able to carry the movement needs to be documented by further research since previous observers do not discuss the *process* of development in any detail, rather they simply *observe* that one phase follows another. A typical comment is that of Schutz (1958) concerning the affection phase: "Finally, following a satisfactory resolution of these problems of control, problems of affection become focal." Schutz does not tell us how the problems of control become resolved or by what process the group moves to the next phase. However, it may not require as much justification to assert that a group will face special problems at the beginning and at the end of its life. For example, at the beginning of the training group, when the leader fails to assert himself, Bennis and Shepard (1956: 420) observe, "The ambiguity of the situation at this stage quickly becomes intolerable for some." Or Mills (1964: 78), describing the termination of a group, says, "The fact of separation forces a complex set of demands and issues."

Finally, with the L-A-I-G sequence in mind, we can go back to Mann's (1967) description of group development to observe the fit between his phases and the four functional categories. His first stage of "initial complaining" is primarily the "L" stage as group members seek a definition of the situation. The second stage of "premature enactment" reflects the members' first attempts to use their new skills in the analysis of interpersonal behavior (A phase). The enactment is "premature" because members have not yet reorganized themselves in a way that frees them from dependence on the trainer. This is done in the next phase of "confrontation" (I). The next-to-last phase of "internalization" is "G" as members carry out the work of group analysis. This is followed in Mann's scheme by a final phase of "separation and terminal review" which brings the group again to "L."

REFERENCES

Bales, R. F. (1970) Personality and Interpersonal Behavior. New York: Holt, Rinehart & Winston.
–––––– (1955) "How people interact in conferences." Scientific Amer. 192, 3: 31–35.
–––––– (1954) "In conference." Harvard Business Rev. 32: 44–50.
–––––– (1953) "The equilibrium problem in small groups," pp. 111–161 in T. Parsons et al., Working Papers in Theory of Action. New York: Free Press.
–––––– (1952) "Some uniformities of behavior in small social systems," pp. 146–159 in G. E. Swanson et al. (eds.) Readings in Social Psychology. New York: Holt.
–––––– (1950) Interaction Process Analysis: A Method for the Study of Small Groups. Reading, Mass.: Addison–Wesley.
–––––– and A. P. Hare (1965) "Diagnostic use of interaction profile." J. of Social Psychology 67 (December): 239–258.
Bales, R. F. and F. L. Strodtbeck (1951) "Phases in group problem solving." J. of Abnormal Social Psychology 46: 485–495.
Bennis, W. G. and H. A. Shepard (1956) "A theory of group development." Human Relations 9: 415–437.
Bion, W. R. (1961) Experience in Groups: and Other Papers. New York: Basic Books.

Borgatta, E. F. (1963) "A new systematic interaction observation system: behavior scores system (BSS system)." J. of Psych. Studies 14: 24–44.

_____ (1962) "A systematic study of interaction process scores, peer and self assessments, personality, and other variables." Genetic Psychology Monographs 65: 219–291.

_____ and A. P. Hare (1965) "Diagnostic use of interaction profile." J. of factors in the interaction of small groups." Sociometry 16: 239-252.

Carter, L. F. (1954) "Recording and evaluating the performance of individuals as members of small groups." Personnel Psychology 7: 477–484.

Couch, A. S. (1960) "Psychological determinants of interpersonal behavior." Ph.D. dissertation. Harvard University.

Coyle, G. L. (1930) Social Process in Organized Groups. New York: Smith.

Dewey, J. (1933) How We Think. Lexington, Mass.: D. C. Heath.

Dunphy, D. C. (1964) "Social change in self-analytic groups." Ph.D. dissertation. Harvard University.

Effrat, A. (1968) "Editor's introduction." Soc. Inquiry 38 (Spring): 97–104.

Freud, S. (1949) Group Psychology and the Analysis of the Ego. New York: Liveright.

Hare, A. P. (1969) "Four dimensions of interpersonal behavior." (unpublished)

_____ (1968) "Phases in the development of the Bicol Development Planning Board," in S. Wells and A. P. Hare (eds.) Studies in Regional Development. New York: Bicol Development Planning Board.

_____ and A. Effrat (1969) "Content and process of interaction in Lord of the Flies." (unpublished)

Hare, A. P., N. Waxler, G. Saslow and J. D. Matarazzo (1960) "Interaction process in a standardized initial psychiatric interview." J. of Consulting Psychology 24: 193.

Heinicke, C. and R. F. Bales (1953) "Developmental trends in the structure of small groups." Sociometry 16: 7–38.

Horsfall, A. B. and C. M. Arensberg (1949) "Teamwork and productivity in a shoe factory." Human Organization 8, 1: 13–25.

Landsberger, H. A. (1955) "Interaction process analysis of the mediation of labor-management disputes." J. of Abnormal Social Psychology 51: 552–558.

Lanzetta, J. T., G. R. Wendt, P. Langham, and D. Haefner (1956) "The effects of an 'anxiety-reducing' medication on group behavior under threat." J. of Abnormal Social Psychology 52: 103–108.

Leary, T. (1957) Interpersonal Diagnosis of Personality. New York: Ronald.

Lennard, H. and A. Bernstein with H. C. Hendin and E. B. Palmore (1967) The Anatomy of Psychotherapy: Systems of Communication and Expectation. New York: Columbia Univ. Press.

Mann, R. D. (1967) Interpersonal Styles and Group Development New York: John Wiley.

Matarazzo, J. D., G. Saslow, R. Matarazzo, and J. S. Phillips (1957) "Stability and modifiability of personality patterns during standardized interviews," in P. A. Hoch and J. Zubin (eds.) Psychopathology of Communication. New York: Grune & Stratton.

Mills, T. M. (1964) Group Transformation: An Analysis of a Learning Group. Englewood Cliffs, N.J.: Prentice-Hall.

Parsons, T. (1961) Article, pp. 30–79 in T. Parsons et al. (eds.) Theories of Society. New York: Free Press.

_____ et al. (1953) Working Papers in the Theory of Action. New York: Free Press.

Plank, R. (1951) "An analysis of a group therapy experiment." Human Organization 10, 3: 5–21; 4: 26–36.

Psathas, G. (1960) "Phase movement and equilibrium tendencies in interaction process in psychotherapy groups." Sociometry 23: 177–194.

Schutz, W. C. (1958) FIRO: A Three-Dimensional Theory of Interpersonal Behavior. New York: Holt.

_____ (1955) "What makes groups productive?" Human Relations 8: 429–465.

Slater, P. E. (1966) Microcosm: Structural, Psychological, and Religious Evolution in Groups, New York: John Wiley.

Stock, D. and H. A. Thelen (1958) Emotional Dynamics and Group Culture. Experimental Studies of Individual and Group Behavior. New York: New York Univ. Press.

Stone, P. J., D. C. Dunphy, M. S. Smith, and D. M. Ogilvie (1966) The General Inquirer: A Computer Approach to Content Analysis. Cambridge, Mass.: MIT Press.

Talland, G. A. (1955) "Task and interaction process: some characteristics of therapeutic group discussion." J. of Abnormal Social Psychology 50: 105–109.

Theodorson, G. A. (1953) "Elements in the progressive development of small groups." Social Forces 31: 311–320.

Tuckman, B. W. (1965) "Developmental sequence in small groups." Psych. Bull. 63 (June): 384–399.

Van Zelst, R. H. (1952) "An interpersonal relations technique for industry." Personnel 29: 68–76.

III. WHO LEADS A T-GROUP AND HOW?

Perspectives on Trainer and Member Roles

INTRODUCTION

There are no simple answers to the dual questions in the heading above: Who leads a T-Group? And how? This introduction to trainer and member roles leaves many issues untouched, or only hinted at. But the issues involved are so central to the laboratory approach that we cannot avoid at least beginning to unravel them. Our hope is that this beginning will provide a useful foundation for the elaborations that need to be built on it.

THE TRAINER'S ROLE

Conveniently, we focus on the trainer of a T-Group, who plays a variety of roles that are diverse and may be conflicting. This diversity and potential for conflict are approached in this chapter from a variety of perspectives. Some notion of the present ball park is suggested by three major polarities which the T-Group trainer must successfully manage.

- The trainer must function as an expert, and he must also project himself as a person.
- The trainer must function in the role of an "Outsider" in bringing his skills and knowledge to bear in encouraging a group into some learning opportunities while discouraging exploitation of others, and he must also be an "insider" so that he can participate meaningfully in the life of a group so as to be more helpful.
- The trainer will be a central person in a T-Group because he has special skills and "has been there before," but he must work hard to help a group increasingly trust and rely on its own resources.

These three polarities usefully frame important insights into the question: Who Leads a T-Group, and How? But we do not intend the polarities to do everything, and some limitations of the present focus on the trainer deserve special and early notice. First, the focus on the trainer should not obscure the goal of participation by all other group members in the leadership function. Although the trainer will be a central figure in all T-Groups (and although we emphasize that centrality here), learning how to effectively share leadership functions among group members is a major goal of T-Group experiences. That goal receives major attention at a number of other points in this volume.

Second, the three polarities do highlight issues that are especially relevant for trainers, but they also apply in various degrees to all other members of a T-Group. For example, nobody is "just a participant" or just an "insider" in a T-Group. Every person brings with him a variety of identifications and memberships; and every person decides to variously "get on board" or to withdraw from a T-Group at various times. In sum, every person in a T-Group is an "outsider" *and* an "insider" in diverse senses. The focus here is primarily on one set of insider/outsider demands, those directed at and/or experienced by the trainer. Similar demands can be felt by all group members, however, and sometimes acutely so.

Third, the three polarities merely illustrate the broader range of diverse and conflicting demands that inhere in the trainer's role. But the illustration should economically suggest the complex force field in which the trainer operates. This selectivity simplifies reality, but hopefully not at the expense of distorting it.

What is it that a trainer does, and how? Robert Tannenbaum, Irving R. Weschler and Fred Massarik[1] have suggested that the role of the trainer can be conceptualized into five broad functions. They picture the trainer as designing appropriate learning opportunities, establishing behavioral models for group members, introducing new values, facilitating communications flow, and participating as an expert on groups. The trainer, in sum, is a "professional helper" who, in order to meet the

---

[1] R. Tannebaum, I. R. Weschler and F. Massarik, *Leadership and Organization* (New York: McGraw Hill, Inc., 1961).

complex demands of the group situation, requires a guided theory and diagnostic vocabulary.

The need for a guiding theory and a diagnostic vocabulary can be reinforced by sketching the intricacies of one of the trainer's major responsibilities, diagnosing what goes on in a T-Group. Bradford, Stock, and Horwitz provided a detailed perspective on the issue in an early article that dealt with diagnostic problems in groups.[2] The acute demands made on the trainer are obvious. Thus the trainer must not only hear and retain the *content* of group interaction, he or she must seek to identify the *processes* that lie beneath the obvious. If the content of a group discussion dwells on how difficult it is to really get started, for example, adequate diagnosis must isolate the processes underlying the lackluster performance. Numerous processes could be operating. Consider only two.

- Group members accept the trainer but have low trust in one another, because they fear rejection by peers but trust authority figures.
- The members have a problem with authority figures and cannot express their feelings about the "incompetence" of the trainer, who has not inspired them out of their lethargy.

How effectively the trainer makes his diagnoses will significantly influence the course of T-Group development. A trainer who diagnoses Process 2 when Process 1 exists, for example, confronts group members with a major dilemma, especially early in the life of a group. Should they be "good group members" and own up to Process 2, thereby hedging against rejection by the powerful trainer but only at the expense of being false to their own sense of what exists? Or will they reject the trainer's interpretation and own up that Process 1 is really operating, which requires that they raise the issue of rejecting the trainer when they themselves fear rejection?

Note, however, that T-Group dynamics provide a valuable crutch for fallible trainers. For many practical purposes, "bad" interventions are only unanticipated learning opportunities. In the case above, for example, either trainer intervention can generate important learning opportunities for some members, no matter which diagnosis is really correct, providing that trainer and members fully analyze the intervention. Of course, a trainer may create too many unanticipated learning opportunities for the taste of members of his T-Group. But he, at least, can also learn from that.

That the trainer comes to a T-Group as a person as well as an expert, as a participant in the group process as well as an observer external to it, enormously complicates the delicacy of the trainer's roles. Indeed, if Carl R. Rogers is even approximately correct, the trainer will be successful only as he

---

[2] Leland P. Bradford, Dorothy Stock, and Murray Horwitz, "How to Diagnose Group Problems," *NTL Selected Reading Series:* Vol. 1, *Group Development* (Washington, D.C.: NTL Institute for Applied Behavioral Science, 1961), pp. 32–50).

blends involvement with clinical insight, the person with the expert. For Rogers, a person in the helping professions will be successful as he is:[3]

- *Congruent,* that is, as he is aware of his feelings and reactions, that he can be them in his interpersonal transactions, and that he can communicate them if appropriate;
- *Empathic,* that is, as he can understand the private worlds of the people whom he seeks to help, and as he is also able to communicate some of that understanding;
- As he experiences a warm, positive accepting attitude towards others involved in any helping relationship, that is, as he has *positive regard* for them; and
- As he feels such positive regard *unconditionally.*

Rogers derives these attitudes or experiential elements of guidance basically from his work as a counselor and psychotherapist, but he notes their applicability to the variety of helping roles. These include "psychotherapist, teacher, religious worker, guidance counselor, social worker, clinical psychologist. . . ."

Rogers' insights may be summarized, and an implication may be noted. For Rogers, the viability of any helping sequence is influenced if not determined by the nature and quality of the interpersonal relationship. By extension, the trainer of a T-Group must similarly bring himself as both a professional and a person to the training situation in order to enhance its efficacy. The potential conflict may be serious, and there are no easy ways to avoid it. The T-Group trainer requires a guiding theory and diagnostic vocabulary as a professional, for example. However, the learning involved in gaining them may only make it harder for the trainer to emerge as a person. Life is a paradox, as Peanuts might say.

Fortunately, much has been learned about the trainer's role over the almost 30 years of experience with sensitivity training. The challenge facing the trainer is formidable. In a mid-sixties article Gordon L. Lippitt and Leslie E. This[4] summarized much of this learning. Stressing that the quality of what is learned in the laboratory learning group is heavily but not solely dependent on the trainer, they emphasized four major points:

- The manner in which group composition affects the trainer role.[5] The need, for example, for trainers to provide emotional support for learning if the group members do not have the resources to supply it;
- The need for trainers to be able to shift from one role to another depending on the needs of the situation. For example, the trainer should be able to move appropriately from being a process diagnostician to a group standards protector to a group member;

---

[3] Carl R. Rogers, "The Interpersonal Relationship: The Core of Guidance," *Harvard Educational Review,* Vol. 32 (Fall, 1962), pp. 516–29.

[4] Gordon L. Lippitt and Leslie E. This, "Leaders for Laboratory Training: Selected Guidelines for Group Trainers Utilizing the Laboratory Method," *Training and Development Journal,* March, 1967.

[5] Roger Harrison, "Group Composition Models for Laboratory Design," *Journal of Applied Behavioral Science,* Vol. 1, No. 4 (1965), pp. 409–32.

- The need for trainers to be aware of "traps" that may await them in the group. An example of a trap would be to permit, if not encourage, a group to tilt toward a mode that supports clinical diagnosis of members by members; and
- The need for trainers to resolve problems that surround the question of when or when not to intervene—"to make it happen or to let it happen."

TRAINER STYLES: A CASE STUDY

Any understanding of the complexities of the trainer role must stress two elements: enormous variation around a stable central core of empirical knowledge about what exists and about what values are desirable. This compound characterization also applies to the selection, "Observations on the Trainer Role: A Case Study," which is taken from a book by Robert Tannenbaum, Irving R. Weschler, and Fred Massarik. The selection is based on a paper by Jerome Reisel.

Both the variation and the central core of "Observations on the Trainer Role" may be illustrated expeditiously. In major senses, there is no such thing as *the* trainer style. The selection focuses on two trainers, both of whom had reputations as successful professionals. Their diverse personal needs, skills, and styles variously helped or hindered their efforts to exploit learning opportunities for the T-Groups with which they worked. Trainer I was self-effacing toward himself and his work, and his successes tended to be presented as results of a happy serendipity or of profound luck. Trainer II had a contrasting and powerful need to have his groups produce, to see his groups progress. If Trainer I seemed to come upon success by happy accident, Trainer II chased success with grim determination. The common products of these variabilities were mixed: each style got certain results at the expense of others. The moral is obvious. No trainer style is foolproof. The only applicable wisdom is for each trainer to be increasingly in touch with the mixed consequences of his or her style, and to work over the long run to shift the balance continually toward intended and helpful consequences.

"Observations on the Trainer Role" also sensitively sketches the central core that defines the common arena in which the trainer variabilities above become manifest. In a number of major senses, that is, important basic similarities permit reference to the trainer approach. For example, the selection stresses the trainer's basic role in introducing to T-Group members an orientation toward group process. This central feature of sensitivity training involves a shift in patterns of perception by group members, for the trainer variously encourages their attention to the way things are done as opposed to what is done. As might be expected, both trainers in the present selection induced an emphasis on process in their own distinctive and human ways, with a mixed record of successes and failures in realizing what they sought.

D. R. Peters and Linda M. Joslyn in "Transference Phenomena in Laboratory Training Groups" take us into more depth concerning some intricate decisions that a trainer may have to make relative to member-trainer relationships. They suggest that the phenomena of transference in groups was neglected in the early days of group training, largely because trainers tended to be either educators or social psychologists and thus did not have a clinical orientation. The authors link the manner in which a trainer may deal with transference to the particular model of training group in which the behavior is occurring. Thus, for example, in a group process-oriented group the trainer's reactions to transference might be slight or non-existent unless the behavior inhibits the group. In a personal growth lab transference behavior might receive major focus as a block to authenticity. At the crux of this problem, as for any other the trainer confronts, is the question, "What is important for this group at this moment in its life?"

CO-TRAINING: A TEAM APPROACH TO THE TRAINER ROLE

The practice of co-training in a T-Group was early associated with a craftsman-apprentice relationship. Part of the training of new trainers had to do with their working with one who had experience and skill. Indeed, this practice continues today. Craig and Joan Lundberg, however, in "Encounter Co-Training" make a case for this model of trainer role as one that has value far beyond the need to train neophytes. Three types of advantages are noted that may accrue to a group when the co-training model is employed: (1) learning is enhanced through member association with different trainer styles, (2) the diagnostic capability of the single trainer is multiplied, and (3) the co-trainers provide a support network for each other, particularly in cases where the group is part of a larger client system. The authors also note some potential dysfunctional consequences of co-training. Untoward effects of co-training can be expected when the trainers are incompatible, when they become overly dependent on one another, or when they are seen by the group as a coalition, either fighting the group or working on their own problems at the expense of the group. The Lundbergs feel that a cost-benefit analysis weighs in favor of co-training and also that further study is needed to conceptualize the practice more adequately.

THE TRAINER OF YOUR CHOICE: NEGOTIATING WHO WILL WORK WITH WHOM

Almost universally when people go to a lab, staff assignments have already been made and participants have little or no choice over whom their trainer will be. Carol Heine, Bernard Lubin, Jerry Perlmutter, and Alice Lubin discuss a polar opposite experience in "Negotiating for Group and Trainers." Their article is a description of a two-week training laboratory, the first part of which was devoted to a design by which trainers and participants would negotiate the formation of the groups and the trainers who would work with them. The concept behind the design, encouraging choice and the development of role contracts, is an intriguing one. Not only was the process reinforcing of T-Group values, the authors also suggest that productive learning outcomes were associated with it, as well. In addition, because the design called for an early sharing of personal resources, the authors feel that this contributed to the absence of severe stress during the remainder of the laboratory. Regardless of whether or not this process of negotiating for leaders and groups becomes widespread, it is clearly illustrative of the type of experimentation with new learning models that goes on in the field.

A final note is needed in this introductory section to "Who Leads a T-Group and How?" It has to do with whatever relationship may exist between trainer style and the development of psychiatric problems or "casualties" among group members. Research[6] that was part of a much larger study[7] suggests that differences in trainer style may be a more potent factor in the development of psychiatric casualties among group members than the particular type of group setting in which the problem occurs. For example, people in groups the style of whose trainer was characterized as "aggressive stimulator" seemed to develop more problems than did those whose trainer style was described as "love," somewhat irrespective of the particular focus of the group or ideological "school" of which it was a part.

The major study of which these findings are a part has been criticized on a number of grounds.[8] Nevertheless, the findings are thought-provoking and should encourage researchers and practitioners to look more closely at the group phenomena with which they are dealing, the better to understand it and, thus, to improve practice.

---

[6] I. D. Yalom and M. A. Lieberman, "A Study of Encounter Group Casualties," *Archives of General Psychiatry,* Vol. 25 (July, 1971), pp. 16–30.

[7] M. A. Lieberman, I. D. Yalom and M. B. Miles, *Encounter Groups: First Facts* (New York: Basic Books, Inc., 1973).

[8] William C. Schutz, "Not Encounter and Certainly Not Facts," *The 1974 Annual Handbook for Group Facilitators* (Iowa City: University Associates Publishers, Inc., 1974).

10. Observations on the Trainer Role: A Case Study

JEROME REISEL

Seeing different trainers at work can be most revealing. Each has his own personality, his theories of training, and different skills in varying degrees of competence. Some act as catalysts; others as sources of wisdom; others as counselors; still others as teachers. Some respond to the overt, conscious needs of their trainees; others to what appear to them as more significant unconscious wants and drives. Some actually do what they think they do; others give lip service to one mode of operation while actually performing in another. Some are blocked by their own personality difficulties from helping their trainees face up to similar problems within themselves; others appear reasonably well adjusted in the interpersonal arena and are not bothered by undue tensions in the efficient execution of their jobs.

Direct appraisal of the trainer role in human relations training programs has generally been neglected, despite the fact that both leadership theory and leadership method have received considerable attention in the literature devoted to group behavior. For the most part, research on group processes has tended to recognize the trainer implicitly, but to ignore his explicit behavior. This has sometimes led to the erroneous impression that events occurring in a training group are only indirectly affected by the trainer's activities.

STUDY PURPOSE

We aim here to present a way of looking at the trainer role, to identify and describe problems which are most likely to be encountered particularly by those who undertake a sensitivity training assignment, and to demonstrate the basic premise that the trainer is a potent factor in the total interaction of his group. His influence, it appears to us, must be given serious consideration if full-scale understanding of the training process is to be achieved.

This [article] is based on a paper, "The Trainer Role in Human Relations Training," by Jerome Reisel, delivered before a meeting of the Western Psychological Association, San Diego, Calif., April, 1959.

In order for sensitivity training to be effective, conditions must be set up which allow for an integration of emotional and cognitive learning. From the trainer's point of view, his task is primarily one of creating an atmosphere conducive to learning. He also must assess how much can be learned by the group with which he works. For every group encountered, the trainer is apt to vary his objectives in some degree. If his training function is to be well carried out, his efforts must be based on an accurate assessment of group potentials. This is his core problem, and it is by no means a simple one. This view of the training role stresses trainer sensitivity in the selection of appropriate goals as a factor of key importance in increasing the likelihood of his doing an effective job.

In his work, the trainer cannot avoid involvement in the flow and counterflow of activity of his group. It is only in this fashion that he picks up the cues that should enable him to provide the kind of assistance that will help the group to work out conflicts that arise. His capacity for discovering cues and his ability to determine an appropriate course of action on the basis of these findings are, we believe, direct functions of his personality.

This case study focuses on the trainer, so far as his role is defined by what he perceives and how he acts on these perceptions. A clinical frame of reference is used. Viewing training behavior in its psychodynamic aspects immediately admits trainer personality as a fundamental variable in the process of human relations training. The clinical approach also challenges the validity of the notion that all the structural and functional properties of such groups can be studied meaningfully apart from the trainer.

Two key hypotheses underlie the clinical point of view. First, the trainer is a constant source of motivational stimuli for the group; second, the stimuli put forth by the trainer are a direct function of his total personality organization.

The assertion that the trainer is a constant source of motivational stimuli for the group implies that the trainer is always a force for encouragement, facilitation, hindrance, or inhibition to the group. By tracing the source of these motivational stimuli to the personality organization of the trainer, one is able to assess his behavior as a function of his needs, beliefs, values, and attitudes. Thus, his training role is the result of a constellation of such factors as the degree and kind of intelligence he possesses; his imaginative capacity; his direct responsiveness to the environment; his outlook toward past, present, and future; the presence and amount of anxiety within him; his range of emotional reactions; and his general pattern of character traits.

It should be added that the hypothesis of a close functional relationship between trainer and group should not lead to the inference of a one-to-one relationship. If it did, a "great-man" theory would provide the necessary and sufficient condition for comprehending all group phenomena—which it does not!

SUBJECTS AND METHOD

The subjects of this investigation were two trainers, both of whom are men of established reputation in the field of human relations training. They have contributed substantially to the literature on group behavior and are currently active as trainers in various training programs. They are frequently engaged as speakers by organizations or groups representing business, labor, education, government, etc. Neither of them is a clinician, and their knowledge of dynamic psychology and its methods comes mainly from academic study with training experience providing a second source of information. Both were aware of the nature of this study, but they have not dictated or influenced its form or content in any way.

The study was carried out by a clinical research psychologist who observed the subjects as they worked with two sensitivity training groups in an academic setting. These particular training groups consisted of seniors and graduate students who were planning to enter such fields as labor relations, personnel management, administrative nursing, business management, public service, and teaching.

Each training group consisted of twenty-four persons. In both groups the men outnumbered the women by about three to one. Each group was organized in a manner that allowed for free and spontaneous interaction during the meetings. Formal course material was in the form of prescribed readings on which the group members were examined at specified times during the sixteen-week semester. Lectures were not given. Each training group had thirty two-hour sessions.

During the semester, there was a subdivision of the members within each group into smaller groups for the purpose of working out a project related to the course content. This work was accomplished in out-of-class time. The small groups were organized on the basis of mutual interest in a topic. The kinds of problems chosen had to do with such matters as the introduction of change, the nature of effective leadership, or the relation between morale and productivity. In each case, the small group had to decide upon a substantive content to illustrate the topic (e.g., one small group concerned with effective leadership studied the activities of two well-known athletic coaches; another dealt with the use of interpersonal influence on the top-management team of a medium-sized company; a third studied the sources of resistance to the introduction of a highly efficient modern appliance).

The psychologist attended all sessions for both training groups, a total of 120 hours in all. He was introduced to each group as a research person, and they were advised that questions could be asked of him at the end of the semester if the group members so wished. The psychologist observed the group and trainer from a point outside the circle of the group. The content of all sessions was recorded on tape so that a complete group history would be available.

After each of the group sessions, each trainer met individually with the psychologist for about thirty to forty-five minutes. These interviews were taped. The meetings with the psychologist were essentially a series of depth interviews, and although these often had a frankly therapeutic quality, no attempt was made to use them for psychotherapy. A total of sixty interviews took place, thirty with each trainer.

The data of this study are essentially qualitative. The use of a clinician who acted as observer and interviewer led to the accumulation of information dealing with the experiences of the trainers as they carried out their jobs.

THE PERSONALITY OF THE TRAINERS

So far as this study is concerned with a description of the training role in terms of the problems attendant on it, the following personality sketches tend to emphasize sources and manifestations of trainer anxiety. This leads to the kind of presentation which focuses on weaknesses and deficiencies rather than on strengths and skills. A one-sided view such as this has the advantage of highlighting the relationship between trainer personality and the problems associated with the training role. It has the disadvantage of making the trainers appear inefficient.

The trainers under observation are not generally anxious individuals. They are, however, subject to anxieties in much the same fashion as many another person. Their anxieties stem in part from an intense need to improve their already substantial skills rather than from a lack of training ability. It is also quite likely that being subject to observation and interview helped to build tensions in them.

In working with the trainers, care was taken to avoid the assumption that successful trainers had to have the same personal characteristics or, for that matter, any special set of qualities. Furthermore, it was not assumed that the personality structure of the successful trainer reflected some form of optimal emotional adjustment.

The interviews with these two trainers served the purpose of helping them to evaluate their training behavior in terms of its conscious and unconscious determinants. The context for these evaluations was always in terms of trainer efforts to provide an experience designed to enable the group members to learn about the effect of interpersonal factors as these were manifested in their group activity. The extent to which the members were able to learn how their actions affected each other could serve as a yardstick for trainer effectiveness.

In this phase of the study, the clinician's task was to help the trainers identify some of their resistances to facing how they really felt about what transpired in the groups. The role of unconscious needs in the trainers, their connection with what the trainers saw themselves as doing, the influence of these needs on the group—all these factors proved interesting and worthy of detailed exploration.[2]

TRAINER I

Perhaps the most striking characteristic of this trainer was his self-effacing attitude toward himself and toward his work. He was constantly surprised by his successes and looked upon them as some sort of profound luck. Though exceedingly skillful in handling his group, he had difficulty in accepting himself as skilled, as if to do such a thing would be to commit the sin of pride. A warm and friendly person, he played the role of a benevolent, kindly father figure for his group. He was highly sensitive and alert to the needs of the group members, and he could communicate this with facility.

As it turned out, these character traits served to mask considerable underlying anxiety over the expression of hostility. As will be seen, many of his problems arose as a consequence of an intense need to be liked and a fear that lack of affection is tantamount to rejection. His role of trainer was carried out without full awareness of the fact that it brought him the attention and respect that gratified his powerful need for affection. His behavior was of a kind that unconsciously averted any direction of hostility toward him. He could deal with expressions of resentment and anger if he was sure that these feelings were not directed at him, or if he deliberately engendered them.

Consciously, he was aware of a hampering passivity within him that led him to deal with heavily emotion-laden situations by exercising excessive caution. He had a tendency to blame himself for this and to react to it with some anxiety and lowered mood. It was almost as if his expectation of failure was so great that it led to a fear of success.

In a sense, his effectiveness as a trainer was due to the fact that he provided a protected environment where the trainee's basic needs were satisfied. Most people have conflicts over the expression of hostility, and in such an environment there is little impetus for anger. This trainer's group

---

[2] Prior to and during the four-month period when the research was being carried out, contact with the trainers was limited to the clinician-trainer relationship. Every effort was made to maintain an attitude of clinical objectivity.

achieved success almost as a present to the trainer for his kindness in helping them to avoid any unpleasantness.

The trainer's basic consideration must be whether or not the group members learn enough to enhance their abilities in interpersonal relations. Any other concerns must be viewed as superfluous and therefore a distortion of reality stemming from the trainer's intrapsychic conflicts. In this instance, clinical observation makes it appear that this trainer's doubts were unfounded—he was effective; the group was helped to work within its limits, and it reached its training goals with a sense of cohesiveness and integrity.

TRAINER II

This trainer was characterized by a powerful need to produce. He could not mask this, and in his desire for the trainees to gain the kind of insights he felt they should, he seemed driven by almost voyeuristic impulse to see results. Intense, serious, highly responsive emotionally, in his role as trainer he showed a kind of ambivalence that rendered him indecisive at one moment, fully in command at the next. In discussing his activities in the group, he seemed to encounter blind spots with which he tried to deal by intellectualization and projection. Much as trainer I seemed to come upon success as if by accident, trainer II chased it as one would a will-o'-the-wisp.

Urged on by powerful drives to be seen as successful both by himself and by others, this trainer frequently tried to overextend himself. For example, it was not enough for him that he was highly intelligent; his intelligence had to scintillate. He seemed engaged in a constant competition for some goal that would gain him recognition. One might say that he used training techniques with the efficiency of a surgeon and took it for granted that his patient must survive if the technique was correct. He approached his work with a zealous sincerity and an intense faith. To the observer it seemed that, in trying too hard, he was creating problems where there might be none.

The facade of flourishing activity in this trainer indicated some concerns about his adequacy and his ability. Prone to feelings of insecurity and upsurges of anxiety, he found in the training role a way of dealing with strong conflicts over authority. By identifying with the authority role and then consciously trying to avoid being authoritarian, he attempted to prevent the anxiety consequent to being forced to compete for recognition. He enjoyed the power of his position but tended to deny the existence of this power by not using it.

Although apt to experience somewhat excessive tensions, these were periodic and he managed to complete his training task with good results.

His purity of motive and his intensity of purpose communicated themselves to the majority of the group members. His behavior in the group encouraged the members to fight him, to block him, to reject him; but they seemed unable to hate him. He provoked their hostility unconsciously despite his difficulty in handling resentment, and then neutralized its adverse effects by accepting such expression. In his group this behavior took the form of living dangerously by attacking resistances and rousing affects. At the same time, however, he was perspicacious enough to protect those who had low anxiety tolerances.

Most of the learning in this trainer's group took place on an unconscious level, thus frustrating his need to see results. As he explored this need, he gradually came to accept the notion that productive ends can come about as a result of nonverbal insights as well as by means of the usual "aha!" experiences. In one sense, most of his problems as a trainer were traceable to his diffuse anxieties inducing, perhaps, too many critical incidents in his group, thereby giving the impression of too much going on rather than too little.

SOME KEY TRAINING PROBLEMS

The foregoing descriptions of the trainers make it evident that they differed markedly. The kind of impact each had on his trainees could be attributed to personality differences—to different ways of handling the anxieties which the training situation caused for them. Still, the problems they encountered were largely the same. This should not be surprising, inasmuch as both were in a situation where the general objectives and training methodology were largely the same. What seems to be a contradiction of the notion that trainer problems are a function of trainer personality (i.e., if trainers differ in personality, then problems should differ) is only apparent. Actually, it is the manner of handling the problem that differs. It is on this level that personality enters; and individual variations in dealing with problems—problems that were the same for both—are what produced differences in impact.

In observing these two trainers in action, five major common problems were uncovered. Each can be viewed as a potential source (or a consequent) of trainer anxiety and difficulties: the first is *time limitation;* the second is *group composition;* the third, *exposure and vulnerability;* the fourth, *reconciling behavior and theory about group functions;* and finally, the fifth, *content versus process orientation.*

This list is by no means exhaustive, but it represents the major problems confronting the trainers under consideration here. These problems will be encountered by all trainers in varying degree. Certainly every trainer is faced with the necessity of achieving his objectives within a specific period with a particular group. Every trainer must also decide how much to give of himself, that is, how deeply personally to get involved. He must face the fact that what he wants to do and what he actually does may not coincide; finally, he has to take a stand on how much structure to provide for his group and at what level of depth he will help it to operate.

TIME LIMITATION

Every trainer is somehow concerned with whether his training goals will be achieved in the time allotted. The time variable is a real one, and it cannot be avoided by the trainer. It can be a source of trainer anxiety if he is driven by powerful needs to achieve. Temporal reality then becomes a threat because its implacability signifies a constant possibility of failure.

The time dimension, if it is a source of trainer anxiety, can account for numerous critical incidents occurring in the group. This proved to be the case with trainer II, but not with trainer I. The decisive factor was the way in which the trainers organized the didactic aspect of the group experience.

Trainer I organized his course so that none of the meetings was devoted necessarily to outright discussion of training materials. This meant that the group members were held responsible for completing their readings and their small group projects by certain specified dates. There were examinations to cover the readings, and these took place at a designated time. Reports on small group projects were to be completed no later than the date for the final examination. The members of the group tried to make an issue of these requirements, but the trainer stood fast and they did not press their point. As a consequence, the group meetings were free to take any direction desired by the members (including discussion of course content if they wished), and a tense and urgent need to meet deadlines was avoided. Trainer I treated the trainees as adults who were presumed to have a sense of responsibility and an ability to meet it. He also prevented the arousal of anxiety within himself by identifying with the realistic elements of the teacher role, thus enabling him to act with authority and deflect any challenges that might lead to a stirring up of his passive conflicts.

Trainer II was in constant fear that he would fail to help the group have a positive learning experience; this created difficulties, because it was communicated to the group in terms of expressed impatience with them and a frequent resort to training gadgetry in order to speed them along. For this trainer, the limitation of time was an important source of anxiety. His need for achievement had to be realized in terms of objectively discernible goals. In the process of achieving these goals, the trainer perceived the group as hindering and blocking itself in the decision-making process. This seemed a direct affront to him. He could not blame the group *in toto* for this recalcitrance, because this would mean his shouldering too much guilt.

So he declaimed against the strictures of a reality that inhibited his freedom. The academic pressures were seen allied with time against him. The developmental tendencies in the group were pushed rather than allowed to emerge in a natural fashion. The latitude of experimentation in the group was narrowed, and the cohesive atmosphere so desired by the trainer seemed missing.

GROUP COMPOSITION

Group composition is also a factor with which the trainer must deal and to which he must adjust himself. Meeting with a newly organized group for the first time, a trainer is generally curious to see "what he has." He is then confronted with the delicate task of using his perceptive skills to determine what his expectations ought to be. Further, he must be ready to accept the idea that so many unknowns enter into the phenomenon of group composition that he can never know precisely how a given set of events manages to occur. The trainer is limited, in his task, by the nature of the materials with which he has to deal. Within this limitation, he must set his goals in terms of what can be achieved rather than what ought to be achieved.

Trainer I was very sensitive to the needs of his group members. He had a good capacity for empathizing with them and helping them to see the manner in which their reactions affected themselves and others. He represented a form of reality that was acceptable to the group because it was not perceived as threatening. As a consequence, the group generated little in the way of organized resistance to the trainer's efforts to exert influence. His characteristic methods of averting anxiety in himself were generally so effective that few of his needs were projected onto the group, and he could seem calm, self-assured, and helpful. He kept his distance from the group by being assiduously protective. By mobilizing very little of the anxiety potential of the group, few crises were precipitated; the trainer knew where he stood, ambiguity was averted, and no disruptive tendencies emerged in strength.

The group that trainer II had to work with seemed, for the most part, less mature and more demanding than that of trainer I. If trainer II was the spark, the group was the fuel; needless to say, this led to pyrotechnics. Whereas group I was characterized by sobriety, control, and warmth, group II was characterized by excitement, frequent aimlessness, and heat. The members tried to avert the arousal of anxiety and resisted the trainer's efforts to help them toward insight into what they were doing. This may have represented rejection to the trainer and seemed to rouse his anxieties above threshold level; thus he created renewed anxiety in the group, and a vicious cycle was instituted. Although this condition can be attributed partly to the trainer's personality, it cannot wholly be laid at his feet. Without benefit of any evaluations of group composition, it is felt that most observers would agree (if afforded the opportunity to compare both training groups) that the source of the trainer's difficulties with this group lay in his stars, as well as in himself. If he could have accepted the fact that the group, by dint of its own make-up, was going to be limited in its attainment of goals, he might have avoided many other conflicts in the course of working with it.

EXPOSURE AND VULNERABILITY

The training role, if it is to reach its objectives, generally involves the arousal of affects; this is in order that the emotional elements in the learning process be made conscious. The rousing of affects is equivalent to grabbing a tiger by the tail. Pressures to deal with feelings are generally experienced as something painful by most people, since their development has proceeded largely by a process of successive repressions. The trainer thus becomes a noxious influence for most and a delight to some. The net effect is that he is subject to a host of displaced attitudes and projections from the group members—the target of a wide variety of feelings, many of them negative and hostile, some protective, some loving, others even seductive.

The trainer, by his very position as the original center of authority in the group, cannot avoid being the target of a certain amount of hostility. In both groups, the members could be described in three different ways with reference to their relationship with the trainer: those who were hostile to authority, those who were submissive, and those who seemed to have no major conflicts regarding their relationship with authority.

Both trainers had considerable conflict over the expression of hostility especially when it was directed toward them.

Trainer I showed his fear of hostility by openly encouraging it ("you can call me an SOB if you feel like it"), thereby serving to inhibit its expression. By this procedure, Trainer I also enabled himself to justify the appearance of hostility so that it would not be sudden and unaccepted if it occurred. Trainer II handled hostility either by ingratiating himself with the group ("See, I'm really not a bad guy") or by backing down under pressure ("if the group doesn't want a final exam, there won't be any"). Both trainers resorted to meetings with certain group members outside of class, partly in order to lessen the growing hostility in these persons. Trainer II also used the rationalizing device of imputing most group manifestations of hostility to irrational elements within the hostile members.

Trainer I, despite his adequate surface handling of hostility, seemed to have a much deeper conflict with such expressions. In his group, he did not avoid dealing with hostility when it arose, but he was decidedly uncomfortable with it. In interviews, he recognized this difficulty and made a strong effort to probe its sources in himself. As has been suggested, he skillfully avoided tying in the authority-dependence problem to that of hostility and for the most part led the group to by-pass the usual struggle for leadership among its members. To be sure, there was much discussion of leadership, but it was always on a fairly intellectual level. This trainer was bothered by one or two group members who tried to take control of the group once they perceived the existence of a power vacuum created by him. He acted protective toward these people even though he did not really feel that way. This neutralized their ability to be angry with him, and when they turned on someone else in the group, the trainer handled the situation more effectively.

Trainer II stirred up hostility, often without being aware that he was doing so. It was difficult for him to see himself as authoritarian, and he projected such tactics onto other group members. Nevertheless, his overt behavior was frequently dictatorial in a subtle way. He would write lists of things on the board with the conscious purpose of helping the members to be sensitive to their resistance techniques. If they then ignored what he wrote or paid lip service to his list, he would point out this behavior and wonder what it could mean. Another device used by him was to give a summary of his observations at the very end of the hour. He thus preserved the last word for himself and averted any possibility of rebuttal. Until given an opportunity to deal with these patterns, this trainer was unaware of their unconscious sources and saw them merely as a part of his usual training practices.

The trainer is confronted with the task of ascertaining whether or not certain of the group members are apt to be greatly threatened or unduly aroused by the emphasis he places on interpersonal factors in trying to attain his training goals. If certain group members become disturbed by what happens to them in the group, they are apt to seek out the trainer for advice, support, and reassurance. The trainer is forced to deal with the fact that a member is looking to him for help. He must have some basis for assessing the degree of upset in the member and then act in a manner designed to be most helpful. He thereupon engages in supportive therapy, much in the manner that a personal counselor, doctor, priest, or other person in a similar role is frequently called upon to do. Part of his responsibility is to know enough about psychodynamics to sense that something is wrong and to suggest referral to an individual or agency if additional help is needed.

Both trainers were constantly faced with the fact that their roles had heavy therapeutic connotation. They were exposed to a great variety of projections, but at times they could not deal with them as intensively as they would have liked. In this vulnerable position, they were forced to carry these projected feelings without any freedom to ascertain the degree to which they were motivated by irrational sources. Both trainers were thus compelled to strengthen their own defenses in order, paradoxically enough, to avoid being defensive in their activities with the group. This was a great burden for them to bear and created considerable feelings of frustration and ambivalence in both men. Trainer I, for example, discussed his tendency to avoid heavily emotion-laden situations and berated himself for being fearful of plunging in and doing something to clarify the atmosphere that seemed to be smothering group progress. He took the blame upon himself and felt as if he were failing in some serious way. He was prone to socialize and "buddy up" to the group members during breaks in the meetings and made it clear, rather more often than necessary, that he would be available, should "any problems come up" which the group members might wish to talk over with him individually. On the one hand, he could not deal as effectively as he desired with the fact that his position necessitated some arousal of anxiety, because his conception of his role limited the degree to which he could engage in this activity. And if he did arouse anxiety, he wanted it understood, in effect, that he had to, but was willing to make this up to the group members by taking a personal interest in them. It was demonstration of a set of circumstances in which a combination of position as trainer and trainer dynamics united to intensify a sense of vulnerability and hamper efficiency.

TRAINER FUNCTIONING THEORY VERSUS BEHAVIOR

In undertaking the task of training a group in the principles and practices of human relations, the trainer has certain formalized conceptions about individual and group behavior. He has, in effect, a set of coordinated hypotheses which help him both to understand and to predict what may happen in the group during the course of its development. To the degree that his expectancies are realized, there is confirmation of his hypotheses—he feels confident and assured, there is little extraneous conflict, and anxiety is minimal. Should the patterns of group interaction veer off, however, then the trainer is apt to experience uncertainty and, if he is so predisposed, become anxious.

Both trainers in this study employed the same theoretical approaches. Without going into any detailed discussion of theory, their formal approach may be described as falling under the rubric of perceptual approaches to group behavior. This means that they utilized hypotheses derived from Lewinian field theory and Rogerian personality theory as the major basis for conceptualizing both their activity and that of the group. They tended to play their roles in terms of the permissive, accepting, nondirective leader who, by the very nature of his activity, would provide an atmosphere conducive to the effective realization of the integrative potentials inherent in the group. Essentially, each perceived his role as one of climate production and control. In its broadest sense, they were providing the living experience of democracy in action, and their problems arose when it became apparent that neither they nor many of the group members were prepared fully to accept the implications of such an atmosphere.

Trainer I managed to fulfill the requirements of nondirective leadership rather well; yet he was bothered by a tendency to take a more active and interpretive role. This reflected a desire to overcome the passive trends in his personality. If he could only be aggressive without becoming anxious in the process! He ruminated over his tendency to avoid risking involvement in touchy matters brought up by the group. He was aware that he afforded the group protection without demanding the right to control it in return. He was disturbed if the activity of the group seemed lifeless, inert, or aimless. If he was ignored by the group, he blamed himself for being insensitive or for having defective timing. Despite an accurate understanding of his training techniques and the theoretical implications of these methods, he was disquieted by a persistence of dictatorial attitudes and behaviors in many of the group members. His expectations led him to believe that the light of heaven would eventually be perceived by all. In reality, he recognized that this was not the case, nor would it ever be; yet in good conscience he was unable to challenge the conceptualizations he had incorporated into his own way of perceiving. For him, the nondirective technique was consonant with his personal needs to avoid anxiety by remaining passive and on the side lines.

Trainer II had a tendency to use most of the techniques that were at his command. He often felt saddled by a theory that was somewhat inimicable to his personality. He had to defend it as vigorously as possible in order to free himself to attack it later in the course of the training sequence. He would resort to terms such as "hidden agenda," "consensus," and "group responsibility," especially at those times when his group was failing to act in accordance with expectations induced by theoretical constructs. For example, one of the well-established hypotheses about group behavior is that in the early phases of a group's existence there always occurs a struggle for power. Cohesiveness cannot come about until this struggle is resolved in some manner. This trainer was on the lookout for signs of cohesiveness because this would mean that he was effective in his role. He was unaware that his own behavior was preventing his state of affairs from coming into being. He needed to see his expectations confirmed, and this need was so strong that it led him to punish the group for failing to come through. In this instance, it was not a case of theory failing the trainer, but rather one of the trainer imposing his own needs on the theory. Group theory was a highly valued vehicle for him; yet if the facts as he perceived them didn't seem to fit, it was the fault of the theory and not his own.

It is interesting to note that as the trainers became aware of the interrelationships between their personal needs and their theoretical expectancies, both chose to act along lines more consistent with opposite sides of their personalities. Trainer I could take more directive actions in his group without becoming anxious. Trainer II became less needful of being in charge.

INTRODUCING AN ORIENTATION TOWARD GROUP PROCESS

A sensitization procedure is essentially a method for evoking responses to previously neutral stimuli. In human relations training, these responses take the form of new perceptive patterns. Increased social perceptiveness implies a shift in the way one looks at things so that more effective behavior can occur. In the training groups, this shift is manifested by attention to the *way* things are done rather than by a focus on *what* is done. This is commonly denoted as the problem of *process* versus *content* orientation. It is the trainer's task to facilitate this perceptual shift within the group.

Ordinarily, a group tends first to concern itself mainly with content, because this is consistent with its notions of logical procedure. To engage in a discussion on a given topic provides one with a sense of continuity and focus; one knows where one is and where one is going. The members do not as yet know each other, nor are they clear on how their goals are to be achieved. It is a period of acclimatization and/or organization.

Typical of the content phase are discussions of group organization. How shall the group get started? What is the agenda? Will there be a chairman? Will somebody act as observer? Should these people volunteer or be elected? How can human relations theories be tested in the group? Questions like these are raised and worked over, and the group members have an opportunity to size each other up. The trainer also uses this period in order to see "what he has" (the group-composition problem) and to determine how he can introduce a change from structural concerns (content) to emphasis on the forces at play within individuals and the group (process).

In this respect the trainer's task is analogous to that of the psychotherapist. Both are involved with the question of dealing with either content or process. Generally, there is little emphasis placed upon content after the initial phases of either group experience or therapy. If the experience is successful, group members as well as therapy patients gradually come to perceive the implications hidden behind the manifest content of their behavior. Insight occurs not on the basis of analyzing content per se but rather from the way in which it is presented and utilized. Sensitization in human relations training is comparable to insight in therapy; that is, new behavioral patterns emerge as a result of awareness of stimuli that had had little or no evocative power previously.

The shift from a content to a process orientation in the training group is illustrated by two brief interchanges that took place in one of the groups.

Early in Training

Bill: Don't you think—after the way we have been floundering—that . . . maybe we ought to have a chairman?

Mary: I agree—maybe a chairman can put some order into what's going on here.

Jack: Quite so—we've got to have some organization to get things done around here.

Later in Training

Bill: Earlier I suggested that we have a chairman and well . . . some of you agreed that it was a good idea. But . . . we never got around to doing it. Now —I'm suggesting it again.

Mary: I think, Bill, I was one of those that agreed with you then, but now I get a feeling that *you* are uncomfortable if things aren't done in a highly organized way . . . I mean, just for the sake of organization.

Jack: Bill, I feel Mary really has a point here. Besides—the way you've acted on other things gives me the impression that you're annoyed if people don't pick up your suggestions. Maybe you want a chairman so that it's easier for you to get your own way. What do you think?

The first example represents a concern with the content of what was said. Bill, Mary, and Jack combined to work out some structural organization in the group. The second example shows how there is an emergent concern with the way Bill does things, and there is some effort to recognize his needs and motives for wanting a chairman. The latter reflects a process orientation.

Both trainers had the problem of educating the group members in the nature of group process and providing them with an impetus to deal with the transactions of the group in terms of the forces at work.

Trainer I limited his contributions to a clarification of content in the early phases of the training and, as soon as possible, shifted to remarks designed to reflect feelings and ignore content. He deliberately avoided responding to cues designed to trap him into being the orthodox professor, thereby maintaining a certain amount of ambiguity about his role as trainer. He was expected to be concerned with content because the expectations of the group were those of students relating to a teacher.

When the group could not identify him with its stereotyped conceptions of what he would be like, it became easy for him to make the shift toward the process aspects of group behavior.

As has already been stated, trainer II was intensely concerned with the development of "insight into process." For him, such insight was the significant indicator of a successful training experience. At the same time, he could consider himself effective if such insights occurred. He saw insightful behavior among the group members as so necessary that he became anxious when the group seemingly was deliberate in resisting such valuable knowledge. There were times when the group was accused by him of "being blind," "having it laid in their laps and not seeing it," etc. The intensity of his overreactions to resistant and fractious behavior of the trainees gradually came to be seen by the trainer as a projective defense against the anxiety he might experience if he failed to achieve his training goals. He became aware of the fact that the greater the tendency on his part to impose his needs on the group, the greater would be its resistance to any change-producing insights. His need to see results was analogous to that of the therapist who must cure all his patients; in both instances the likelihood of an unfavorable result is increased.

Actually, the creation of frustration and the mobilization of some anxiety are necessary for change. Trainer II apparently tended to create excessive anxiety in his trainees so that many of them became fearful and hid behind the facade of a content orientation. Those of his trainees who had good capacity to withstand frustration reacted positively to the training experience. Trainer II saw these persons as "effective," and in fact they were. Such trainees took the load off the trainer and helped the group to attain a process orientation by their activity during the meetings. Seeing some of his trainees "successful," from his point of view, helped to reduce his tensions, and he could thus become more effective by becoming less of a threat to the group.

CONCLUSIONS

The key conclusions of this study are, first, that the five training problems which have been identified and described may well be encountered by all who do human relations training in general and sensitivity training in particular; and second, that these problems arise from the situational context of the training.

The first conclusion is essentially to hypothesize that having problems is a requisite for the trainer. It implies that every trainer is going to have the problem of attaining his training objectives in a given period of time, and that his objectives will be conditioned by the nature of the group membership. His position requires some skill in dealing with hostile expression in its wide variety of forms. His trainer-leader role invites the trainees to displace attitudes and project feelings onto him. His conceptual grasp of the trainer role may lead him to expect certain outcomes, and if these are not forthcoming, there may be frustration and anxiety. The teaching of others to perceive behavior in terms of motives and dynamics rather than in terms of manifest content is always difficult and sometimes impossible.

The second conclusion is that if these five problems are invariably associated with the conditions of training, then they are aspects of reality existing prior to, and independent of, the trainer. On the surface this might appear as an easy opportunity for the trainer to disclaim any responsibility for his failures, inasmuch as the matter would seem to be out of his hands; by the same token, he could not accept any credit for the achievement of his objectives. Actually, what is implied is that the realities of the training situation include certain general difficulties which the trainer must confront. His personality accounts for the *intensity* with which a problem is manifested. It does not account for the presence of the problem.

From a case-study standpoint, this report has many interesting facets. Persons who serve as sensitivity trainers have a vital interest in developing and utilizing their ability to exercise influence (leadership) in order to help people be more sensitive and skillful in the handling of interpersonal relations. These are not the ordinary goals of leadership activity. There are strong overtones of social responsibility in this kind of teaching-leadership function.

A descriptive study of this kind raises many more questions than it answers. This is probably as it should be. The questions are not limited to sensitivity training alone, but should be applicable to other areas of interest with regard to the phenomena of interpersonal relations.

At this point little is known about the common qualities of trainer personality that are requisite for success. Certainly selection of trainers is apt to be more refined if there is some recognition of the personality correlates necessary for efficient dealing with problems associated with the training role.

Much has been said and written about those who have been subjected to influence, either on an individual basis or as members of groups. One need only consider the abundance of research on educational methods, group dynamics, and psychotherapy. Perhaps the shift of focus away from those who are influenced and onto those who attempt to influence may provide fresh insights on a problem that, for all its obviousness, has no lack of complexity and subtleness.

11. Transference Phenomena in Laboratory Training Groups

D. R. PETERS and LINDA M. JOSLYN

SCENARIOS

As a trainer of a T-Group, imagine that close to the end of the first meeting you are suddenly confronted by a participant who previously had been quiet. He indirectly attacks you as being ineffectual and derelict in your duty to help the group get started. Another member nods in apparent agreement with this, but the group starts onto another topic . . .

In the third session of the group, the members begin talking about the ways the role of trainer has affected them. One man says to the trainer, "I have admired the way you quietly control the group. I've felt if people started getting out of hand in here that you'd step in and keep us from getting off the track."

Which of the following strategies comes closest to what you think the trainer should do in each of the 2 situations above?

(a) Ignore the incident unless it seems to be receiving widespread attention or support or unless it recurs.

(b) Consider this incident as important and a useful learning opportunity. Thus: (1) gather some systematic data about authority and power relationships in the group; or (2) inquire about the assumptions of the group regarding the trainer role; or (3) reflect the content and the feelings back to the individual member and check out your understanding of what he meant; or (4) confront the individual member with your immediate personal reactions about what he said to you; or (5) interpret the reaction and focus on eliciting and exploring the deeper reactions of the person and others toward yourself.

These incidents, not uncommon events in groups, exemplify instances of what could be usefully viewed as transference-based reactions. Whichever strategy of intervention you might have chosen from the above will reflect not only personal style but a particular training and learning theory underlying what you do in the role of a trainer. In this paper we will focus on the occurrence and treatment of transference phenomena in several contemporary models of laboratory training and examine the possibility of interventions consistent with the related assumptions about learning in each model.

Reprinted from *Interpersonal Development*, Vol. 1, 1970, pp. 203-215.

INTRODUCTION

T-Group trainers, psychological consultants, and organizational change agents have often noted instances in which organizational or group members reveal peculiar and seemingly inappropriate perceptions of them or respond to them as if they were someone else. Such distorted perceptions and inappropriate responses often resemble behaviors classified by the clinician as transference phenomena—a term which may connote more intense or disturbed affective states than are usually generated during a training laboratory.

The attention given this topic in the laboratory training literature to date is sparse and needlessly limited in scope, perhaps in part because of the education and/or social psychology background of many early pioneers and theorists. Only in the context of "self-analytic" groups has the concept been explicitly mentioned, and little attention has been given to its applicability to most types of laboratory training. Neither has it been demonstrated how a broader understanding of transference may be related to a variety of laboratory learning models and trainer interventions. However, we join many colleagues in considering the transference phenomena very relevant to the dynamics of laboratory learning groups.

The concept of transference had its inception in Freud's observations during individual psychoanalysis and was denoted as: ". . . the unrealistic roles or identities unconsciously ascribed to a therapist by a patient in the regression of the psychoanalytic treatment and the patient's reaction to this representation derived from earlier experience" (*Menninger*, 1958, p. 81). Later many other theorists, including *Sullivan* (1954), broadened the concept to refer not only to phenomena related to the analyst and the analysis, but to several other forms of inappropriate transfer of affect and perception based on the person's earlier experiences.

We shall employ *transference*, then, in this broadened way, consistent with the current usage of most therapists, to refer not only to the simple transferring of attitudes from real-life figures, but also to the distortion of interpersonal reality in response to one's needs and fears (*Yalom*, 1970). As such, transference in training groups may be considered a special case of need-motivated perception—similar to that occurring in all significant interpersonal relationships.

In the training laboratory there are elements designed to "unfreeze" participants (*Schein and Bennis*, 1965), notably, isolation from everyday events and the absence of familiar structures. These factors and the absence of direct guidance from a traditional leader create mild anxiety for the participants. This facilitates regression and projection, allowing wide sway for motives to distort the perceptions of important, cathected, and minimally-cued persons, particularly trainers ((*Peters*, 1966). Transference is demonstrated most clearly and particularly in incidents involving reactions to the lack of structure, attitudes toward the trainer, stereotyping of other members, resistance to feedback, rigid stances and impasses, and issues of jealousy, favoritism, possessiveness, etc.

Whether or not one wants to perceive and deal with the transferred element in the ongoing stream of perceptions and reactions, the ubiquitous distortions still exist and play a role. One of the reasons why such reactions are important in the context of laboratory learning is that interpersonal distortions tend to be repetitive and self-perpetuating. For example, a member with a derogatory self-image, through selective inattention, may distortedly perceive another member (or the trainer) as a harsh, rejecting figure. If the member then acts in terms of his perceptions (e.g. with servility, antagonism, defensiveness, etc.) the other is likely to be "pulled" into relating as he expected; thus, a self-fulfilling prophecy is created and distortions continue and compound. In such cases group development and member learning will be hampered.

Our position is that it is essential to be aware of the transference element in all T-Groups, rather than to ignore or overlook its existence. This permits the choice of whether and how to approach it; this also reduces the likelihood of the trainer's own reactions to it (and counter-transference) remaining unclear and muddying the issue. Two of our goals here are to facilitate awareness of transference phenomena in different types of training groups and to suggest methods of intervention compatible with varying theoretical positions about experiential learning.

ANALYSIS

In order to consider the concept of transference within the broad spectrum of laboratory training settings, it becomes necessary to conceptualize and differentiate some of the major variations of what are commonly called "T-Groups." We will set forth 5 major versions of laboratory training: the "instrumented" group, the "classical" T-Group, the interpersonal relations group, the personal growth group, and the self-analytic group. (While this classification is a useful one, it is not the only possible way of depicting the variations within laboratory education.) In each type of group, there are some explicit or implicit assumptions about learning which are more or less characteristic of the model. (Trainers or lab staff tend to emphasize a particular "learning theory" but may use one or two other ones adjunctively in any given laboratory.)

Each version of laboratory training will be examined with reference to (1) the extent and nature of transference potential and the attention to the phenomena in practice, (2) theoretical emphasis upon transference (or related) phenomena, and (3) implications for trainer strategy and interventions. We will focus here primarily on transference phenomena in the member-leader relationship and will give only secondary attention to the interlacing of member-member transference and to counter-transference.

MODEL 1. INSTRUMENTED GROUP LAB—
"ACTION RESEARCH"

The first major variation of laboratory training to be considered here is the "instrumented laboratory" design, such as pioneered by *Blake and Mouton* (1962). Data from self-administered instruments provide for feedback which steers the group development and participant learning.

The theory of learning which is most used in this version of laboratory training has been described as the "dilemma-invention-experimentation-feedback" approach by *Blake and Mouton* (1962). Learning means the recognition of group problems, invention and experimentation with new procedures, and the gathering and analyzing of data for feedback on group processes. This approach is related to the general model of "action research." It is usually focused more on group-level learnings than individual-level learning, and it emphasizes the acquisition of skills and cognitive understanding.

In this model the trainer or staff member in attendance removes to the role of a resource person, providing conceptual tools and methodological inputs for collecting, analyzing, and feeding back data about processes and problems in the group. The implications of this model, and the underlying action-research theory, suggest that the trainer as an individual be minimally visible, although his role as resource person is manifest and somewhat well structured.

Theory and instrumentation lend a moderate amount of structure to these groups. Participants thus tend to display less anxiety in them than in groups following different models. As a result, the regressive potential for transference seems to be lower and the phenomena appear less frequently. Indeed, such authors as *Blake and Mouton* do not explicitly use the term "transference." They do mention, however, that the attitudes of dependence or counter-dependence which are often expressed toward a traditional trainer do occur sometimes toward other participants in the group, perhaps on the basis of some similarity to the staff or identification with staff-related attitudes.[1] In such instances, the trainer or staff person

---

[1] Several years ago, the senior author observed students in an instrumented T-Group reacting toward the instruments themselves in a way which strongly suggested displaced transference reactions. Initially, a few members of the group viewed the instruments with substantial awe, almost reverence. Later on, during a phase of some frustration and pressure upon the author to "help the group out," one participant got up, strode to the wall and tore down one of the charts with great vengeance and apparent satisfaction. These emotional reactions to the instrumentation or the design of the laboratory (which subtly functions like a "trainer surrogate" in terms of influencing what goes on) are an analogue to the familiar transference reactions to the psychotherapist.

might well devote some attention to issues of power and authority relationships within the group prior to further progress on problem solving. A model 1 trainer, then, can insert a lecturette to conceptualize these conscious reactions or design an instrument to assess them and feed back to the group. However, he would probably not interpret the data for the group but would leave the interpretation and generalization processes to the members.

In summary, while transference reactions are very much present, they tend to occur less frequently in model 1 than in other models, and to be somewhat displaced in form. They represent only one of many important development dilemmas. To the extent that transference reactions and authority issues can be dealt with legitimately in this framework, it is most often under circumstances in which the group is experiencing an impasse blocking further progress. Under this model, the authority issues and transference reactions will be viewed as one among many important dilemmas upon which the participants need to work. Nevertheless, the effective trainer will choose to deal with them. He may do so without jeopardizing his model 1 training stance by using indirect or impersonal methods, i.e. through lecturettes and instrumentations.

MODEL 2. THE CLASSICAL T-GROUP—
THE "INQUIRY PROCESS"

In the classical model of laboratory education, the T-Group is conceived as an "experimental" situation to which empirical and inductive methods of investigation are applied.[2] (It is this version which has sometimes been contrasted to therapy groups by clinicians such as *Frank* (1964), *Durkin* (1964), and *Horwitz* (1964). The theory of learning most typical to the classical T-Group assumes that learning occurs best through the development of new attitudes toward the learning process itself and toward the systematic use of data from interpersonal and group phenomena. This may involve sensitization and recognition of formerly unnoticed behavior about the self and others (*Schein and Bennis*, 1965). Members may be instructed in "participant observation" with the outcome of training seen as a better understanding of "learning how to learn." Representative of this view would be the writings of *Bradford et al.* (1964) and of *Miles* (1959). The distinction between this theory and the preceding one is slight but it lies in its primary emphasis on the *learning process* itself,

---

[2] Probably the best descriptions of this model, which grows out of roots in adult education and applied group dynamics, are in the first 7 chapters of *T-Group theory and laboratory method* by Bradford, Gibb and Benne. For a historical overview see the recent article by *Lubin and Eddy* (1970).

in other words "learning how to learn," rather than upon action research to solve specific group dilemmas.

In this model the trainer participates in the group and may serve multiple educational functions. One of the primary elements of the role centers on process observations of the here-and-now dynamics of the group. Although transference phenomena arise, partly from frustration of dependency needs, the trainer role does not encourage this, as the emphasis is upon group member processes and the trainer gradually moves into more of a member role during the group.

In relation to transference phenomena in the classical T-Group model, a trainer would avoid much analysis of this aspect of the group's process unless it were impeding progress and development of the group. If transference-based reactions become blocking issues, however, the trainer could choose to note certain member-leader perceptions and actions which seem at variance with the current group situation, i.e. seemingly inappropriate generalizations from earlier learning situations. The trainer could point out such inappropriate attitudes to the group, talking in terms of "group attitudes," "group needs," and "group conceptions" of the trainer and his leadership role (*Bradford et al.,* 1964).

In brief, this model makes no particular effort to elicit transference reactions nor does it stress their analysis, unless they are particularly detrimental to group functioning. The emphasis here is on group process issues. However, transference-based reactions may become an issue. If so, it is only one of many issues, according to this outlook, and the trainer handles it in a group-centered and "learning-style" fashion rather than psychodynamically.

MODEL 3. THE INTERPERSONAL RELATIONS LAB— "VALID COMMUNICATION"

This model of laboratory training developed as an outgrowth of the evolution (*Lubin and Eddy,* 1970) from the classical "group process" orientation (model 2) toward a focus on the nature and quality of interpersonal relationships established by individual participants. The theory of learning most often associated with this model is concerned with the establishment of valid communication and authentic relationships. Thus, the entire range of participants' interpersonal behavior, including communicative meanings, distortions and inconsistencies becomes the focus.

The intellectual heritage of this theoretical approach is rooted in the interpersonal theories of *Sullivan* (1954), *Rogers* 1959), and others (*Bennis et al.,* 1968, section I) and the T-Group development theory of *Bennis* (1964). One may readily assume that transference phenomena are assigned a more significant role in such laboratories than in the preceding models.

Sullivan considered the relationship between doctor and patient, therapist and client, or leader and member as an interpersonal process in which clear and open communication between the involved participants formed the keystone of growth. Transference phenomena, which *Sullivan* termed "parataxic distortions," should therefore be distinguished as such. These distortions occur whenever "the *real* characteristics of the other fellow . . . may be of negligible importance to the interpersonal situation" (*Sullivan,* 1954, p. 26). Thus, when "whole sets of imaginary others" become involved in any two-way communication, the result is surely not one in which conscious awareness of one's experiencing and accurate communication are likely to occur. When *Rogers* discusses the process of growth toward congruence and authenticity, he does not explicitly conceptualize it in terms of lessened transference. However, he does describe the individual at the "fixity" end of the process continuum as one who construes experience out of his past and is rigidly unaffected by the actualities of the present (*Rogers,* 1958). Thus, his theorizing evinces an appreciation of the significance of transference reactions.

A model 3 trainer will probably choose to make specific use of the occurrence of such intrapersonal communication distortions. He might make a direct interpretation and check for consensual validation by the members. Or he might follow the less directive approach of a here-and-now reflection of the distortion of the group member, a Rogerian approach.

In sum, then, model 3 proponents will be more concerned with transference phenomena whenever it seems relevant to the ongoing stream of communication. Tactics of confrontation, however, could be directive or non-directive. In either case, the model 3 trainer would aim to clear up such intrapersonal distortions within the person, or interpersonal distortions of communication within ongoing relationships.

MODEL 4. SENSITIVITY TRAINING—
"PERSONALITY DEVELOPMENT"

The goal of personal change and development of individual participants is foremost in the laboratories designated as "sensitivity training," "personal growth" and some of the new "encounter groups." (For a representative description of the sensitivity training version, see *Weschler et al.* [1962]). The learning outcomes center around self-actualization, self-awareness, and sensitivity to emotional dynamics of self and others, in contrast to the relative emphasis on group dynamics, cognitive understanding and behavioral skills found in the first two models. The theoretical underpinnings for this approach come from various sources, such as emotional dynamics, interactionist communication theory, humanistic psychology, and existentialist and gestalt therapy.

Trainer behavior in this kind of model generally tends toward an active, visible, here-and-now, confrontative style. Such a trainer may choose to use himself as an "instrument," registering his reactive feelings and thoughts toward members and sharing these reactions. In so doing, the trainer becomes, then, both a powerful figure and a "knowable person." Remaining a central figure, he tends to elicit reactions to authority; but knowing the reactions and feelings of the person in this role tends to reduce group members' magical fantasies and anxiety, projection, and regression. (*Horwitz* [1964] has distinguished between trainer and therapist behavior along similar lines of knowability and centrality in the group.) Thus, the amount of transference potential in such groups is substantial but not extreme. Transference reactions occur with moderate frequency and intensity here and contribute directly and legitimately to learning goals of such groups.

At times, a model 4 trainer might want to attend immediately to a members' manifestation of transference reaction. At other times, the trainer here will be less concerned with transference reactions. For example, when transference feelings about the trainer seem less important to a member's personal growth than learnings about himself in other areas, e.g. how he handles anger or his sensitivity to certain verbal and non-verbal cues from others—then such transference reactions would not be attended to immediately. In other words, in the personal growth model, the emphasis placed on the interpretation of the transference phenomena in the group largely depends on the particular needs of different individuals and the group.

In model 4, transference could be conceptualized in terms of the member's past experience with significant others. The reactions may be considered as unconscious attempts to re-establish earlier crucial relationships (*Bugental,* 1965), reflecting a lack of existential courage to be authentic. The implication for trainer intervention is that he pay special attention to evidences of dependence, complaining, counter-dependence, rebellion, etc.—as each of these reactions restricts the degree to which members can permit themselves to experience the trainer as the individual he really is. For example, when members express concern that the trainer fulfill his "duty" to the group (as in the first scenario) or suggest he "make something happen," the model 4 trainer is likely to intervene. He could, perhaps, interpret members' apparent needs to "run away from uncomfortable feelings by turning him into a sort of superhuman" who would protect them from hurting. This implies that group members were anxious and searching for a messianic deliverance, an "easy way out" of authentic relations with him and between themselves as fallible human beings.

In general, the emphasis in this model is toward noting and confronting all transference reactions that could restrict personal growth by reducing authentic relations, existential realities, and the rights of each person, including the trainer, to "be" and to "do his own thing."

MODEL 5. SELF-ANALYTIC GROUPS— "UNCONSCIOUS MOTIVATION"

The 5th model of training groups is the self-analytic group, in which participants study the evolving structure and processes of their group as a miniature society. In the academic version of this model (e.g. the Harvard Social Relations course described by *Mann* [1967]) the goal is understanding the basic intra- and interpersonal dynamics and structure of human relationships. In the therapeutic version (e.g. *Bion*, 1959) the goal of understanding is coupled with the interest in facilitating the therapeutic "work" of the group. The commonality in both versions is the group as a microcosm whose natural processes are the legitimate focus of contemporaneous analysis.

The theory of learning most often associated with such groups focuses on unearthing and analysis of attitudes, feelings, and motivations which are unconscious (or pre-conscious) and unattended to by group members. The goal is increased understanding and insight into the fundamental assumptions and dynamics underlying key group and interpersonal events. This theory has its intellectual heritage in the psychoanalytic approach to group analysis and might be paraphrased by the psychoanalytic dictum, "where *id* was, there shall be *ego*." Representative of such an approach as applied to training groups and laboratory education are theorists such as *Whitman* (1964), *Mann* (1967), and *Bion* (1959).[3]

Bion's version (1959) of this self-analytic model,[4] being the most group-centered, identifies 3 group-shared, emotional modalities or "group mentalities"—which are present in early and middle phases of group development before the group becomes a mature "work" group. These emotional modalities and their associated assumptions correspond to unconscious processes in individuals which are activated by their inclusion in an unstructured group. Thus, his writings deal extensively with transference

---

[3] *Whitman* (1964) refers to the unconscious motivations involved in the focal conflicts shared by the group and variously experienced by individual members; while *Bion* (1959), on the other hand, is primarily concerned with the unconscious motivations and assumptions which the members are sharing at a given time, i.e. the "group mentality," a notion essentially analogous to the individual unconscious.

[4] A full understanding of his conceptualization of transference reactions in groups rests upon a knowledge of Melanie Klein's theory of personality, which lies beyond the scope of this paper. The conceptualizations offered by *Bion* have been important influences on the work of others, such as *Stock and Thelen* (1958) and *Mann* (1967).

phenomena in his groups (though he hesitates to label them explicitly as such) in terms of a "class of member reactions which implicitly or explicitly presupposes the ascendency of needs stemming from a primitive unconscious level of intrapersonal and interpersonal functioning" (*Bion*, 1959).

With regard to the trainer role, *Whitman* (1964) and *Frank* (1964) imply an optimal degree of openness with which a trainer should interact in a T-

TABLE 3.1
TRANSFERENCE IN MODELS OF LABORATORY TRAINING

Model	Representative of model	Theoretical emphasis on transference	Attention in application or practice	Strategy of intervention
1	Instrumented lab. *Blake and Mouton* (1962)	None, although 'authority issues' are mentioned	Infrequent— negative attitudes to the lab design as a 'trainer surrogate'	Design instruments, gather data, or make cognitive input. Group interprets data 'on its own'
2	Classical HR lab. *Bradford et al.* (1964), *Miles* (1959)	Little emphasis Term not used	Ignore these reactions unless they inhibit the group	Intervention focused on group assumptions about leadership, not on individual member reactions
3	Interpersonal lab. *Bennis et al.* (1968) *Rogers* (1959) and *Sullivan* (1954)	Moderate emphasis although *Rogers* does not employ the term; *Sullivan* refers to 'parataxic distortions'	When relevant to increasing interpersonal congruence and valid communication	Help members discover distortions in the 'here and now' perceptions of trainers and others
4	Personal growth lab.; 'Sensitivity training' *Weschler et al.* (1962)	Important as a form of resistance to being 'authentic' in here-and-now relations. Term occasionally used	In proportion to special learning needs of individual participants	Attend to dependence on the leader, resistances, stereotyping, etc. Remove blocks to authenticity. May utilize specialized nonverbal techniques
5	Self-analytic group *Mann* (1967) and *Whitman* (1964)	Important in terms of 'group focal conflicts' and group development	Important— seldom overlooked	Reflection or interpretation which is direct, analytical; at individual or group level.
	Bion (1959)	Primary in theory although term not used	Substantial emphasis	Analytical, direct, persistent; at group level

Group. This level—somewhat more than the analyst's poker-faced impassivity but less than the gregarious, extremely open approach of some proponents of encountering methods—will create a slightly lesser amount of ambiguity, member anxiety, regression and, hence, fewer transference feelings than would occur in a group therapy setting. (*Horwitz* [1964] makes a similar point here.)

In such a self-analytic training group, transference phenomena are important entry points and levers for the development of insight. Transference in the member-leader context would be conceptualized here as the members' idiosyncratic perceptions of the leader which are really more appropriate to other persons in their life and not attributable to culturally learned expectations about the "helping person." In the self-analytic group transference phenomena can serve therapeutic goals as means by which members learn how their reactions to important others "back home" are colored by their experience with significant other persons earlier in their lives. The analysis of transference in the member-leader interaction provides an important means of introducing this insight. In this regard the difference between model 5 and psychoanalytic group therapy is very slight; however, in analytic group therapy, the transference relationship and phenomena are typically seen as the crucial, if not sole, means to this insight (*Durkin*, 1964).

The implications for practice in Model 5 are similar to, but more extensive than, the preceding two models. The trainer concerns himself with evidence of what *Mann* (1967) calls "dependent complaining," "counterdependent flight," maneuvers to manipulate the leader and, in short, with all of the members' impulses and feelings toward him. However, the model demands that the trainer's style be more passive, reflective, and analytical than in any of the preceding theories. The trainer will choose to keep his "personality" largely out of the picture, inserting himself or intervening in a reflective, didactic fashion while making interpretations at the group (and sometimes individual) level.

The preceding analysis is summarized in tabular form in Table 3.1.

CONCLUSION

The preceding discussion emphasizes several points with reference to transference phenomena in laboratory training groups. (1) What is clinically referred to as "transference phenomena" has been subject to a paucity of theoretical and technical explication by authors in the area of laboratory education. In view of this, our concern has been to explore the utility and implications of the concept, rather than to dismiss it or rename behaviors for which it stands. We hope that this analysis will stimulate further theoretical and empirical examination of this aspect of laboratory training group process. (2) The thesis was developed that transference is a concept which is generally applicable to laboratory learning situations. Several different models of laboratory training were described along with the learning theory typically utilized. (3) The analysis indicated that phenomena will occur with different frequency (and the manifested form will vary) depending on the type of laboratory and the trainer role. The models were rank-ordered in terms of their extent of theoretical emphasis and the likelihood of their eliciting transference phenomena in actual laboratory settings. (4) A variety of possible trainer intervention strategies which would be consonant with a particular type of laboratory and learning theory have been suggested. Our intention has been to stress the desirability of specifically linking transference intervention strategy with an overriding learning theory and laboratory model. Implicit in this is the belief that to be maximally effective the trainer's interventions should be consistent with the theoretical framework and laboratory model within which they are employed.

REFERENCES

Bennis, W. G.; Schein, E. H.; Steele, F. I., & Berlew, D. E.: *Interpersonal dynamics: Essays and readings on human interaction,* rev. ed. (Dorsey, Homewood, Ill. 1968).

Bennis, W. G.: Patterns and vicissitudes in T-Group development; in Bradford, Gibb and Benne *T-Group theory and laboratory method,* pp. 248–278 (Wiley, New York 1964).

Bion, W. R.: *Experiences in groups* (Basic Books, New York 1959).

Blake, R. R. & Mouton, J. S.: The instrumented training laboratory; in Weschler and Schein *Issues in human relations training,* vol. 5, pp. 61-67 (National Training Laboratories–National Education Association, Washington 1962).

Bradford, L. P.; Gibb, J. R., & Benne, K. D. (ed.): *T-Group theory and laboratory method. Innovation in re-education* (Wiley, New York 1964).

Bugental, J. F. T.: *The search for authenticity* (Holt, Rinehart & Winston, New York 1965).

Durkin, H. E.: *The group in depth* (International Universities, New York 1964).

Frank, J. D.: Training and therapy; in Bradford, Gibb and Benne *T-Group theory and laboratory method,* pp. 442–451 (Wiley, New York 1964).

Horwitz, L.: Transference in training groups and therapy groups. *Int. J. Gr. Psychother. 14:* 202-213 (1964).

Lubin, B. and Eddy, W. B.: The laboratory training model. Rationale, method, and some thoughts for the future. *Int. J. Gr. Psychother. 10:* 305-339 (1970).

Mann, R. D.: *Interpersonal styles and group development: An analysis of the member-leader relationship* (Wiley, New York 1967).

Menninger, K.: *Theory of psychoanalytic technique* (Basic Books, New York 1958).

Miles, M. B.: *Learning to work in groups* (Columbia University, New York 1959).

Peters, D. R.: *Identification and personal change in laboratory training groups*. Cambridge, Mass. MIT Microreproduction Laboratory, Doctor. Diss. (1966).

Rogers, C. R.: A process conception of psychotherapy. *Amer. Psychol. 13:* 142–149 (1958).

Rogers, C. R.: A theory of therapy, personality and interpersonal relationships, as developed in the client-centered framework; in Koch *Psychology: A study of a science,* vol. 3, pp. 184–256 (McGraw-Hill, New York 1959).

Schein, E. H. and Bennis, W. G.: *Personal and organizational change through group methods. The laboratory approach* (Wiley, New York 1965).

Stock, D. and Thelen, H. A.: *Emotional dynamics and group culture* (New York University, New York 1958).

Sullivan, H. S.: *The psychiatric interview* (Norton, New York 1954).

Weschler, I. R.; Massarik, F., and Tannenbaum, R.: The self in process. A sensitivity training emphasis; in Weschler and Schein *Issues in human relations training* (National Training Laboratories–National Education Association, Washington 1962).

Whitman, R. W.: Psychodynamic principles underlying group processes; in Bradford, Gibb and Benne *T-Group theory and laboratory method,* pp. 310–336 (Wiley, New York 1964).

Yalom, I. D.: *The theory and practice of group psychotherapy* (Basic Books, New York 1970).

12. Encounter Co-Training

CRAIG LUNDBERG and JOAN LUNDBERG

With the development of applied behavioral science steadily advancing, the field can be characterized, as most new fields, as frequently having its practices leading its body of knowledge.

Laboratory training has been central to the development of a reliable, systematic body of experience and theory related to the behavioral science-

Reproduced by special permission from the October, 1974 *Training and Development Journal,* pp. 20–22, 24–26. Copyright 1974 by the American Society for Training and Development, Inc.

based, planned-change process. We are specifically referring to the intense small group experience known as the T-Group, basic encounter group or the sensitivity training group.

Those of us who facilitate or train such groups seem to share two outlooks. On the one hand, we personally find training to be rewarding and growthful, and on the other hand we tend to systematically reflect on these experiences in efforts to conceptualize our practices. In the following pages we shall share our thoughts on the usefulness of, and on the problems of, facilitating group activity by a team.

At the present time, quite a large share of laboratories utilize groups that are led by a team of co-trainers. As yet, the pitfalls and benefits of co-training are mostly matters of private opinion or informal discussion. Since co-training is prevalent and within the experience of almost all trainer-facilitators, we believe it deserves some conscious attention (Steele, 1969).

EARLY DEVELOPMENTS

Encounter co-training originally came about as a device to develop inexperienced trainers. As the facilitating of the intensive group experience was initially a rather intuitive activity, the one way new trainers could learn was directly from their experience as trainers, and this clearly was enhanced by their observing a skilled trainer and by having this person monitor the new trainer. Obviously, this practice follows the traditional development pattern of apprenticeship. This function of trainer development not only was the earliest purpose of co-training but probably remains as the main purpose at the present time. In this light, co-training tends not to be viewed as a necessarily desirable component of laboratory design.

In the following pages we shall promote the position that the benefits tend to exceed the pitfalls of dual facilitation, and therefore should become a more standard feature of laboratory training. Our argument is that beyond new trainer development, utilizing co-trainers offers the possibility of a better learning experience for participants, and, in addition, promotes the means whereby experienced trainers continue to develop their skills.

EFFECTIVENESS FOR GROUP MEMBERS

The presence of two trainers in an encounter group does not merely double the amount of some uniform skill available, but actually introduces qualitatively different advantages to the group beyond those available when there is only one trainer. In this section we wish to elaborate on three major types of benefits; those accruing from the existence of two trainer styles, those associated with opportunities for additional trainer practices and the benefits available to organizational client systems.

ADVANTAGES OF MULTIPLE STYLES

Perhaps the most obvious advantage of having co-trainers in a group is that they can complement each other's style of facilitating, thus compensating for, or overcoming individual blindspots and shortcomings in technique or knowledge.

It is relatively common to find that one trainer attends more naturally to group process and dynamics while another tends to focus on individuals. Or similarly, one trainer who stresses conceptual matters complemented by a partner who relies on his or her intuitive skills.

Anne and Lee were discussing over coffee some events in the group that they were leading. Anne mentioned a pattern she had seen among various pairs of members. This sparked Lee to diagram some conceptual ideas on a napkin. Anne quickly saw that Lee's ideas helped her make sense of the behavior she'd seen and suggested he make them an input to the group. Lee did this, stimulating not only some useful encounter but also prompting Anne to initiate this sequence of events several times more.

When there are co-facilitators, group participants have an increased opportunity to not only observe multiple styles of training, but more important, have different styles after which to model their own behavior. Trainers clearly are "significant others" for their groups and when two such persons are actively demonstrating useful behaviors, participants have more chances to identify with and imitate models of experiential learning (Lundberg, 1973-74).

When there are co-trainers, the modeling of effective interpersonal behaviors is more probable because the co-trainers can promote it through their interaction, encountering and confronting one another. This can be significant for group progress in that it is one important way to introduce and legitimize conditions crucial to group development such as trust, openness and levelings (Gibbs, 1964).

Early in a weekend lab, Rock, one trainer and a graduate student of Steve's, the other trainer, was pointed out by a group member as always nodding after Steve made an occasional point of clarification. Rock then spoke of his respect for Steve and that he saw Steve in a "father's role." Rock and Steve then conversed about their feeling of being "father" and "son," the exchange ending with their hopes that each would note when the other seemed to slip into those roles. This incident prompted others in the group to use family role terminology to indicate their perceptions and feelings of one another as well as the co-trainers.

Co-facilitators are seldom identical in age, origins, ethnicity, sex or other occupational or social characteristics. This fact of being different offers to group participants the chance not only to watch these people encounter one another with its attendant modeling opportunities, but also increases the probabilities of at least one trainer being different from themselves. Learning to relate in new ways to significant others, who differ in varying degrees from oneself, has utility for back home learnings for participants as well as reducing the "specialness" of the trainer role associated with particular personal and/or social characteristics. Also, with one another, co-trainers can exhibit, for the group's observation and discussion, key role relations from the wider culture such as age and sex roles.

ADDITIONAL TRAINER PRACTICES

When there are *two* trainers, their group is served by the simple fact that two heads and bodies responsible for facilitating the group exist. The joint "memory bank" of co-trainers is undoubtedly larger, increasing the likelihood of seeing the connections between current and past group behavior. The fact of having two sets of experienced eyes and ears increases the probability of more accurate perception of events.

Doubling the perspective on what has and is occurring in a training group means fewer trainer errors by omissions. Under some designs there is more energy available for the facilitating role. For example, trainer alertness is enhanced during marathons because one trainer can "rest" briefly while a partner "works." This advantage is shown too when an individual requires special effort which would mean the rest of the group would have to wait if there were only one trainer.

Sue and Bud were co-training a marathon of teenagers and high school teachers. During a break, after a long night, Sue was sought out by Lucy, a student. Lucy was experiencing a depression related to her parents. Finding a quiet room they began an hour-long, tear sprinkled dialogue. Bud, though missing Sue at the end of the break, took up with the group. At a convenient time he went looking for her. A glance told him Sue and Lucy were working hard, so he gave a sign of support to them and went back to working with the group.

FLEXIBILITY INCREASED

The role flexibility of facilitators is measurably increased with co-training. Beyond offering a choice of facilitating models at a point in time, co-training permits great role flexibility over time. It is not uncommon to see the two trainers begin with a group, one being initially perceived as the "tough" trainer and the other the "warm" trainer, and then, in the course of the group's life, having a switch in roles occur, with the obvious learning possibilities for the members. This alternating of facets of the training role, augmented by the chance to slip out of it on occasion when "backed up," serves to model role flexibility and the expansion of role repertoire is often a desired goal for members.

When actively working, one facilitator tends to be more *focal* than the other. This provides the less-active trainer unusual on-the-spot opportunities to review the development of the group and its members. From this less focal position, a trainer can sometimes perceive cues that a partner cannot. These advantages accrue to the group because the "second" trainer may be able to focus on processes involving his or her partner under fire in the group. This position has an advantage too when audio or visual equipment is being used. The less active trainer can do whatever "chores" are necessary in conjunction with the equipment.

Designing "in situo," that is the assessing of the group's progress and designing while training is going on, is more possible in co-led groups. This can allow for a design that is more responsive to group needs. Related to this activity is the powerful effect on the group when the trainers design or clinic together in front of the group, showing dramatically their concerns for the group. Such "fish bowl" training tends to reduce the mystique which surrounds training, to show in another way the human qualities of the trainers, as well as their being open-minded and influenced by the group. Getting their design ideas out in the open increases the group's sense of participation in their own destiny—something valued by many trainers.

During the group, Mark leaned over to his co-trainer Mary and whispered an idea for an intervention. Mary smiled her agreement and Mark sat back to wait for an opportunity to intervene. In a few minutes Mary spoke to the group saying that some of them may have noticed when Mark whispered to her; Mary then invited Mark to make his request to her openly. Mark did this and he and Mary went on to discuss its merits—with group members then adding their opinions and finally initiating the proposed activity for themselves.

AUTHORITY ISSUE

The consensual validation and support trainers can offer to one another is the source of other advantages to the group that co-facilitating offers. For example, when the inevitable authority issue is raised, with two trainers only one tends to get the brunt of the group pressure. The co-trainer may help the group by supporting members as well as his or her partner, and especially be helpful in aiding the group when it processes that significant sequence of behaviors. Again the opportunities to learn by modeling abound.

Tom, Vera's co-trainer, late in a marathon in which he had been challenged much more than usual, was feeling tired and rather isolated. At a lull in the work Tom asked Vera for some comforting, she came over to him, held him in her arms and stroked his hair. Tom relaxed knowing that while it might look unusual to the group, he knew he needed the contact very much. The group's discussion then turned to the humanness of trainers and the utility of asking for what one wants.

During this discussion several group members ventured their own requests to others and both exhibited and received caring behaviors.

It happens occasionally that a trainer and participant get blocked in reaching one another. The presence of a co-trainer can be facilitating to both parties in this instance, or where one trainer works a difficult issue in which he or she is central for the group's progress. Thus the co-trainer intervenes as a third party (Walton, 1969).

Ken and Gary co-trained a group of desegregation specialists, most of whom were mature blacks. Gary too, would continue to act after the group in an advisory capacity to these people. One group member, Buzz, had been in a graduate course instructed by Gary, in which he received a very low grade. Late in the group Buzz seemingly attacked Gary about his grade, with Gary defending himself with " there and then" content. Ken intervened asking the group what was going on in the "here" and "now." Quickly the group helped Gary and Buzz to see that their "private" matter was actually related to an unresolved trust issue that was shared by many group members.

One of the prime detractions from effective training occurs when a trainer either unconsciously or selfishly services his or her own needs and hang-ups through the group. A co-trainer may act as a brake or barrier to such personality serving, hence protecting the group members' own learning from being subverted by the other trainer.

SOCIAL SYSTEMS ADVANTAGES

Training in a team has certain advantages when the encounter group is part of a larger client system as in executive and organizational development. The size of the system the group is drawn from or embedded in, and the cruciality of the group-system relations usually means effort needs to be expended by the trainer in diagnosing system problems. This is especially true in designing appropriate systems instrumentations and interventions, in monitoring group-systems relations, in the follow-up so often mandatory, etc.

Often, in such work, one or more of the OD team are system members. The outside co-trainer not only brings perspective to the program and objectivity to the group, but his or her presence aids in legitimizing the trainer role of the insider, thus enabling group members to see their colleague as performing a necessary, if not previously familiar, role and thus taking the sting of distrust away.

Having a co-worker can be useful to trainer and client alike when trainers experience the anxiety or fear of confronting prestigious or monolithic groups such as in industry or family work (Clark, 1969). In other special groups, where pairs or teams of people make up the group's membership, the existence of a co-trainer relationship offers an advantage to the group. Working in a relationship, working through pair conflicts and working to improve the co-trainer relationship provides a modeling opportunity for participants of couples groups, management teams, etc.

TRAINER GROWTH, DEVELOPMENT

We wish to break with the point of view that sees co-training as merely an *apprentice* activity for the development of new, inexperienced facilitators. It can be *the* potent developmental experience for the trainer intern to be sure, but this limited conception of co-training tends to hide the more general function of trainer development, a process we assume to be continuously desirable. Here we urge consideration of the view that training in tandem has certain potential benefits to new and experienced trainers alike.

CONTINUING DEVELOPMENT

Working with an experienced trainer has obvious benefits to the less experienced trainer if he or she is open to learning and if there is an adequate clinicing of their joint efforts. Yet, skilled facilitators may learn and increase their skills from associates who bring fresh vision and new insights to what may have become a familiar or routine exercise. One major source of such learning comes from having someone to provide continuous feedback on training effectiveness. Having to articulate one's interventions, intentions and consequences sometimes results in process insights which were previously undiscovered. The presence of another trainer with his or her own style can prompt useful self assessment. Sharing experiences too, offers a way of keeping up with new developments in the field.

Beyond professional development, co-facilitation has potentiality for personal growth. A trainer may be able to work some personal issues into the group if he or she has a skilled partner. One opportunity exists which is unavailable to solo trainers; namely when the co-trainer represents some aspect of one's own hang-ups and thus provides the stimulus to examine it.

Mike and Jim were co-training an advanced personal growth group and Jim began to sense some uncomfortableness around Mike's seemingly flirtatious actions toward a couple of attractive females. Going to eat one evening, Jim spoke of this to Mike which stimulated an examination of both Mike and Jim's behaviors with the females in the lab. Jim had to face his own, to that point, undetected attracting behaviors and eventually his own feelings regarding his masculinity, a matter eventually worked in the group.

The opportunity to see one's own hang-up, in relief so to speak (plus the responsibility of clinicing for development with the other), can be positively therapeutic. This could be as simple as finding you can work with or adapt to a trait in another you assumed you could not. For example, a male co-training with a female who "isn't your type" whom you would never choose to work with, but who turns out to be both competent and attractive for the things you previously avoided in females is a common experience.

RISKING AND RENEWAL

When two trainers bring their repertoires of experience and technique to a group, they have a reservoir to draw on which is larger than the simple sum of their contributions. In the face of crisis especially, co-trainers find that synergy exists and that timely creative interventions and designs often result. The support available from a colleague can permit a facilitator to attempt interventions which might appear risky if he or she were working alone.

The confidence inspired by a co-trainer not only reduces fear of failure and encourages new interventions, but also encourages a trainer to extend him or herself emotionally, to be more authentic, more genuine, exposing more emotions, as well as increasing investment in clients. This "back-up" function results in new behaviors which are a source of continuing growth (Rabin, 1967).

Training is often demanding work, if not emotionally draining. Peers who share directly in training, even more than other lab staff, enhance the vital unwinding. The closeness engendered by co-training seems to carry over to after hours. A co-trainer has both the incentive as well as the insight necessary when a partner requires "cooling-out." This opportunity for reciprocal servicing can contribute to a facilitator's renewal.

Thus far, we have focused our attention on the benefits to training and trainer development of two facilitators working together. These benefits are substantial, to be sure, yet co-training is not without its dangers and it is to these potential pitfalls we now turn.

PROBLEMS AND PITFALLS

Facilitating encounter groups in duo presents several potential problems which can hinder or even retard groups and can be dysfunctional for trainers. It is to this we now turn. One issue, not related to the co-training relationship per se, is the *economics* of having two trainers. There is no way to argue that the advantages of co-trainers can be economically justified. This no doubt will deter their use. Until we can research the learnings from encounter much more adequately, this issue will have to be a matter of personal judgment. Hence, we have to be content with simply mentioning it.

One possible problem with co-training occurs when the trainers do not keep their "out-of-group behavior" from clinicing their own behavior, relaxing or talking diagnostically about the group. When co-trainers consult with one another to solve group problems and "impart" these solutions to the group, members tend to feel "handled" and such maneuvers often backfire (Stroller, 1969). Better to consult with the group and get their help in resolving the conflict openly.

We also know that even smoothly coordinated facilitators get into relational difficulties on occasion. These present little threat to group processes if the co-trainer team has the sensitivities and mechanisms for "working-through" and often benefits the group when they share in this activity.

DYSFUNCTIONAL CONSEQUENCES

When there are major incompatibilities of trainer personality or style, at least when these lead to excessive competitive or combative behaviors, we anticipate the dysfunctional consequences for the group. Such trainer behavior absorbs group energy and raises anxiety, and it permits unhealthy flight and permits the rationalizing of hostility. Undesirable modeling also occurs when the co-trainers are functionally identical in style and/or personality. Here the monolithic effect of these particular trainers may unduly influence participants into believing there is an "ideal" way of behaving in the group.

Another possible danger in co-training stems from facilitators who grow overly dependent on one another. This can result, for example, in accepting the other's interventions uncritically or letting him or her fall into routine habits of training. At the extreme, over-dependency fosters sloppy and passive training to more outright waiting for one's partner to do "his or her thing" on cue. Dependency leading to uncritical-lazy training is one thing, and dependency that leads to active defensiveness or over-controlling behavior by facilitators is quite another.

In the latter case the facilitator-group relationship is one of distance and wariness, caution and self-interest. Similarly, the fear of judgment sometimes experienced by junior co-trainers in intern programs can result in frustration about their own development. They tend to feel controlled by their senior's style. The consequences for the group are patent.

When co-trainers become a coalition, several pitfalls exist. One extreme condition occurs when the trainers work their own issues at the expense of the group. The opposite condition, when trainers team up to fight their group, is also detrimental. Sometimes co-trainers hit it off and work well together and with their group, but are perceived as "cliquish" by the rest of the staff, resulting in discordant staff relations.

While noting co-trainer support and closeness, we should mention that if this is all the group experiences, they may feel distanced from the trainers and perhaps even discount their credibility. Exclusive positive support between trainers can be seen as not caring enough for group members or as not reflecting their "real" relationship. This skepticism leads to trust reduction. It has long been acknowledged that co-trainers can evolve in an enveloping intimacy which can be personally and/or professionally disruptive. Whether the co-trainers are of the same sex or not, this danger is always present.

CONCLUDING NOTE

We have explored the benefits of facilitators working in pairs beyond simply training apprentice trainers. We have argued for an extension of the practice of co-training for both continuing trainer development, and to underline the potential benefits accruing to participants. We acknowledge that facilitating personal growth and group development through laboratory methods is still primarily an art. We have suggested that dual facilitators be more often considered as a standard element of laboratory design. To be sure, there are pitfalls that must be recognized and avoided. But, we believe the benefits of co-training we have outlined enable facilitative skills and group member learning to be enhanced in a positive, productive fashion.

In conclusion, let us return to our opening remarks. Our own experience tells us that co-training has been both growthful and satisfying, very often beyond the individual training experience. We not only urge more co-training, but particularly urge other facilitators to reflect on their co-training endeavors and to further contribute to conceptualizing this practice.

REFERENCES

Clark, J. V., Task Group Therapy: Interventions and Problems of Practice. Unpublished paper. U.C.L.A. Graduate School of Business Administration, 1969.

Culbert, S. A., Trainer Self-Disclosure and Member Growth in Two T-Groups, *Journal of Applied Behavioral Science,* 1968, Vol. 4, No. 1, pp. 47–73.

Gibb, J. R., Climate for Trust Formation. In L. P. Bradford, J. R. Gibb and K. D. Benne (Eds.), *T-Group Theory and Laboratory Method: Innovation in Re-education.* New York: Wiley, 1964, pp. 279–309.

Lundberg, C., Toward Explicating Trainer Interventions: An Emphasis on Reducing Incongruities, *Interpersonal Development,* Vol. 4, No. 2, 1973/74, pp. 42–50.

MacLennan, B. W., Co-Therapy, *International Journal of Group Psychotherapy,* 1965, Vol. 15.

Mintz, E., Special Values of Co-Therapists in Group Psychotherapy, *International Journal of Group Psychotherapy,* 1963, Vol. 13.

Rabin, H. M., How Does Co-therapy Compare with Regular Group Therapy, *American Journal of Psychotherapy,* 1967, Volume 21, p. 250.

Steele, F., Consultants and Detectives, *Journal of Applied Behavioral Science,* 1969, Volume 5, No. 2, p. 198.

Stroller, F., A Stage for Trust. In A. Burton (Ed.) *Encounter,* San Francisco: Jossey-Bass, 1969, p. 93.

Walton, R., *Interpersonal Peace-making: Confrontation and Third-Party Consultation,* Reading, Mass.: Addison-Wesley, 1969.

13. Negotiating for Group and Trainers

CAROL HEINE, BERNARD LUBIN, JERRY PERLMUTTER, and ALICE LUBIN

Accumulating evidence points to the importance of group composition and trainer style as determinants of differential participant learning in laboratory education (Harrison & Lubin, 1965; Lieberman, Yalom, & Miles, 1972), and to trainer style in the occurrence of severe stress reactions (Lieberman & Yalom, 1971; Yalom, 1971).

Lab staffs usually form groups before participants arrive, balancing demographic variables (sex, age, occupation, etc.) and separating people from the same organization, particularly those who, from the application materials, seem to have working relationships. Trainers are normally assigned to groups composed of members with whom they have no institutional affiliation or personal acquaintance. These practices satisfy the criterion of heterogeneity but address themselves only minimally to the issue of finding the optimal match between trainers and participants.

We recently had an opportunity to include participants and trainers in the decision process of composing T-Groups and assigning trainers, and we want to describe and comment upon that process.[1]

Our overall objective was to provide conditions that would encourage participants to value the exercise of choice and to take responsibility for

Reprinted from *Social Change,* Vol. 4, No. 2, 1974, pp. 3–6.

[1] During the past few years some H-1 labs have included participant choices with heterogeneity restrictions set out by staff for group formation, but the involvement of participants in the staff assignment process, to our knowledge, has not been previously reported.

their growth and learning. Specifically, we wanted to (1) assist participants in forming their own T-Groups as a result of informed choice; (2) provide a format for staff and groups to negotiate staff assignments to groups; (3) make explicit the criteria for the above choices; and (4) highlight, through direct experience, many facets of group process, e.g., inclusion, formation, and group boundary issues.

The design included five phases:

1. Developing a sense of self
2. Developing a sense of self in relationship to others
3. Practicing commitment to relationships of varying degrees of temporariness
4. Negotiating for group formation (the formation of more permanent relationships for the two-week period)
5. Negotiating for trainers.

SENSE OF SELF—FROM A LITTLE PIPE CLEANER

This phase took 40 minutes, divided into two 20-minute periods. First, there was a 5-minute period of "alone" time, to help members become more aware of their feelings. They were asked to remain seated, close their eyes, relax and think why they had come to this lab, and become aware of how they were feeling right at that moment. Then they were asked to open their eyes and select (without verbal interchange) a colored pipe cleaner that best represented their current feeling. They were then asked, first, to form groups with those who had selected the same color, and then to "become" that color and talk about themselves in relationship to "their" color. This process took about 20 minutes. The groups were of different sizes: some had 15 members, some as few as 4, and one group comprised persons who had no color-mate. Most of the trainees participated though a few elected to observe and listen.

After this exercise, participants were asked to say good-bye to one another and then to twist their pipe cleaner into a shape that expressed how they felt at that particular moment. They were told that the important thing was not how it looked but that it represent themselves. (There were extra pipe cleaners for this exercise, and participants could incorporate other colors if they wished.) All were then asked to mill around and group according to similarities in shapes, "become" their shape, and talk about the "selves" represented by it. This exercise complete (some 20 minutes), they were asked to say good-bye and to mingle informally once again.

Comments on Phase 1

Different types of data were produced by the first phase of this design. Some focused upon how the person felt when he or she selected and then shaped the pipe cleaners, as opposed to how the participant usually felt.

Some people talked about the color or the shape as symbolic of a larger aspect of themselves. For some, the constructions touched upon life themes or issues they were working through. Some commented on their response to the task itself: "I haven't done anything like this since I was a little kid," or "I wouldn't have guessed such meaningful material would come from a damn little pipe cleaner."

The exercise was useful for an early identification of participants who came for irrelevant purposes or who seemed to be high risks in terms of potential stress reactions; e.g., one individual was identified as such by the depth of a depressive verbalization about the color he chose.

SELF IN RELATION TO OTHERS

This phase was divided into two sections: (1) two nonverbal pairings and (2) the initial forming of T-Groups. In section one, each person was asked to mill about and become acquainted nonverbally (but without touching) with others, since participants were to form a series of pairing relationships for the next 20 minutes. They were first asked to pair with a person to whom they were attracted. Each dyad was to sit down, talk about their mutual attraction, and try to specify its basis. In the second pairing, participants were to find a person very different from themselves; in the third, someone with whom they felt uncomfortable. Each pairing and discussion was allotted 10 minutes.

Comments on Part 1, Phase 2

First impressions, an important source of data in interpersonal and group relationships, were exchanged, worked with, and used in later choices.

TEMPORARY RELATIONSHIPS—TRAVELING COMPANIONS

After dinner (7:30 p.m.), a general orientation to the evening task was given. The overall goal was to form T-Groups by 10:00 p.m. Participants and staff would take part in selecting and in negotiating for T-Groups and trainers.

Participants were asked to sit in a relaxed position, close their eyes for 5 minutes, and then visualize their ideal group, including what it said and did. Participants were then instructed to write their goals, limits, and personal resources on newsprint, which they taped across their chests, like the front half of a sandwich board. While music played, people milled around for 20 minutes and read one another's signs, after being told that they would soon form dyads of temporary "traveling companions."

Participants then negotiated a dyad through nonverbal mutual choices based on information from the newsprint. Phase 2 ended after the traveling companions took an additional 10 minutes to outline the information they needed from others in order to know whether they wanted to be in T-Groups with them.

Since staff were free to participate as they wished during this phase, their participation was variable: some milled, some paired with participants, and some simply listed goals, limits, and resources.

Comments on Part 2, Phase 2

The listing of limits was useful but difficult for some people, and there were statements about no "nude groups," no "touchie-feelie" activities; nevertheless it provided the staff with an immediate sense of where participant anxieties lay. Listing and sharing "goals" served to orient participants in the work of the lab and also provided data for later negotiations and a format for establishing criteria for selection of other group members. Psychotherapy and previous group experience, the latter usually meaning some group psychotherapy experience either as therapist or patient, were listed by several as resources. The presentation of those data was thereby legitimized, and in later T-Group sessions, useful discussions of the differences between group psychotherapy and group training occurred.[2]

Staff members who did not list their goals, limits, and resources had low visibility in the community. The two trainers who chose not to do so were the last to negotiate a staff assignment. Our recommendation, based upon this experience, is that staff list goals, limits, and personal resources but that they not pair, so as to keep confusion to a minimum.

LONG-TERM RELATIONSHIPS—THE T-GROUPS

The first task given each pair in this phase was to develop information upon which they could base decisions about whom they wanted to work with during the next two weeks. (The 10 p.m. deadline for forming five T-Groups and selecting trainers for them was repeated.)

The following restrictions on group composition were presented: number of groups (five); group size (not more than 13 members); sex ratio (about even in each group); and no group could include spouses, workmates, or friends. In addition, there would be two co-training pairs; i.e., if one member of each was accepted, the other would be included automatically.

---

[2] Although the characteristic casualty rate for NTL labs is low (Lubin & Eddy, 1970), discussions with the lab counselor at the end of the two weeks revealed that he had received no referrals from our community for psychological consultation.

When most of the initial groups were too large, the criteria were repeated. Group-to-group negotiations occurred spontaneously, and some individuals offered to serve as consultants.

Staff resisted participant attempts to depart from the group composition criteria, particularly number and size of groups, giving the rationale of trying to assure sufficient "on air" time for each group member. An exciting dynamic of testing authority and structure occurred when one group insisted on retaining a 14th member, which staff finally accepted.

Each T-Group discussed the way in which it had formed and its apparent characteristics as a group, and then reported to the entire group.

NEGOTIATING FOR TRAINERS

The participants were instructed to initiate negotiations with staff for trainer assignment. Groups interviewed trainers individually, and some trainers interviewed groups. Some of the questions asked of trainers were: What is your training style? How do you see working with a T-Group? What are your training goals? What are your criteria for a successful experience? What do you get out of training? Do you do nonverbals? Gestalt? The meaning of co-training to each trainer? What is your impression of this group?

Some questions trainers quizzed group members on were: How hard does this group plan to work? How willing is this group to look at what it's doing? (This question prompted a meaningful discussion of the concept of "process.") What are the group goals? What common theme do you share? Members' previous experience in groups? How much work does the group expect to do versus how much do you expect the trainer to do? How much responsibility are you willing to assume for your own learning?

The lack of structure in the negotiation process facilitated learning about negotiating and interviewing for both trainers and participants. By the second interview the process was considerably refined, as participants and trainers became more experienced.

The last group and the last set of trainers settled for each other as a consequence of the rapidity with which other options were closed—a sobering experience on which to embark a two-week relationship. This experience led to the "lean and hungry phenomenon," where an initial sense of failure resulted in sustained processing of the "how and why" of what happened—with much eventual benefit to the overall experience of the group and trainers.

Contracts were then negotiated for each group; e.g., nonverbal techniques would be employed only if the trainer first checked with the group, speculation about early childhood causality would not take place, and the "here-and-now" concept could be extended beyond the immediate situation when appropriate.

CONSUMER TESTS

Some of the advantages of this design have already been noted: Participants were able to make informed choices about the composition of their group and the selection of their trainers; negotiations between groups and trainers regarding assignment were provided; useful information about participants, staff members, and group and trainer expectations were exchanged; and a number of issues concerning group formation and group boundaries were worked through. The early sharing of personal resources seemed related to the absence of severe stress reactions during the two weeks of the laboratory.[3] For example, information about experience in psychotherapy—either as patient or as therapist—was shared and influenced some of the choices involved in group composition and trainer negotiation, and the negotiation process for trainers resulted in appropriate matches of trainers and trainees with regard to expected levels of risk and kinds of techniques.

The same aspects of the design mentioned above as advantages seemed, in some cases, to produce unwanted results. The method of group composition seemed to result in one group's, for part of the first week, adoption of super-cohesion characteristics to the extent that it resisted analysis of group-level phenomena and developed myths about its origin and special characteristics. (This particular group was able to explore and work through both of those issues during the second week.) Another group discovered—well into the training week—that two verbally dominant members, rather than the group as a whole, were primarily responsible for the choice of the trainer. Near the end of the first week, when discussion revealed that some participants had second thoughts about the value of their influence in trainer assignment and felt deprived of experience with other trainers, an opportunity to work with other trainers was provided for many during the second week, when new groups were formed for two sessions.

IMPLICATIONS FOR STAFF DEVELOPMENT

The staff development value of this design should be emphasized. Staff unanimously agreed that, although uncomfortable at times, a great deal of

---

[3] Such data are difficult to use meaningfully in the opening phases of a T-Group; i.e., some people present their previous group experience as a status ploy and others avoid mentioning it for fear of creating overdependence upon themselves.

stimulation and learning took place for them during the opening session. Clichés were challenged, and, on both sides, considerable modeling of "straight talk" occurred. The interview and negotiation process provided a crucible in which trainers were confronted with questions that forced them to search deeply for concise statements of their training philosophy, goals, style, and expectations for the group. In addition, the fast-moving, tense, marketplace atmosphere pressured trainers to confront groups about their expectations and their willingness to engage in a sustained learning effort.

REFERENCES

Harrison, R. L., & Lubin, B. Interpersonal perception and interpersonal behavior in training groups: A study in group composition. *Journal of Applied Behavioral Sciences,* 1965, *1,* 13-16.

Lieberman, M., & Yalom, I. Dimensions of leader behavior. In B. Berzon and L. N. Solomon (Eds.), *The encounter group: Issues and applications.* San Francisco: Jossey-Bass, 1971.

Lieberman, M., Yalom, I., & Miles, M. The impact of encounter groups on participants. *Journal of Applied Behavioral Science,* 1972, *8,* 29-50.

Lubin, B., & Eddy, W. B. The laboratory training model: Rationale, method, and some thoughts for the future. *International Journal of Group Psychotherapy,* 1970, *20,* 305-339.

Yalom, I. D. A study of encounter group casualties. *Archives of General Psychiatry,* 1971, *25,* 16-30.

IV. WHAT CONCERNS ARE THERE ABOUT T-GROUPS?

Goals, Methods, and Results

INTRODUCTION

IV. What Concerns Are There About T-Groups?
Goals, Methods and Results

The development of the concept and methodology of laboratory training has been accompanied by controversy as well as acceptance. This is not surprising. Indeed, such controversy is in part a signal measure of the impact of the T-Group as a social and educational innovation. In part, also, the controversy is a mixed bag of acute insights into a developing approach and of misguided caterwauling. Separating the one from the other is a major challenge.

How the controversy over T-Groups is handled will go a long way toward determining the use made of the laboratory approach. Certainly, the controversy can be very productive. For example, concern has been expressed about the goals and values of sensitivity training, its methods, and its results. Later sections will redirect attention to these three targets. For now it suffices to note that these are vital issues, and concern about them on balance can provide useful guidance for the laboratory approach. In some part, this is because the concerns come both from people who are associated with T-Groups on a professional basis as well as from those who are outside looking in, so to speak.

"INSIDER" CONCERNS ABOUT T-GROUPING

The concerns about T-Groups that are expressed by those professionally involved in sensitivity training have a familiar ring. They resemble the concerns found among any group of professional people. Insiders question their precise mission and role, and they often differ about the specific ways and means of achieving their common goals. This phenomenon of in-group controversy can be seen not only in the social and behavioral sciences, but in the biological and physical sciences as well. Perhaps the most familiar example in the behavioral area is found in the different schools of thought in the field of psychotherapy. Here we find classical Freudians, neo-Freudians, Jungians, Adlerians, Rogerians, and behavioral therapists, to mention a few of the most prominent conceptual approaches. Adherents of several of the positions frequently debate; they may sometimes deride each others' compe-tence; and they often make no secret of the "fact" that *their* framework is the most promising one.

Examples of other insider concerns are easy to come by. In the field of public education, for example, controversy and conflict rage unabated. Not only do differences exist over method—team teaching, the self-contained classroom, and programmed instruction, to mention a few—but serious questions are raised about the goals of education itself. Should the schools be 3-R-oriented? Or should they be primarily concerned with social adjustment, college preparation, serving as family surrogates—or what? Similarly, the technology of transplanting hearts has triggered profound conflict within the medical profession. Nor do things go smoothly in biology, space science, or astronomy.

The point of these examples is dual. First, it would be difficult to find any field of scientific or applied scientific endeavor in which differences and conflicts do not exist among the scientists or the practitioners. The differ-ences often spring from divergent theoretical positions, but they may also be rooted in contrasting value systems. Much of the time, the variant positions are expressed rationally, through well-documented argument. On other occasions, however, proponents and opponents zealously and mutually disparage the professional competence or even the persons of the "other side." Second, such controversy typically accompanies dynamic efforts to meet environmental challenges, and may generate significant advances. Some of the controversy is inevitably so much strutting and feather-pruning by would-be cocks of the walk, of course.

Steven F. Feinberg, in "Some Questions about Ethics and Responsibilities in Sensitivity Training," writes from the perspective of a recent participant in T-Groups and a trainer in training. His view is that of an insider and, as Lakin[1] before him, he suggests that many of the ethical and responsibility considerations involved in sensitivity training have been spawned by success; that is, by the tremendous popularity of sensitivity training as a vehicle for personal learning. These considerations are related to participants, objectives of learning, and trainer competency and behavior. Feinberg's selection, which was written specifically for this book, ends with a plea to professionals to get their house in order. As we noted in an earlier edition of this volume in addressing the ethical problems in the field, "The questions will not just quietly wait on judicious scientific resolution."[2]

Rosabeth Moss Kanter raises "insider" ethical and practical issues concerning women in laboratory groups. In "On Ending Female Tokenism in T-Groups," she takes the position that women, particularly if their presence is token, have difficulty in performing competently (using their resources fully), because they have been and are cast in one of four female stereotypes: the "mother," the "sex object," the "pal," or the "iron maiden." The effect of these stereotypes is to alter the characteristics of the group, thus the interaction among and behavior of members. Kanter suggests that the problems of women in male-dominated groups bear similarity to any minority problem, but they are compounded by sexual issues. The mere reading of this selection should give men cause to examine their own feelings and behavior with women in groups, whether they be training or work groups.

"OUTSIDER" CONCERNS ABOUT T-GROUPING

Concerns and criticisms about T-Groups and sensitivity training that come from people not professionally involved in the area also have been voiced, and in this sense the laboratory approach also has ample company. For instance, the goals, methods, and competencies of people involved in public education are continually being scrutinized by parents of school children. The wisdom of devoting huge sums of money to space exploration also has been questioned by many groups.

As with insider concerns, those of the outsider can serve variously useful purposes. In any case, these concerns will exist and they should be responded to. The rationale is uncomplicated. First, our pluralist society not only permits but encourages divergence in goals and values, which increases the likelihood that every field of work will have its critics. Indeed, our general

---

[1]Martin Lakin, "Some Ethical Issues in Sensitivity Training." *American Psychologist*, Vol. 24 (Oct., 1969), pp. 923–28.

[2]Robert Golembiewski and Arthur Blumberg (Eds.), *Sensitivity Training and the Laboratory Approach*, 2nd edition (Itasca, Ill.: Peacock Publishing Co., 1973), p. 274.

philosophic position is that every interest *should* have its critics. Second, issues expressed by outside publics about a particular field can be of value. At the very least, such issues can serve as some indicator as to the adequacy of a field's communications with those outside its own fold.

"Outsider" concerns about sensitivity training have three major motivators. The first resides in the very nature of the technology itself. By definition, the major thrust of the laboratory approach is toward emotional and behavioral processes, not cognitive ones. That is, the aim of a T-Group experience is to encourage people to be more aware of the feelings and behavior of themselves and others. Of less concern is that people learn a body of subject matter that has been developed by someone else. This very point, combined with the uniqueness of its methodology, makes communicating about a T-Group experience less than satisfactory for those people who have not had direct experience with it. So a common attitude develops among people. "If you can't tell me about it so that I can understand it, there can't be much to it." Relatedly, it is difficult to be very concrete even about an individual's experience in a T-Group. The person feels he has learned something, in the vast bulk of the cases. But it may be a fugitive something, even if it is personally very real, such as being more free to accept and confront feelings that had previously been denied. Sometimes the learning is simply that the person listens better, or is less defensive about his work. Some of these results are hard to measure, and they are harder to communicate about. Even the major success stories of dealing with a person's inner life space are not the kind of thing that makes headlines, although even minor failures may draw major attention.

The moral of the telling is plain enough, as is its associated danger. The end product of sensitivity training has a multidimensional subtlety and elusiveness with which professionals will simply have to live. The danger is that this fact will be used as a rationalization to excuse the failure to try to communicate effectively about the subtlety and elusiveness.

Second, some people who have been involved in T-Groups have had learning experiences that are minimal or negative, or even traumatic in a few cases. Such outcomes inspire external reactions that are critical or even damning, and understandably so.

These no-learning outcomes present a formidable challenge even though it is true that in a significant sense T-Groups sometimes get the worst of it. Consider the array of educational experiences. For example, not everyone can or does learn algebra or French. "I had a miserable time with it," they may explain. Or they may say "I guess I lack the aptitude. I just couldn't learn algebra." Or they may question the competence of the teacher. But no-learners are not likely to say that algebra is bad, or to advise others not to learn algebra. In other words, people easily accept that there are individual differences in capacities and in predispositions to do well in one kind of academic learning or another. "He's clever at math," we could say, "but she is not." But we are less willing to acknowledge individual differences in emotional capacities. On the emotional level, it seems that there is a general feeling that we are all pretty much alike. "People are people." Given this assumption, if one person's experience in a T-Group was not productive for him, it follows that the same will be true for his neighbor.

People, however, are not people. Not enough is yet known about who will profit from which designs of sensitivity training experiences, but major differences seem to exist in the capabilities of specific people in various combinations to profit from specific learning designs.[3] And *vive la difference.* Moreover, refinements still need to be made in ways of filtering out persons who might find a T-Group experience beyond their abilities to cope. For example, all reputable sensitivity training programs caution against its use as a therapy substitute. These cautions are not foolproof, obviously. And like all learning environments—schools, the army, and so on—the T-Group may be the place where an ego is revealed as seriously shaken. The stress of a T-Group may even precipitate the onset of a psychotic break for some few people. But so might a thousand other stress situations, if the individual is that vulnerable. It could happen to any of us, in fact, and in very much worse places. The typical T-Group provides an unusual opportunity for emotional support in such cases, and perhaps no other environment is so geared toward developing helping relationships. These can be vital resources for emergency care, if necessary. Indeed, just this environment of support and warmth has convinced many people that they required help beyond the competence of their T-Group.

Third, the value system underlying sensitivity training differs from many dominant value systems in our culture. This encourages rejections of the laboratory method, if only because it is easier than changing these dominant value systems. For example, Argyris sees the "pyramidal values" as dominant in our organizations.[4] These values emphasize man's rationality to the exclusion of his emotions, and rather clearly indicate that hierarchical power and control alone are sufficient to channel man's productive energies. Man, according to this value system, cannot be trusted to produce on his own. The value system associated with a T-Group experience is different. It assumes the legitimacy of man's emotions, and sees them as part and parcel of his work life. It also includes an emphasis on sharing power, which denies the pervasive notion that hierarchical control is alone sufficient or even necessary to ensure man's productivity.

Such differences in value orientations can reasonably account for a person having a nonproductive experience in a T-Group. For example, consider a

---

[3]Revealingly, see William C. Schutz, *FIRO-B* (New York: Rinehart, 1958).
    [4]Chris Argyris, "T-Groups for Organizational Effectiveness," *Harvard Business Review,* Vol. 42 (April, 1964), pp. 60–62.

person who basically accepts the pyramidal values and who is in an organization which reflects those values. Such a person is likely to see a T-Group experience as artificial, as not applicable to the workaday life and, therefore, as a waste of time. And, of course, such a person would be absolutely correct, from his point of view.

The point for us is a direct one. Concerns about T-Groups from outsiders can help define differences in such value-orientations. The payoff of careful listening is patent, then. Greater sensitivity to such differences in values will help determine who can have a useful laboratory experience, and perhaps who should. Such information is particularly valuable for assessing the usefulness of applications of the laboratory approach in schools or businesses or other organizations.

THREE SPECIFIC CONCERNS

Attention now will be shifted toward explicitly documenting what learning potential exists in a variety of concerns about T-Groups, coming from "outsiders" as well as "insiders." The focus, in turn, will be on goals, methods, and results of sensitivity training. The editors do not share all the concerns in the selections that will be introduced, but they are representative and do deserve attention.

A. Goals of T-Grouping

Within the professional group associated with sensitivity training, total agreement does not exist about training goals. In Chapter I, for example, the point was made that sensitivity training was neither therapy nor a substitute for therapy, at least as far as the NTL Institute for Applied Behavioral Science is concerned. In "Conditions for Competence Acquisition and Therapy," Argyris discusses the issue in some depth. The goals of sensitivity training are seen as competency acquisition, for people who may be characterized as more or less open and growth-oriented. On the other hand, therapy is aimed at survival of people who are more or less closed; its aim is to stop or even delay an already serious degeneration. The conditions for learning in these two situations are different, and they require different kinds of learning experiences and different learning theories. In brief, competency acquisition is concerned with creating situations in which an individual can experience psychological success, where the information that is exchanged is directly verifiable, minimally evaluative, and minimally contradictory. In contrast, the therapeutic situation is marked by knowledge that is only indirectly verifiable, by knowledge that is evaluative, and by a learning approach which can lead to psychological failure, according to Argyris' model.

But Argyris does not speak for a united network of professionals engaged in sensitivity training, to say the least. Differences over the goals of training seem to be related to the history of the development of sensitivity training as a technology and of the NTL Institute as an organization. In the early years, the people who were most closely associated with T-Group training, indeed its very innovators, were primarily social psychologists. Their primary interest was in group processes and behavioral skills. The focus of their efforts as trainers was dual: on helping people understand groups better; and on improving the ways in which people worked with and in groups. Of necessity, part of this learning process involved developing a deeper awareness of self in relation to others. But the focus was on the group. As time went on, however, members of other disciplines became attracted to sensitivity training. They came primarily from clinical and industrial psychology, with a sprinkling of psychiatrists. Their concerns were more individual than group-oriented. Existing T-Group practice reflects both emphases in various combinations.

This developmental history frames an issue of consequence for professionals interested in T-Group: the relative attention that should be given to individual and group dynamics. To a degree, the outlines of the professional skirmish line are clear: the issue is sometimes one of emphasis and sometimes one of essence.

The individual/group issue has been highlighted in a published exchange between David H. Jenkins[5] and James V. Clark.[6] Jenkins argued that sensitivity training is drifting toward therapy; that this drift was contrary to its original intent; and that the continuation of the drift would be harmful to the profession and the clients it serves. Clark does not see the issue similarly. In fact, he does not seem to treat the circumstances Jenkins describes as an issue, suggesting instead that the course of T-Group development makes varied demands on the trainer. At times, he suggests, it is most appropriate to give attention to the conscious, "here-and-now" group processes. At other times, particularly when individual dynamics seem to be inhibiting group growth, attention needs to be given to those unconscious, "there-and-then" individual problems. If there is a middle conceptual ground in the argument, it may well be found in the selection concerned with transference by Peters and Joslyn that is included in our discussion of the role of the trainer. These authors suggest that the extent and quality of interventions related to unconscious individual processes should be a function of the thrust of the lab and inferentially, of the expectations of the group members.

Controversy over goals is not confined to the professionals. External criticism about T-Group goals tends to stress two issues. First, there is the point of view that trainers really want to encourage the molding of individuals into mere spokes in the wheel of a conforming group. Second, T-Groups are often

---

[5] "Excerpts from a Letter," *NTL Human Relations Training News*, Vol. 6, No. 1 (1962), pp. 2–3.

[6] "Some Troublesome Dichotomies in Human Relations Training," *NTL Human Relations Training News*, Vol. 6, No. 1 (1962), pp. 3–6.

said to constitute an invasion of privacy under the guise of scientific respectability.

These two issues contain an element of truth, but the quality of that truth is strained. No doubt, for example, "the group" often becomes "the thing" in a laboratory. Pressures *are* put on people to conform to group norms. But the laboratory approach emphasizes a unique set of norms. Thus a maturing group typically recognizes the value of dissent, and begins to learn from criticism. Similarly, T-Group norms imply openness about feelings and reactions, including any generated by pressures to conform, and they also encourage each member to "do his own thing." For these are the ways other group members will learn about his reactions and ideas, and hence about their own. In addition, one would be hard put to find a trainer who would support the idea that the aim of sensitivity training is to get people to learn how important it is to conform. Quite oppositely, in fact, the position of most or all trainers is that a T-Group experience can help a person fully recognize the group pressures that are being exerted on him. And the T-Group experience can help that individual learn to behave in ways that will enable him to preserve his values and, if he wishes, still work to be an integral part of the group.

Questions about the invasion of privacy in a T-Group are easy to understand. For example, T-Group members are encouraged to be open about their feelings of hostility, happiness, sadness, anxiety, or whatever, induced by what has happened in the group. Most people find that learning to express their feelings openly is freeing and, at times, exhilarating. Pressures encouraging this exposure of self can be threatening for anyone, at various levels, and when those pressures are great enough, a real invasion of privacy may follow. Typically, T-Group members are more cautious than hasty in encouraging feedback and disclosure, and the trainer can be crucial in holding the overzealous in check. But the danger of pushing too far is a very real one, against which event the basic safeguards are T-Group norms. These norms sanction openness about feelings, even feelings about invasion of privacy; and T-Group norms also emphasize trust and help and considerate response to the feelings of fellow group members.

Many question the conformity and invasion of privacy that are said to be associated with T-Groups. A brief sketch of one source illustrates the genre, an article from the police chief's magazine, *Law and Order.*[7] Essentially, the article proposes that the T-Group experience is a behavioral science fad that is being foisted upon an unknowing public. Group therapy is seen as legitimate, but sensitivity training is described as "group confession and group criticism" which seeks to undermine the personal convictions of

---

[7]W. Cleon Skousen, "Chief, Watch Out for Those T-Group Promoters," *Law and Order Magazine,* November, 1967, pp. 10–12, 70.

T-Group members. The article sees the goals of behavioral science as understanding and predicting human behavior, but it pictures sensitivity training as destroying American culture and as devoted to challenging and discrediting the Judaeo-Christian value system of T-Group participants.

B. Methods Used in T-Groups

Concerns about the methods used in T-Groups come mostly from the professional trainer group. They are related to differences in opinion about the goals of training. The specific point at issue here is the use of "personal growth" experiences generally, and "nonverbal techniques" specifically, in the T-Group as a means of developing both behavioral and emotional data around which members can interact. Nonverbal techniques cover an enormous range. For example, one design might be called "Jungle." Participants are told to adopt the characteristics of some animal, and imagine themselves in a jungle. And you "let her rip." Or various physical encounters—like Indian wrestling—can be arranged to test for trust, aggression, or whatever. Or the individual might be asked to express himself by dancing to recorded music. Typically, brief discussions follow each such design-element, which involves large numbers of participants.

Cyril Mill and Miriam Ritvo direct attention to this class of designs in their "Potentialities and Pitfalls of Nonverbal Techniques." Their intended view is a balanced one. Such techniques can deepen a learner's experience, but that power also implies major costs. For example, conveniently available designs might encourage a trainer to trigger socioemotional dynamics that are either beyond his own competence to manage, or which were more engaging than they were relevant to some specific learning goals. Perhaps the most telling caution in the selection by Mill and Ritvo, indeed, is one directed at each user of nonverbals. Why are you using nonverbals?, is the question they urge on all trainers. The ideal is their use to highlight or isolate dynamics that help learners work toward their own goals. One alternative motivation is that of a trainer more or less intent on guru status by making "big things" happen for participants, whatever their readiness.

The broader philosophical and ideological issues involved in these insider concerns about methods can be suggested by a sketch of Chris Argyris' argument.[8] His position essentially questions some basic assumptions of William Schutz,[9] and others. Schutz assumes that

- It is of positive value for a person to be able to experience his world in a completely open manner;

-----
   [8]Chris Argyris, "On the Future of Laboratory Education," *Journal of Applied Behavioral Science*, Vol. 3, No. 2 (April, 1967), esp. pp. 163–83.
   [9]William C. Schutz, *An Approach to the Development of Human Potential*. A report of the 1963 Continuing Human Relations Laboratory, Bethel, Maine (August 15, 1963). See also his *Here Comes Everybody* (New York: Harper & Row, Publishers, 1971).

- Experiencing one's world in primarily a cognitive manner leaves a person somewhat incomplete; and
- The unconscious is crucially important in learning and development.

Argyris questions the validity of these assumptions, both as they apply to the goals of sensitivity training and as they encourage heavy use of nonverbal methods. Perhaps the biggest issue, as Argyris sees it, is the changed role of the trainer in a sensitivity training experience that involves a heavy loading of nonverbal experience. The trainer becomes very much a director of learning, which may induce conditions of psychological failure. That is, the learning achieved may be below the learner's aspiration level if motivating forces outside the person are primarily responsible for the learning. Under such conditions, Argyris suggests that "personal growth" experiences can have serious unintended consequences which are in conflict with T-Group goals. These include

- The development of high dependence on the trainer may develop;
- The strengthening of narcissism among the participants is likely;
- An increased emphasis on there-and-then diagnosis is probable; and
- Decreases in the generalizability of learning of other situations are likely.

Argyris' concerns, then, relate to the power of "personal growth" or "nonverbal" learning designs, and to the appropriateness of a heavy reliance on them. First, he feels a heavy reliance on such techniques can raise serious conflicts with T-Group goals. Second, and far more difficult, heavy use of nonverbal designs encouraged their use by unskilled and unqualified people who have experienced them as participants in a laboratory.

C. Results of Sensitivity Training

Questions have been raised about the efficacy of sensitivity training, both by insiders and outsiders, from data that supply ammunition to both proponents and opponents. Most people who take part in sensitivity training report their experience to have been very worthwhile. Some describe it as the most meaningful and exciting experience of their life. This is not the whole picture, however, particularly with regard to people who go to a lab as part of their organization's program of management development. The real question about such people, regardless of the high value they received personally, is whether or not their experience results in behavioral change that will enable them to do a better job in their organization. Relevant evidence is mixed.

The traditional case against the usefulness of T-Groups in both senses sketched above may be detailed. Odiorne's well-known approach serves our purpose.[10] He rests his criticisms on several criteria of sound training. He opens his critique by suggesting that sensitivity training (more accurately, the

---

[10]George S. Odiorne, "The Trouble with Sensitivity Training," *Training Directors Journal,* Vol. 17 (October, 1963), pp. 9-20.

professional group involved in it) is a closed system: "The most damaging criticism of sensitivity training is that it has built into its system an automatic rejection of orderly, rational, conscious criticism. This itself is a dangerous rigidity which should be corrected first." He then states that sensitivity training is not training, as measured by the following five criteria:

- In good training the desired terminal behavior can be identified before the training begins.
- The course of change is comprised of some logical small steps in good training.
- The learning and learner are under control in good training.
- There are selection standards for admission in good training.
- Results are evaluated in good training.

Sensitivity training just does not measure up to any of these criteria, Odiorne concludes. His conclusion rests on anecdotal data obtained from former T-Group participants or third-party reporters, which reflects the undeveloped state of the research literature when Odiorne wrote in 1963. Odiorne closes with the suggestion that business executives call a moratorium on the use of sensitivity training in their organizations until behavioral scientists reassess and overhaul the technology. This volume should aid the reader in evaluating Odiorne's conclusion.

A second kind of criticism of the results of sensitivity training maintains, oppositely, that it works too well in quite specific ways for which most of the world is not yet ready and in ways that the organizational world might do well to reject. Louis A. Allen, in "The T-Group: Short Cut or Short Circuit?," is quite clear that the T-Group may, indeed, be an effective tool for changing behaviors, attitudes, and values. But he also pointedly indicates that the resulting changes are in all likelihood antithetical to the values implicit in the current management style of organizations in our society. In particular, Allen suggests that T-Group attitudes and values transferred into action will erode management prerogatives of direction and control to the detriment of the enterprise. There are points in his paper where Allen, we believe, overstates his case. At other times his statements of fact seem questionable. For example, "The T-Group," he says, "is the one common feature to all organizational development programs." None the less, the cautionary flags he raises for managers considering a sensitivity training program for their firm are well worth noting. He raises questions that need to be attended to.

The last selection in this chapter deals with a type of result of T-Group experience that is unintended and untoward. Our concerns here are with what have come to be known as psychological casualties of T-Groups or sensitivity training. It is the rare individual who does not experience some sort of personal stress during the course of a T-Group's life. For some the stress may be minor. Others may experience it as a major, if transitory, emotional upset. The huge majority of participants seem able to cope with the stress they experience and learn from it. A minority, however, apparently find their coping mechanisms inadequate—suffering, at times, severe psychological trauma that may require some sort of psychotherapeutic help, short- or long-term. Judgments concerning the size of this minority vary, running from less than one per cent to over nine per cent.

Cary L. Cooper's "How Psychologically Dangerous Are T-Groups and Encounter Groups?" is a review and critique of a number of studies that have been conducted on the personally disruptive effects of T-Groups. Cooper points out that a shortcoming of the data used to substantiate the "dangerous" charge is that most of it is either of the anecdotal or paper-and-pencil test variety and that little of it is behavioral.[11] On the basis of his review, including what behavioral data is available, Cooper concludes that charges of T-Groups being psychologically dangerous have not been proved and that, indeed, they may be less stressful than other taken-for-granted parts of life—the taking of university examinations, for example. He does not, however, brush the problem aside, but suggests the need for more research and the development of systematic screening procedures for potential participants.

The evidence, then, regarding the degree to which participation in a T-Group may cause psychological casualties is conflicting. To brush off the problem as minimal would be ostrich-like. To consider it apocalyptic would be somewhat unreal. We can only reinforce the already mentioned references to the need for some sort of screening and more refined research.

---

[11]A glaring exception to this statement is the study conducted by Morton Lieberman, Irwin Yalom, and Matthew Miles reported in *Encounter Groups: First Facts* (New York: Basic Books, Inc., 1973). These authors would probably suggest that Cooper is a bit too sanguine about the problem.

14. Some Questions about Ethics and Responsibilities in Sensitivity Training

STEVEN F. FEINBERG

A number of explanations have been offered to account for the proliferation of intensive, small group experiences. One is that they represent a reaction to the increasingly impersonal nature of our large and complex society. A second is that such group experiences are filling a void left by the trend away from the extended family and the accompanying transient nature of the nuclear family. It is also possible that the development and utilization of experience-based learning methods is an attempt to counterbalance our "current preoccupation with objective, mechanistic, cognitive, computerized education" (Combs, 1970, p. 235); an educational format in which "our preoccupation with the information half of the learning equation has dehumanized our schools, alienated our youth, and produced a system irrelevant for most students" (p. 236).

Regardless of the reasons, sensitivity training is very much in evidence today. However, its continuing expansion into a variety of divergent forms has been accompanied by an increase in the number of questions concerning ethics and responsibility in the field of sensitivity training. This article is an examination of some of these questions.

A BRIEF BACKGROUND

Included among the features that have been and continue to be fairly characteristic of human relations training is the emphasis on feelings, a "here-and-now" orientation, and the encouragement of immediate feedback. With these characteristics certain general purposes are often cited. They include: increasing the participant's awareness of feelings as well as impact on, and reaction to, others; learning more effective ways of expressing one's feelings and in so doing, improving interpersonal communication and interpersonal relationships; learning to be more open and genuine or authentic; reducing or eliminating defensive behavior; and understanding how groups operate and develop.

With the growth and expansion of the field of sensitivity training, a wide variety of methods have been incorporated into the process of trying to achieve these aims and aims that are more situationally specific. Furthermore, a number of different types of groups utilize various combinations of

Written expressly for this volume.

these methods. Some of the more common types are: T-Groups, encounter groups, marathon groups, and sensory awareness groups. These different types of groups are often noted more for their similarities and their lack of specificity regarding distinct methodologies than they are for their differences. This view appears to be voiced not only by the general public, but also by members of the various professions and academic disciplines involved in the field of small group training.

REACTIONS TO SENSITIVITY TRAINING

The term "sensitivity training," which was one of the first terms used to describe the intensive, small-group training approach to learning, is now used to describe a wide variety of small group activities and its meaning has become rather nebulous. For many it is a rather volatile term that invokes extreme reactions, both positive and negative, concerning the group movement.

Included among the extreme negative reactions is the depiction of sensitivity training as a communist plot and a form of brainwashing aimed at weakening support for our democratic principles (Allen, 1968). Somewhat less extreme, but still negative, is the blanket condemnation of sensitivity training by some members of the helping professions. Many of these professionals have either heard of or treated former group participants who, either during or shortly following their participation in intensive groups, suffered psychotic episodes, lost their jobs, left their spouses, or attempted suicide. On the extreme positive side are gross, unsupported claims, expressed by both laymen and professionals, regarding training group effectiveness. Such claims are often accompanied by emphatic denial of possible risks to participants of intensive group experiences.

In considering some of the extreme lay opinions, positive claims, which may refer more to the emotional experience than to any learning outcomes, are often voiced in ways that are not only characteristic of religious fervor, but also seem to carry with them religious connotations. This doesn't seem so surprising, given the decline of the centrality of formal religion in our modern way of life and the not infrequently expressed notion that today's psychiatrists and clinical psychologists are serving in the role formerly held by spiritual leaders in the various religious denominations. This also seems to have carried over into the group movement. Kurt Back (1972), examining the development of sensitivity training and the encounter movement, points out that "the group leader in sensitivity training has thus assumed the function of the healer, priest, or shaman in earlier societies" (p. 214). With regard to the extremely positive opinions held by professionals, some of these beliefs may be due, in part, to the relative brevity of many group experiences and the limited emphasis placed on obtaining follow-up data so that "any psychological decompensation manifesting itself after the end of the group would be unlikely to come to [the group leader's] attention" (Lieberman, Yalom, and Miles, 1973, p. 168).

On the other hand, the extremely negative reactions of some professionals may be due to the fact that while they hear about those groups in which a participant has experienced some degree of emotional distress and has then sought out professional help, they are not apt to hear about the many other groups that are effective or at least don't cause participants to suffer any ill effects. The combination of these two factors may therefore produce a picture of sensitivity training that is not at all representative, but which does result in negative reactions on the part of some professionals. Regardless of the possible reasons for the various extreme reactions, their very prevalence does little to bring about greater understanding of specific aspects of sensitivity training.

SOME ETHICAL GUIDEPOSTS

To set the stage, or perhaps more accurately, raise the platform from which ethical questions can be asked, a brief review of some of the commonly voiced responsibilities of the professions and practitioners in the field of sensitivity training is required. Included among the more general responsibilities of those professions involved in group work is the continued integration and utilization of "values from the orientations of science, democracy, and of processes of giving and receiving help" (Benne, 1975, p. 46). Such values represent an emphasis on the continuing development of theory and methodology, as well as on refinement of ethical standards that place high priority on the adequate training of group practitioners.

With regard to the more specific responsibilities that group leaders have, both to their clients and to the professions themselves, is the necessity that they be quite clear in their own minds as to what their training goals and objectives are. Once they have clarified their objectives, they are then in a position to select those methods that will help them to achieve their goals. (The term "methods," as used here, refers to those behaviors group leaders may display during the life of the group as well as the various techniques they may employ.) The decision regarding objectives is determined, to a large degree, by the values that trainers hold. This implies that group leaders need to be cognizant of their own value orientation. Not only must group leaders have an adequate understanding of training theory and training design that has specific relevance to the group participants, they must also be well aware of the range of consequences that may result from the procedures they have chosen to utilize within the group, and must be able to relate this to their own limitations as group trainers.

In summary, group leaders must be well-trained with regard to theory, training design, and appropriate procedures, and must be aware of the range of possible consequences of the procedures. They must have a clear understanding of their limits and values as trainers, and their values must be in agreement with the ethics of their profession. When these conditions are met, their objectives will likely be worthwhile, and the potential hazards associated with the path to those objectives will be greatly minimized.

QUESTIONS PERTAINING TO ASPECTS OF SENSITIVITY TRAINING GROUPS

Specifying objectives, describing procedures to realize those objectives, and clarifying the responsibilities associated with the procedures and objectives are important ingredients in any developing field of study. To do so, however, does not prove either the inherent worth of the objectives or the effectiveness of the procedures. Nor does it guarantee that the responsibilities will be accepted, or imply that no other issues need to be dealt with. The current condition of the field of sensitivity training not only provides support for this view, but raises a number of ethical questions in the process.

Questions Concerning Objectives

One primary T-Group objective is to achieve "openness" in the group. Indeed, part of the mythology surrounding human relations training is that it will provide an emotionally uplifting experience characterized by "openness," which may frequently get mistranslated into "let it all hang out." Requests for openness may also be misunderstood. For example, when group members request openness from their fellow participants, they may really be asking to have various emotional needs met, such as needs for affection, respect, or admiration (Stanford, 1972). Even where there is clarity regarding the meaning of the term, however, group members who are "open" about positive feelings that they have for themselves or positive characteristics that they believe they possess may be seen as threatening by other group members. In addition, when openness involves the expression of negative feelings toward other group members, the recipients respond with hostile reactions and may also experience extreme discomfort.

Such occurrences are not uncommon in sensitivity training groups. How viable can such an objective be when it is often misunderstood, when it can result in hostility or emotional discomfort, and when being "open" can serve to threaten other group members? Furthermore, are trainers being irresponsible if they don't take time to clarify such terms, even when group members indicate that they know what these terms mean? Should trainers set limits as to how "open" members can be? How aware must trainers be of the potential vulnerability of group members with regard to their receiving negative feedback? If trainers feel such data concerning participants are needed, how is the data to be obtained?

Another question that can be raised about T-Group objectives concerns the decrease or elimination of participants' defensive behavior. While it is possible that the utilization of various defense mechanisms may contribute to participants' limited awareness of aspects of themselves or others, defense mechanisms are employed by virtually everyone and in some cases help individuals to deal with anxious feelings within the group. To attempt to "break down" participants' defenses may cause individuals even greater difficulty in gaining awareness of themselves or others. Furthermore, the inappropriate utilization of defenses by participants may be indicative of psychological impairment. An attempt by the group to decrease or eliminate such defenses may result in participants experiencing severe emotional distress and may necessitate therapeutic intervention.

These points raise the question, how much information do trainers need to have regarding participants' vulnerability? Additionally, and also with regard to openness, what effects will the realization of these objectives have on group members' ability to function in the outside environment? Will group members who have been rewarded within the group for being open with regard to feelings, either positive or negative, receive the same rewards from family, friends, and those individuals with whom they work? How great an emphasis have trainers placed on developing skills to enable participants to differentiate between situations where the strong display of emotions is appropriate and when it is not? Even in those groups where there is such an emphasis, how can trainers determine how well participants have developed such skills? In those cases where such determinations can be made, what can or should trainers attempt to do when they find that some members are not able to differentiate between such situations? Is it enough to merely point out the potential hazards before the group ends, and if so, how often is this done? In those groups where an emphasis is placed on "breaking down defenses," what risks does this pose for participants whose defenses help them to deal with hostile and potentially dangerous elements in their outside environment? It is quite possible that trainers have little knowledge about such aspects of group members' outside environment, and if they do, does this imply that they should help participants to "build up" their defenses before leaving the group? In what way could this be accomplished? It might be argued that if participants' defenses were very important for survival, the likelihood that they could be broken down would be small. If this is the case, and it may well be, then whose objectives would be served by such a group?

Questions Concerning Group Composition and Screening Procedures

An issue that has prompted some debate concerns the potential hazards that exist when a sensitivity training group is composed of participants who are not strangers to each other, participants who may have social or business relationships with other members outside of the group. With regard to business relationships, Gazda, Duncan, and Sisson (1971) suggest that trainers be aware of the potential risks involved when close business associates are in the same group. Shostrom (1969), however, in presenting guidelines for prospective group participants, is much more emphatic and states the individuals should "never participate in a group encounter with close associates, persons with whom [the individual has] professional or competitive social relations" (p. 38). What are some of the potential risks that such cautions suggest? Will a business relationship be enhanced as a result of joint participation in a sensitivity training group, or will some members feel they have "revealed too much" and, by so doing, have placed greater stress on the relationship—stress that may even lead to a desire to terminate the relationship or, in some cases, to leave the job? Furthermore, while prospective participants may have considered such risks and may therefore be very reluctant to join a group, it is quite common for training groups to be held within a business organization for just that purpose of improving working relationships. What are these individuals to do when the boss "strongly suggests" that they participate? These questions have implications for trainers not only with regard to potential risks, but also concerning the issue of conducting groups when participation is not voluntary.

A special case involving these issues can be found in some university settings where students are required, as part of a course, to participate in a training group experience. Is it responsible behavior on the part of trainers to conduct groups where participation is "mandatory?" As is the case with business associates, what are the hazards when participants have social relationships with other group members? How might such social relationships affect the development of the group? Might there be a greater tendency for scapegoating? Furthermore, where grades need to be given, how is student participation to be "evaluated?" If instructors serve as group trainers, will this inhibit, or in some other way affect the manner in which students participate in the group? Conversely, to what extent might students' behavior in the group affect instructors' perceptions of them in other settings?

Another issue associated with group composition, which was alluded to in the discussion of objectives and which often receives criticism, is the lack of screening of participants. Yet, except in those cases where prospective group members display rather obvious signs of psychological impairment, in what way is screening to be done? Do trainers need to conduct extensive interviews with prospective participants to determine if admission to the group should be refused, or to help trainers to be better prepared to deal with problems that group members may experience? Should group leaders have such diagnostic skills? If so, how many of them do? When trainers do employ some form of interview procedure for prospective members, how much emphasis is placed on determining whether the desired goals of the members are consistent with the trainers' goals? In those instances where interviews are conducted for this latter purpose, prospective members may be unclear as to what their goals are. What responsibility do trainers have for helping members clarify their goals and, in those cases where trainers do help in this clarification process, what happens when the group members' goals turn out to be different from the goals of the trainers? Should trainers then encourage members to drop out of the group? What effect might this have on the rest of the group members? Furthermore, while it may be argued that group leaders have a responsibility to inform prospective members as to their objectives and methods, how specific can they be without jeopardizing the realization of their objectives?

Questions Concerning the Use of Techniques or Exercises

The growth and diversification of sensitivity training has been accompanied by the creation and increased use of techniques or exercises within the intensive group experience. These techniques may involve some or all of the participants and include a wide variety of activities such as fantasizing, physical contact, dancing, and other nonverbal behaviors. Mill and Ritvo (1969) suggest that such exercises can serve as "one more link for making contact with self and others" (p. 1) and that "professionalism is promoted when their use stems from a theory of training, when their selection is relevant to a theory of learning, and when they fall meaningfully into a coherent design which meets the needs of the participants" (p. 1). Unfortunately, numbers of individuals who are inadequately trained lead groups and utilize various techniques. These individuals are often previous group participants who find that "simple" exercises can bring about exciting effects. But these people may have little, if any, understanding of the theory associated with these exercises nor of the potential dangers associated with their use. Moreover, the motivation of such individuals in using these techniques may stem from a desire to impress the participants in order to gratify their own needs. When this is the case, their behavior is clearly irresponsible. What is not so clear, however, is that while a great number of techniques for use in groups have been developed and are used by "qualified" trainers, "little research evidence is available to validate their use or to tell us when they may be most appropriately employed" (Gazda, Duncan, and Sisson, 1971, p. 642).

What implications does this have for professionally trained group leaders who incorporate techniques within their groups? Do they need to collect follow-up data to find out if any participants have suffered ill effects? When the use of a technique produces unexpected problems or crises for group participants, are the trainers capable of helping the participants to get through the crisis? If not, do they have appropriate referral sources?

SOME GENERAL CONCERNS

As is the case with many potentially humanizing innovations, the excitement and enthusiasm that has accompanied and contributed to the growth of sensitivity training has also overshadowed many of the potential hazards. In addition, the rate of increase in the use of group procedures has taken place much more rapidly than has the development of theory, methods, safeguards, and evaluating procedures. For example, Lakin (1973) points out that in some of the newer formats for sensitivity training there is little opportunity or encouragement for the group to examine and deal with possibly inappropriate usage of influence and power by the trainers (a safeguard that represented an aspect of the philosophy associated with many of the earlier training laboratories). Some group members may experience strong emotional reactions to the trainers' power without having the chance to discuss these reactions. Group members may also experience strong feelings resulting from techniques that trainers have used without having an opportunity for working through these feelings. The lack of such opportunities raises the issue of trainers' ethical responsibility for members' learning as well as members' welfare.

Related to the issue of trainers' responsibility for members' welfare, some trainers may not realize or else ignore the possibility that members may experience severe problems as a result of participation in the group. Other trainers are simply unwilling to accept any responsibility for negative consequences and, instead, voice the opinion that all individuals must accept responsibility for themselves. Furthermore, some group leaders express the view "that extreme psychological discomfort, even to the degree where professional aid is required, may not be a failure but an accomplishment of the group," and that it may simply represent a "stage of personal growth" (Lieberman, Yalom, and Miles, 1973, p. 168). Do group leaders inform prospective members of the possible risks involved or express their opinion regarding participants' responsibility for themselves? If participants are informed of the possible risks, does this then absolve group leaders of any responsibility? How long might it take participants to move out of this "stage of personal growth?"

The potential hazards as well as the refusal on the part of some group leaders to accept any responsibility for the discomfort that participants may experience raises the question, how adequately trained are group leaders in the field of sensitivity training? A common characteristic of virtually every developed profession is the training and licensing or certification of its practitioners. Within the field of human relations training, however, some confusion exists regarding what the phrase "adequately trained" really means.[1] This confusion seems due, in part, to the number of different professions and academic disciplines that are involved in the area of group work. Not only do these professional and academic areas differ with regard to their developmental histories, their philosophical orientations, and their specific aims, but also, within each area can be found a variety of theoretical frameworks. Furthermore, many of these areas differ with regard to their use of terminology. This often results in similar activities being described by different names, while different activities are referred to by the same name. Beymer (1972) states this last point much more succinctly, "the present state of the literature of group work is a semantic disaster area" (p. 488), and things seem not to have changed too much since Beymer made his comment. This confusion seems to have greatly hindered both the clarification of training requirements and the establishment of ethical principles. Does this confusion represent a lack of cooperation among the various areas involved? If it does, how can cooperation be improved? Has any attempt been made to standardize the terminology? Don't the potential hazards represent a responsibility of the professions as well as of the practitioners?

Also contributing to the problems in the field of sensitivity training are the confusion and misperceptions of the general public. A partial cause of this seems to be the increasing use and misuse of psychological terminology in everyday conversation. While many technical terms have been incorporated into modern-day language, during the process the meanings of many of them have undergone modification. As psychological terminology is sometimes employed to describe aspects of sensitivity training, the modification and distortions of these terms have brought about confusion regarding sensitivity training so that it is seen as different things by different people—a situation, as noted above, which also exists within the professions themselves. For example, many individuals regard sensitivity training as a form of group therapy and join training groups to obtain therapy. A number of group trainers also consider sensitivity training a form of therapy. The question, with regard to the confusion of the general public concerning sensitivity training, seems to be, how useful would an attempt be to better inform the public, given the lack of agreement and confusion of many of those individuals who conduct groups?

A FEW CLOSING COMMENTS

Today the field of sensitivity training is marked by confusion, conflict, controversy, and caution. While the importance of utilizing procedures that stem from a well-developed theoretical framework is stressed, little empirical

---

[1]An exception is the International Association of Applied Social Scientists, established in 1971. It takes, as one of its major responsibilities, the accreditation of trainers, and has developed procedures for assessing adequacy as a trainer.

evidence exists to support claims of effectiveness with regard to many of the theories and accompanying training designs that are currently in use. Furthermore, as Lieberman, Yalom and Miles' extensive and well-documented study concerning encounter groups points out, it has been found that potential risks for group participants do exist and negative outcomes are not uncommon. Given such findings, how much longer will those professionals involved in the field of sensitivity training tolerate its current condition? What can they do to improve the present situation? What are they doing now? These may be the most important ethical questions pertaining to sensitivity training.

REFERENCES

Allen, G. Hate therapy: Sensitivity training for "planned change." *American Opinion,* January 1968, pp. 73–86.

Back, K. W. *Beyond Words.* Baltimore: Penguin, 1972.

Benne, K. D. Conceptual and moral foundations of laboratory method. In K. D. Benne, L. P. Bradford, J. R. Gibb & R. O. Lippitt (Eds.), *The laboratory method of changing and learning.* Palo Alto: Science and Behavior Books, 1975.

Beymer, L. Confrontation groups: Hula hoops? In R. C. Diedrich & H. A. Dye (Eds.), *Group procedures: purposes, processes, and outcomes.* Boston: Houghton Mifflin, 1972.

Combs, A. W. Sensitivity education: problems and promises. *Educational Leadership,* 1970, *28,* 235–237.

Gazda, G. M., Duncan, J. A., & Sisson, P. J. Professional issues in group work. *Personnel and Guidance Journal,* 1971, *49,* 637–643.

Lakin, M. Some ethical issues in sensitivity training. In R. T. Golembiewski & A. Blumberg (Eds.), *Sensitivity training and the laboratory approach* (2nd ed.). Itasca, Ill: F. E. Peacock, 1973.

Lieberman, M. A., Yalom, I. D., & Miles, M. B. *Encounter groups: First facts.* New York: Basic Books, 1973.

Mill, D. & Ritvo, M. Potentialities and pitfalls of nonverbal techniques. *Human Relations Training News,* 1969, *13,* 1–3.

Shostrom, E. L. Group therapy: let the buyer beware. *Psychology Today,* May, 1969, pp. 36–40.

Stanford, G. Openness as manipulation. *Social Change: Ideas and Applications,* 1972, *2* (3).

15. On Ending Female Tokenism in T-Groups: Group Norms, Process, and Sex-Role Issues

ROSABETH MOSS KANTER

The small training group has long been viewed as particularly suited to help *men* develop new behavioral repertoires and self-insights counterbalancing the stereotypical tendencies of the male role. Where the male role stresses instrumental leadership (a task and power orientation), T-Group norms emphasize learning the expression of feelings; where the male role stresses analytic and intellectual reasoning, T-Group norms emphasize learning to pay attention to emotions; where the male role stresses an identity based on task achievement, T-Group norms emphasize learning to receive and be influenced by feedback from others; where the male role stresses aggression and competition, T-Group norms emphasize learning collaboratively. And so on, in its many extensions, the small training group is a dramatic tool in the reeducation of men.

NORMS AND NUMBERS

But the very norms that offer new learning for men are *already* a stereotypical part of the female role: expressive leadership, nurturance and support, emotional reasoning, talking immediately and directly to one another, intuition, cooperation. Thus, what is dramatic new learning for men in a T-Group setting may be support for continuation of a stereotypical sex role for women (see Table 4.1). Thus, while men may need help in learning about relationships and emotional expression, women need help in learning just the *opposite:* to experience their power, to develop task orientation, to intellectualize, to behave "impersonally" and address large groups, to become invulnerable to feedback, to own and value their own ambitions as well as their responsibilities to others.

The major implication of this for laboratory trainers and process consultants who design workshops and training sessions is the need for very different agendas for men and for women. Trainers and consultants must modify their own styles, for example, to help men in the all-male groups learn about relating to others and to help women in the all-female groups learn about boundaries; men and women in the mixed groups could be encouraged to see each other in the light of these new behavior possibilities

Reprinted from *Social Change,* Vol. 5, No. 2, 1975, pp. 1–3.

TABLE 4.1

Male Stereotypical Role Tendency	T-Group Norm	Female Stereotypical Role Tendency
Instrumental leadership; task and power orientation	Learn to express feelings	Expressive leadership; nurturance and support
Analytic reasoning; intellectualizing	Learn to pay attention to feelings	Emotional reasoning; intuition
Generalizing	Learn to speak for yourself	Personalizing
Identity based on achievement; how others see self less important	Learn to receive and be influenced by feedback	Identity dependent on feelings of others toward self; status traditionally based on relationships
Attention to issues of large systems; in a group, remarks impersonal and indirect	Learn to talk personally, directly to others	Attention to small number of others; in a group, remarks addressed personally to another
Anger and blame externalized; vengeance sought	Learn to take personal responsibility for own behavior	Blame internalized; difficulty expressing anger
Physical distance; hostility-violence in crowded conditions	Learn comfort with physical contact	Greater comfort with being touched; cooperation under conditions of crowding
Fear of failure in the organizational world; get ahead at all costs	Learn to value human concerns	Ambivalence about success in the organizational world; concern with people
Aggression; competition	Learn to behave cooperatively	Cooperation; support
Exhibit strength; hide weakness	Learn to show vulnerability	Exhibit weakness; hide or repress strength

and consequently, to redefine their usual modes of interacting with one another.[1]

The second important group issue concerns the sex ratio of the group. The relative proportions of men and women in a group of any kind have many behavioral consequences. Recent social psychological research has confirmed the common-sense notion that all-male, all-female, and mixed-sex small groups differ in their conversational content, process, and relationship styles. Themes in all-male groups include competition, aggression, violence, victimization, practical joking, questions of identity, and fear of self-disclosure. Almost a third of the statements in the all-male groups in one study were addressed to the group as a whole, signaling an avoidance of intimacy; references to relationships were more often impersonal than in the other groups. All-female group themes included affiliation, family, conflicts about competition and leadership, and seeking information about relationships;

---

[1] Since most trainers and consultants are male, they are probably not sensitive to the special needs and issues of women, and they must modify their styles and assumptions.

there were more references to self than in all-male groups, and references to relationships were more often personal. In the mixed groups, men were more tense, serious, and self-conscious; spoke less of aggression; and engaged in less practical joking. There were more references to self for both sexes and more talk of feelings, but the women generally spoke much less than the men. Sexual tensions were noted in the mixed groups; heterosexual contact was valued, and concerns were expressed about being attractive to the opposite sex.

A skewed sex distribution will have its own effects on the dynamics of the group. Two quick generalizations can be made. When a man is the rarity in a group, he is likely to be central, to be deferred to and respected. When a woman is the rarity, she is likely to be isolated, to be treated as trivial. Effective intervention in such situations may depend upon understanding these dynamics as a function of the group, and not necessarily of the individuals involved.

FOUR FEMALE STEREOTYPES IN MALE-DOMINATED GROUPS

Perhaps the most frequent circumstance training staffs face above the blue-collar regions of organizations is that of the solitary or virtually solitary woman in a male-dominated group. The "token" woman may have difficulty with competent performance because she is cast in one of four stereotypical roles: the "mother," the "sex object," the "pet," or the "iron maiden." I will discuss these at length because of their importance for characterizing group dynamics—whether we are talking about women in a small training group setting or the few women beginning to trickle into formerly all-male organizational preserves.

"Mother"

A solitary woman sometimes finds that she has become a "mother" to a group of men. They bring her their troubles, and she comforts them. The assumption that women are sympathetic listeners and can be talked to about one's problems is a common one in male-dominated organizations (even though when the therapeutic role is monetized, it is more often performed by a man). This role is comparatively safe; the mother is not necessarily vulnerable to sexual pursuit nor to competition for her favors.

This typecasting of woman as nurturer has three consequences: 1) The mother is rewarded by her male colleagues primarily for service to them and not for independent action. 2) The dominant, powerful aspects of the maternal image may be feared by men; thus the mother is expected to keep her place as a noncritical, accepting, "good" mother, or lose her rewards. The ability to differentiate and be critical is often an indicator of competence in workgroups, and the woman-as-mother is thus blocked from demonstrating her own competence. 3) The mother becomes an emotional specialist. This provides her with a place in the life of the group. Yet one of the traditionally feminine characteristics men in positions of authority often criticize in women, as people trying to change the status of women in industry can attest, is excess "emotionality." Though the mother herself might not ever cry or engage in emotional outbursts in the group, she remains identified with emotional matters rather than with critical, independent, task-oriented behaviors.

"Seductress"

The role of seductress or sexual object is fraught with more tension than the maternal role, for it introduces an element of sexual competition and jealousy. The mother can have many sons; it is more difficult for the sex object to have many lovers. Should the woman cast as sex object[2] share her attention widely, she risks the debasement of the whore. Should she form a close alliance with any man in particular, she arouses resentment—particularly so because she represents a scarce resource; there are just not enough women to go around.

A high-status male (staff member, manager, professor, or other) can easily become the "protector" of the still-virgin seductress, gaining through masking his own sexual interest what the other men cannot gain by declaring theirs. But this removal of the seductress from the sexual marketplace contains its own problems. The other men may resent the high-status male for winning the prize and resent the woman for her ability to get an "in" with the high-status male that they as men could not obtain. Although the seductress is rewarded for her femaleness and is ensured attention from the group, she is also the source of considerable tension. At the same time, her perceived sexuality blots out all other characteristics.

"Pet"

The "pet" is adopted by the male group as a cute, amusing "little thing" and symbolically taken along on group events as mascot, a cheerleader for the shows of male prowess that follow. Humor is often a characteristic of the pet. She is expected to admire the male displays but not enter into them; she cheers from the sidelines. Displays of competence on her part are treated as special and are complimented just because they are unexpected (the compliments themselves can be seen as reminders of the expected rarity of such behavior). One woman reported that when she is alone in a group of men and speaks at length on an issue, comments to her by men after the meeting often refer to her speech-making ability rather than to the content of what

---

[2] That is, seen as sexually desirable and potentially available. Seductress is a perception; the woman herself may not be consciously behaving seductively.

she said (e.g., "You talk so fluently"), whereas comments the men make to one another are almost invariably content or issue oriented.

Such attitudes on the part of men in a group encourage self-effacing girlish responses on the part of the solitary woman (who, after all, may be genuinely relieved to be included at all) and prevent her from realizing or demonstrating her own power and competence.

"Iron Maiden"

The "iron maiden" is a contemporary version of the stereotypical roles into which strong women are placed. A woman who fails to fall into any of the first three roles and, in fact, resists overtures that will trap her in a role (such as flirtation) may consequently be responded to as "tough" or dangerous. If she insists on full rights in the group, if she displays competence in a forthright manner, or if she cuts off sexual innuendoes, she may be asked, "You're not one of those women's libbers, are you?" Regardless of the answer, she may henceforth be regarded with suspicion, undue and exaggerated shows of politeness (by inserting references to women into conversations, by elaborate rituals of not opening doors), and distance— for she is demanding treatment as an equal in a setting in which no person of her kind has previously been an equal. Women who become trapped in the "iron maiden" role are often behaving in healthy, self-actualizing ways, but the male response may stereotype them as tougher than they are (hence the name I've provided) and may trap them into a more militant stance than they would personally prefer.

EVERYWOMAN: ALONE, COMPETING

I am speaking, of course, of *stereotypes* and deliberately caricaturing the patterns and their response. I see the notion of the four roles as "sensitizing concepts" that make sense out of much subtler real-life behavior. What all four ideal conceptions of the roles and their real-life manifestations have in common is that they serve to isolate the solitary woman—one of one, two, or three in a much larger group of men—from the mainstream of group interaction. They prevent her from demonstrating competences that contrast or conflict with the stereotypical role. Some of the roles, further, arouse resentment in the very male colleagues who, at the same time, might be promoting such stereotypical behavior. And finally, each of the roles engenders in the woman conflicts that can easily interfere with effective performance.

The token woman lacks other women with whom to generate a "counter-culture" to the male-dominated culture, a critical mass which could provide support and its own indicators of status. If status and power positions are the monopoly of men then the woman remains dependent on men for inclusion and for reward.

Further, to the extent that the presence of only a handful of women indicates that few places in the group are open to women, the solitary woman herself may have very ambivalent responses to other women, who represent a threat of replacement. Thus, a token woman may still feel that her fate and future rest on "making it" with the men. Her possible antagonistic response to the few other women present heightens the conflicts both in her and in them.

Finally, a woman seen as All Women (because of her aloneness) carries an extra burden of responsibility if she perceives that her performance in the group will help determine whether women can, in fact, be effective in the new positions opening to them. This cannot help but engender additional anxiety, not to mention the tendency to be too critical of her female colleagues.

MASS AND MODEL

The special problems of incorporating women into male-dominated groups are partly those of any very small minority interacting with a powerful majority, but they are also compounded by the sexual issue that can arise when the majority is male and the minority female. What are the possible solutions that would help ease the strains of such a situation and permit women to exercise their full competence unencumbered by stereotypes and role traps? A first step is to attempt to talk openly in a workgroup about sexual majority-minority problems. I call this a *partial* solution because I think some of the sexual questions involved are difficult to talk about and often only poorly understood by the participants themselves. Second, include female role models in powerful positions in or around each group. These women should have real status and in addition be capable of understanding the interactional dynamics in the group so that they can give the female participants feedback about how their behavior might contribute to the role traps. The third step is awareness on the part of male staff—awareness of their own reinforcement of female stereotypes (e.g., by adopting the "protector" role toward the solitary woman) and of how to confront the stereotyping process in group members. Fourth, end tokenism. Wherever possible, include a "critical mass" of females in every work or training group —more than two or three, and a large enough percentage that they can help reduce stereotyping, change the culture of the group, and offer support without threatening one another.

16. Conditions for Competence Acquisition and Therapy

CHRIS ARGYRIS

The acquisition of interpersonal competence and therapy are viewed as learning processes that differ in terms of several key dimensions. The former is especially relevant for those who are competence or growth oriented. Competence acquisition *requires psychological success, the giving and receiving of information that is directly verifiable, minimally evaluative, and minimally contradictory.* Therapy *is especially relevant to those who are survival or deficiency oriented. Such individuals may best be helped by indirectly verifiable knowledge, knowledge that is evaluative and can lead to psychological failure. Competence acquisition requires a group setting whose internal milieu is different from that of therapy.*

During the past several decades new reeducational activities have been and are being developed to help human beings increase their interpersonal competence. It is the thesis of this paper that these *interpersonal competence acquisition activities* will take on increasing importance in programs of positive mental health; that they will eventually become the main resources offered in a program of positive mental health; that they will be integrated with, but kept differentiated from, *therapeutic activities;* and that each will be offered under defined conditions. Indeed, even the practitioners will have to show that they manifest a certain minimum level of interpersonal competence.

In this paper I should like to present a theoretical framework that outlines the conditions under which interpersonal competence can be acquired. In order to give concreteness to the theoretical framework, I shall use laboratory education in general and T-Groups in particular as examples of competence acquisition activities (Argyris, 1962; Bradford, Gibb, & Benne, 1964; Schein & Bennis, 1965).

DEFINITION OF INTERPERSONAL COMPETENCE

The objective of competence acquisition is to provide individuals with opportunities to diagnose and increase their interpersonal competence.

Reproduced by special permission from *The Journal of Applied Behavioral Science,* Vol. 4, No. 2, "Conditions for Competence Acquisition and Therapy," Chris Argyris, pp. 147–177, 1968, NTL Institute for Applied Behavioral Science.

Invited paper for Association for Research in Nervous and Mental Diseases, December 1967, New York. The author is indebted to Drs. Seymour Sarason, Dan Levinson, Douglas Hall, and Edward Lawler for their helpful comments.

Interpersonal competence is the ability to cope effectively with interpersonal relationships. Three criteria of effective interpersonal coping are:

1. The individual perceives the interpersonal situation accurately. He is able to identify the relevant variables plus their interrelationships.
2. The individual is able to solve the problems in such a way that they remain solved. If, for example, interpersonal trust is low between A and B, they may not have been said to solve the problem competently unless and until it no longer recurs (assuming the problem is under control).
3. The solution is achieved in such a way that A and B are still able to work with each other at least as effectively as when they began to solve their problems.

TRANSFER OF LEARNING AS CRITERION OF COMPETENCE

The test of interpersonal competence therefore is not limited to insight and understanding. The individual's interpersonal competence is a function of his ability (and the ability of the others involved) to solve interpersonal problems. This criterion implies that to test the interpersonal competence developed in a learning situation, the individual(s) must show that the learning has transferred beyond the learning situation. The aim therefore is to change behavior and attitudes in such a way that observable changes can be found in solving interpersonal problems outside the learning situations. Transfer of learning is a central aspiration in competence acquisition.

ELEMENTS OF TRANSFER OF LEARNING

Providing the conditions for the maximum transfer of learning is extremely difficult in the interpersonal area. First, it takes much practice to develop interpersonal skills because they are complex, and much unfreezing is usually required. If the individual is to be internally committed to the new learning he must have come to the conclusion that his old modes of behavior are no longer effective, a conclusion that needs to be based on actual experiences in the learning situation in which he used his old modes of behavior and found them wanting.

Second, the individual must develop new modes of behavior that have also been tested and found more effective than the old. These new modes of behavior must have been practiced often enough so that the individual feels confident in his ability to use them.

Third, the individual must develop new modes of adjunct behavior that may be called for in the practice of his new modes of behavior. For example, if the individual learns to express his feelings of anger or love more openly, he may also have to develop new competence in dealing with individuals who are threatened by such openness. It is important, therefore, for the individual to learn how to express these feelings in such a way that he minimizes the probability that his behavior will cause someone else to become defensive, thereby creating a potentially threatening environment.

This suggests a fourth criterion: namely, the probability that A will behave in an interpersonally competent manner is not only a function of his own confidence in his abilities to do so; it is also a function of the others' confidence and willingness to behave in an interpersonally competent manner. For example, the writer's interpersonal competence scores have been found to vary immensely depending upon the situation in which he was placed. Quantitatively his scores have ranged from 150 to 390, where the lowest score obtained is 10 and the highest 390 (Argyris, 1965). Interpersonal competence, therefore, is an interpersonal or situational ability and not simply an individual or personal ability. This does not mean that each individual cannot learn skills that will help him behave more competently. It means that such skills are necessary but not sufficient.

Finally, the probability is very low that an individual can be taught everything he needs to know in order to behave competently in most of the situations in which he will find himself. The variance and complexity of life are too great to predict a situation adequately ahead of time. Therefore, *the most important requirement in obtaining transfer of learning is to generate, along with the knowledge of any specific behavior, the basic skills needed to diagnose new situations effectively and those needed to develop cooperation with others involved to generate the competent behavior appropriate to the situation.*

Experience and theory relevant to competence acquisition suggest that there are several key elements in the learning situation if these five requirements are to be fulfilled. The individuals must learn how to (*a*) communicate with one another in a manner that generates minimally distorted information, (*b*) give and receive feedback that is directly validatable and minimally evaluative, (*c*) perform these skills in such a way that self-acceptance and trust among individuals tend to increase, and (*d*) create effective groups in which problem solving may occur.

GENERATING MINIMALLY DISTORTED INFORMATION

It seems self-evident to state that the information needed for competent problem solving should not be distorted. Altering behavior on the basis of distorted feedback would tend to make the individuals distorted, which, in turn, would tend to increase the probability that future feedback would be given or received in a distorted manner.

Self-Awareness and Self-Acceptance. The minimum requirement that each individual must meet (if he is to provide minimally distorted information) is that he manifest a relatively high degree of *self-awareness* and *self-acceptance.* The more an individual is aware and accepting of those aspects of his self which are operating in a given situation, (*a*) the higher the probability that he will discuss them with minimal distortion, and (b) the higher the probability that he will listen with minimal distortion. For example, if A is aware and accepting of his predisposition to control others, he will tend to listen to the impact that he is having upon others without distorting what others are saying. Moreover, he will also tend to provide another controlling individual with feedback that is minimally distorted by his own similar problem in that area.

How is the individual to increase his self-awareness and self-acceptance? By receiving minimally distorted feedback from others about his impact upon them and their willingness to be accepting and understanding of his behavior, even though *he* may not be. Thus we have what is known as inter-personal bind. Helpful feedback depends partially upon self-awareness and self-acceptance; yet these two factors depend upon helpful feedback!

How is this circular process broken into? This is a key task of the educator. Presumably he has a higher degree (relatively speaking) of self-awareness and self-acceptance against which the individuals can interact. His bind is that if he is not careful he can easily become the focus of attention. Everyone will tend to turn to him for valid information; and this dependency could lead to awareness but hardly to confidence, on the part of the learners, that they can create their own conditions for self-awareness and self-acceptance. The educator strives to create conditions under which the learners will turn to one another as resources. In so doing the educator makes two important assumptions about each individual. Each is assumed to have a constructive intent. Each is capable of learning from others, *if* he receives the kind of information that is helpful and *if* the proper group atmosphere is developed.

Acceptance and Trust of Others. One of the major initial tasks of the educator is to create conditions under which the learners can become aware of and test the validity of these two assumptions. If these two assumptions are not validated for each individual in the learning situation, the processes of competence acquisition will not be highly effective. This test is very difficult to make during the early stages because most of the learners are expecting the educator to control their learning, to tell them what to do, to provide them with agendas, and so on. If he behaves in any other way, he may easily be perceived as hostile, noncaring, or ineffective.

The withdrawal of the expected directive leadership, agenda, and status at the beginning of a T-Group experience is a strategy of the staff member to emphasize that he really means to help the participants come to trust in one another's intentions to be constructive, in their capabilities to learn, and to develop an effective group. The point is made forcefully at the outset, not because the educator enjoys the drama of his apparent withdrawal and the resulting social weightlessness, but because he has learned that such behavior on his part is so strange that individuals do not tend to believe him unless he behaves in this way with purpose and thrust. The educator strives not to be seduced from this stance by individuals who accuse him of being perplexing, cruel, and or ineffective. His major response during this period is, in effect, "I can understand that you may feel that if I have any concern for you I will help you out of this predicament. But may I point out again that I am assuming that a deeper predicament is to learn to rely on all of our strengths and not to become focused primarily on me."

As soon as the learners realize that the educator means what he says, they usually turn to one another for help "to get the group moving." Those who begin to take the lead also expose their behavior, which becomes the basis for learning because it provides material to be diagnosed and discussed. Thus Mr. A may dislike the initial social weightlessness and may appoint himself as chairman. He may, somewhat demandingly, begin to define an agenda. The educator may eventually use this here-and-now situation to help the members explore their feelings about Mr. A. This could lead Mr. A to realize the impact he has had on others. It could also help the others to explore their different reactions to Mr. A (some welcome his behavior and some dislike it), as well as their feelings about beginning to be open. Another task would be for the members to explore the group process. For example, how was the decision made to develop an agenda? Did Mr. A check to see whether he had the commitment of the members? What happens to decisions made uni-laterally?

The point is that no matter which approach is taken in the group the educator used the here-and-now to maximize members' feelings of respon-sibility for their learning. It is primarily *their* behavior that they explore. It is *their* behavior that defines the goal. It is *their* responsibility to choose whether they will learn from the situation and, if so, how, and how much. To be sure, early in the history of this type of learning, some people resent the fact that the educator does not prevent them from going in what he "knows" will be an ineffective direction. However, as the members see the importance of being self-responsible, as they feel the internal confidence that is developed from experiencing self-responsibility, as they come to trust others in the group, they become much more understanding of the educator's strategy not to interfere. Indeed, by the end of the first week, it is not uncommon for group members to caution an educator against too early intervention on his part to "pull them out of a difficulty." They have come to trust their capacity to do this "on their own" and to value the intrinsic satis-faction that goes along with such learning. Moreover, they may also have begun to learn how it is possible for them, in another situation, to "withdraw" in order to help others help themselves.

Conditions for Psychological Success. The word "withdrawal" is placed in quotation marks because it is not true that the educator withdraws in the sense of becoming uninvolved or being nondirective. The withdrawal from the expected leadership style is purposive action. The educator is deeply involved in creating the kind of environment which, if the learners decide to enter, will lead to important learning. What is that environment? The answer to this question identifies one of the underlying characteristics of competence acquisition mentioned at the outset. *No matter what is being learned substantively, it should be learned in such a way that it is accomplished by feelings of psychological success and confidence in self and others, and in the group.*

The educator manipulates the environment (*never* the people) so that the individuals, if they decide to enter the environment, are offered frequent opportunities to—

1. define their own learning goal,
2. develop their paths to the goal,
3. relate the goal and the paths to their central needs, and
4. experience a challenge in achieving the goal that stretches their present level of abilities (Lewin, Dembo, Festinger, & Sears, 1944).

The educator is actively striving to create the learning conditions which will lead participants to an increase in trust and confidence in themselves and in their group. As the trust of self, of others, and of group increases, the probability of giving and receiving valid information increases; and so does the probability of self-awareness and self-acceptance, which in turn increases the predisposition for more experiences of psychological success.

GIVING AND RECEIVING HELPFUL INFORMATION

Feedback may be undistorted but not very helpful in creating behavioral change, self-acceptance, and an effective group. In order for information to be most helpful it should be directly verifiable and minimally evaluative.

Directly Verifiable Information. It is important to distinguish between information that can be verified directly by self and others versus information that can be validated by reference to some conceptual scheme. The first type of feedback includes categories of behavior that are directly *observable*,[1] the second utilizes categories that are inferred. The more the information used in the learning situations is composed of *inferred* categories that refer to a conceptual scheme, the greater the dependence of the individuals upon the conceptual scheme if they are to verify the information that they are using. If, for example, the conceptual scheme is a clinical framework, then the individuals must turn to the educator for help because he knows the scheme. (Indeed, is not a great part of therapy learning the conceptual scheme of the therapist?) This dependence *decreases* the *probability* of experiencing psy-

---

[1] I am indebted to Dr. Alvan R. Feinstein (Yale Medical School) for clarifying this distinction and recommend to the reader his book, *Clinical Judgment* (Baltimore, Md.: Williams & Wilkins, 1967).

chological success and trust in others and in the group because the key to success, trust and effectiveness lies in knowing the conceptual scheme, which is in the mind of the therapist. For example, if B learns from the therapist that his hostility is probably an attempt to deal with authority figures and that the transference phenomenon is actively present, he will be unable to verify these inferences unless he learns the conceptual scheme used by the therapist. Moreover, even if he learns the scheme, B will soon find that he is using inferred categories for which relatively unambiguous tests are not available. He is being diagnosed, "interpreted," and advised with the use of concepts that he understands vaguely and which have minimal operational actions to test their validity. He may indeed come to feel that the very process of testing the therapist's inference could be interpreted as resistance.

Information, therefore, should be as far as possible directly verifiable. However, to generate information that is directly verifiable by nonprofessionals as well as by professionals requires that it remain as close as possible to observable data. For example, B learns that when he behaves in X manner (asks questions, evaluates others), A feels attacked. B can then turn to other members of the group and ask whether they see him behaving in X manner and, if so, whether they also feel attacked. He may learn that some see him behaving in X manner and some see him behaving in Y manner; he may learn that some feel attacked and some do not. Finally, he may learn that of those who do *not* feel attacked, several feel this way because X type of behavior is not threatening to them. Others may find Y type of behavior threatening.

One of the crucial learnings that B obtains is that his behavior is rarely perceived in a unitary fashion and that its impact varies widely. He may then ask the members to describe what kind of behavior they would not have found threatening. This information may lead B to alter his behavior. It may also lead him to decide to behave in X or Y manner but, the next time, to show awareness that his behavior is having a differential impact.

In the section preceding we distinguished two kinds of inferred categories: one that was related to a formal-theoretical framework (he is projecting; she is ambivalent) and the other that was related to the personal values of the individual (he is nice; she is sweet). There is a third way that formal or personal theory may be used to verify the information that is given. There are many writers who are beginning to stress the use of more directly observable categories. For example, the therapist may say to the client, "I think you are kidding yourself." "It sounds as if you would like to kill that individual, you are so angry." The function of such *attributive* interventions is to attribute something to the person, which the therapist infers exists, about which the client is more or less unaware. Such an intervention may use relatively observable categories but they are based upon a theoretical framework. Thus, if the patient asks, "Why do you say I am kidding?" he may receive a reply, "Because you are denying such and such." Or, if he asks, "Why do you think I want to kill so and so?" he may be told, "You sounded very angry and I felt that you were afraid to say what you truly felt." It now becomes apparent that the former intervention was based upon the concept of denial; the latter, on a concept of some category of psychological blockage.

Any intervention that attributes something to the client that he has not already mentioned (in some directly verifiable form) is based upon the therapist's inferences about the inner states of the client. Such an intervention is also of the inferred variety even though it may initially be placed in the language of observed categories.

Telling the client what may be "inside" himself that is "causing" his problems, even if *correct,* will tend to lead to psychological failure because the client, if he is to be rational and self-responsible, must assign the primary responsibility for the insight to the therapist who guessed correctly what was "in" the client. If the therapist, however, intervenes and reveals the raw data from which he inferred that the client is unaware (kidding himself) or is not expressing openly that he may want to kill someone, then the client is able to judge for himself the possible validity of the influence attributed to his behavior.

This comment should emphasize that the meaning of here-and-now in competence acquisition is significantly different from the meaning of here-and-now in many psychotherapeutic activities. Some psychotherapists tend to use the here-and-now to help the client discover the unconscious structure active in the present but created in the past. Others use here-and-now to help the client see that he uses the relationship to involve the therapist as a more or less unconscious object. Finally, others (Ezriel, 1952) use the here-and-now data to generate enough evidence to make an interpretation to the patient. He may be projecting, they say, or he may be identifying with such and such a person, and so on.

In all these examples the here-and-now data are used to help the professional generate interpretations that go far beyond the directly verifiable observed category. This point cannot be made too strongly. To date, the overwhelming number of psychotherapists' works read by the author has led him to the conclusion that, unlike his emphasis on observed categories, therapists use interpretations of the here-and-now variety which are composed of *inferred* categories.[2]

Minimally Evaluative Feedback. The second major characteristic of helpful information is that it be minimally evaluative of the recipient's behavior. There are two reasons for this requirement. First, such information reduces the probability of making the receiver defensive, thereby creating

---

[2] William Glasser may be closer to this view, but he gives examples in terms of there-and-then in his *Reality Therapy* (New York: Harper & Row, 1965), pp. 75 ff.

conditions favorable to an increase in accurate listening. Thus laboratory education does not value the communication of all information. It values that openness which will help the individuals receiving feedback to learn. Second, minimally evaluative information describes how the receiver feels about the sender's messages without describing them as "good" or "bad." This places the responsibility for evaluation, if there is to be any, on the individual trying to learn about himself. He, and only he, has the responsibility of deciding whether he plans to change his behavior. Again, placing the responsibility on the individual increases the probability that if he changes, since it is his decision, he will tend to experience a sense of psychological success.

Requiring minimally evaluative feedback does not mean that evaluation is harmful. Evaluation of behavior and effectiveness is necessary and essential. The point is that one ought, as far as possible, to create conditions under which the individual makes his own evaluation and then asks for confirmation or disconfirmation. If the individual first makes his own evaluation, then even if it is negative, a confirmation by others of its negative quality can lead to growth and inner confidence in one's capacity for correct self-evaluation (Argyris, 1962, pp. 140–143).

What this implies is that an individual should take the initiative in seeking confirmation and should "own up" with his evaluations before others do so. "Going first," if it is to be successful, requires that several conditions be met. The individual should be unconflicted and accepting about his evaluation of himself. If he is not, others will sense it and may tend to withhold their true feelings. This tendency to withhold, in turn, will be a function of their view of the individual's readiness or capability to receive accurately and use effectively the evaluative comments that he is requesting. Thus, "going first" requires less courage and more competence, so that the individual has created, by his behavior, the conditions under which others would trust him to use their evaluative feedback competently.

Minimally Contradictory Messages. A third major characteristic of helpful information is that its meaning be unconflicted or consistent. Information that contains contradictory messages will tend to decrease the effectiveness of interpersonal relations. This point was illustrated by Bateson and Reusch (Bateson, Jackson, Haley & Weakland, 1956) in their concept of the double bind. When A says to B, "I love you, but get lost," B will receive two contradictory messages which place him in a bind. Does A love me, or is he lying? Is love associated with distance? How will I judge which part of A's message is valid? In the extreme case, a high frequency of double binds may contribute to neurotic or psychotic behavior, because man's basic need is to be competent and he therefore abhors situations of imbalance. As Brown (1962) concludes ". . . human nature abhors imbalance. . . . A situation of imbalance is one that calls for mutually incompatible actions . . . Imbalance in the mind threatens to paralyze actions" (pp. 77–78).

The acquisition of interpersonal competence requires that the individual learn to minimize the contradictory messages that he intentionally or unintentionally communicates to others. The contradiction or imbalance can exist between (a) words and feelings, (b) words and feelings versus behavior, and (c) verbal versus nonverbal behavior. For example, A may say, "I do not feel rejected," yet say it with a cracking voice or emphasized so strongly that the receiver may infer that A is hurt and does feel rejected. Or A may say that he likes B or wants to work with B, yet he does not make or take opportunities to establish working relationships. When A asks B, "Do you *really* mean to say that you are not angry?" his message may be received as being open for information about, yet also disbelieving, B.

The area of nonverbal behavior is especially important in competence acquisition. Individuals tend to be unaware of the messages that they communicate to others by their facial expressions, body positions, and body tenseness. If these are viewed as being beyond the control of the sender, the receiver may place a heavy reliance on them, especially when the trust in the relationship is low. (Since I do not trust him, I will trust that behavior over which he has least control.) These nonverbal cues are used in such a way that the receiver will not tend to confront the sender with the knowledge that he is transmitting contradictory messages. The receiver may then hide his true assessment of the relationship with the sender by withdrawing or by responding with a contradictory message. The latter action will create a bind; the former may also create a bind, especially if there is an overt message indicating that "all is fine."

If the receiver attempts to confront the sender with the bind which his messages are creating for him (the receiver) and if the sender is either unaware of or defensive about his nonverbal behavior, then the sender will tend to deny or question the validity of the receiver's inferences. The defensive reaction will, in turn, either confirm the receiver's view of the sender's defensiveness or (if the reaction is interpreted as valid) will make the receiver question himself (Why am I distorting the sender's messages?) when, in fact, his question was valid. If the receiver is in some kind of power or authority relationship that obviates his questioning the sender, then the receiver could eventually come to mistrust himself and/or the sender.

THE EFFECTIVE GROUP AND ITS USE FOR
INDIVIDUAL CHANGE

A careful analysis of the activities described above will suggest that competence acquisition requires the development of effective groups. For example, the individual requires minimally distorted and immediately validatable feedback. If he is to understand his impact upon others then he needs to receive valid information from others. In order to obtain valid information, the others should be minimally defensive. Assuming that the selection process has eliminated those who are so defensive that they cannot learn from others (see next section), then the major source for defensiveness becomes the group. If the members cannot decide on a sequence of topics acceptable to all—who will receive the first feedback—or if they are unable to judge the constructive intent of the members, then their problem solving could become so ineffective that they would become frustrated and angry with one another. Under these conditions, minimally distorted, immediately verifiable information will rarely be generated. *Although competence acquisition focuses on helping individuals become more interpersonally competent, the very nature of personality (its incompleteness without others, the need for consensual validation, and so on) makes an effective group central to the learning processes.*

This conclusion leads naturally to two questions. What is an effective group? How can one utilize an effective group to facilitate individual growth?

Beginning with the first question, there are four major dimensions of group effectiveness:

1. The members focus on defining group goals that "satisfy" the needs and utilize the important abilities of the individual members. Adequate time is spent to make certain that the goals represent a challenge to the group as well as to the individuals and that the members are internally committed to the achievement of the goals.
2. Attention is paid, whenever it is necessary, to the group processes. For example, are the members' contributions additive? Do the members focus on the history of the group in order to learn from its successes and failures, from its internal conflicts, from its problem solving? Are the members owning up to their ideas and feelings? Are they open to new ideas and feelings? Are they experimenting and taking risks?
3. Norms are generated that reward the individuality of each member, that show respect and concern for the members' ideas and feelings, that facilitate and maintain a sense of trust.
4. Leadership is shared so that each member is leading the group when his skills are the most pertinent to the achievement of the group goals.

The next question is: How may an effective group be used as a medium for individual behavioral change? Cartwright (1951), on the basis of a review of the literature, suggests several conditions under which a group may be a more effective medium for change. There needs to be a strong sense of belonging to the same group, including a *reduction* of the normal gap between teacher and student, doctor and patient, et cetera, so that the faculty and students feel as members of one group in matters involving their growth. This means that the staff member must strive to become a member of the group without giving up his expertise. This is a difficult task because, as we have seen, so many of the members come to the group with different expectations. As was pointed out above, the staff member strives to develop membership by withdrawing initially and dramatically creating a situation in which the members must turn to one another as resource people. As their trust and confidence in themselves and in their group increases, their need to see the staff member as a godlike, distant figure decreases.

A second way to earn genuine membership was also described above. The staff member makes as many of his contributions as possible at the level of observed categories, with minimal distortion, and focused on how he sees the world (and not what is "in" others or what "the" group is doing). Every one of his contributions is then subject to verification by the other members. As all the other members learn how to use both of these strategies effectively, they will begin to feel closer to one another, including the staff member. Indeed, one of the crucial ways in which a staff member earns his membership is by making several interventions which are not verifiable or are found to be in error. This helps the group come gradually to realize that he is not infallible and that the staff member needs *them* to check his own effectiveness.

As the members begin to trust themselves and one another, as their group functioning becomes more effective, the group becomes more attractive to each member. As the group becomes more attractive it meets the second condition defined by Cartwright. The more attractive the group is to its members, the greater is the influence that the group can exert on its members.

Cartwright (1951) also suggests a third condition: namely, that a strong pressure for change in the group can be established by creating shared perceptions by the members of the need for change. Again, examples of how a staff member creates opportunities for these pressures to develop were described in the previous section. If, at the outset, the staff member creates an opportunity for the members to "take over"; yet if, in the process, they exhibit interpersonally incompetent behavior, it will lead to their becoming frustrated. If they feel a need to be competent and their intent is constructive, then these experiences will become a major source of shared perception of the need for their change.

If the staff member follows the strategy of helping the members develop their own plans, define their own learning goals, generate their own level of aspiration (psychological success), then we have created the fourth condition mentioned by Cartwright. Information relating to the need for change, plans for change, and consequences of change must be shared by all relevant people in the group.

We conclude, therefore, that individual learning cannot be separated from group effectiveness, and (happily) the conditions required for each are overlapping but highly consonant. This suggests that the arguments for individual versus group learning may be off the mark. Moreover, it may not make much sense to plan a learning experience that focuses on only one level of learning. Both levels of learning must be experienced to some degree of effectiveness if learning is to occur at either level. One may wish to *begin* at the group or at the individual level; but if a whole learning experience is to be developed, the interdependencies of each type on the other must be brought out and mastered. This is especially relevant to transfer of learning. When an individual finds himself in a situation outside the learning context, the other members of that situation will not focus on individual or group phenomena simply because this one individual learned to do so in his laboratory. Under these conditions the individual may feel frustrated and experience a greater sense of failure than the members who had never attended a laboratory, since their level of aspiration, related to their interpersonal competence, may be realistically lower than his.

Another implication is that the learning experience should last long enough and be designed in such a way that the learners can be exposed to "pairs" of interpersonal and group phenomena. Moreover, one may predict that if the staff chooses to ignore the individual or the group phenomena during the learning experiences, the learners will have to make up the deficiency in their own informal way. For example, a recent delegation to a Leicester-Tavistock conference reported that they spent many off-hours discussing their learning about interpersonal competence and about the usefulness of the experience: two topics never scheduled formally (and rarely informally) by the faculty. A group experience recently conducted by the writer, which did not concentrate on group phenomena during the formal sessions, led many members to spend many of their informal hours focusing on that subject.

COMPETENCE AND SURVIVAL ORIENTATION LEAD TO DIFFERENT SYSTEMS

At the beginning of this paper two conditions of competence acquisition were defined. The assumptions are that the individuals have (*a*) a constructive intent and (*b*) a genuine desire to learn, to become interpersonally more competent. It was noted that the lower the constructive intent to learn, to a lesser degree the conditions of competence acquisition apply. Why would individuals have different degrees of willingness to learn?

A detailed discussion of this question would lead beyond the main thrust of this paper. However, a brief note is necessary in order to build the position. Individuals can be described as predisposed or oriented toward increasing their competence or toward protecting themselves in order to survive. Maslow (1954) describes the former as growth motivation, the latter as deficiency motivation. The more the individual is competence oriented, the more he will tend to focus on those activities that enlarge his self and increase his self-acceptance and confidence. The individual becomes more of an *open* system. In the area of interpersonal relations, the activities involved in the growth and acceptance of self may be conceptualized as the seeking of a sense of interpersonal competence (White, 1959).

Developing a sense of interpersonal competence is intrinsically satisfying; it provides much of the motivation for growth and learning in interpersonal relationships. However, the individual will tend to be free to focus on competence acquisition only to the extent that he feels his survival problems are resolved (i.e., they do not control his present behavior). Thus human beings "graduate" into, and (once having done so) strive to maintain, competence acquisition orientation. They will return to survival orientation only when they experience threat. A survival orientation is primarily one of the protection of the self. The individual, through the use of defense mechanisms, withdraws, distorts, or attacks the environment. In all cases the end result is to reduce the probability that the individual will learn from the environment. This, in turn, begins to make the individual more closed and less subject to influence. The more closed the individual becomes, the more his adaptive reactions will be controlled by his internal system. But since his internal system is composed of many defense mechanisms, the behavior will not tend to be functional or economical. The behavior may eventually become compulsive, repetitive, inwardly stimulated, and observably dysfunctional. The individual becomes more of a *closed* system. The greater the proportion of the individual's behavior that falls into this category (closed), the more he approximates the conditions that Kurie (1961) has described as neurotic behavior.

It is important to emphasize that individuals are *not* being viewed as being *either* closed *or* open. People are not totally open or closed. Nor is all openness effective and all closedness ineffective. An individual may be quite open to learning about his authority relationships but not in his capacity to create mistrust. Another individual may be open to learning more about how to express his feelings and suddenly become closed when he realizes he has reached the point beyond which further expression of feelings could lead to an uncontrollable state. He prefers to postpone further expression of feelings until he has learned to manage the new feelings that he has already expressed.

The important point, from a theory of learning, is that the educator and the client need to be able to differentiate between that learning which evolves around problems and issues about which the individual is more or less open or closed. Each state of affairs requires different interventions by which to encourage learning. Thus, as we shall see in a moment, it may be necessary to use inferred evaluative interventions under certain conditions if the individual is to gain insight and unfreeze. However, if one is to go beyond insight and unfreezing, then one will have to utilize competence-oriented learning conditions. These learning conditions may be inhibited if mixed with too strong a component of interventions designed to unfreeze closed (survival-oriented) behavior. The problem is *not* that it may be difficult for the educator to cope: he may be quite competent to shift from one level of intervention to another. The problem is within the group. Until the members become much more competent they will find the mixture confusing. One of the basic reasons is that interventions designed to unfreeze closed behavior tend not to create conditions for psychological success, directly verifiable information, minimally evaluative feedback, and effective group functioning. The members will feel challenged enough to learn how to be competent in terms of these conditions. Moreover, they will feel the pressure stemming from the reality that their learning experience is limited in time.

The Closed System as Response to Threat. If the situation in which the individual is placed is confirmed as threatening, then closedness may be a functional response. Individuals may become more closed for social reasons. Empirical evidence has been presented (Argyris, 1962, 1965, 1966) that there seems to be a general tendency for people to create social systems that are closed and reward survival orientation. It is therefore possible for the individual to behave in a closed manner because it makes sense; it is functional in a closed system. This type of closedness we shall call *external* to indicate that it comes primarily from the social system. An individual who is closed for external reasons has not internalized the systemic values to such a point that he cannot differentiate closedness from openness. He is able to go back and forth from more open to more closed behavior depending upon the situation. In a T-Group, for example, an externally closed individual will resist openness initially until he can assure himself that the T-Group is truly an open system. The individual whose survival orientation stems from personal reasons may be called *internally* closed. This individual is unable to become open even when he is provided with a situation in which openness is relevant and functional. He has generalized that the world is threatening far beyond the situation where threats have existed or do exist.

VARIATIONS OF CLOSEDNESS

A threat could produce momentary closedness if it is of short duration, or it could produce long-lasting closedness if it is present over an extended period of time.

The degree of closedness will tend to vary on the basis of whether the source of threat is related to inner, peripheral, or central aspects of the self. Peripheral aspects are those that have a low potency for the individual, while inner aspects tend to have a high potency. We assume that one must pass through the peripheral in order to arrive at the inner aspects of the personality. The central aspects can be peripheral or inner. The key differentiating property is that change in a central part will tend to create changes in the surrounding parts, be they inner or peripheral.

Whether or not the source of the threat is from within or from without determines the problems an individual faces in dealing with threat. When the threat emanates from within, an individual faces problems different from those faced when the threat comes from the external environment.

Finally, the degree of control the system is able to manifest (in our case, individuals) over the threat determines the degree of closedness. The less control he has over the threat, the greater is the probability that the individual will become closed. Closedness will also increase as the potency of the parts involved increases and as the duration of the threat increases.

It should be clear, therefore, that it is a gross oversimplification to think of open and closed individuals. What is more likely is that individuals are more or less closed or open, both in degree and in time. The more an individual seeks the processes of competence acquisition, the more open he may be said to be. The more an individual resists these processes, the more closed he may be said to be. *The point to be emphasized is the hypothesis that the more open an individual can be, the more he can learn from competence acquisition activities; the more closed, the more he may need therapy, at least as the initial step toward competence acquisition.*

To summarize, the probability of learning to behave more competently *and* to transfer this learning beyond the learning situation increases—

1. as the *client's* self-awareness and self-acceptance increase, as his acceptance and trust of others increase and

2. as the *educator* is able to create, in the learning situation, conditions of
   a. psychological success
   b. directly verifiable information
   c. minimally evaluative feedback
   d. effective group functioning (group goals are congruent with member needs, attention to group processes, norms of individuality, concern, trust, and shared leadership).

3. *These conditions for effective learning* feed back to help increase and strengthen the individual's self-awareness and self-acceptance and his acceptance and trust of others; which, in turn, increases the probability that

4. the *members* will take increasing responsibility and manifest greater competence in creating conditions of effective learning, which will further

5. provide the *members* and *educator* opportunity to practice and deepen their competence as well as their confidence in creating the conditions elsewhere.

Some readers may wonder whether we are suggesting that feelings of pain, fear, and self-accusation should not occur in the learning session. Is this learning experience one that emphasizes "sweetness and light"? To reply briefly: Anyone who has experienced, either as an educator or a member, the difficulty in creating conditions for effective learning, the embarrassment of realizing how incompetent one can be, the blindness to one's own impact upon others, or the capacity to unintentionally prevent the reception of valid feedback can testify to the existence of feelings of pain, fear, and confrontation of reality.

A second and more important point is that the strategy presented in this paper suggests that the educator should not focus directly on creating such feelings as pain or fear or other. He should focus as much as possible on creating the conditions described above. If, while he does this, fear, pain, anguish, or frustration occurs (and they will occur), he helps the members to express these feelings and to understand the basis of such fears. Past experience suggests two important causes of these feelings: (a) the awareness of one's blindness to (b) the degree of one's interpersonal incompetence. The awareness of such conditions provides internal motivation for further work on increasing one's interpersonal competence.

THERAPY

To give therapy means more than to change behavior. The word "therapy," according to the dictionary, means "to cure"; to cure means to restore to a healthy condition. In terms of this model, an unhealthy individual exists, or unhealthy aspects of an individual exist, when he has become primarily a closed system and when there seem to be no validatable reasons, in the present, for his closed orientation. An individual may need therapy when he is unable to marshal internal or external resources in order to become aware of the relevant factors causing his problems, solve them in such a way that they remain solved, and accomplish these two states without reducing the present level of problem-solving effectiveness (within himself or between himself and others).

The behavior of the closed individual tends to be focused on survival rather than on learning, it is repetitive and compulsive rather than adaptive and functional, and it tends to be adhered to either with a very weak or very strong sense of responsibility.

The individual who has had to survive by becoming relatively closed may have difficulty in focusing on his here-and-now behavior or in learning from exploring the impact of his behavior upon others. Since he is defensive he will not tend to give competent feedback or be able to receive with minimal distortion feedback that is helpful. Indeed, the relatively closed individual will tend to seek feedback that confirms the rationality of his having to be closed. Finally, if his self-confidence and trust are low, then he will tend to be unable to set realistic reeducation goals. He will tend to focus either on skin-surfaced, phenotypic changes or he may strive to change behavior that is difficult to change easily. In the former case his level of aspiration will be low; in the second case it would be too high. In both cases, the result will be psychological failure.

A relatively closed individual may, if left to his own devices, generate those kinds of learning experiences that will tend to make him even more closed. He may also frustrate members who are less closed and capable of learning but who do not know how to deal with him effectively. The more closed the individual is, the more he may require learning experiences which are controlled, guided, and interpreted by the therapist. If a person is closed to learning, then he needs someone to begin this learning for him and to use techniques which will help him see connections that hitherto he was unable to see.

One can see how the therapists have developed such techniques as free association, dream analysis, and analysis of slips of the tongue. If one is dealing with a relatively closed system, he may need to utilize devices to diagnose what is behind the wall of psychological defenses that keep the individual from behaving more competently. One can also understand the need for interventions in which the therapist is interpreting in order to tell the client what is probably causing his problem. Interpretations that suggest to the person hypotheses about himself that he is not aware of are, therefore, one of the major skills of a therapist. Moreover, there is the possibility that a person who is sick, in despair and internal panic, may find interpretations that seem to try to understand his problems and show concern on the part of the therapist very supportive. At the outset, the process of making interpretations may be helpful even if the interpretations are neither testable nor even correct, because they may represent a concrete sign of someone reaching out. I doubt whether descriptive, immediately verifiable feedback would, during the early stages, be seen as supportive.

However, according to our model, the more a therapist successfully interprets for the individual, the more he is responsible for the hunches and interventions that lead to insight for the client, the more the client will learn about himself under conditions of psychological failure and minimal essentiality. If it is the therapist who helps to define the problems and their explanations, then the patient must attribute the success of his therapy to the therapist.

The more closed an individual is—the more compulsive his behavior—the lower the sense of interpersonal competence will tend to be. The lower his interpersonal competence, the lower will be his problem-solving effectiveness. Under these conditions, the individual may develop a lack of confidence in himself and a perception that the environment is primarily a hostile one. This, in turn, may cause the individual to withdraw, to become even a more closed system.

ON THE IMPORTANCE OF HISTORY

The more closed the individual the less effective he will tend to be in his problem solving and the less confidence he will tend to have in himself. Once this state of affairs has continued for any length of time, not only will the individual tend to perceive himself to be highly incompetent but he may also have come to believe that he is beyond reach in terms of becoming a learning or open system and generating a competence orientation. The conclusion that one is not able to learn is deeply threatening. It implies a lack of credibility and trust of self.

Under these conditions, the individual needs help to learn exactly how he developed himself into a closed system, so that he can ascertain whether it is possible for him to become a more open learning-oriented system. It is at this point that exploration of personal history may become especially important. Unless the individual can rationalize his having begun the processes that have led to his closedness, he will tend to mistrust himself deeply, because he will see himself previously moved and possibly still influenced by factors beyond his control. Under these circumstances the exploration of his past can be very important. If he can discover the initial conditions that led him to choose a survival orientation, he can begin to feel that he is, or can be, a rational human being with potential for effective problem solving. This kind of reeducation requires the exploration of defense mechanisms, since it has been primarily through the use of defense mechanisms that the individual has made of himself a closed system.

Insight into one's historical experiences will not, of itself, lead to increased competence in behavior. Competence acquisition requires a different set of conditions. Historical explorations are *necessary* for individuals who are primarily closed systems, but they are not *sufficient* to cause the individual to become more competent.

For the person who is closed, we should also keep in mind that the less acceptable he is to himself, the more it may be necessary to place him in a situation in which the therapist is free to hypothesize openly what may be "in" the individual that is keeping him closed. Understanding the therapist and patient relationship in terms of transference and counter-transference, seeking data under free association (a process which the therapist hopes will give him insight into the wall of defenses making the individual closed), interpreting behavior in terms of symbols used (straight objects representing the male and round objects the female), exploring dreams and slips of the tongue—all these become essential instruments of exploration when the therapist evaluates the individual as "out of touch" with the valid causes of his problems and therefore unable to solve them.

Historically oriented, dynamically based therapy makes three very important assumptions about the patient which influence the nature of the therapeutic process. 1. The individual is so closed that he cannot learn very much about his problem by focusing on his here-and-now behavior. Indeed, his here-and-now behavior may be a facade hiding the underlying problems. 2. The individual probably became closed as a result of threatening experiences in his early life. He has managed to lose awareness of these experiences in order to live with himself as a relatively competent individual. 3. Conditions 1 and 2 make the individual a poor risk in providing help to others. In short, the therapist and the patient (rightly) mistrust the patient's capacity to portray himself accurately; and yet the therapist, and perhaps the patient, assumes that the individual can be helped to do so.

SOME CRITERIA IN SELECTING THERAPY OR COMPETENCE ACQUISITION

Does this imply that an individual skilled in competence acquisition should never attempt to help clients who are very closed? On the contrary, the professional should always be as aware as possible of the limitations and strengths of competence acquisition and therapy. He should strive to develop as many data as he can on the level of closedness of the client.

One way to develop these data is to create the environment that permits and encourages the experience of psychological success and to note the individual's reaction. If his reaction is one of increasing fright and withdrawal, then one may begin to wonder whether the individual is not more closed than open, at least in terms of the problems he is trying to solve. The educator may use these criteria to judge the degree of openness or closedness of the individual.

1. He can surface a genuine dilemma the individual (or group) is facing. If the individual does not feel some sense of imbalance, even some slight motive for the resolution of the dilemma, then he may be more closed than open.
2. Another criterion is to feed back any inconsistencies and gaps in the individual's behavior and obtain his reaction. If he confirms that they are inconsistencies and gaps but experiences little need to correct an inconsistency or close a gap, then the individual may be more closed than open. If the individual denies the existence of the inconsistency or gap, then he is still potentially open because new data could be generated to determine whether the educator or the individual is correct.
3. To the extent that competence-oriented feedback is given and it is experienced as threatening, the individual may be more closed than open. Also, if survival-oriented feedback is given and the individual accepts or values it, he may be more closed than open.

HELPFUL AND HARMFUL FEEDBACK

The definition of competence-oriented feedback is information that is (a) minimally distorted, (b) directly verifiable, and (c) minimally evaluative. Survival-oriented feedback is information that is (a) interpretive and based

Intervention or Feedback	Open	Closed (Externally)	Closed (Internally)
Competence Oriented	Helpful	Helpful but will be resisted initially	Not helpful
Survival Oriented	Not helpful	Could be helpful in terms of awareness, not in terms of effective behavior	Could be helpful in terms of awareness, not in terms of effective behavior

Figure 4.1. Feedback: Types and Effects on Individuals

on inferred categories, (b) evaluative, and (c) contributory to insight with psychological failure.

This criterion implies that competence-oriented feedback may or may not be viewed as helpful. Competence-oriented feedback will probably be viewed as helpful by individuals or groups who are more open than closed. Survival-oriented feedback with a system that is largely open will probably not help; but it will probably not be harmful, as long as it is not continued. An overload of survival-oriented feedback to an individual who is competence oriented could lead to his becoming confused, feeling less competent, and ultimately losing confidence in himself, because he is accustomed to dealing with observed categories that are directly verifiable. To the extent that the therapist uses inferred categories that are not verifiable (and insists that this is the way to help the client), the client's foundations for interpersonal competence may be shaken.

Another condition potentially harmful is exposing the client to both survival- and competence-oriented information without clearly differentiating between types and telling him why this is being done. If the professional insists that both of these kinds of information are part of the same process of knowing oneself and verifying one's perceptions, he could place the relatively rational client in difficulty because the client realizes that this is not the case.

Survival-oriented feedback will probably be resisted initially by an individual (system) who is externally closed. Once the individual realizes that he is in a situation in which openness is functional, he will find competence-oriented feedback helpful. This is the situation that is most typical of T-Groups composed of individuals who have never been in such learning situations before. Survival-oriented feedback (interpretation, evaluative feedback, intervention under conditions of psychological failure) may be helpful, at best, in providing to the individual an awareness of his problem. The awareness or the resolution (if there is one) of the problem will not tend to generalize beyond the learning situation.

Finally, competence-oriented feedback will not tend to be helpful to an individual (system) that is internally closed. The individual is so closed that minimally evaluative, here-and-now intervention will probably not penetrate his defense structure. It is under these conditions that therapy may be necessary.

THE TERMINATION PROCESS

If the educator or others provide competence-oriented feedback such as described above and the individual remains or becomes even more defensive, then the next step is for the educator to own up to his feelings of inadequacy and invite the client to help him decide whether he (the interventionist) can, in the long run, be of help to him. "I am trying to be helpful, but everything I do that *I* see as helpful seems to have ineffective results in our relationship. How do you experience my behavior and our relationship?" The beginning of the termination process, therefore, occurs when the interventionist asks the client to join him in a dialogue about his (the interventionist's) feelings of inadequacy and failure. If the client confirms the interventionist's feelings, then the latter should offer to withdraw from the relationship *or* change (if he is competent to do so) to a therapeutic strategy. The latter alternative probably should be taken only if the interventionist is competent in therapy and if the client can be separated from other clients who are ready for competence acquisition. Maintaining a competence and therapeutic orientation in the same group is extremely difficult for the interventionist, and it could be confusing to those attempting to acquire more competence. The resulting confusion and difficulty could be used, by the client who may need therapy, for the purpose of resisting it.

If the client disconfirms the interventionist's feelings of failure, then the latter may ask the client to give him some examples of how the interventionist has been of help. This dialogue could provide more data for the interventionist to test the hypothesis about the degree of closedness in his relationship with the client. One should point out a methodological imperative at this point. The interventionist, if possible, should not confront the client with his feelings of inadequacy and failure without having his behavior first evaluated by another interventionist who is not involved in the situation. The writer usually utilizes a tape of a session for the other interventionist to use as data. Naturally, he does not tell his professional colleague ahead of time his feelings of inadequacy nor his evaluation of the client's degree of closedness.

Whether the client chooses to confirm or disconfirm, the interventionist should use this "last try" as still another independent test of his hypothesis. He looks for any signs of competence acquisition in this episode. Perhaps the client begins to show some *searching, openness, concern,* which could lead to an increment of trust in the relationship, as well as self-confidence on the part of both. It may be that under the conditions of a genuine potential termination the client may see that his opportunity to learn (in this context) is endangered. If so, he may begin to become more open by talking about his fears, his closedness, and his frustrations with the interventionist. If he does this, the interventionist maintains the relationship. If the client continues to be closed, then the interventionist may decide to terminate his part of the relationship.

The interventionist should never confront the client with a possibility of termination until he has tried everything that he has at his command. When one threatens termination, the client may become angry and condemn the interventionist for being cruel and impatient. If the interventionist does not genuinely feel failure, his strategy will be exposed, by the client's confrontation, for what it is: a trick to get the client to move faster toward openness.

SUMMARY

Therapy and competence acquisition have similar objectives: to help individuals behave more competently. Each change activity differs from the other primarily in terms of the learning conditions that it creates and, therefore, in terms of the different clients who can be helped by experiencing it.

Competence acquisition is more relevant when the subjects are conflicted enough so that (a) they are less survival oriented and more competence oriented and (b) they are able to generate for and learn from one another, because of their ability to communicate minimally distorted, directly validatable, and minimally evaluative information is such a way that (c) they are able to come to trust themselves and the other group members as resources for learning.

Therapy is more relevant when the subjects are so conflicted that (a) they are more survival oriented, (b) they must explore the genesis of their here-and-now behavior, (c) their defensiveness is so great that evaluative and interpretive behavior is necessary to help them break through their closedness, and (d) they, therefore, require a professional with whom to dialogue (or to monitor the dialogue).

REFERENCES

Argyris, C. *Interpersonal competence and organizational effectiveness.* Homewood, Ill.: Irwin-Dorsey, 1962.

Argyris, C. *Organizational and innovation.* Homewood, Ill.: Richard D. Irwin, 1965.

Argyris, C. Interpersonal barriers to decision making. *Harvard Business Review,* March–April 1966, 84–97.

Bateson, G., Jackson D., Haley, J., & Weakland, J. Toward a theory of schizophrenia. *Behavioral Science,* 1956, *1,* 251.

Bradford, L. P., Gibb, J. R. & Benne, K. D. (Eds.) *T-Group theory and laboratory method: Innovation in re-education.* New York: Wiley, 1964.

Brown, R. Models of attitude change. In Roger Brown, *et al.* (Eds.), *New directions in psychology.* New York: Holt, Rinehart & Winston, 1962.

Cartwright, D. Achieving change in people: Some applications of group dynamics theory. *Human Relations,* 1951, *4,* 381–393.

Ezriel, H. Notes on psychoanalytic group therapy: II. Interpretation and research, *Psychiatry,* May 1952, *15,* 119–126.

Kurie, L. S. *Practical and theoretical aspects of psychoanalysis.* New York: Praeger, 1961.

Lewin, K., Dembo, T., Festinger, L., & Sears, P. Levels of aspiration. In J. M. V. Hunt (Ed.), *Personality and behavior disorders.* New York: Ronald Press, 1944. Pp. 333–378.

Maslow, A. H. *Personality and motivation.* New York: Harper & Row, 1954.

Schein, E., & Bennis, W. *Personal and organizational change through group methods: The laboratory approach.* New York: Wiley, 1965.

White, R. W. Motivation reconsidered: The concept of competence. *Psychological Review,* 1959, *66,* 297–334.

17. Potentialities and Pitfalls of Nonverbal Techniques

CYRIL MILL and MIRIAM RITVO

It is possible to identify several trends in training style which have been reflected in changes in trainer behavior over the past decade, as well as changes in the design of laboratories. For instance, role playing was once much more popular than it is now. "Rogerian mirroring" is rarely used today as a form of trainer behavior. A rising trend is the use of nonverbal techniques (NVTs). By NVTs we refer to a specific group of devices which have mushroomed in the past several years, including those which may be categorized under movement, fantasy, improvisation, psycho-motor experience, the use of plastic media, and acting out such as wrestling and pillow pounding. "Nonverbal techniques" is actually a misnomer, for words are used in many of these methods, but we choose to retain the label as words are often used in these techniques in a free-associative manner and are seldom employed for direct, purposeful communication. Let us recognize that nonverbal techniques are popular today and probably will continue to be so. The writers use them regularly, both as T-Group interventions and as larger

Reprinted from *Human Relations Training News,* Vol. 13, No. 1 (1969), pp. 1–3.

elements in laboratory designs. An NVT can be one more link for making contact with self and others. However, precautionary notes should be made to maximize their potential for learning.

The best potential of NVTs is realized when they are used professionally and not as a matter of whim or fad. Professionalism is promoted when their use stems from a theory of training, when their selection is relevant to a theory of learning, and when they fall meaningfully into a coherent design which meets the needs of the participants.

When are NVTs appropriate? Skilled trainers see them as useful to gain physical release for emotion, to demonstrate and give overt expression of feelings, and to reduce inhibitions or break down dysfunctional barriers to participation in a greater than usual range of life experiences. Not all training participants are ready—particularly at the beginning of a laboratory —for some of the atypical behaviors that may be elicited. Group contact, touching, extraordinary postures are sometimes assigned in a mass way as a "universal good," ignoring individual timing and readiness for such actions. If one submits to this in a state of unreadiness, one can experience feelings of great tension and personal violation when the opposite should be the result. This may be the case even within the T-Group:

> In a group with an inexperienced trainer, a girl stated that she felt warm and open toward a man in her group. When he found this hard to believe, the trainer suggested that she sit near him and hold his hand. When she resisted, the trainer interpreted that she really was not feeling warm and open toward him. The trainer may, in fact, have misjudged her readiness to act out her feelings in this way.
>
> A contrasting example is of a woman who, seated on a davenport between a priest and a nun, was struggling through distressful sobs to tell of her intimate concerns. The priest and nun sat rigidly, staring straight ahead, immobilized by her emotion. The trainer commented, "I think Julia needs some comforting." This released the priest so that he took her in his arms, while the nun patted her shoulder and held her hand. They subsequently discussed their chagrin at not being able to do so spontaneously and related it to their life style of avoiding physical contact.

What are the trainer's motivations for introducing NVTs either into his T-Group activity or into the total laboratory design? Many trainers who gradually have experienced some of these techniques subsequently have tried them, found them useful, and through an accumulation of experience include them as a natural part of their current competence. Unfortunately, an amateur can sometimes make a "good show" with NVTs. When NVTs are used primarily to make the trainer look good, the motivation is, of course, suspect.

Participants sometimes press for NVTs. Perhaps they have had a previous experience with a "nonverbal weekend" workshop and want a repetition. Or they have heard sensational accounts of this style of training and want to see what it is like. A trainer who is sure of the theoretical basis for what he is doing will easily resist this kind of persuasion until the appropriate time in accordance with the overall learning design. Trainers of a more cognitive bent need not be intimidated by the antiverbal bias of some new enthusiasts. "Real" experience is not just preverbal or postverbal. There are indeed both verbal and nonverbal forms. Out of context and in the absence of learning or design orientation, NVTs take on the aspect of a cult, with resulting deprofessionalization.

We have noted an increasing sophistication among laboratory participants. With some groups the trainer need hardly do more than wonder aloud about feelings that are blocking participation, for members to begin, of their own accord, to flail away at one another with rolled newspapers, or get into pushing and shoving matches, or move across the room for a kiss and embrace. The trainer role may, instead of trying to induce open behavior of this type, consist of setting limits to prevent physical or psychic injuries, aiding group members to avoid coercion, or examining pressures toward group conformity. Some groups slide into a group norm where a member does not feel that he has "arrived" unless he has cried openly. The trainer may want to help the group examine whether, in fact, tears are the price of membership.

If NVTs are valuable and useful, is there a danger of over-popularity? It is our estimation that the greatest value of NVTs is their novelty. They are possibly never so potent, as learning vehicles, as when first encountered. Thus a first exposure in a meaningless context can bring about a marked reduction in emotional impact at a later, more serious attempt to explore oneself through these media.

What are some guidelines for the use of NVTs? We suggest that the trainer be able to provide, with some sophistication, an answer to three questions: (1) *How does your selection and use of an NVT fit into your understanding of the way people change (learning theory);* (2) *what position does this NVT hold in the context of the laboratory goals toward which you are working (training design);* (3) *what immediate and observable needs at this time with these participants does this NVT meet (specific relevance)?* The trainer who asks—and answers—these questions of himself may avoid some of the pitfalls which lie in the path of all of us.

NVTs are potent because they open up and encourage the expression of emotions and behavior which typically have been suppressed. The Protestant Ethic, however, which may be giving way slightly to the new morality, demands restraint in most people. Even the new morality frowns on "losing your cool." The potency of NVTs suggests that they present a danger for those participants whose defenses have been covering a fragile stability. It is regrettable, therefore, not only to see NVTs wasted as training gimmicks in incidental get-togethers but to see such potency applied in possibly dangerous ways. Aggressive wrestling can produce sexual overtones which may not be recognized by the group leader. In mass nonverbal games many strong emotions can be aroused too numerous to note or control as well as being out of the awareness of the trainer. Such feelings, if acted out outside of the session, may have unfortunate and lasting consequences in the life of the participant. The use of NVTs requires a careful accumulation of proficiency just as T-Group leadership does.

One of the more difficult aspects of NVTs is to determine how to get the best learning results from them. A most frequently cited learning result is that they "help you to understand the nonverbal communication of other persons better." However, research long ago showed that accuracy of interpretation of nonverbal expression of emotions falls only slightly above the level of chance. The most we hope to accomplish in laboratory training is to make persons aware of the presence of the vast amount of nonverbal behavior that usually is overlooked. Meaningfulness is attached to it through verbal exploration. In laboratory language this means that the "processing" of an event is as important as the event itself.

There may be an existential value to some nonverbal experiences. Some trainers believe that they can stand alone in accordance with the principle that "it is better to have loved and lost than never to have loved at all." The feeling tone resulting from some nonverbal exercises is so intense and at the same time so fragile that to discuss it would be to talk it out of existence. On the other hand, some trainers hold that the unanalyzed experience quickly fades away, and the experience which cannot be verbalized cannot affect interpersonal behavior regardless of the intrapersonal warmth that may have been generated.

Trainers are thus faced with a decision—to process or not to process. If the training goal is to acquire learnings that are transferable to other, real-life situations, we hold that the chief value comes from the verbal discussion which follows. It can take the form of a brief encounter group or a full T-Group session, but there is a need to extract meaning from NVT experiences.

In the case of the individual participant, an NVT is always uncertain in its outcome. Nonverbal expression can produce primitive and regressive responses and energies. Pillow pounding, for instance, may be good catharsis, but the internal context may have nothing to do with the physical manifestation. How responsible must a trainer feel for what is going on? In conducting a fantasy exercise, can the trainer be a participant-observer? We think not. For most NVTs the trainer is observer only, excluded from much of the event which is internal to the participants. The trainer must rely upon mediating clues such as autonomic responses, breathing, flushing, decrease in coordination, or in verbalisms suggestive of morbid content, and symbols —bizarre or benign—in order to maintain some degree of contact with members' experience.

In summary, we believe that enthusiasm is no substitute for firm theoretical foundation. Trainers can encourage participants to use NVTs sparingly in their home organizations, just as they have been cautioning participants not to set up a T-Group as a means of solving back-home problems. It is preferable that the trainer who employs NVTs have knowledge of principles of human behavior, especially in regard to feelings and emotions. NVTs are extremely useful when applied selectively and with clinical judgment. They are best applied with care in a design where the trainer takes responsibility for aiding the participants to derive maximum learning benefits.

18. The T-Group: Short Cut or Short Circuit?

LOUIS A. ALLEN

Training or T-Groups have initiated a revolution in management education in the past ten years. Termed by Carl R. Rogers as one of the most significant social inventions of the century, the movement is now on the point of bringing about major changes in the practice of management itself.

Because there are serious questions of both fact and value inherent in the use of T-Groups, I believe it is time to take a closer look at this phenomenon. How do such groups relate to management practice? Specifically:

Is there evidence supporting the use of such a powerful therapeutic tool to change behavior on the job?

Are such changes and their implications fully understood by the employees and executives directly affected?

Is the process of change reversible when mistakes are made?

What are the implications of changing a person's attitudes and value systems, often without his concurrence?

"T" FOR TWO-EDGED

What is a T-Group? First, the background. Commonly known as sensitivity training, and encounter groups, as well as by other names, T-Groups owe much to the work of Kurt Lewin, a German psychologist who fled the Nazis and emigrated to the United States where he worked at Harvard and the Massachusetts Institute of Technology. Impetus for the group approach

Reprinted from *Business Horizons*, August, 1973, pp. 53–64.

developed during World War II, when psychotherapists recognized that the needs of returning servicemen were not being filled by the one-to-one relationship of conventional psychotherapy. Wilfred Bion and other therapists experimented with group methods in military hospitals. They found that treatment in groups helped emotionally damaged people to unlearn old patterns and find better ways to cope with their environment. At M.I.T., Lewin continued the development of group methods, and, after his death in 1946, the work was continued by the National Training Laboratories.

The T-Group is generally small, consisting of eight to twelve people who meet once or twice a week for a couple of hours, for a period of anywhere from two weeks to two years, under the guidance of a qualified leader. More concentrated courses are quite common. The mechanism of the T-Group is simple in concept, but in operation it is as complex as human emotions. People meet, observe one another's thoughts, feelings, and actions, and then comment fully and honestly on what they see. This helps the individual to see himself as others see him. Group pressure motivates him to change—hopefully for the better.

Tobias Brocher, an international authority on group processes with the Menninger Foundation, describes the T-Group as a temporary closed and sheltered social system within which the individual is forced to discharge repressed feelings in front of other members. As these feelings are expressed, they are questioned and analyzed by the group, which acts as a mirror, reflecting to the individual the personality the members see. The individual then recognizes the deficiencies in the picture he sees of himself and becomes unhappy enough to change, a process that may require him to question the value system that underlies his behavior (Brocher, 1972).

The purpose of the T-Group session is to help the individual actualize himself—to become what he is capable of becoming. He does this by learning to express his feelings deeply and honestly, in the expectation that the members are eager to help him and will receive his confidence with sincerity and understanding. The fully sensitized individual is said to function thereafter with great autonomy. According to its advocates, T-Group training makes democracy a reality; it encourages self-actualization by encouraging the individual to use his full capabilities and to express his individuality. Group effort, group objectives and group decision making are the preferred modes for achieving this.

T-Groups fall into three categories: those that are therapeutic, and those intended to promote personal improvement and organization development. Group psychotherapy is a recognized branch of medicine, with rigorous qualifications and high standards. The T-Group is used by psychotherapists both as a training method and as a treatment for certain types of patients. Such T-Group techniques as unfreezing and feedback have been incorporated into clinical practice. In psychotherapy, both the therapist and the group help the individual examine and assess his underlying sense of values, on the assumption that people tend to behave in terms of their values and beliefs.

Personal improvement T-Groups concentrate on short-span, highly intensive emotional experiences in an attempt to help people better understand their feelings and beliefs and to change behavior by modifying these beliefs. Their contexts range from laboratories for top executives to "feelies" and "fornies" for the avante garde. These groups have been the subject of considerable controversy.

The T-Group is the one feature common to all organizational development (OD) programs. OD, as described by Warren G. Bennis, is "a complex educational strategy intended to change the beliefs, attitudes, values and structures of organization" (1969).

THE UNBUTTONED MIND

What happens to people who participate in T-Groups? Therapeutic groups in competent hands have achieved significant results, although these results are open to the same scrutiny as any other current method of psychotherapy. Irwin D. Yalom of the Stanford University School of Medicine, for example, finds that T-Group therapy helps patients understand and accept themselves and others, and work more effectively. It increases functional flexibility, improves self-control, and enhances personal comfort and confidence. While observable, these results have not been scientifically measured. "A new approach to measurement of outcomes is needed," Yalom notes (1970).

T-Groups have also made impressive contributions in helping to change individual behavior of so-called "normals." Because the process is cathartic and highly emotional, it has either rabid supporters or rabid derogators. Most evidence is anecdotal. The immediate response, typically euphoric, is described by Rogers, who quotes one T-Group graduate as saying: "I feel truly alive and so grateful and joyful and hopeful and healthy and giddy and sparkly. I feel as though my eyes and ears and heart and guts have been opened to see and hear and feel more deeply, more widely, more intensely." (1967)

The opportunity for emotional catharsis is undoubtedly one of the significant aspects of sensitivity training. In my personal experience, I have seen the strong feeling of liberation and release when an individual finally levels in a T-Group. The opportunity to tell and to be heard in a sympathetic, supportive atmosphere arouses intense emotion; I have seen mature, seasoned executives "spill their guts" and wipe away tears. In many ways, the experience is undoubtedly very close to religious conversion.

Casualties of the Method

Powerful tools have dangers as well as benefits. Managers considering T-Groups should be warned of the potential hazards. The most potent influence generated by the T-Group is the pressure to conform, the dynamic underlying both unfreezing and brainwashing. As the group becomes cohesive and the members become more open, candid, and supportive, the pressure to "get with it" is almost intolerable. The cohesive group becomes a closed society. Its members seal their ranks against any individual who insists on remaining independent; he can come for the ride, but he is not one of the club.

I have observed that a group under a strong leader will tend to reflect the values and goals of the leader. In a leaderless group, such as the T-Group, some norm must be found that is acceptable to the group as a whole; this can just as easily be the lowest as the highest common denominator in attitudes, values, and actions. I have watched as nonswearers have been pressured to swear, the naive to become cynical, and the friendly to become hostile. This is as true for company presidents in an executive T-Group as it is for members of a street corner gang.

This tension gives rise to psychological dangers. In the emotional pressure cooker that some groups become, participants can be badly shaken and even suffer lasting damage. Members of the group, encouraged to be completely frank and candid about themselves and their feelings toward others, may harass and badger an individual until he becomes greatly disturbed, according to Louis A. Gottschalk and E. Mansell Pattison (1969). The result may be emotional breakdowns or acute psychotic withdrawal reactions, as well as sadistic and exhibitionistic behavior. At times, the participant does not show the symptoms of damage until he returns to the job.

Another danger is that each person tends to see and understand others in terms of his own values, so that T-Group members of necessity feed back an inaccurate or even distorted picture to some individuals and group pressure conditions the individuals to accept it. As Yalom points out, this may become a self-fulfilling prophecy: the individual may develop mannerisms and behavior traits to fit this debased self-image and be damaged rather than helped by the group experience.

Virtually all disabling casualties occur in encounter groups conducted by leaders without proper psychiatric training; in the hundreds of sessions conducted by the National Training Laboratory over the past two years, the casualty rate is reportedly low—only one or two per year. Unfortunately, the great majority of sessions are conducted by leaders who are neither competent nor qualified.

Because the T-Group is a social system that is both closed and short-lived, the culture that develops in it may have little carry-over in real life. "The T-Group may foster a concept that anything goes," warn Gottschalk and Pattison. "Exposure and frankness, attack and vulnerability may become premium values. Often little attention is paid to the necessity for support and nurturance." They go on to say that "the participants may return to their organization with 'new ways of being' only to find that the new self is not accepted by the old work group." Some executives who have tried the new approach say that the problem of reorienting everybody to think and act in the same open, trusting fashion is almost insuperable. Not everyone wants to hear blunt and honest evaluations of what they are and do.

The president of an international basic materials company put it to me succinctly: "Our top people all tried to become open, frank, candid, trusting, and supporting. They worked hard at consensus, participation, and group decision making. It didn't take. Neither our managers nor our people could change that completely." He went on to say that managers who did succeed in changing their styles no longer fit in with the rest. "After a year, one vice-president keeps saying, 'But we agreed to level with one another,' at our executive council meetings; however, even the most willing of us find we can't easily change the defenses and the personality traits of a lifetime."

Are there basic reasons why the T-Group life style may be difficult to graft on to the American character? Many competent observers believe that the restless, individualistic culture that has developed in the United States is inimical to the close, confiding personal relationships T-Group trainers advocate. And if people are pressured to change, will the same divisiveness, frustration, and conflict appear that always accompany the forceful intro- duction of new culture traits?

The late Abraham Maslow strongly advocated the long-run benefits "of trying to be honest, of trying to be intimate, of trying to learn to expose our- selves." However, he recognized that this might be so alien to the United States character that it could be inculcated only with difficulty, and he had no prognosis of what the ultimate result might be (Maslow, 1965).

NEW VALUES VERSUS OLD

The T-Group technique has made unquestioned contributions to psy- chotherapy; positive behavioral changes can result. Even its extreme mani- festation in nude and marathon groups probably does no more harm than other pastimes that titillate a predictable segment of the population. My primary concern is with the use of this powerful, but still primitive, tool to bring about fundamental changes in organizations. I am convinced it has already set in motion far-reaching and, in many cases, unrecognized changes in the culture of U.S. corporations.

Behavior change is desirable if the new behavior improves on the old. But the fact is that the precise nature of the behavior changes that T-Group training brings about is unpredictable. Furthermore, what are the conse- quences of such changes?

What really worries many executives I know is this use of sensitivity training for planned efforts throughout the enterprise to change the instru- mental values of the organization into the expressive values preferred by academic organizational theorists. While they do not question the value of T-Group as a means of improving interpersonal skills, these executives question the use of this technique to change the value system of business. Of greatest concern is that there is no scientific consensus on whether the new, expressive values are more effective than the old, instrumental ones. In fact, current behavioral science research is beginning to accumulate evidence that some of the changes in values that are being advocated can be destructive rather than helpful.

This new value system derives, at least in part, from Rousseau, and has been filtered through both holism and organismic theory. It contends that people are good, creative, and hard-working, but that their institutions stunt and distort them. Chris Argyris of Harvard University voices the common belief that conventional organizations psychologically hobble people. He contends that management has purposefully developed the pyramidal, hierarchical organization as a "strategy designed to give the greatest influence over persons, information and instrumentalities to the higher-level positions and that the control increases with higher levels." Argyris feels this "strategy creates a complex of organizational demands that tend to require individuals to experience dependence and submissiveness and to utilize few of their relatively peripheral abilities" (Argyris, 1964).

We can get a better idea of what all this is leading up to if we look at the kind of organization that respected organization behaviorists recommend and that some are working with great energy and dedication to realize. First, the purposes of the organization will be determined by employees, not by managers. Subordinates will set their own objectives; the manager will help and catalyze, not direct. This is supposed to lead to a radical change in the purposes of business organizations. The idea of economic gain and profit is condemned and supplanted by an enterprise that would exist to fulfill the desires of its employees, not its owners. As Jay W. Forrester expresses it: "The primary objectives of the corporation would change from the already diluted idea of existence primarily for profit to the stockholders and toward the concept of a society primarily devoted to the interests of the participants."(1965).

The process of management itself will be radically altered in this new organization. Managers will no longer be held accountable for securing effective results through their own team, peers, and staff groups. Instead of having responsibility for planning, organizing, leading and controlling the efforts of others, they will act as a sensitive and sympathetic interface between groups. The new content of the manager's job is described by Edgar H. Schein: "The manager's role shifts from planning, organizing, motivating and controlling to acting as an intermediary between the men and higher management, listening and attempting to understand the needs and feelings of his subordinates, and showing consideration and sympathy for their needs and feelings" (1970).

The organization structure is to change. Pyramidal organization, hierarchy, and functional specialization will disappear. "In today's technologically dominated world, pyramidal concepts no longer have any credence," says Ronald Hainsworth, an expert with Esso Petroleum in England.[1] The new mode will utilize matrix, circular, and linking-pin structures. Final decisions will be made, not by accountable managers, but by specialists with the greatest technical knowledge of the area in question.

How do these new values work out in practice? First, does the effort spent on making people happier finally appear on the bottom line? So far, as shown below, the evidence is mostly negative. In particular, new findings forcibly uproot the long-established assumption that happy, satisfied people are the most productive; they throw into question the idea that effective managers are friendly and well-liked, and they give better insight into the real dynamics of higher performance.

ARE HAPPY PEOPLE PRODUCTIVE?

Satisfied people are not necessarily the most productive. On the contrary, when people do good work, they become happier and more satisfied because of it. Research by David Cherrington, J. Joseph Reitz, and William E. Scott, Jr. (1971) makes clear that programs designed to make people happier and more satisfied at their work can be a waste of time and money: such programs have no direct influence on improved performance.

The reason is simple. People are happiest and most satisfied when they work to achieve their own personal objectives. However, if performance and productivity are to improve, each individual must give first priority to achieving the organization's objectives. Just as the football coach's long and punishing practice sessions may not make his players happy or satisfied, but will help them win games, so management plans and control aimed at better performance may make people temporarily unhappy, but they help improve productivity and, in the long run, increase the rewards available to each person.

Other findings by behavioral scientist Ralph Stogdill reinforce this point. The objective of the organization is not to create satisfied employees who will then be productive because they are happy, Stogdill points out. The real objective of any enterprise is to survive and grow and, as a means to this end, to help people actualize their best abilities. If a manager follows the now popular prescription and tries to generate happiness and satisfaction, as Stogdill puts it, "he can be surrounded by loyal, happy workers, but lose money on his operations" (1969).

In a recent survey, Charles N. Greene of Indiana University concluded that programs leading to greater personal satisfaction and happiness—openness, trust, and warm and friendly relationships—do not cause improved perfor-

---

[1]Quoted in "Is the Pyramid Crumbling?" *International Management* (July 1971), p. 10.

mance; in fact, he states, "increasing subordinates' satisfaction will have no effect on their performance" (1972). What he does emphasize is that the reward a person receives for his work is the important motivating factor. A manager can secure improved performance by giving people appropriate rewards for good work performed currently—and withholding rewards if work is substandard. This motivates subsequent performance.

According to T-Group values, relaxed and friendly leaders result in high productivity; however, new evidence demonstrates that high productivity encourages leaders to relax and become friendly. The effective manager will often take action to accomplish objectives, but this may not engender friendliness; in fact, he must not only encourage and inspire, but sometimes also impel people to perform unpleasant but necessary tasks.

When a manager makes a real effort to become friendly, open, and supportive and to "level" with members of his team, many good things occur: they become more loyal to him, cooperate better, and develop higher morale. But this has to be balanced with the fact that, when pressure is on to achieve results, members of the team will often join ranks to work for ends *they* believe are most important—and this may have little to do with management's commitment. If the friendly, supportive manager tries to swing the group to see management's view, they may level him to impotence.

On the basis of his research, Reed M. Powell of Ohio State University concluded that "as group members become more interrelated and as their influence upon one another increases, the formal directive leadership pattern within the group erodes. The group members tended to neutralize the leadership thrust" (1971).

This finding was reinforced by a business gaming experiment by Deep, Bass, and Vaughn (1967), which has implications for executives who feel that managers should be on the most familiar terms with their subordinates. The experimenters concluded that "better interpersonal relations tended to go hand in hand with poorer business decisions" because people who worked for the friendliest leaders tended to follow their own preferences and showed little inclination to work hard at forecasting, planning, meeting schedules, and other tasks vital to group success. Leaders who were friendly and very much one of the boys could not organize or control the group effectively and, as the researchers put it, "could not needle them for the required amount of work that each had to do if adequate decisions were to be made."

EVERYBODY'S BUSINESS

Further conflict between T-Groups and business values lies in the relationship between the individual and the organizations to which he belongs. Since the purpose of the individual is to satisfy his personal needs and desires and that of the organization is to accomplish its objectives, some conflict is unavoidable. Each individual belongs to a number of organizations: family, church, educational, social, and business. Obviously, he cannot be fully committed to all, nor integrate his personal objectives fully with any one; whatever fulfillment he achieves will come from home life, hobbies, pastimes, and community service, as well as the work environment. It is fallacious to assume, as most T-Group theorists seem to do, that the business organization can provide for all the individual's needs and wants and that it is to blame if he fails to actualize them.

The variety of choice is already great. Even among business organizations the individual can find endless diversity; if his needs are unsatisfied, he can move to another environment without restriction. That such mobility is a fact shows the difficulty of satisfying these varying and often fast-changing demands. Because the needs of individuals do differ so widely, I believe that we need and should encourage diversity; we need approaches that are entrepreneurial, competitive, cooperative, authoritarian, permissive, and more.

Only in an open society can selective pressures work to evolve the form that is of greatest utility to the greatest number. A closed humanistic society, to my mind, is little better than a closed authoritarian one. To be free is to be able to seek a father figure as well as to find a soul mate.

A potential casualty if the T-Group movement becomes general is the dilution or loss of the unique blend of aggressiveness and creativity that has made the culture in the United States the most productive in history. The hallmarks of this culture are evident: entrepreneural drive, competitiveness, respect for hierarchical authority, the work ethic, reward for achievement, and little sympathy with failure. Sensitivity trainers are united in finding these attitudes undesirable:

Frederick Herzberg (1966) looks at the chart rooms of duPont, the automated systems of Xerox, the cost controls of GM, and sees the system creating "instrumental men" and resulting in "an almost inhuman society."

Warren Bennis (1966) has contended that many methods used by professional managers—including hierarchical organization, written definitions of responsibility and authority, and the concept of accountability—make people subordinate, passive, and dependent and are "hopelessly out of joint with contemporary realities." He believes that T-Groups and organization development, conducted by behavioral scientists, are an ideal means of accomplishing the fundamental changes he envisions.

Chris Argyris (1964) of Harvard University, a leading organizational researcher and theorist, says that the "formal organizational structure, managerial controls and directive leadership used by most business managers tend to decrease rather than increase effectiveness."

These assertions are unproven. There is no evidence that an organized enterprise can continue to function without hierarchy, formalized structure, accountability, direction, and controls. Warren Bennis voiced an impossible ideal: "The problem is to find a form of association in which each, while uniting himself with all, may still obey himself alone, and remain free as before" (1961).

PROMISE AND PERFORMANCE

How has the T-Group ideology worked out in practice? There has been considerable success in changing the attitudes and values of both students of management and practicing managers, but the outcome of attempts to translate these values into action has ranged from limited success to disaster.

Two examples most often cited are Texas Instruments and TRW, Inc. In both cases, however, the change effort has centered on improvement of planning and control, participation, communication, and delegation, rather than on dramatic new forms of management or organization. Texas Instruments, for example, has recognized the central importance of planning and control skills, management process activities that the modern theory of organization minimizes. It has delegated an increased share of planning and control responsibility to first-line operators and coupled this with an adaptation of methods improvements. This strategy is itself a primary tool of industrial engineering and a direct outgrowth of the operations logic developed by Frederick Winslow Taylor and widely used during World War II as job methods training.

The Systems Group of TRW, Inc., helps people to be open and frank in resolving problems, to level instead of dissembling or playing games when personal conflict is imminent, and to create an environment that encourages both individual and group growth and development. This work has been emphasized in the Redondo Beach, Calif. group which concentrates on high technology aerospace projects and is staffed mostly by highly educated scientists and engineers.

The group minimizes the formalized organization structure, detailed procedures, and impersonal controls necessary in more highly standardized components of the same company. However, the systems group has found no successful replacements for conventional organization. It uses matrix organization structures, a form of project divisionalization, with multiple project team membership. While highly flexible in nature, the matrix organization is basically hierarchical, even though the designations are "team members" and "team leaders" instead of "superior" and "subordinate." The company maintains functional specialization to encourage the development and application of advanced technologies.

The systems group has found that it cannot operate without division of labor, span of control, hierarchy, and staff-and-line relationships. It has adopted behavioral techniques as a useful extension, but not replacement, of its conventional management. In reporting on the TRW experiment, the Conference Board notes, "While the company reports that sensitivity training speeds up the interpersonal learning process for many people, it does not regard it as a prerequisite to effective management." The Conference Board (1969) further quotes a TRW manager as follows: "Some people benefit more than others. For those who find the experience meaningful, it has significance in this environment where work content changes rapidly and where most work programs are of relatively short duration."

A widely publicized experience is that of Non-Linear Systems, Inc., a San Diego electronics company, which has implemented T-Group techniques for about ten years. It has been cited frequently in the literature. Initially, the excitement of introducing the new T-Group program, coupled with a booming economy, yielded excellent results for Non-Linear Systems. But when a slump hit in 1970 and the pressure was on, the new techniques failed.

Both blame and excuses have been generously offered. The evidence indicates, however, that executives were so friendly they were reluctant to fire people; employees had so much authority that they could not relate their group efforts to those of the company as a whole; financial planning and controls took a back seat to the effort to create autonomy and independence. "I may have lost sight of the purpose of business, which is not to develop new theories of management," the president of Non-Linear Systems, Andrew F. Kay, is reported as saying. Or, as consultant Richard Farson commented, "I think we know now that human relations don't have a lot to do with profit and productivity . . . That is a fact we must accept."[2]

WHAT MANAGEMENT IS NOT

The T-Group ideology has serious implications for today's business. What will happen, for example, if the respect now accorded the work ethic is replaced by single-minded pursuit of self-expression? If people are encouraged to act spontaneously and emotionally, what will become of the rationality, standardization, and system basic to scientific and technological advance? Is the attempt to find a new definition of man going to undermine the foundations on which the questioning culture has been built?

The United States is the most efficient and successful generator of material wealth the world has known. This success has made possible the resources and freedom necessary to develop and enrich emotional and spiritual life. Our problem now is not with the machine and its technology as such: they have served their purpose with surpassing effectiveness. Where we fall short is in our ability to establish the goals we must achieve if man is to grow beyond his biology and technology. Without these goals we cannot work rationally to create an enduring society.

If management is to be changed and improved, we must first decide what we are changing. What is management as it is practiced by real people in the real world? Most competent professionals would agree that it is not a style or

---

[2]These two quotations are from *Business Week* (January 20, 1973), p. 100.

a set of personality characteristics, but, rather, mastery of the work necessary to plan, organize, lead, and control the efforts of others. Improvement requires the same approach as upgrading any other skill.

It suggests, first, an analysis of the concepts, principles, and techniques that help a manager to perform these kinds of work most effectively. It would necessitate defining and using a commonly understood management vocabulary. Given this base, a company would determine what system of management it would adopt, audit its current management practice to identify strengths and weaknesses, and then systematically help its people to improve their knowledge, attitudes, and skills to attain the standard of performance desired. Increasingly, this is being recognized by behavioral scientists as well as professional managers.

Improvement in management, as in other forms of human endeavor, requires changes in attitudes and habits from intuition to rationality, from self-interest to concern for others. It demands unending effort, self-discipline, and humility, qualities that traditionally have underlain the most successful organized undertakings. This is straightforward, logical, and difficult, which is probably why easier alternatives are popular.

THE T-GROUP IN USE

The T-Group as Fad

The disquieting truth is that the enthusiasm of some T-Group and laboratory training people is taking on a faddish character. The T-Group is becoming the "in" thing. Companies that have already "done" decision making, the grid, and MBO are now on the T-Group or OD kick.

Fads in management development are accepted because most managers have not thought through their needs or objectives. Many executives I have talked with, for example, are intimately familiar with every aspect of a product being developed or a new assembly line, but are only vaguely familiar with what is being done to change the very character of the organization.

Too often, management education is undertaken because management recognizes that human resources are important and there is social pressure to do something about it. Confused by the welter of contradictory claims and the paucity of scientific evidence, the top executive may accept any panacea that is offered. Currently, this is the T-Group and organization development.

A great many executives are supporting T-Group activity in one or more of its varied forms without recognizing that they are changing the beliefs, and, with them, the behavior patterns, that have supported their past growth and profitability. Some, in fact, would be startled to learn that the training classes whose existence they have noted only in the approval of budgets are systematically teaching that management regards the average man as stupid, lazy, and irresponsible, that the company's form of organization is both obsolete and inhuman, and that their planning and control system is an anachronism.

I asked one company president whom I have known for years to identify the single most important factor in his company's success. "Our control system," he told me. "It helps us get the right people, it keeps our planning on track, it alerts me to problems before they become crises."

"What would you say," I asked, "if I told you that your supervisors and managers were being taught that centralized controls are both undesirable and unnecessary; that first-line supervisors can be trusted to control their own operations completely and that the only information that should go to higher level managers is that which the foreman see fit to release?"[3] The president expressed his disbelief, but investigated, and the T-Group program in his company was unceremoniously discontinued.

If You Must Use T-Groups

T-Groups and sensitivity training have an important, if limited, role. Through the processes of unfreezing, feedback, and group pressure, the T-Group can dramatically change a participant's beliefs and values. To the thoughtful executive, the changing of basic beliefs is more than a matter of philosophical debate. The nature of these new values is significant, for, once established, they will lead to changes not only in leadership style, but also in the organization structure; the decision-making, planning, and control systems; the methods of compensation; and the competitive capability of the marketing effort. The new values may well result in abandonment of methods now in use to stimulate performance in favor of such new and unproven methods as decision by consensus, nonhierarchical organization, personal controls, and nondirective leadership.

Because T-Groups can change values rather drastically, the executive must decide in advance what his objectives are. Is the enterprise primarily an economic agency of society and is its first obligation to provide the goods and services society demands of it? Recognizing that the means are now at hand to engineer a culture that will enable the individual to actualize himself more greatly than at any previous period in history, what role should the business enterprise play? Can it contribute by serving as the testing ground for new theories of human behavior? Or will this experimentation endanger its productivity and its effectiveness in a world which is still highly nationalistic and competitive?

These are great issues, but the executive needs to make them his personal concern if he is to make sound value judgments. Values, after all, are the very fiber of an enterprise; to change them, even knowingly, may endanger the entire structure. As Thomas J. Watson, Jr. of IBM has said, "The beliefs of IBM, far more than technical skill, have made it possible for our people to

---

[3]An approach recommended by Argyris (1964), pp. 245–46.

make the company successful" (1963). The values that will shape the society of the future are best achieved by rational evolution from the best we now have to more effective forms.

Whatever the decision, the T-Group still has a useful place. It helps people to understand themselves and to work more effectively with others. Under competent leaders, it can help to change and enrich the lives of participants. But the enthusiasm of its advocates must not be permitted to get out of bounds. Louis A. Gottschalk (1966) concludes, after extensive experience with T-Groups, that the procedure requires much more study to determine what changes it can induce and the influence of these changes. In particular, he warns that "its application to the remedy of social and psychological problems should be more strictly limited and both its participants and trainers should be more carefully selected." When a T-Group centered program is indicated, the executive must answer two questions.

Who Is the Leader? Although the leader is the critical factor in sensitivity training, many leaders practice without clearly committing themselves to the beliefs they are attempting to inculcate and without the necessary personal or professional qualifications. Unqualified leaders have done more to jeopardize sound practice than any other factor. Too often, the trainer's only preparation has been his participation in a T-Group or a short course in methodology. He may have had little or no business exposure or experience in real life. His value system may be based on a conviction that corporations are ruthless exploiters of people. Often he has a missionary zeal to inculcate nobler feelings and aspirations in others.

The difficulty of finding and training qualified leaders is evidenced by an estimate given to me by a University of Pittsburgh researcher that, although some 2,000 T-Groups function in the thirteen western states, there are not many more than two dozen properly qualified trainers in this area. Because of the lack of professional requirements for leadership and ethical standards, there is little incentive for prospective leaders to spend time in training.

A sound background will include specialization in psychiatry or group psychotherapy, graduate work in a field heavily oriented to the behavioral sciences, or special qualifications based on experience in leadership and interpersonal relations. For business practice, a minimum of five years of meaningful experience in a corporation is desirable. Although the National Training Laboratory has issued a set of standards for the use of the laboratory method, there are no official requirements. Anyone can pronounce himself qualified and conduct sessions.

Restricting the practice of unqualified leaders is an urgent matter. Without the proper background, the leader may miss vital cues as individuals get into difficulties or as the group takes the reins and gallops into quicksand. Even if a leader is trained and qualified, he may still run into problems because of his own biases or his tendency to vent his feelings of hostility or compensate for his own deficiencies. Tobias Brocher (1970) warns of individuals who become leaders because of a personal need to act out their own psychopathology.

The goal of the T-Group determines the type of leader needed. If the objective is therapy, a qualified psychiatrist or clinical psychologist, trained in group methods, should be hired as a group leader. If the objective is training and development, the professional background of the trainer need not be as intensive. Brocher points out, however, that it is always desirable to have available a psychiatric consultant who can help in case of casualties.

Who Are the Participants? It is as important to screen participants as leaders. Therapy involves treating and correcting emotional problems; training aims at developing knowledge, attitudes, and skills. People with emotional problems should join therapy groups; mature, balanced personalities do best in training and development sessions.

For development groups, careful prescreening is necessary to select members who are able to be objective about their own feelings and actions as well as those of others—people who are capable of full emotional involvement in the proceedings. Although some companies require the entire management group to go through sensitivity training, Yalom emphasizes that group members "must be able to send and receive communications about their own and other members' behavior with a minimum of distortion; they must, if they are to convey accurate information and be receptive about themselves, have a relatively high degree of self-awareness and self-acceptance." Clearly, T-Groups are not for everyone.

Business organizations are caught up in a worldwide questioning of the purposes of organized enterprises in a changing society. This is leading to a rethinking of the value systems that shape the nature of institutions. In the United States, one of the most dynamic instruments of this change is the T-Group or sensitivity training. A proven and useful technique for therapy in the hands of qualified psychotherapists, the T-Group is also used for changing the beliefs and the management methods of organized undertakings. In fact, because of its central and dominating influence, the business enterprise has become the priority target.

It is now time for top executives to examine the purposes and methods of this movement more closely and to assess the results already achieved. The urgent need now is to decide rationally the proper ends and means for this powerful tool so that its uncontrolled implementation does not prejudice the firm's effectiveness and success.

REFERENCES

Argyris, C. *Integrating the Individual and the Organization.* New York: John Wiley and Sons, 1964, p. 58.

Behavioral Science, Concepts and Management Applications. New York: The Conference Board, 1969, p. 163.

Bennis, W. G. A Revisionist Theory of Leadership. *Harvard Business Review* (January-February 1961), p. 146.

_____. *Changing Organizations.* New York: McGraw-Hill, 1966, p. 308.

_____. *Organization Development: Its Nature, Origin and Prospects.* Reading, Mass.: Addison–Wesley, 1969.

Brocher, T. Orientation on Group Dynamics. *Psychiatric Communications.* No. 1 (1970), p. 4.

_____. *Personal Communication,* December, 1972.

Cherrington, D. J., Reitz, H. J. and Scott, Jr., W. E. Effects of Contingent and Non–Contingent Reward on the Relationship between Satisfaction and Task Performance. *Journal of Applied Psychology* (December, 1971), pp. 531–36.

Deep, S. D., Bass, B. M. and Vaughn, J. A. Some Effects on Business Gaming of Previous Quasi–T–Group Affiliations. *Journal of Applied Psychology,* LI, No. 5 (1967), pp. 426–31.

Forrester, J. W. A New Corporate Design. *Industrial Management Review* (Fall 1965), pp. 5–17.

Gottschalk, L. A. Psychoanalytic Notes on T-Groups at the Human Relations Laboratory, Bethel, Maine. *Comprehensive Psychiatry* (December 1966), pp. 472–87.

Gottschalk, L. A. and Pattison, E. M. Psychiatric Perspectives on T-Groups and the Laboratory Movement: An Overview. *American Journal of Psychiatry* (December 1969), p. 101.

Greene, C. N. The Satisfaction–Performance Controversy. *Business Horizons* (October 1972), p. 34.

Herzberg, F. *Work and the Nature of Man.* Cleveland, Ohio: The World Publishing Co., 1966, p. 35.

Maslow, A. H. *Eupsychian Management.* Homewood, Ill.: Richard D. Irwin, 1965, p. 160.

Powell, R. M. and Schlacter, J. L. Participative Management: A Panacea? *Academy of Management Journal* (June 1971), p. 172.

Rogers, C. R. Process of the Basic Encounter Group. In J. F. T. Bugental, *Challenges of Humanistic Psychology.* New York: McGraw-Hill, 1967, pp. 262–76.

Schein, E. H. *Organizational Psychology.* Englewood Cliffs, N.J.: 1970, p. 59.

Stogdill, R. M. Individual Behavior and Group Achievement—A Behavioral Model of Organization. Paper presented at the annual meeting of The American Psychological Association, Washington, D.C., September 3, 1969.

Watson, Jr., T. J. *A Business and Its Beliefs.* New York: McGraw-Hill Book Co., 1963, p. 69.

Yalom, I. D. *The Theory and Practice of Group Psychotherapy.* New York: Basic Books, 1970, pp. 60–81 and p. 380.

19. How Psychologically Dangerous Are T-Groups and Encounter Groups?

CARY L. COOPER

STUDIES INDICATING PSYCHOLOGICAL DISTURBANCE FOLLOWING THE GROUP EXPERIENCE

In a report by a Task Force Commission of the American Psychiatric Association (1970), entitled *Encounter Groups and Psychiatry,* the authors state that the only available evidence to evaluate the psychiatric effects of T-Groups and Encounter groups is based on anecdotal reports or some 'simple' empirical studies (inadequately designed) which consist generally of no pretraining or follow-up measures. An example of this type appeared in the *Archives of General Psychiatry* entitled Acute Psychosis Precipitated by T-Group Experiences (Jaffe & Scherl, 1969). This consisted of case studies of two ex-T-Group participants each of whom the authors claim 'suffered an acute transient psychosis precipitated by attendance at an intensive T-Group'. One of these had no previous record of psychiatric treatment and the other was undergoing treatment during training. A detailed account was given of the patient's background and of how the group experience aggravated the underlying psychiatric condition. The authors avoided the trap of suggesting that these failures were typical consequences of this methodology and they proceeded in a constructive way to offer guidelines 'to help diminish the number of severe reactions similar to those described', which included screening of participants by interview and questionnaires, voluntary participation, clear statements by trainers of goals and methods, and follow-up of ex-participants. Although these case histories and ground rules are very interesting, they do not help us to understand the nature or extent of the problem. Are T-Group and Encounter groups psychologically disturbing? If so, how large is the casualty rate? Are certain people more vulnerable than others? Are certain forms of group experience more likely to lead to breakdown? Are the personality characteristics of the leaders or trainers associated with psychological disturbance following these groups?

In the late 1960's these questions remained unanswered, as more and more articles of a descriptive or anecdotal nature appeared raising the same issues: 'Psychiatric Perspectives on T-Groups and the Laboratory Movement' (Gottschalk & Pattison, 1969), 'How Sensitive Is Sensitivity Training' (Crawshaw, 1969), 'Some Ethical Issues in Sensitivity Training' (Lakin, 1969), 'Sensitivity Training: Should We Use It?' (Mann, 1970). One of the first attempts to

Reprinted from *Human Relations*, Vol. 28, No. 3, pp. 249–260.

examine the psychological consequences of these groups empirically was carried out by Reddy (1970). Using the Tennessee Self-Concept Scale (Fitts, 1965), which consists of 100 self-descriptive statements and provides measure of psychological disturbance (the Number of Deviant Signs scale or NDS), he studied two T-Groups and compared them with a psychotherapy group and a control of students taking an introductory course in psychology. He found that the participants in the two T-Groups showed significantly more changes in the direction of greater pathology from pre to post-test, while the psychotherapy and control group did not. Although this study is the first of its kind to deal directly with this problem, the results are limited. First, there was a pre-test NDS score difference between the T-Group and the psychotherapy group subjects with, as one might expect, the psychotherapy group scoring significantly higher. This meant that the T-Group participants had a greater chance of obtaining higher scores on the post-test than the participants in psychotherapy. Second, and more importantly, an increase in the NDS score may indicate a greater willingness to admit more psychologically disturbing or threatening material to one's consciousness which may indicate the realization of T-Group goals (i.e. greater openness and enhanced self-awareness) and not psychological disturbance or stress.

A much more comprehensive study was carried out by Yalom & Lieberman (1971). They studied 209 university undergraduates in 18 encounter groups which met for a total of 30 hours. Leaders were selected for the groups from a range of different schools of group work; two NTL[1] Sensitivity Training groups, two Gestalt Therapy groups, two Psychodrama Groups, one Psychoanalytical group, two Transactional groups, one Sensory Awareness group, two Marathon groups, two Synanon groups, two NTL Personal Growth groups, and two Encounter groups. The participants completed a battery of questionnaires before, during, and after, and at a follow-up period six-eight months after the group experience. There was (i) no pre-group screening of students, (ii) random assignment of participants to groups, and (iii) all the participants were informed before entering the study that 'participation in encounter groups sometimes results in considerable emotional upsets' (intended to minimize the psychological risk to participants). The two main purposes of this research were to find out the extent of encounter group casualties and the relationship between the type of encounter group and the casualty rate. A casualty was defined as:

'An individual who, as a direct result of his experience in the encounter group, became more psychologically distressed or employed more maladaptive mechanisms of defense, or both; furthermore this negative change was not a transient but an enduring one, as judged eight months after the group experience.'

---

[1]NTL stands for the National Training Laboratory, which is the main focus of T-Group training in North America.

Seven measures were used to operationalize the 'casualty suspects.' They were: request for psychiatric aid, drop-outs from groups, peer evaluation, self-esteem drop, subjects' testimony, psychotherapy, and leaders' ratings. On the basis of these criteria a list of casualty suspects was compiled and eight months after the group experience each suspect was interviewed by telephone. If an individual was judged during the telephone conversation to have had a psychologically destructive experience he was invited in for an in-depth interview. The suspect was considered a casualty after the interview if three conditions were met: (1) if he/she was judged to have undergone some 'psychological decompensation', (2) if it was persistent, and (3) if the group experience was judged to be the responsible agent. A total of 104 casualty suspects were identified of which 79 were contacted by telephone (the others were not located). Of these 16 students were considered to be 'casualties', which represent 7.5 per cent of the 209 students who began the groups (9.4% of the 170 who completed the groups). In addition, they found that the casualties were not evenly distributed across the types (for example, six groups had no casualties, three had two, and one had three). It was determined that the ideological school of the leader was not the main factor in the skewed distribution but that the leadership style of the trainer/facilitator contributed most of the variance. Leader behaviour was determined by participant questionnaires (designed to get at the symbolic value of the leader to participant), and by observer ratings of leader behaviour, style and primary focus. They came up with seven basic styles, which cut across ideology; aggressive stimulators, love leaders, social engineers, laissez-faire leaders, cool-aggressive stimulators high structure leaders, and encounter-tape (this included two groups which had as their leader the Bell and Howell encounter tape, with the encounter group instructions coming from the tape) leaders. They found that the aggressive stimulators style of leadership produced seven of the 16 casualties (44 per cent of the total). They represented not only the most casualties produced but the most severe ones. These leaders or trainers were characterized by high stimulus input, intrusive, confrontive, challenging but demonstrating, high positive caring. They were the most charismatic but were also authoritarian and often structured the events in the group.

This study is a useful beginning to this most important line of research. The casualty figure of roughly eight per cent, which in terms of the authors' methodology is a conservative one (due to lack of contact with 25 casualty suspects), is an appreciable rate. There are several aspects of the design of this research, however, that must be taken into account before drawing any firm conclusions. First, as the authors themselves admit, the random assignment of students to groups may have increased the risk of psychological disturbance. Second, the decision to categorize the 'suspect' subjects into 'casualties' was based on subjective criteria, that is, self-report by the subjects and the authors' judgement of 'psychological decompensation' and not on measurable observed behaviour. No evidence is given to validate the authors' judgements. And finally, it is arguable that informing T-Group or encounter group participants about the possibilities of 'considerable emotional upsets' before the start of the experience minimizes the psychological risk to participants. It may, in fact, have the reverse effect by creating an expectation (which is later converted into a group norm) of intensive psychotherapy, which may not have been established without this intervention.

STUDIES INDICATING THE ABSENCE OF PSYCHOLOGICAL DISTURBANCE FOLLOWING SENSITIVITY TRAINING AND ENCOUNTER GROUPS

One of the early studies in this area was carried out by Lubin & Zuckermann (1967). They took pre- and post-test measures of changes in anxiety (A), depression (D), and hostility (H) derived from the Multiple Affect Adjective 'Check List' in four T-Groups. They found that initially all three of these dimensions increased as the emotional involvement of the participants increased and then it decreased by the end of the experience. In a later study (1969), they compared the level of emotional arousal in T-Groups with these levels in perceptual isolation experiments of six, eight, and 24 hours. They found that the highest A, D, and H levels in four different T-Groups were significantly lower than the levels of the same emotions aroused in all three of the perceptual isolation situations. Lubin & Lubin (1971) extended this research to compare the level of emotional arousal produced by T-Groups with the stress evoked from university examinations. Using the same, A, D, and H scales, they had seven undergraduate university classes complete the Checklist on a non-examination day and just prior to a scheduled examination. Seven T-Groups completed the scales just prior to the opening of a T-Group and at the end of each T-Group session throughout the one-week experience. For the comparisons, data were used from the single session in each T-Group in which mean scores on A, D and H were highest. Pre-T-Group and non-examination day scores were controlled for initial group differences. They used T tests between T-Group stress scores and college examination stress scores and found that in approximately 80 per cent of the cases the college examination stress means were significantly higher than the T-Group means. This seems to indicate that stress was greater, in most instances, just prior to a university examination than during the most stressful session of a T-Group.

Another similar study (Pollack & Stanley, 1971) focussed on a more positive dimension and examined changes in coping behaviour after T-Groups. The authors compared 28 students who participated in a 24-hour marathon T-Group with a control group matched in terms of age, sex, and education (none of who had ever been through sensitivity training). The

Sentence Completion Test was used as a means of separating those who personally and specifically confront aggressive and sexual stimuli (coping) from those who characteristically avoid such confrontations (Pollack, 1966). Results indicated a significant increase in coping scores after the T-Group training; whereas there was no change observed in the control subjects.

Although this study and the previous three in this section provide encouraging results for the advocates of T-Groups and Encounter Groups, they all suffer from the same methodological disease, the paper and pencil test. There is nothing wrong in principle with such tests but they rely heavily on being properly validated and, in many instances, the groups or criteria utilized in the validation procedure may not justify the use of terms such as stress, coping, etc. Whenever possible therefore it is preferable to use measures linked to actual or observed behaviour. The study by Ross, Kligfeld & Whitman (1971) does just this. They carried out a survey in the city of Cincinnati, Ohio, a community in which extensive T-Group and Encounter Group activities have developed in the five years prior to the study. They sent a series of questionnaires to 162 psychiatrists in the greater Cincinnati area, who were known to be seeing psychiatric patients (they were the entire membership of the Ohio Psychiatric Association). One of the questionnaires asked the psychiatrists to report any cases in which a patient's 'psychotic reactions or personality disorganizations, whether transient or long-lasting, seemed to be consequent to participation in nonstructured groups (either T-Groups or Encounter Groups) in the preceding five years'. A total of 148 of the 162 psychiatrists in the community responded which was a very high rate of return, 91 per cent. Nineteen separate patients were reported as becoming psychotic or acutely disorganized after group training. In order to get a general estimate of the size of the total population of T-Group participants from which these cases came, all the organizations in the city of Cincinnati known to sponsor such groups were contacted. The authors were given figures for numbers of separate persons participating in such groups over the preceding five years which totaled 2900. Thus, as the authors state, 'the 19 who became acutely ill and were brought to psychiatric attention represent 0.66 per cent of the population thought to be at risk'. This study is very convincing in view of the large sample obtained and the criterion measure, which was based on observed overt behaviour.

This result, suggesting that the dangers of T-Groups are not alarmingly great, was confirmed by the author in two studies assessing psychological stress (Cooper, 1972a; 1972b). In the first study, 16 final year psychology students volunteered for T-Group training during the beginning of their final university year, while the remainder of the students (16 in all) served as a control group. There were no significant differences between the T-Group and control students with respect to sex, age, social class, or on any of the scales of the 16 PF personality inventory. The training consisted of a three-day T-Group. Psychological stress was assessed in terms of the frequency of visits to the Student Health Service doctors, visits judged by them to be symptoms of psychological disturbance. Visits to the doctor for T-Group and control students were examined during the term after training and compared to the same term in the previous year. If the T-Group was disturbing one might expect an increase in visits (judged to be related to stress) to the doctor immediately following training. The results indicated no significant difference between the T-Group and control students either before or after training. However, in the second or follow-up study, the same 'visiting' data was collected on these 32 students during the last term of their final year at university. During this term, U.K. students take a number of final examinations, which attempt to assess their performance over the whole of their three years at university. Visits to the doctor (judged as stressful by the doctor) during this term, it can be argued, provide a measure of the ability to cope with stress. Examination of the data during this period of stress, indicated that T-Group students tended to visit their doctor less often with symptoms of stress than the controls. In addition, the number of T-Group students with more than one visit to the doctor dropped significantly from the term preceding training to the period of stress or examination term. These results are consistent with Ross, Kligfeld & Whitman (1971) that in behavioural terms T-Group training may not immediately cause psychological stress or disturbance and may, in fact, help the participants to cope better. This later finding would have to be confirmed on a large sample and with populations other than students before one can safely generalize. In fact, the reduction in frequency of visits to the doctor during stress may not mean that these students coped better with stress but that they sought other sources of support during this period of stress (examination term), for instance, with other students who participated in the T-Group. In fact, informal observation suggested this as a real possibility.

The author did another study (Cooper, 1974) using both a personality inventory and a behavioural measure of psychological disturbance. This was done not only to test further the extent of distress from training in a non student group, but also to explore the relationship between these two different indices. The study was carried out on 30 members of the helping professions (social workers, probation officers, psychiatrists, nurses, etc.) who were attending a one-week residential T-Group course. Two measures of disturbance were used; (1) the Eysenck Personality Inventory—Neuroticism Scale, given before and after the training; and (2) a Behaviour Change questionnaire comprized of items judged (by psychiatrists) to be related to psychologically disturbing behaviour, completed by the participant and his close family and friends two weeks after the group experience. Although participants showed increases in their EPI neuroticism scores as a result of training, these individuals were not seen by their family and friends during the two weeks following training as psychologically distressed on any of the items in the questionnaire. In fact, a large number of trainees saw themselves and were seen by their close relatives and friends as slightly better able to cope with personal and family problems, slightly more happy, better able to get on with their children and significant other persons, and better able to communicate. This provides some support for the notion that paper-and-pencil test measures of increased psychological disturbance may, as suggested earlier, reflect increases in willingness to self-disclose or openness and not in disturbance.

And finally, the most recent study in this area (Posthuma & Posthuma, 1973) compared the impact of three encounter groups (N = 24) with changes in a 'placebo control' group matched control group with some group experience, mainly on a content-level, but with no here-and-now confrontation, N = 23) and an untrained matched control group (N = 26). All the subjects were associated with the Unitarian Church community in Canada. A behaviour change index was designed by the authors and filled out by all the subjects at the end of the group experience and six months later. The index included subscales on social, vocational, health, personal, and domestic categories. Although the measure was a self-report measure, the authors analyzed the responses independently to determine 'real change in behaviour' (Sampled independent assessments were correlated at r = .95, p < .01). The main purpose of the study was to assess the frequency of *negative* behaviour change reported in the encounter and control groups just after and six months after training. There were five main findings. First, 90 per cent of the encounter group, 62 per cent of the placebo, and 52 per cent of the control subjects reported one or more positive change after the experience (x^2 = 7.79, p < .05). Second, significantly more encounter group participants than placebo controls reported positive change at the end of the group. Third, after six months the reported occurrence of three or more positive changes declined and the differences between the encounter group, placebo, and controls were insignificant, 62 per cent, 60 per cent and 43 per cent respectively. Fourth, fewer negative changes were reported and by fewer subjects than was the case with positive change. At the end of the training, 33 per cent of the encounter group participants, 24 per cent of the placebo, and 33 per cent of the controls reported one or more negative changes in behaviour. And finally, by the end of six months the proportions reporting one or more negative change were 33 per cent, 48 per cent and 52 per cent for encounter group participants, placebo, and controls (no significant differences between them). The authors conclude 'thus in the present study at least the encounter group experience does not provide more psychological distress than what would normally occur in people coping with the exigencies of life'. Although the results of this study provide further support for the protagonists of encounter groups, the research has several methodological shortcomings. First, the measure labelled Behaviour Change Index is not really a *behavioural* measure, in fact, it is simply a self-report measure which contains all the problems of any such measure—social desirability and unconscious self-deception biases. It is much preferable when using measures of this sort to provide for some kind of consensual validation, by means of other people reporting on the behaviour of the subject. Second, the authors should not have analyzed or coded the data themselves, it would have been preferable to have given the data for coding to independent judges unaware of the nature and hypotheses of the study. And finally, the data in the published study was presented in a form, overall per cent positive and negative change, which may have obscured far more interesting material particularly in terms of change on each of the five categories of the Index. The value of this study is limited by these issues.

CONCLUSION

At the moment, the cries that T-Groups and Encounter Groups are psychologically dangerous and in Gottschalk's (1966) opinion 'psychiatrically disruptive to almost half the delegates in a group' have not been proved. In fact, as we have seen, there is some evidence that indicates that it may be less stressful than university examinations or perceptual isolation experiments, or indeed, that it may enable participants to cope better with sexual and aggressive stimuli and stressful periods in their life. Before we can say anything definite, however, it is important to develop and improve on the research that already has been done and that has been outlined in this article. In particular, research is needed which utilizes behavioural measures. In the meantime, we have no alternative but to implement some of the suggestions made by Jaffe and Scherl described earlier in the paper, for instance, a systematic screening procedure for potential participants who may be at risk. It is hoped, however, that these safeguards do not totally inhibit the potentially beneficial effects of such groups (Cooper & Mangham, 1971).

REFERENCES

American Psychiatric Association (1970). *Encounter groups and psychiatry.* Washington, D.C.: A.P.A.

Cooper, C. L. & Mangham, I. L. (1971). *T-Groups: a survey of research.* London: John Wiley & Sons.

Cooper, C. L. (1972a). An attempt to assess the psychologically disturbing effects of T-Group training. *Brit. J. soc. clin. psychol. 11*, 342–345.

Cooper, C. L. (1972b). Coping with life stress after T-Groups. *Psychol. rep. 31*, 602.

Cooper, C. L. (1974). Psychological disturbance following T-Groups: Relationship between Eysenck Personality Inventory and family/friends judgements. *Brit. J. social work, 4*, 39–49.

Crawshaw, R. (1969). How sensitive is sensitivity? *Amer. J. Psychiatry, 126,* 870–873.

Fitts, W. H. (1965). *Tennessee Self-Concept Scale: Manual.* Nashville, Tenn.: Department of Mental Hygiene.

Gottschalk, L. A. (1966). Psychoanalytic notes on T-Groups at the human relations laboratory, Bethel, Maine, *Comprehensive psychiatry 71,* 472–487.

Gottschalk, L. A. & Pattison, E. M. (1969). Psychiatric perspective on T-Groups and the laboratory movement: an overview. *Amer. J. psychiatry, 126,* 823–839.

Jaffe, S. L. & Scherl, D. J. (1969). Acute psychosis precipitated by T-Group experiences. *Arch. gen. psychiat. 21,* 443–448.

Lakin, M. (1969). Some ethical issues in sensitivity training. *Amer. psychologist 24,* 923–928.

Lubin, B. & Lubin, A. W. (1971). Laboratory training stress compared with college examination stress. *J. appl. behav. sci. 7,* 502–507.

Lubin, B. & Zuckerman, M. (1967). Affective and perceptual-cognitive patterns in sensitivity training groups. *Psychol. rep. 21,* 365–476.

Lubin, B. & Zuckerman, M. (1969). Level of emotional arousal in laboratory training. *J. appl. behav. sci. 5,* 483–490.

Mann, E. K. (1970). Sensitivity training: should we use it? *Trg. Development. J. 24,* 44–48.

Pollack, D. (1966). Coping and avoidance in inebriated alcoholics and normals. *J. abn. psychol. 71,* 417–419.

Pollack, D. & Stanley, G. (1971). Coping and marathon sensitivity training. *Psychol. rep. 29,* 379–385.

Posthuma, A. B. & Posthuma, B. W. (1973). Some observations on encounter group casualties. *J. appl. behav. sci. 9,* 595–608.

Reddy, W. B. (1970). Sensitivity training or group psychotherapy: the need for adequate screening. *Int. J. grp. psychother. 20,* 366–371.

Ross, W. D., Kligfeld, M. & Whitman, R. W. (1971). Psychiatrists, patients and sensitivity groups. *Arch. gen. psychiat. 25,* 178–180.

Smith, P. B. (1971). The varieties of group experience. *New society. 443,* 483-485.

Yalom, I. D. & Lieberman, M. A. (1971). A study of encounter group casualties. *Arch. gen. psychiat. 25,* 16–30.

V. WHERE CAN T-GROUP DYNAMICS BE USED?

Applications in the Home, School, Office and Community

INTRODUCTION

V. Where Can T-Group Dynamics Be Used?
Applications in the Home, School, Office, and Community

Exploiting the full usefulness of T-Group dynamics involves getting them out of the laboratory and into production, as it were. "The critical question . . . is the question of transfer," Winn notes. "How does one," he queries, "transfer one's insight, the deeper understanding of group phenomena, the realization of how one's behavior affects others, from a 'micro-culture' of a laboratory into the outside world?"[1] There is no denying that the effects of a T-Group experience are usually meaningful and "learningful," that is, but therein lies the rub. How can the full meaning and learning be applied to a person's life space, as opposed to being encapsulated as a precious moment or two spent on a lofty but remote "magic mountain"?

Note that the issue is not the utopian one of making all life a T-Group. Sometimes, a T-Group can be set up in the "real world." Other times, the challenge is to variously approach the T-Group model as an ideal type, to apply the laboratory approach. This more subtle transfer problem is dual: to find real-world processes that are the same as or analogous to, those tapped in a T-Group; and to apply to those processes knowledge and experience gained from the laboratory approach. Sometimes the transfer is simple and direct, as when I say: "I would like my relations with Joe to be like those I experienced in a T-Group, and I have some idea of how to go about it." Sometimes the transfer is complex and indirect, as when a large organization is involved.

The following editorial comments and selected readings will approach the transfer issue from four vantage points. First, some major experiential learnings with transfer will be sketched. Second, the role of the "change agent" in facilitating transfer will be introduced. Third, two types of transfer will be outlined. Fourth, several examples will be presented of attempts to transfer T-Group dynamics into a variety of contexts, including the home, schools, complex organizations, and the community.

TWO PERSPECTIVES ON TRANSFER

The traditional approach to transfer has been a gentle one, proceeding from "stranger" to "family" T-Group experiences. A stranger experience is just what the name implies, a T-Group composed of people who did not know one another before and who are not likely to have regular contacts after their group disbands. The rationale for beginning with the stranger experience is direct, and apparently compelling. Three major elements in that rationale suggest both qualities.

- Strangers will find it easier to be open with one another, there being no long-standing and perhaps unavoidable relations that must be preserved at any cost.
- Strangers are not burdened by longish histories whose detail may obscure the underlying social and emotional dynamics.
- Risks should be easier to take, given that the members anticipate no future.

[1]Alexander Winn, "The Laboratory Approach to Organization Development: A Tentative Model of Planned Change," p. 1. Paper prepared for delivery at the British Psychological Society, *Annual Conference* (Oxford, England: September, 1968).

Of late, however, a number of transfer attempts have started the other way around. These transfer attempts have started with "family groups," that is, those whose members live together or work together. Husband-wife pairs have been used to compose a T-Group, for example,[2] as have superiors and their subordinates from the same organization.[3] T-Group learning is directly applicable to back-home situations, in such cases, which is the major value of a family group. The supporting counterrationale also has its compelling qualities.

- Family groups maximize the chances that insights will be embodied in corrective action with someone who matters in a long-run sense, which is distinguished from having an insight in a group that will soon disband.
- Family groups in organizations minimize fantasies that the trainers will carry tales to the person's superiors, for at least some of those superiors will be present.
- Family groups increase the chances that an organization's norms will reinforce and support T-Group learning, whereas stranger experiences permit far less confidence about such an effect.

The basic decision about the way to approach transfer—whether initially through stranger or family experiences, to note only two approaches—has its major benefits and risks, obviously. Thus the risk of feedback and self-disclosure are both greater in a family group, just as the potential returns are greater. Perhaps the only generalization is that the family groups become more useful as the values of the involved individuals or groups are consistent with values underlying the laboratory approach. If individuals or groups are less "culturally prepared," the approach via stranger experiences becomes increasingly reasonable. At some undetermined point, indeed, that cultural unpreparedness might be so great as to argue against any attempt to apply the laboratory approach. The chances of success would be too slim, even if more harm than good did not result.

THE CHANGE AGENT: AN EVOLVING PROFESSION DEVOTED TO TRANSFER

Since the transfer problem is so critical in the full use of the laboratory method, it is no surprise that a new profession has begun evolving to do the job. The role is that of the "change agent," and it may truly be classified as a modern phenomenon. Indeed, the legitimate appearance of the change agent may be dated as October 7, 1963, when a large classified ad appeared in the *New York Times.* That advertisement is an early recognition that a growing body of professionals is preoccupied with the transfer problem, with searching for ways and means to apply the accumulating results of the behavioral sciences in a wide variety of contexts.

---

[2]George B. Leonard, "The Man & Woman Thing," *Look,* December 24, 1968, pp. 62–72.
[3]Winn, *op. cit.*

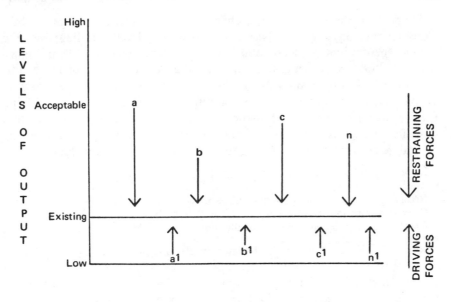

Figure 5.1. A Generalized Force-Field Analysis

The change agent as a person, as a professional, and the processes in which change agents engage have received increasing scholarly attention over the past several years. An early paper by Warren G. Bennis[4] presented a valuable profile of this evolving profession. He highlighted the idea that the assumptions that change agents make about their work both channel diagnostic effort and exclude potentially significant phenomena.

Bennis' ideas are reflected indirectly in Noel M. Tichy's "How Different Types of Change Agents Diagnose Organizations." Tichy describes a recent study of the diagnostic emphases of four types of change agents. These are the Outside Pressure Type, the Organization Development Type, the Analysis for the Top Type, and People Change Technology Type. In this questionnaire study the manner in which change agents conceived of their role was related to differences in the factors they choose to emphasize in their diagnosis, and these differences were related, in turn, to differences in value orientations and change techniques. Inferentially, Tichy's findings support those of Bennis. The relationship between diagnostic emphases and change interventions tends to be a self-reinforcing cycle. This is so particularly when the intervention is successful as its very success creates the possibility that important problem elements in the group or organization may be overlooked.

[4]Warren G. Bennis, "Theory and Method in Applying Behavioral Sciences to Planned Organizational Change," a paper read before the Conference of International Operations Research Associations, September 14, 1964, Cambridge, England.

Stripped to the essentials, the change agent diagnoses and prescribes. Consider the simple case of persistent low output levels. In diagnosis, the change agent might use such notions as "force-field analysis." As in Figure 5.1, the low level of output is conceived as a "quasi-stationary equilibrium," which is the resultant of an existing balance of forces, some driving output higher and other forces restraining any increases. After identifying the various forces and estimating their significance, as represented by vectors of different lengths in Figure 5.1, the change agent can choose among the several general strategies available to him. These strategies include:

- Increasing old driving forces;
- Adding new driving forces;
- Reducing the number and strength of old restraining forces;
- Converting previous restraining forces into driving forces;
- Employing various combinations of the four strategies above.

The several strategies have different payoffs and problems, but the change agent must act so as to effectively manage several processes, whatever the mix of strategies he employs. Roughly, the change agent's challenge has three components: to induce employees to "unfreeze" so that they are able to give up the attitudes and behaviors supporting the low level of output; to permit them to develop appropriate new attitudes and behaviors; and to reinforce these new attitudes and behaviors that support a higher level of productivity, to "refreeze." Since the change agent typically operates under significant pressure of time, and in very complex networks of opposing forces, the challenge of effectively managing these general processes of change is a numbing one.

The change agent also must keep in mind a variety of guidelines governing change in complex systems, as if he did not have enough with which to concern himself. Six of these guidelines may usefully be noted here.[5]

- To change a subsystem or any part of a subsystem, relevant aspects of the broad system also must be changed.
- To change behavior at any level in an organization complementary and reinforcing changes usually must be made at organization levels above and below that level.
- The place to begin change is at those points in the system where stress and strain exist. Stress may give rise to dissatisfaction, and thus motivate change in the system.
- If thoroughgoing changes in a hierarchical structure are to be made, they usually should start with the policy-making body or as high in the hierarchy as possible.
- Changes in both formal and informal organization typically are involved in any process of change.
- Planned change is likely to be more effective if persons at many organization levels participate in fact-finding and in diagnosing needed change, as well as in formulating and reality-testing goals and programs of change.

---

[5]NTL Institute for Applied Behavioral Science, "Change Does Not Have to Be Haphazard," *Reading Book* (Arlington, Va.: NTL Institute, 1968), pp. 68–70.

A conclusion about the role of the change agent is there for the making. If transfer is crucial in extracting fuller value from the laboratory, the role of the change agent is a vital one in midwifing that transfer.

Herbert A. Shepard's "Rules of Thumb for Change Agents" represents some reflections on his own consulting experience or in situations where "you are just being yourself trying to bring out something that involves other people." The "rules of thumb," of course, are not precisely that. They are bits of advice or things to think about that have made sense to Shepard and they have a distinct humanistic flavor, as well as one that might be called hard-nosed. An example of the latter is, "Don't argue if you can't win" meaning that it's a good idea for the change agent to avoid win-lose strategies "because they deepen the conflict instead of resolving it." And the humanism shines through in "Rule VIII: Capture the Moment", as Shepard suggests that change agents, in order to take advantage of the total situation, must have their hearts as well as their heads in tune. Having one's heart involved means being able to have full access to one's own experience of the self in the situation so that the moment will be captured more often.

TRANSFER IN SEVERAL MODALITIES: TWO VARIETIES

Thus far, we have intentionally been unspecific about what "transfer" means. We will change this unsatisfactory state of affairs. Recall that two kinds of transfer were broadly described earlier in this chapter. The first kind is relatively simple and direct but uncommon: to set up T-Groups in the real world, thereby improving interpersonal and intergroup situations. The second kind of transfer is more subtle and typical. It involves attempting in various contexts to engage processes and to gain results that are characteristic of T-Groups, in which attempts T-Groups are used sparingly or not at all. In this second kind of transfer, the T-Group serves as a kind of ideal model of what human relations can be like. The job is to approach in life those processes and results characteristic of that ideal model.

Richard E. Walton[6] has described a narrow but significant case of transfer of T-Group processes in his work with interpersonal conflict resolution. In a case study, he analyzed how two administrators worked toward resolving some issues between them with the help of a consultant. Transfer in this case took place at a variety of levels. For example, both parties involved had previous T-Group experiences. Consequently, they had at least been exposed to the values of the laboratory approach, and thus no doubt had direct experiences about how feedback and self-disclosure can be used to work toward resolution of issues between people. Relatedly, the "third party" consultant served as a kind of conscience about these values and, perhaps, as

---

[6]Richard E. Walton, "Interpersonal Confrontation and Basic Third Party Functions: A Case Study," *Journal of Applied Behavioral Science*, Vol. 4, No. 3 (1965), pp. 322–344.

a reminder of their sanguine effects. The third party, in short, helped encourage feedback and disclosure.

There are other convenient ways of showing how the third-party approach attempts to tap some basic dynamics analogous to those encountered in a T-Group. Crudely, the purpose is to minimize degenerative communication sequences and maximize regenerative ones. The sketches below suggest the closed-system nature of the two kinds of sequences. The two men in Walton's study seemed locked into a degenerative sequence, which fed on itself. The consultant's strategy was to try to reverse the sequence, apparently beginning in this case by building trust. That is, the consultant was seen as possessing useful skills. Moreover, the consultant was very conscious of attempting to be impartial, although he had stronger ties to one of the men. Similarly, both men effectively raised their trust in each other by the very act of agreeing to meet with the consultant. Such factors seem to have set the stage for beginning to reverse the degenerative communications between the two men. That is, increased trust had the effects of reducing the risk of relating authentically, as well as encouraging heightened openness and owning by the two principals about their feelings toward one another. These effects provide the basis for building a regenerative communication cycle.

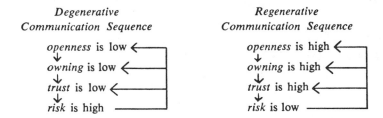

In another context, Walton[7] has suggested that the T-Group provides a person with the opportunity to learn how and when to choose behavioral strategies that are distributive or integrative. Distributive situations are competitive, win-lose affairs. In the T-Group they tend, over time, to be minimized in favor of an integrative or collaborative model of behavior.

A second variety of transfer of T-Group dynamics is both more complex and comprehensive. Overall, Organization Development (OD) programs based on the laboratory approach strive to create a work environment in which individual needs can be met in the process of meeting organizational needs.

Organization Development (OD) programs face an uphill battle, for the values commonly guiding interpersonal and intergroup relations in organizations are uncongenial to the values underlying the laboratory approach. This

---

[7]Richard Walton. "How to Choose Between Strategies of Conflict and Cooperation," *NTL Institute: Reading Book* (Arlington, Va.: NTL Institute, 1967), pp. 57–62.

point is easily supported. Argyris does the job well in discussing the "pyramidal values" that he sees as dominant in public and business organizations.[8] He emphasizes three pyramidal values.

- The crucial human relationships at work are those related to getting the technical job done.
- Effectiveness in human relationships increases as behavior becomes more rational and clearly communicated. Expression of emotions is associated with ineffectiveness.
- Human relationships are most effectively influenced by controls and rewards/punishments that reinforce the two values above.

Argyris does not like some of the major consequences of these pyramidal values. Thus he notes they imply decreases in giving and receiving information about executives' impact on one another. Moreover, Argyris envisions decreases in risk-taking and openness, which can be associated with degenerative communication sequences. Finally, as trust and risk-taking decrease, subordinates will tend to become more dependent upon superiors. This can rigidify organizations.

Argyris proposes an alternative set of values, which supplements the pyramidal values but does not replace them. He details three such values.

- Important human relationships not only relate to achieving the organization's objectives but also relate to maintaining the organization's internal system and adapting to the environment.
- Human relationships increase in effectiveness as *all* the relevant behavior (rational and interpersonal) becomes conscious, discussable, and controllable.
- Direction, controls, and rewards and penalties are important. But human relationships are most effectively influenced through authentic relationships, internal commitment, psychological success, and the process of confirmation.

What is the vehicle for aiding people in organizations to learn and implement these alternative values? And what are the specific goals of such learning and implementation? Previous selections provide the answers. Thus the T-Group is an important vehicle for establishing that individuals prefer such alternative values, as well as for demonstrating that individuals can develop attitudes and skills appropriate for these values. These alternative values then can guide attempts to build organizations that are more need satisfying.

TRANSFER OF T-GROUP DYNAMICS IN VARIOUS CONTEXTS: HOME, SCHOOL, OFFICE, AND COMMUNITY

The various modalities of transfer have been applied in a variety of contexts, which variety is the present focus. The transfer often involves the direct use of T-Groups, but it may be based on various learning designs that

---

[8]Chris Argyris, "T-Groups for Organizational Effectiveness," *Harvard Business Review,* Vol. 42 (March/April, 1964), p. 61.

attempt to engage T-Group dynamics without using T-Groups. The transfer of T-Groups and/or their dynamics to various contexts may be characterized in terms of two themes, rapidly growing acceptance and significant challenge to traditional patterns of organizing collective action.

The escalating acceptance of T-Groups can be illustrated easily by the growing number of applications in "organizations" of two extreme sizes. Thus the T-Group has been used to help improve relations between husband-wife dyads, and with substantial effect to judge from available reports.[9] At the other extreme, T-Groups have been used variously to improve relations in complex organizations. For example, all kinds of organizations have provided their personnel with "stranger" experiences in T-Groups. In addition, large organizations increasingly are making "cousin" experiences available to their employees.[10] Cousin groups are formed of members of the same organization who are roughly of the same rank but who do not work together. Even the popular press has felt it appropriate to note the phenomenon, via articles such as "It's OK to Cry in the Office."[11] Finally, T-Groups have been increasingly used to develop "family" units or "teams" among individuals who work together and are hierarchically related. One such experience, for example, concluded that work units can profitably share a T-Group experience, given appropriate conditions.[12] Some of these conditions are:

- If a substantial level of trust exists among members of the work team, the training will be more effective than a stranger experience.
- The presence of the boss reduces the concern of participants that the trainer will carry tales to him.
- T-Group training will be more effective in family groups if the emphasis is on improving interpersonal relations and communications for the sake of the organization, rather than the personal growth of the individual.

Applications also fall everywhere in between the two extremes of dyads and complex organizations. Thus T-Group experiences have been utilized to help teachers improve the interpersonal and intergroup climates in their classrooms, with marked success.[13] Less direct applications of the laboratory method, in addition, have successfully sought to improve black/white relations.[14] And the list could be extended to include virtually all of man's collective activities.

---

[9]Leonard, *op. cit.*

[10]Robert T. Golembiewski and Arthur Blumberg, "Sensitivity Training in Cousin Groups: A Confrontation Design," *Training and Development Journal,* Vol. 23 (Aug. 1969), pp. 18–23.

[11]John Poppy, "It's OK to Cry in the Office," *Look,* July 9, 1968, pp. 64–76.

[12]Arthur H. Kuriloff and Stuart Atkins, "T-Group for a Work Team," *Journal of Applied Behavioral Science,* Vol. 2, No. 1 (1966), p. 64.

[13]Richard A. Schmuck, "Helping Teachers Improve Classroom Group Processes," *Journal of Applied Behavioral Science,* Vol. 4 (December, 1968), pp. 401–36.

[14]Eugene B. Nadler, "Social Therapy of a Civil Rights Organization," *Journal of Applied Behavioral Science,* Vol. 4 (September, 1968), pp. 281–98.

Applications of T-Group dynamics also raise serious challenges to traditional ways of organizing collective effort, however, which fact implies problems for any attempts at transfer. Even "an organization which is sincerely interested in the growth of its members," Schein notes, may nevertheless generate "organizational conditions and forces which decrease

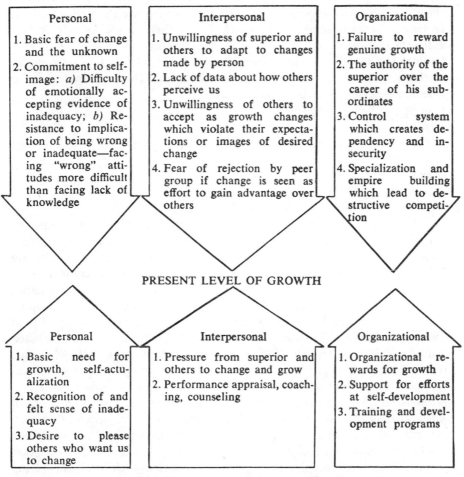

FORCES WORKING TOWARD BLOCKING GROWTH

Personal	Interpersonal	Organizational
1. Basic fear of change and the unknown 2. Commitment to self-image: *a)* Difficulty of emotionally accepting evidence of inadequacy; *b)* Resistance to implication of being wrong or inadequate—facing "wrong" attitudes more difficult than facing lack of knowledge	1. Unwillingness of superior and others to adapt to changes made by person 2. Lack of data about how others perceive us 3. Unwillingness of others to accept as growth changes which violate their expectations or images of desired change 4. Fear of rejection by peer group if change is seen as effort to gain advantage over others	1. Failure to reward genuine growth 2. The authority of the superior over the career of his subordinates 3. Control system which creates dependency and insecurity 4. Specialization and empire building which lead to destructive competition

PRESENT LEVEL OF GROWTH

Personal	Interpersonal	Organizational
1. Basic need for growth, self-actualization 2. Recognition of and felt sense of inadequacy 3. Desire to please others who want us to change	1. Pressure from superior and others to change and grow 2. Performance appraisal, coaching, counseling	1. Organizational rewards for growth 2. Support for efforts at self-development 3. Training and development programs

FORCES WORKING TOWARD GROWTH

Figure 5.2. Analysis of Forces Which Work Toward and Which Block Management Growth and Development

From Edgar H. Schein, "Forces Which Undermine Management Development," *California Management Review*, Vol. 5 (Summer, 1963), p. 32.

the likelihood of growth and thus [may undermine] its own efforts."[15] Figure 5.2 sketches the set of forces-in-tension which typically determines the level of real growth in organizations. For example, T-Group experiences may free organization members to be more in touch with their feelings and those of others, to begin to grow effectively in managing their interpersonal and group relations. But unless (for example) their organization's reward and punishment systems reinforce such behaviors, continued growth is unlikely. The real danger is not mere backsliding. Paradoxically, indeed, the failure to reinforce the initial learning experience may so frustrate the individual that he leaves the organization. The dual challenge, then, is to change individual attitudes and the norms of the larger organizations as well.

Applications of T-Group approaches will be illustrated in four contexts and at several levels of organizational complexity. These contexts may be listed in order of their complexity. They are

- The husband-wife dyad;
- The schoolroom;
- The large administrative or industrial organization, whether business or government; and
- The community.

A. To Married Couples

It is entirely to be expected that the T-Group concept would be introduced into family situations. Indeed the practice of conducting "couples' groups" is fairly widespread, though little has appeared in the literature concerning the processes and problems that these groups encounter. In a related vein, Samuel A. Culbert and Jean R. Renshaw describe a creative transfer of laboratory methodology into family life. Their article "Coping with the Stresses of Travel as an Opportunity for Improving the Quality of Work and Family Life" discusses a seminar-research program that focussed on the problems that develop for a married couple when the husband spends a relatively large proportion of his time in business travel. The program was not a T-Group. Its concern was more on intra- then inter-couple interaction. Various exercises were used to enable the couples to gain a better sense of each other in their relationship, to better understand the stresses that each partner felt as a result of being alone due to travel, and to ponder ways they could help each other deal with the stress. The results of the program indicated that the couples involved had increased their problem-solving resources, had increased their ability to cope with travel stresses, and had a positive carry-over into other organizational relationships in which the husband was involved. Culbert and Renshaw note finally that the program format is not necessarily prototypical and that, "Its utility lies in demon-

---

[15]Edgar H. Schein, "Forces Which Undermine Management Development," *California Management Review,* Vol. 5 (Summer, 1963), esp. pp. 23, 29, and 32.

strating the interdependence of the family and the organization and showing that progress can result from meeting issues at that interface head on."

B. In Schools and Training Situations

Applications of the laboratory approach also have proved useful in schools and in training situations, both via the use of T-Groups as well as the use of designs that induce basic dynamics of the approach without resort to sensitivity training.

Rory O'Day describes, in "Reality Teaching: The Self-Analysis Classroom," a teaching situation whose aim is "to help students become more conscious and skillful participant observers of their own lives." O'Day stresses that the self-analysis classroom is not a sensitivity-training group in that its purpose excludes attempts to prescribe or alter behavior. Because the classroom can present a valuable microcosm of the larger society, it can be conceived of as a laboratory through which concepts concerning social systems and individual behavior can be tested against what actually occurs.

The specific goals of the self-analysis classroom are:

- Student self-direction;
- Student independence;
- Thoughtful observation of one's own behavior and the behavior of others; and
- The ability to engage in effective collaborative group action to resolve common learning dilemmas.

The role of the teachers in this classroom setting, though it is not a T-Group, resembles that of the trainer in many ways. The teachers withdraw from active leadership, talk as little as possible, and try predominantly to ". . . help the students move from a position of contradiction to one of synthesis and balance. . . ." Though most self-analysis classrooms have been conducted on the college level, O'Day suggests that the methodology is clearly appropriate to the secondary school. It is important to note, however, that there is a cognitive side of this type of teaching-learning situation and it is best used in the context of some substance such as interpersonal relations or social psychology.

How dynamics associated with T-Groups can be induced into adult and more tense learning situations is illustrated by Thomas H. Patten, Jr., and Lester E. Dorey. They report on the results of a learning design for adults dealing with racial attitudes in "An Equal Employment Opportunity Sensitivity Workshop." The results imply the usefulness of this effort at adult education in an area of critical concern.

T-Group dynamics also have been variously applied to schools[16] as social systems. Fred C. Feitler and Lawrence L. Lippitt describe the thinking and

---

[16]For a wide range of applications of the laboratory approach in schools, see Richard A. Schmuck and Matthew B. Miles, *Organization Development in Schools* (Palo Alto, Calif.: National Press Books, 1971).

programming that went into the development of a fourteen-school consortium change effort. Their selection, "A Multi-District Organizational Development Effort", takes the reader through an account of the first year's training and development activities of the consortium. The program emphasized the importance of training principal and teachers together and its results raised the tantalizing prospect of schools becoming more collaborative organizations than they typically tend to be.

C. In Large Organizations

The purpose of OD (Organization Development) programs is not to make every organization a big T-Group, then, whatever that means. Rather, the purpose is to build into the organization values and processes that are consistent with the laboratory approach. These values and processes, in turn, will guide the development of appropriate practices and structures in a large organization. T-Groups are often used in the "front load" of OD programs, to help build trust and attitudes that will support continual analysis and renewal of the organization. The "back load" of OD programs will include a wide variety of changes in policies and procedures and structure, with their accompanying panoply of training and development efforts. T-Groups or T-Group processes may be variously used in such training and development, as in team-building or making more effective project groups.

Change programs of the OD variety are usually long-term propositions as they typically are concerned with integrating new behavioral norms into the organization's life. In "Durability of Organizational Change" Stanley E. Seashore and David G. Bowers speak directly to factors that may influence the long-term integration of organizational change efforts. They revisited the site (a manufacturing firm) of a major organizational change program that had been started seven years previously and from which their most recent data was five years old. It is important to note that the change program had a heavy participative emphasis. They found what perhaps they had hoped to but were not clearly prepared to find; that is, somewhat surprisingly, the data they collected during their visit clearly implied that the changes had been maintained and had been integrated into the organization. Little, if any, regression had taken place.

Three possible explanations are offered for the non-regression phenomenon. First, in retrospect it appeared as though the original change program contained "lock-in" devices. That is, change efforts were not aimed at human organizational processes, technology, or organizational structure in isolation from each other. Rather, for example, the thrust was ". . . to make structural changes in the organization that matched the work system and that did not violate reasonable assumptions about the values and motives of individual members." The changes, then, were systemic and were, it was hoped, mutually reinforcing—thus setting up counter forces to regression tendencies. A second and somewhat more speculative explanation for the maintenance of the changes is that part of the original program was aimed at helping people analyze their decisions in terms of projected systemic effects. It is possible, the authors suggest, that "An organization habituated at all levels to think about, discuss openly, and to weigh properly the full range of elements in the organizational system might well have unusual capacities for self-maintenance and self-development." The third explanation of the data is that the thorough induction of the participative mode may be by itself an agent of change maintenance. People may get ". . . hooked, know what they want, and lend their effort to maintaining it. . . ." Perhaps, at its root, the prime value of the Seashore and Bowers article rests in the potential for the development of action hypotheses concerning the induction of long-lasting change in an organization.

There are OD efforts that might be described as limited-purpose programs. "Integrating Disrupted Work Relationships" illustrates such limited purpose programs. The goal was a simple one: to help ease the transition for men in an organization who had been demoted, using a design consistent with the laboratory approach. Two points about the piece of action-research dealing with that transition deserve highlighting. First, the demotions induced major trauma in the men, as far as the available measuring instrument was sensitive to reality. Second, the design seems to have been successful in quickly reducing that trauma, not by avoidance but by confrontation. These two findings in turn imply how much there is out there to do, and they also suggest how much can be done, even given our limited present knowledge.

D. In the Community

T-Group dynamics also have been applied in the community, usually with the intention of improving the climate for intergroup relations. Sometimes the arena is a public and dramatic one, as was a six-hour confrontation between the races carried by a metropolitan radio station.[17] Mostly, the arena is private, known only to participants and to close followers of applications of the T-Group. Typically, whatever the arena or however dramatic, the consequences seem pretty much the same: increased understanding of the position of the other person; a better communication between those previously at odds; and a common commitment to try to do for others what the participants experienced. However, little is known about gearing such changes by individuals into the broader community.

In "Community Action Groups Come to the Classroom", Joseph M. Petulla describes how he transferred the "observe, judge, act method" from his work with community groups to the training of college students in urban

---

[17]"Boston Marathon," *Newsweek*, Vol. 73 (January 13, 1969), p. 60.

studies. The relationship of his strategies to individual behavior in a T-Group is elegant if subtle. At issue is helping people to behave less impulsively without regard to consequences and to develop the ability of people to collect all relevant data, analyze the systemic effects of alternative acts—and then act.

The last article in this section, "Working with Hostile Groups: A Reexamination" by James E. Crowfoot and Mark A. Chesler, presents a political-ideological counterpoint to the ". . . well-ordered world of scientifically oriented planned social change. . . ." The vehicle for their views is a commentary they wrote relative to an article by Cyril Mill[18] in which Mill analyzed the sources of dealing with that hostility, to reduce it so to speak. Crowfoot and Chesler say that Mill's position is a classic case of "victim blame." The political perspective on hostile groups treats this hostility as a legitimate symptom of value differences and suggests that it ". . . can be a major source of energy and personal growth. . . ." The problem is to utilize productively the power inherent in hostility, not to dissipate it.

Surely more than one change agent or OD specialist has belatedly discovered that the real function that was performed by his or her activities was to "soothe the troops." Crowfoot and Chesler might comment that in the soothing process grand opportunities for learning and change were lost. So, in a sense, this paper brings this chapter to a close in the way it began, with a focus on the change agent in a way that gives one pause for thought.

---

[18]Cyril Mill, "Working with Hostile Groups," *Social Change,* Vol. 4, No. 1 (1974).

20. How Different Types of Change Agents Diagnose Organizations[1]

NOEL M. TICHY

INTRODUCTION

When asked to describe what he does as a change agent, one respondent said, 'First I gotta figure out what's happening'. He went on to state:

When we move in for system change, we look immediately for grassroots strength, we go right for the throat, that's it, always look at grassroots groups. The second thing we look for is radical mentality. We always look for those two things first. We then immediately begin making contact with grassroots groups and assess their radical mentality . . .

Whatever a change agent's orientation to social intervention, he employs a number of diagnostic dimensions for assessing new situations. Whyte (1967) posits that the organizational models used by change agents are directly related to their intervention strategy. Our study of 133 varied change agents indicates that such a relationship does tend to exist. Different types of change agents do vary in their diagnostic approach.

This paper presents the findings of the portion of an interview and questionnaire study of 133 change agents which focused on how they diagnose organizations. The change agents in our study are individuals whose primary role is to deliberately intervene into social systems in order to facilitate or bring about social change. The respondents are divided into four categories of change agent types. The four category scheme of change agent types was presented in previous work by the author (Tichy, 1972; Tichy & Hornstein, 1976, Tichy, 1974). The categorization scheme was empirically derived to distinguish change agents from each other in terms of their General Change Models (GCM).

The GCM includes a *conceptual component* (how the respondents diagnosed organizations and conceptualized about mediators of change), a *value component* (their change goals and attitudes), and a *change technology* component (the techniques and tactics they used) as well as personal characteristics and concurrent characteristics (where they work and how).

Reprinted from *Human Relations,* Vol. 28, No. 9, 1975, pp. 771–799.
[1]Support for this study came from a National Institute of Mental Health grant, Change Agent Approaches (Grant No. 5RO1MH24159–02); the Faculty Research Fund of the Graduate School of Business, Columbia University; the Center for Policy Research, Inc., New York City; and the Garrett Chair for Social Responsibility, Graduate School of Business, Columbia University. I would like to thank Jack Pogany for his considerable help in conducting interviews and analyzing the data.

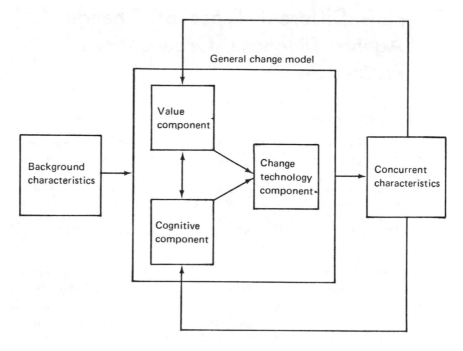

Figure 5.3. Framework for Organizing Change Agent Data

This paper concentrates on the conceptual component of the change agent's GCM. This is the framework change agents use to diagnose social systems. Figure 5.3 diagrammatically presents the GCM and the proposed relationship between its components.

The four types of change agents are: Outside Pressure Type (OP), Analysis for the Top Type (AFT), Organization Development (OD), and People Change Technology Type (PCT). The characteristics of each type were dealt with extensively elsewhere and will be only briefly summarized here.

The OP's[2] focus primarily on changing the way systems relate to their external environment, such as making corporations more socially responsible. They get their leverage for change from outside systems through the application of various pressure tactics, including mass demonstration, civil disobedience, political organizing and, in some cases, violence. Most of them, according to their accounts, work against government units or busi-

---

[2]This category included 8 respondents who worked as part of a national consumers advocate group, 13 respondents engaged in civil rights, women's rights, and peace movement work as nonviolent interventionists, 6 respondents involved in various social change activities resorting at times to violence as an intervention strategy, 3 respondents who were community organizers and 6 union organizers.

nesses and attempt to accomplish as their first goal 'equalization of power in the system or increased responsibility to the general public welfare'. Of the four types, the OP's are obviously the most politically radical, most critical of our society, and the greatest advocates of radical social change.

The PCT's[3] focus their change efforts on individual functioning within organizations. They gain their leverage for change from inside organizations at the top level. The PCT's include the highest proportion of university-based, behavioral scientist respondents. The PCT's are split into three groups in terms of their goals: (1) improved efficiency and output, (2) improved system problem-solving, and (3) power equalization and responsiveness to the general public interest. In order to accomplish their goals, they employ behavioral science technologies which they attempt to get incorporated into a system. They accomplish this by working within organizations as 'expert doers', implementing and operating the technology for the client, such as behavior modification programs.

The OD's[4] are similar to the PCT's in a number of ways. They both share the same leverage point for change, inside at the top of the system; and both have a high proportion of university-based people in the behavioral science area. They do differ. The OD's focus on internal processes, such as group functioning, communication, etc., instead of individual functioning. Also, the OD's are not 'expert doers' but work collaboratively with the client system to help them solve their problems and to improve their system's problem-solving ability. Many OD's label themselves as liberals and have similar patterns of responses on political and social value questions as do the PCT's. They use such tactics as sensitivity training, team building, individual consultation, etc., to affect change in organizations.

Finally, there are AFT's[5] who focus primarily on the system's external relationships with its environment (market, government, consumers, etc.) and whose leverage for change is from inside at the top of the organization. The AFT's work primarily with businesses and government units and reported that they are primarily interested in improving 'efficiency' and 'output' of the systems they work with. Their techniques for accomplishing these goals include recommending technical and structural modifications of organizations. The recommendations are based on analytic type, e.g., operations research, and systems analysis, studies which are fed to the top decision makers, who then legislate the recommended changes. Politically they include the highest proportion of respondents low on societal criticism

---

[3]These respondents included group consultants, need achievement consultants, behavior modification consultants and job enrichment consultants.

[4]These respondents included those who were associated with two major nonprofit institutes and who referred to themselves as Organization Development consultants.

[5]This category consisted of 15 respondents who used operations research and systems analysis, 6 who did policy studies, 7 who were eclectic analytic consultants (Business School professors) and 12 corporate planner consultants.

and low on advocating radical and social change and the highest proportion of conservatives.

As previously presented in Figure 5.3, the conceptual component of the GCM includes a diagnostic category. It is assumed that change agents have conceptual frameworks or models which determine the categories of information used to diagnose organizations. Cognitive theorists, such as Zajonc (1960) propose that 'individuals expecting to deal with information "tune in" cognitive structures which constitute the basis of their commerce with the information'. This article explores the results of a study designed to assess the characteristics of the cognitive structures which change agents employ in diagnosing aspects of complex organizations. The primary focus of the inquiry was whether or not different types of change agents employ different diagnostic models in their change activities.

Often the cognitive structures or diagnostic models are not explicit, as we discovered during our pilot interviews (Tichy & Hornstein, 1976). We therefore had to develop a research methodology which enabled us to uncover change agents' sometimes implicit diagnostic frameworks. Often when faced with the task of articulating their diagnostic models, respondents made comments similar to the following operations researcher who stated:

I have a modest belief that I have a very subtle and sophisticated understanding of orgnizations and how they work. I don't have any formal structure and lots of generalizations. Did you ever play around with making fires? You can get an awful lot of skill in making a fire work, but you try to explain it to someone and it is very hard to do; the same with diagnosing an organization.

Other respondents had less difficulty, yet almost all indicated that their diagnostic approach was based more on artisanship than science. As researchers, we were interested in uncovering the frameworks which they used and comparing them to determine similarities and differences.

METHOD

One hundred and thirty-three well known change agents of apparently varying types were studied by means of questionnaires and interviews. Thirty-four were OD's, forty OP's, forty-one AFT's, and eighteen PCT's. Not all 133 respondents completed the section of the questionnaire on organizational diagnosis. The response rates for this section of the questionnaire were OD's, 33/34; OP's, 36/40; AFT's, 37/41; and PCT's, 18/18. There is no explanation for why PCT's had a higher proportion of respondents answering on this section. The percentages reported in each of the tables are based on the number of respondents who completed the diagnosis questions.

This was an exploratory study, hence the respondents are not a representative sample.[6] They were selected using an *a priori* categorization scheme of

---

[6]Because there is no sample, tests of significance are not appropriate.

change approaches (Hornstein *et al.,* 1971) as well as a sociometric nomination technique. The categories emerged from an inductive analysis of the data. These four categories best accounted for the many differences in the study variables (see Tichy, 1972; Tichy, 1974).

Measurement of Change Agent's Diagnostic Framework

Three aspects of their frameworks were obtained: (1) subcategories of specific pieces of information which they seek in a diagnosis; (2) the major categories of information sought during diagnosis; and (3) the relationship of the diagnostic categories to interventions.

Sub-categories of Information Sought: These represent specific things such as turnover, fiscal characteristics, which a change agent might want to find out about an organization in order to aid in diagnosis. To determine what pieces of information change agents generally seek in their diagnosis, respondents were instructed as follows:

We would like you to assume that you are making initial contact with a system (organization, community, group) with which you are going to work. We are interested in what information you would require in order to begin a change effort with the system. We have provided you with examples of information you might seek in the labels below.

(1) Look at these labels and consider which items you would actually use. Place a check mark on the items you would use.
(2) Add additional items which you would require by writing them in on the blank labels. Specify the information you would require, being as brief and concise as possible.

Put down as many things as you feel are necessary for you in your role as change agent.

The labels included: formal authority structure, informal reward system, span of control, work process-technology and organization of tasks, informal groupings, relation of system to external factors-markets and government, formal reward system, selection of staff, training, organizational culture-norms and values of system members, turnover, satisfaction of members with their jobs, performance evaluation and appraisal of organizational units, interpersonal satisfaction of members, goals of the system, resource limitations, information channels, political leadership, informal leadership, control systems. The labels which were provided represent aspects of social systems commonly discussed in the organizational literature.

Major Categories of Information: These were obtained by asking respondents to organize the labels they selected in step 1 into categories. The instructions were to:

Fold out your label sheet so that you can view it while working on these pages. The task in Step 2 of this section is to arrange the information you have listed as necessary into categories. Look over the labels which contain the items you would use to see if they seem to fall into groupings. Place only these labels into eight or less (no fewer than five) categories using the spaces provided on these pages. Once these labels are in the categories you have designated, give each category a descriptive name in the space provided at the bottom of each block.

Organizational Categories Worked on Directly: This information was obtained by asking respondents to indicate which of their major categories contained elements which they worked on directly.

Developing Common Categories: Because each respondent was instructed to name his own categories, it was necessary to develop a common set of category names. Two judges independently assigned each of the respondent's major categories into one of 14 categories. The 14 categories represented critical organizational dimensions found in the literature, as well as ones that emerged in preliminary analysis of this study. The fourteen categories were later reduced to 12 by combining Psychological and Individual Factors with Personal Selection, and Change Problem Area with the Change Agent's Relationship with the client. The twelve categories which remained and samples of the information items most often included in each are:

Formal Structure, this typically included such items as the formal authority structure, span of control, and control system.
Goals of the System, the primary item in this category was system goals.
Informal System, this category often included such items as informal groupings, informal leadership and informal communication.
Relation to External Factors, information items generally dealt with the system's relationship to its environment in terms of resources, constraints imposed on it by government, etc.
Performance, this included such information items as performance of units, individual performance and turnover.
Psychological and Individual Factors and Personnel Selection, this category was originally two separate categories; (1) psychological and individual factors and (2) personnel selection—they were combined and include such items as satisfaction with job, interpersonal satisfaction and selection of staff.
Change Problem Area and the Change Agent's Relationship to System, this category typically did not include specific sub-categories of information.
Culture, the most frequent information items in this category include organizational culture, informal reward and interpersonal satisfaction.
Resources, the two most frequent information items in this category were resource limitations and fiscal characteristics.
Reward System, this typically included information items on formal reward system and informal reward system.
Leadership, both informal and political leadership were included as information items.
Work Process, the most frequent information items included in this category were work process, information channels, and control systems.

Assignment to categories by the judges was based on two criteria. First, if the respondent's major category name and description clearly corresponded to one of the 14 categories, it was assigned to that category. Second, if the major category name did not correspond, then assignment was based on the specific information items (labels) included in the category. For instance, one respondent called a category the 'skeleton' which did not directly correspond to any of the 14 categories, but upon inspection it included such items as 'formal authority structure', and 'span of control' so judges assigned it to the Formal Structure category.

The judges' independent assignments to categories were compared. The inter-judge agreement was over 85%. The 15% non-agreement or non-overlap items were dealt with by having the judges discuss and decide jointly on which of the 14 categories to assign the item.

Respondent one

Category name: Administration	Category name: Geist	Category name: Grass roots characteristics
Technical competence Selection of staff Information channels Training	Radical mentality Imaginative individuals	Grass roots groups Informal leadership Resistance against disruption and subversion Informal groupings

Category name: Guts characteristics	Category name: Environment	
Goals of system Research and information competence	Political leadership Formal authority structure Resource limitations	

Respondent two

Category name: Organization structure and functioning	Category name: Effectiveness of volunteer group	Category name: Objective technical and social factors
Formal authority Selection of staff Performance evaluation and appraisal of organizational units Selection of staff Span of control Turnover Satisfaction of members with jobs Performance evaluation of individuals	Informal reward system Training Interpersonal satisfaction Informal groupings	Relation of system to external factors Work process Fiscal characteristics Resource limitations Information channels

Category name: Organization of groups	Category name: Goals for change	
Organization culture Informal groupings	Goals of system Political leadership Formal reward system	

Figure 5.4. Diagnostic Categories of Two Outside Pressure Respondents

INTRODUCTION TO RESULTS

In order to provide a flavor of how respondents from each of the four change agent types go about their diagnostic work, several of the models which they created in the questionnaire are presented below along with their comments concerning how they proceed with diagnosis. The category names are the ones given by the respondents before the judges assigned them to the new categories.

Outside Pressure: The two examples are from a respondent involved in radical right wing social change activities and a community organizer who was formerly a union organizer. Their work includes political organizing and confrontation, consulting with and helping develop other groups.

The first respondent describes his diagnostic framework, presented in Figure 5.4, in the following terms:

We look immediately for grass roots strength . . . the second thing we look at is radical mentality. We always look for these two things first. We then immediately begin making contact with grass roots groups and assessing their radical mentality. We look for a third thing which is hard to define, that is, imaginative individuals. We need them more than anything, they have to have that imaginative cast about them . . . If the organization has geist, then they will have the radical mentality; they will have these imaginative individuals.

The grass roots characteristics we look for are resistance against disruption and subversion, informal leadership and groupings. These are things we have learned from our experience as being important.

When we talk about the environment, we are focussing on the external political environment in terms of the political leadership, the formal authority structures and their resource limitations.

The final category is called 'guts'; that is, the goals of the system, and the system's research and information competence. You just do not have anything without that; if these people do not have goals and research competency, they are dead cookies.

The second OP respondent is a community organizer. He discusses his diagnostic framework and the whole approach to diagnosis in the following terms:

One has to maintain some degree of objectivity, yet you can become too objective. If you don't know what the hell the score is in the social system as a whole you have no business being there. If you're such a pure social scientist that you've got to study every aspect, you're not worth a damn as a social activist.

There are certain common factors throughout all social systems. You do not need data about them, however. You can't make cracks where there are whole walls. If you attack a wrong you have to make sure you have done your homework. The framework I presented guides me in doing this. You operate under a certain dogma, you are out for certain basic social changes, and certain basic social forces affect this change no matter what social system you are in, yet you still need data to begin with.

It is obvious from these descriptions of their diagnostic frameworks that how they collect information about an organization guides and constrains the subsequent social interventions.

Respondent one

Category name: Organizational arrangements	*Category name:* Output of system	*Category name:* Strategy
Control systems Formal authority structure Information channels Formal reward system Role expectations	Fiscal characteristics, assets, profits Turnover Satisfaction of members Performance evaluation and appraisal of organizational units	Goals of the system

Category name: Environmental inputs	*Category name:* Social system	*Category name:* Intervening variables
Work process, technology and organization of tasks Resource limitations Relation of system to external factors	Informal reward system Informal groupings Political leadership Informal leadership System culture	Intergroup coordination Conflict resolution methods Patterns of interaction Strength of superordinate goals Cooperation orientation of members

Respondent two

Category name: Formal structure	*Category name:* (Individual) psychological variables	*Category name:* Leadership
Selection of staff Formal authority structure Informal reward system Goals of system	Interpersonal satisfaction of members Work process	Political leadership Organization culture Informal leadership Training

Category name:	*Category name:* Environment—system to external	
Satisfaction of member with job Informal grouping Control system Information channels Turnover Resource limitations Formal reward	Relation of system to external environment Fiscal characteristics	Performance evaluation of individuals Performance evaluation of organizational units

Figure 5.5. Diagnostic Categories of Two Organization Development Change Agents

Organization Development: The OD respondents generally stress the importance of client involvement in the diagnosis of a system. They also stress the importance of working on issues and problems which the client group is feeling a need to work on, not those that the change agent identifies and imposes as his view of what the problems are.

Figure 5.5 presents the diagnostic model which was discussed in the following terms by one OD respondent:

In any one situation, I have all of these categories in the back of my mind, yet I let people in the system tell me which ones I should pay particular attention to in that situation, because they seem to be the things that people have aches and pains, points of friction, complaints, and so forth, around. Those are the things you tend to look more closely at than those things that people don't seem to have any sense of discomfort about.

That does not mean that you don't quickly tend to fill yourself in on these other background factors. I go through a process of interviewing plus collecting documents about the formal structure and the history of the institution as well as available records of other people who have taken a look at it. I do tend to go through the checklist, even though people don't volunteer.

The thing that is hard about diagnosis is that there are many potential things to look at when you go into a system. How you manage the process of obtaining information

Respondent one	
Category name: *Formal system for controlling individuals*	*Category name:* *Organizational task*
Formal authority structure Formal reward system Selection of staff	Goals of system Work process Relation of system to external factors Performance evaluation and appraisal of organizational units
Category name: *Individual satisfaction in roles*	*Category name:* *Informal system norms*
Satisfaction of members with their jobs Interpersonal satisfaction of members Informal reward system Turnover Performance evaluation and appraisal of individuals	Organizational culture Informal leadership
Respondent two	
Category name: *Analysis of problems of child-goals*	*Category name:* *Etiology of the problem*
Assessment of willingness of teacher to change Assessment of children's rewards Parent involvement Observation of teacher/child interaction Observation of children's problems Goals of the system	Information channels Parent problems Developmental history Medical history Resource limitations
Category name: *Training*	*Category name:* *Evaluation*
Informal reward system Formal reward system Span of control Work process: technology and organization of staff Satisfaction of members with their jobs Selection of staff Training Informal leadership	Performance evaluation of individuals

Figure 5.6. Diagnostic Categories of Two People Change Technology Respondents

which people volunteer and what you want to look at in order to round out your understanding to make some sensible suggestions and interventions is the process that I find hard to articulate. I listen for a while; then I ask three or four questions which might pick off an item of these reserve things that I think is apt to tell me more about what this is all about.

In effect, I'm developing a thorough and elaborate diagnosis of the set of factors behind the presenting symptom that people are unhappy about.

A somewhat different OD diagnostic model is also presented in Figure 5.5. The two OD models differ in the emphasis each places on the formal system characteristics of the organization and on the individual and human factors

---

Respondent one

Category name: *Goals*	*Category name:* *Effectiveness*	*Category name:* *Formal organization*

Goals of the system
Potential of the organization
  to serve other goals
Process by which goals were
  set
Social importance of current
  and alternative goals
	View of organization held by
	  its clients
	Performance evaluation and
	  appraisal of organization
	  units
		Formal authority structure
		Work process
		Formal reward system
		Control systems

Category name: *Internal forces*	*Category name:* *Sources of innovation*	*Category name:* *External constraints*

System culture
Informal reward system
Informal leadership
Satisfaction of members with
  their jobs
	Selection of new members
	Training
		Resource limitations
		Relation of system to external
		  factors

Respondent two

Category name: *Formal system definition*		*Category name:* *Functional system*	

Formal authority
  structures
Formal reward structures
Resource limitations
Goals of system
Fiscal characteristics
Information channels
	Political leadership
	Work process
	Performance evaluation and
	  appraisal of organization
	  units
		Internal power structure
		  (informal authority
		  structure)
		Informal leadership
		Organizational culture
		Relationship with other
		  organization in same
		  bureaucracy
			Control system
			Informal reward system
			History of organization's
			  development
			Informal information
			  channels

Category name: *System functions and problems*		*Category name:* *Data base*

Problem definition by
  organization
Relationship between goals
  and output
Performance evaluation and
  appraisal (external)
Methods currently employed
  to achieve output
	Relation of system to
	  external factors
		Existing data concerning inputs and outputs
		Development of new data base

Figure 5.7. Diagnostic Categories of Two Analyses for the Top Respondents

in the organization. Each of these respondents included categories which the other did not. The first respondent has categories called 'organizational arrangements', 'system output' and 'goals'—none of which are included in the other's scheme. The other, however, has categories labeled 'leadership' and 'individual/psychological variables' not included in the first's scheme. It is not surprising to discover that the first OD respondent stresses organizational re-design in his intervention work, while the second stresses increased interpersonal competence and team effectiveness.

People Change Technology: The two examples of PCT diagnostic frameworks include that of an achievement motivation trainer and that of a behavior consultant.

The achievement motivation trainer explained that the categories, Respondent One in Figure 5.6, are general guidelines for diagnosis and that because he works primarily with individuals, it is not always necessary for him to systematically collect data in each of the categories.

The second respondent, a behavior modification consultant, uses the categories presented in Figure 5.6 for his diagnostic activities. His orientation to change is reflected in his diagnostic categories. He works in school systems to change children's behavior. His diagnostic categories directly reflect the steps he goes through in setting up a behavior modification programme.

Analysis for the Top: Two AFT diagnostic frameworks are presented in Figure 5.7. The categories for Respondent One in Figure 5.7 are used by a change agent who describes his approach in the following terms:

The kind of agent I am is oriented toward change by means of working directly with or for governmental agencies, applying to these agencies a variety of more or less sophisticated formal analytic techniques, not looking first and hardest at questions of efficiency—to distinguish me from typical management consulting firms—but first and hardest at questions of effectiveness, what is it the organization is trying to accomplish and why; does that make sense? What are alternative goals?

It is clear from the above self-description that the first two categories, Goals and Effectiveness, in Figure 5.7 are central to this change agent's approach.

The other AFT respondent's categories also presented in Figure 5.7 are from a change agent engaged in similar activities. He described his approach as beginning with:

Identify policy problems, define a subset of those problems; establish priorities; define alternative solutions; compare alternatives on the basis of anticipated (estimated) benefits/cost, estimate implementation feasibility; specify the range of uncertainty, recommend one or more options for experimentation or implementation. Participate in implementation and remain involved as innovation succeeds or fails.

Diagnosis starts with a look at the items in the first category, 'Formal System Definition'. He views this as the 'initial process, involves learning

TABLE 5.1
THE PERCENTAGE OF OP'S, AFT'S, OD'S AND PCT'S EMPLOYING
DIFFERENT DIAGNOSTIC CATEGORIES

Category name	Organization development type. %	Outside pressure type. %	Analysis for the top type. %	People change technology type. %	Overall
1. Formal structure	85%	59%	69%	71%	69%
2. Goals of the system	33%	50%	47%	55%	45%
3. Informal structure	42%	42%	49%	44%	44%
4. External relationships	45%	42%	30%	39%	39%
5. Performance	39%	44%	49%	39%	43%
6. Individual/psychological variables	42%	31%	31%	55%	38%
7. Change problem area/change problem relation	39%	25%	16%	50%	30%
8. Culture	63%	17%	21%	28%	33%
9. Resources	18%	47%	54%	22%	39%
10. Reward system	18%	14%	21%	11%	19%
11. Leadership	24%	47%	21%	8%	28%
12. Work process	44%	17%	57%	39%	40%
N	(33)	(36)	(37)	(18)	(124)

what an organization (formally) believes about itself'. The second category is then used to aid him in 'learning how the organization really works'.

These examples were given to provide the reader with a sense of how various individual respondents organized the diagnostic categories. These examples provide a backdrop for us to explore the aggregated results.

FINDINGS

The results presented in Table 5.1 indicate that each type of change agent tends to have his own set of yardsticks for diagnosing the health of social systems in order to plan an intervention. The results provide support for going beyond what was found in previous portions of the change agent study: namely, that change agent goals and values tend to determine change technology and strategy. Now it seems that goals and values are also related to what the change agent looks at during diagnosis.

It was proposed that different types of change agents would differentially use the twelve diagnostic categories. Table 5.1 presents the percentage of each change agent type who reported using each of the categories for organizational diagnosis. The five categories reported by all four types as being used most were: Formal Structure (69%); Goals of the System (45%); Informal System (44%); Performance (43%); and Work Process (40%). It is interesting to note that only one of these categories was reported as being used by more than 50% of the respondents. The least used categories were: Leadership (28%) and Reward System (19%). These results certainly suggested that change agents do not all agree on standard diagnostic categories.

The OP's with their power equalization orientation to change, pay more attention than the other types to Leadership (47% compared to 24% for any of the other types), and less to Formal Structure (59% compared to 69% of any of the other types), Work Process (17% compared to 39% of any of the other types) and Individual/Psychological variables. The OD's with their improved organizational problem-solving orientation pay more attention to Culture (63% compared to 28% of any of the other types) and Formal Structure (85% compared to 71% for any of the other types). The PCT's who aim to change individual functioning more frequently collect information about Individual/Psychological factors (55% compared to 42% for any of the other types), Goals of the System (55% compared to 50% for any of the other types), and Change Problem Area and Change Agent's Relationship to System (50% compared to 39% for any of the other types), than the other types and less frequently collect information about Resources and Leadership. Finally, the AFT's who are system productivity and output oriented, more often than the other types, collect information about Work Process (57% compared to 44% of any of the other types), Resources (54% compared to 47% for any of the other types) and Performance (49% compared to 44% for any of the other types).

The different yardsticks or categories stressed for each type turn out to be quite consistent with other aspects of the orientation to change. The OP's are the only ones who focus on leadership, which is no surprise, given the political nature of their approach. Goals and resources are also important in assessing a target system's power. The OD's, on the other hand, are the only ones to focus so heavily on the Culture during diagnosis; again given that their approach is often characterized as a 'cultural change' approach (Hornstein, 1971), this bias is understandable. The PCT's are the only type to focus heavily on Individual/Psychological factors which is consistent with what they do in their interventions. The AFT's focus heavily on Performance, also consistent with an emphasis on system efficiency and productivity.

Which Categories Each Type Works on Directly: Table 5.2 provides a summary of the four major categories which each type reported working on directly as part of their intervention. By focusing on the categories which

TABLE 5.2
TOP FOUR CATEGORIES EACH CHANGE AGENT
TYPE WORKS ON DIRECTLY[1]

Item rank	Organization development type. % Choosing category	People change technology type. % Choosing category	Analysis for the top type. % Choosing category	Outside pressure type. % Choosing category
First	Culture—50%	Informal structure—38%	Formal structure—32%	Leadership—31%
Second	Formal structure—42%	Individual/Psychological variables—31%		Goals—23%
Third	Informal structure—35%	Change problem area—31%	Goals—29%	Formal structure Informal structure —19%
Fourth	Change problem area—31%	Formal structure—31%	Performance—29%	Culture
N	(26)	(13)	(28)	(26)

[1] Each respondent named more than one category.

respondents report changing, we are able to begin bridging the gap between change agents' diagnostic approaches and their change approaches. Before we discuss how their diagnostic models correspond to their intervention approach, we will briefly summarize the findings reported in Table 5.2.

The OD's top change categories are Culture and the Formal Structure, followed by Informal Structure and Change Problem Area and the Relationship of the Change Agent to the System. The PCT's first category is Informal Structure followed by Individual/Psychological Factors, Change Problem Area and Change Agent Relationship to System and Formal Structure. The AFT's reported working directly on the Formal Structure and Work Process most, followed by Goals and Performance next. For the OP's, Leadership comes first; then Goals and, finally, Formal Structure, Informal Structure and Culture.

DISCUSSION

Now that we are familiar with the diagnostic framework associated with each of the four change agent types, we will examine these frameworks as they relate to the overall GCM's. How do the change agents' diagnostic approaches fit with other aspects of their approach? How much are subsequent interventions influenced by what a change agent looks for in the first place? Each of the four change agents' GCM's will be discussed in terms of how congruent their diagnostic model is with other aspects of their approach, e.g., change goals and change techniques they use. Finally, each diagnostic model will be discussed in terms of possible dysfunctional biases.

When considering the OP's diagnostic categories in relation to their GCM, the categories seem to be quite congruent. The most commonly used diagnostic categories are Formal Structure, Leadership, Goals and Resources. These are all reflected in literature associated with various OP approaches (Alinsky, 1971; Nader, 1971). Once OP's obtain information about these characteristics of the target system, many reported that they attempted to alter the Leadership and the Goals of the system. These change targets are worked on through the use of pressure tactics. Again, this implies a model of organizations and change focused heavily on political power.

The OP approach to diagnosis appears to be influenced by some of the factors proposed in our earlier work (Tichy, 1974) to account for high value and cognition congruence. One factor is that the centrality of their political ideology and values provides not only a driving motivational force but a framework for conceptualizing social relations. Another factor is the unidimensionality of the approach, e.g., power is unequally distributed, it should be more equal: therefore, engage in power equalization tactics. Both of these factors may influence what OP's attend to in new change situations. Furthermore, what they attend to subsequently influences what they decide to work on. It is difficult to prove that this implied self-fulfilling cycle actually exists, yet it makes a good deal of intuitive sense to propose its existence. If you set out paying particular attention to certain variables while ignoring others, it is more likely that you will find support for changing them than for changing factors which have not been examined.

Organization Development GCM: The OD's follow a similar pattern. Their key diagnostic categories, Formal Structure and Culture, are also the organizational variables which they reported most often directly attempting to change.

The OD type focuses heavily on the organization's culture and climate as key to change. The two goals listed: improved problem-solving and improved system efficiency and increased output, are proposed to change due to cultural change. That is, system norms are changed in such a way as to support the on-going diagnosis of the organization and the use of social technologies to improve problem-solving and, as a consequence, improve the system's efficiency and output. The OD type's central diagnostic categories reflect these assumptions. They look at Formal Structure, Culture, External Environment and Work Process. They are the only ones of the four types to focus so much on Culture as a diagnostic category. More revealing is their report that the Formal Structure and Culture are the two factors they work to change most directly. Overall, the addition of the OD's diagnostic approach into their model does not alter the conclusion of our earlier article. The OD's are left with a value/action inconsistency. What they say they should be doing and what they actually do is less congruent for them than for any of the other types. Like the OP's, what they look for during diagnosis is related to what they alter as change agents.

Analysis for the Top GCM: The AFT's diagnostic categories reveal their systems analysis and operations research bias. They focus on the formal structure, work process, resource limitations of the system and its performance. Most reported that change is brought about by working directly on the Formal Structure and the Work Process. As with the OD's and OP's, we see a relationship between what the change agents look for and what they do. Their diagnostic categories and the categories they reported working on directly appear to be quite congruent with the remainder of their GCM.

People Change Technology GCM: Organizational diagnosis focuses primarily on the Formal Structure, Individual/Psychological variables, Goals and the Change Problem area. Following the diagnostic activities, PCT's reported that they generally work most directly on changing the Informal Structure and Individual/Psychological variables. They use such techniques as role clarification, behavioral science training and change in the reward structure to carry out these changes. As with other types, diagnosis and intervention strategies are related.

CONCLUSIONS

This study might be said to support the proposition that different types of change agents view the world through different sets of rose-colored glasses.

There appears to be a relationship between diagnostic categories and subsequent change interventions. This relationship leads to a self-fulfilling cycle in the GCM's. The most important factors which change agents examine during diagnosis tend to be also those things which are worked on most often to create change in the systems. For example, the OP's look at Formal Structure, Leadership and Goals most often during diagnosis and most often work to change Leadership and Goals as their intervention. For the PCT's Individual and Psychological factors are looked at most often during diagnosis and are worked on to create change. The OD's include Culture as one of the most important diagnostic categories and are the only type to work directly on culture as a social intervention. The AFT's look closely at Work Process in diagnosing an organization and also happen to generally change the work process as part of their change strategy.

Are we to conclude that change agents, therefore, are like the blind men who tried to describe an elephant after each touched different parts of the elephant? The answer to this question is yes and no. Like the blind men, change agents seems to have limited perspectives, not only due to their diagnostic frameworks, but also very probably due to real world constraints of time, money and access to certain information. As a result, their diagnoses are partial. They only look at certain aspects of complex social systems. Unlike the blind men, change agents have a greater potential for positive response to their limited perspectives. Before suggesting some of these responses, we will discuss the probable consequences of partial view diagnostic frameworks.

Like specialists in other fields who rely on different diagnostic frameworks, there are subsequent consequences on action. In medicine it is not uncommon to hear of different physician specialists proposing very different medical interventions for the same illness. Similarly, with different change agents, depending on which specialist you go to, you emerge with a different cure. Assuming that some cures are more appropriate than others depending on the symptoms and circumstances, we are faced with the dilemma of determining which cure when.

Knowing that change agents stress different aspects of social systems—both in their diagnoses and in their interventions—is helpful for consumers of change agentry. More and more of us are becoming consumers as increasing numbers of institutions in this society turn to the professional consultant for help in improving organizational functioning. Therefore, consumers beware! Individuals in decision-making positions deciding on the use of professional change agents should be educated as to the different biases associated with different change agents. This at least enables them to have a greater control and understanding of the process, except in the case of OP's who do not collaborate with the target of change.

More generally, the findings of this study underscore a need for a great deal more knowledge, not only about what change agents are doing, but studies evaluating the effectiveness of what they do. These studies could begin to develop needed knowledge about which change approaches work under what sets of conditions. Eventually it may even be possible to develop a general model for organizational diagnosis, one not so wedded to the biases of different types of change agents.

REFERENCES

Alinsky, S. D. (1971). *Rules for Radicals.* New York: Random House.
Hornstein, H., *et al.* (1971). *Social Intervention: A Behavioral Science Approach.* New York: Free Press.
Nader, R. & Ross, D. (1971). *Action for a Change.* New York: Grossman Publishers.
Tichy, N. M. (1972). *Developing an Empirically Based Framework of Change Agent Types.* New York: Unpublished PH.D. dissertation, Columbia University.
Tichy, N. M. & Hornstein, H. (1976). Stand when your number is called: Change agent study. *Human Relations* (In Press).
Tichy, N. M. (1974). Agents of planned social change: Congruence of values, cognitions and action. *Administrative Science Quarterly,* Vol. 19, No. 2, 164–182.
Whyte, W. F. (1967). Models for building and changing organizations. *Human Organizations,* Vol. 26, Nos. 1/2.
Zajonc, R. (1960). The process of cognitive tuning in communication. *Journal of Abnormal and Social Psychology, 61:* 150–167.

21. Rules of Thumb for Change Agents
HERBERT A. SHEPARD

The following aphorisms are not so much bits of advice (although they are stated that way) as things to think about when you are being a change agent, a consultant, an organization or community development practitioner—or when you are just being yourself trying to bring about something that involves other people.

RULE I: STAY ALIVE

This rule counsels against self-sacrifice on behalf of a cause that you do not wish to be your last.

Reprinted from the *OD Practitioner,* Vol. 7, No. 3, Nov., 1975, pp. 1–5.

Two exceptionally talented doctoral students came to the conclusion that the routines they had to go through to get their degrees were absurd, and decided they would be untrue to themselves to conform to an absurd system. That sort of reasoning is almost always self-destructive. Besides, their noble gesture in quitting would be unlikely to have any impact whatever on the system they were taking a stand against.

This is not to say that one should never take a stand, or a survival risk. But such risks should be taken as part of a purposeful strategy of change, and appropriately timed and targeted. When they are taken under such circumstances, one is very much alive.

But Rule I is much more than a survival rule. The rule means that you should let your whole being be involved in the undertaking. Since most of us have never been in touch with our whole beings, it means a lot of putting together of parts that have been divided, of using internal communications channels that have been closed or were never opened.

Staying alive means loving yourself. Self-disparagement leads to the suppression of potentials, to a win-lose formulation of the world, and to wasting life in defensive maneuvering.

Staying alive means staying in touch with your purpose. It means using your skills, your emotions, your labels and positions, rather than being used by them. It means not being trapped in other people's games. It means turning yourself on and off, rather than being dependent on the situation. It means choosing with a view to the consequences as well as the impulse. It means going with the flow even while swimming against it. It means living in several worlds without being swallowed up in any. It means seeing dilemmas as opportunities for creativity. It means greeting absurdity with laughter while trying to unscramble it. It means capturing the moment in the light of the future. It means seeing the environment through the eyes of your purpose.

RULE II: START WHERE THE SYSTEM IS

This is such ancient wisdom that one might expect its meaning had been fully explored and apprehended. Yet in practice the rule—and the system—are often violated.

The rule implies that one should begin by diagnosing the system. But systems do not necessarily *like* being diagnosed. Even the *term* "diagnosis" may be offensive. And the system may be even less ready for someone who calls himself or herself a "change agent". It is easy for the practitioner to forget that the use of jargon which prevents laymen from understanding the professional mysteries is a hostile act.

Starting where the system is can be called the Empathy Rule. To communicate effectively, to obtain a basis for building some strategy, the change agent needs to understand how the client sees himself and his situation, and needs to understand the culture of the system. Establishing the required rapport does not mean that the change agent who wants to work in a traditonal industrial setting should refrain from growing a beard. It does mean that, if he has a beard, the beard is likely to determine where the client is when they first meet, and the client's curiosity needs to be dealt with. Similarly, the rule does not mean that a female change agent in a male organization should try to act like one of the boys, or that a young change agent should try to act like a senior executive. One thing it does mean is that sometimes where the client is, is wondering where the change agent is.

Rarely is the client in any one place at any one time. That is, s/he may be ready to pursue any of several paths. The task is to walk together on the most promising path.

Even unwitting or accidental violations of the empathy rule can destroy the situation. I lost a client through two violations in one morning. The client group spent a consulting day at my home. They arrived early in the morning, before I had my empathy on. The senior member, seeing a picture of my son in the living-room, said, "What do you do with boys with long hair?" I replied thoughtlessly, "I think he's handsome that way." The small chasm thus created between my client and me was widened and deepened later that morning when one of the family tortoises walked through the butter dish.

Sometimes starting where the client is, which sounds both ethically and technically virtuous, can lead to some ethically puzzling situations. Robert Frost* described a situation in which a consultant was so empathic with a king who was unfit to rule that the king discovered his own unfitness and had himself shot, whereupon the consultant became king.

Empathy permits the development of a mutual attachment between client and consultant. The resulting relationship may be one in which their creativities are joined, a mutual growth relationship. But it can also become one in which the client becomes dependent and is manipulated by the consultant. The ethical issues are not associated with starting where the system is, but with how one moves with it.

RULE III: NEVER WORK UPHILL

This is a comprehensive rule, and a number of other rules are corollaries or examples of it. It is an appeal for an organic rather than a mechanistic approach to change, for a collaborative approach to change, for building strength and building on strength. It has a number of implications that bear on the choices the change agent makes about how to use him/herself, and it says something about life.

---

*Robert Frost. "How Hard It Is To Keep From Being King When It's in You and in The Situation", *In The Clearing* (New York: Holt, Rinehart and Winston, 1962), pp. 74–84.

Corollary 1: Don't Build Hills as You Go

This corollary cautions against working in a way that builds resistance to movement in the direction you have chosen as desirable. For example, a program which has a favorable effect on one portion of a population may have the opposite effect on other portions of the population. Perhaps the commonest error of this kind has been in the employment of T-Group training in organizations: turning on the participants and turning off the people who didn't attend, in one easy lesson.

Corollary 2: Work in the Most Promising Arena

The physician-patient relationship is often regarded as analogous to the consultant-client relationship. The results for system change of this analogy can be unfortunate. For example, the organization development consultant is likely to be greeted with delight by executives who see in his specialty the solution to a hopeless situation in an outlying plant. Some organization development consultants have disappeared for years because of the irresistibility of such challenges. Others have whiled away their time trying to counteract the Peter Principle by shoring up incompetent managers.

Corollary 3: Build Resources

Don't do anything alone that could be accomplished more easily or more certainly by a team. Don Quixote is not the only change agent whose effectiveness was handicapped by ignoring this rule. The change agent's task is an heroic one, but the need to be a hero does not facilitate team building. As a result, many change agents lose effectiveness by becoming spread too thin. Effectiveness can be enhanced by investing in the development of partners.

Corollary 4: Don't Over-organize

The democratic ideology and theories of participative management that many change agents possess can sometimes interfere with common sense. A year or two ago I offered a course, to be taught by graduate students. The course was over-subscribed. It seemed that a data-based process for deciding whom to admit would be desirable, and that participation of the graduate students in the decision would also be desirable. So I sought data from the candidates about themselves, and xeroxed their responses for the graduate students. Then the graduate students and I held a series of meetings. Then the candidates were informed of the decision. In this way we wasted a great deal of time and everyone felt a little worse than if we had used an arbitrary decision rule.

Corollary 5: Don't Argue If You Can't Win

Win-lose strategies are to be avoided because they deepen conflict instead of resolving it. But the change agent should build her/his support constituency as large and deep and strong as possible so that s/he can continue to risk.

Corollary 6: Play God a Little

If the change agent doesn't make the critical value decisions, someone else will be happy to do so. Will a given situation contribute to your fulfillment? Are you creating a better world for yourself and others, or are you keeping a system in operation that should be allowed to die? For example, the public education system is a mess. Does that mean that the change agent is morally obligated to try to improve it, destroy it, or develop a substitute for it? No, not even if he or she knows how. But the change agent does need a value perspective for making choices like that.

RULE IV: INNOVATION REQUIRES A GOOD IDEA, INITIATIVE AND A FEW FRIENDS

Little can be accomplished alone, and the effects of social and cultural forces on individual perception are so distorting that the change agent needs a partner, if only to maintain perspective and purpose.

The quality of the partner is as important as the quality of the idea. Like the change agent, partners must be relatively autonomous people. Persons who are authority-oriented—who need to rebel or need to submit—are not reliable partners: the rebels take the wrong risks and the good soldiers don't take any. And rarely do they command the respect and trust from others that is needed if an innovation is to be supported.

The partners need not be numerous. For example, the engineering staff of a chemical company designed a new process plant using edge-of-the-art technology. The design departed radically from the experience of top management, and they were about to reject it. The engineering chief suggested that the design be reviewed by a distinguished engineering professor. The principal designers were in fact former students of the professor. For this reason he accepted the assignment, charged the company a large fee for reviewing the design (which he did not trouble to examine), and told the management that it was brilliantly conceived and executed. By this means the engineers not only implemented their innovations, but also grew in the esteem of their management.

A change agent experienced in the Washington environment reports that he knows of only one case of successful interdepartmental collaboration in mutually designing, funding and managing a joint project. It was accomplished through the collaboration of himself and three similarly-minded young men, one from each of four agencies. They were friends, and met weekly for lunch. They conceived the project, and planned strategies for implementing it. Each person undertook to interest and influence the relevant key people in his own agency. The four served one another as consultants and helpers in influencing opinion and bringing the decision-makers together.

An alternative statement of Rule IV is as follows: Find the people who are ready and able to work, introduce them to one another, and work with them. Perhaps because many change agents have been trained in the helping professions, perhaps because we have all been trained to think bureaucratically, concepts like organization position, representativeness or need are likely to guide the change agent's selection of those he or she works with.

A more powerful beginning can sometimes be made by finding those persons in the system whose values are congruent with those of the change agent, who possess vitality and imagination, who are willing to work overtime, and who are eager to learn. Such people are usually glad to have someone like the change agent join in getting something important accomplished, and a careful search is likely to turn up quite a few. In fact, there may be enough of them to accomplish general system change, if they can team up in appropriate ways.

In building such teamwork the change agent's abilities will be fully challenged, as he joins them in establishing conditions for trust and creativity; dealing with their anxieties about being seen as subversive; enhancing their leadership, consulting, problem-solving, diagnosing and innovating skills; and developing appropriate group norms and policies.

RULE V: LOAD EXPERIMENTS FOR SUCCESS

This sounds like counsel to avoid risk taking. But the decision to experiment always entails risk. After that decision has been made, take all precautions.

The rule also sounds scientifically immoral. But whether an experiment produces the expected results depends upon the experimenter's depth of insight into the conditions and processes involved. Of course, what is experimental is what is new to the system; it may or may not be new to the change agent.

Build an umbrella over the experiment. A chemical process plant which was to be shut down because of the inefficiency of its operations undertook a union-management cooperation project to improve efficiency, which involved a modified form of profit-sharing. Such plans were contrary to company policy, but the regional vice president was interested in the experiment, and successfully concealed it from his associates. The experiment was successful; the plant became profitable. But in this case, the umbrella turned out not to be big enough. The plant was shut down anyway.

Use the Hawthorne effect. Even poorly conceived experiments are often made to succeed when the participants feel ownership. And conversely, one of the obstacles to the spread of useful innovations is that the groups to which they are offered do not feel ownership of them.

For example, if the change agent hopes to use experience-based learning as part of his/her strategy, the first persons to be invited should be those who consistently turn all their experiences into contructive learning. Similarly, in introducing team development processes into a system, begin with the best functioning team.

Maintain voluntarism. This is not easy to do in systems where invitations are understood to be commands, but nothing vital can be built on such motives as duty, obedience, security-seeking or responsiveness to social pressure.

RULE VI: LIGHT MANY FIRES

Not only does a large, monolithic development or change program have high visibility and other qualities of a good target, it also tends to prevent subsystems from feeling ownership of, and consequent commitment to the program.

The meaning of this rule is more orderly than the random prescription—light many fires—suggests. Any part of a system is the way it is partly because of the way the rest of the system is. To work towards change in one subsystem is to become one more determinant of its performance. Not only is the change agent working uphill, but as soon as he turns his back, other forces in the system will press the subsystem back towards its previous performance mode.

If many interdependent subsystems are catalyzed, and the change agent brings them together to facilitate one another's efforts, the entire system can begin to move.

Understanding patterns of interdependency among subsystems can lead to a strategy of fire-setting. For example, in public school systems it requires collaboration among politicians, administrators, teachers, parents and students to bring about significant innovation, and active opposition on the part of only one of these groups to prevent it. In parochial school systems, on the other hand, collaboration between the administration and the church can provide a powerful impetus for change in the other groups.

RULE VII: KEEP AN OPTIMISTIC BIAS

Our society grinds along with much polarization and cruelty, and even the helping professions compose their word of grim problems to be "worked through". The change agent is usually flooded with the destructive aspects of the situations he enters. People in most systems are impressed by one another's weaknesses, and stereotype each other with such incompetencies as they can discover.

This rule does not advise ignoring destructive forces. But its positive prescription is that the change agent be especially alert to the constructive forces which are often masked and suppressed in a problem-oriented, envious culture.

People have as great an innate capacity for joy as for resentment, but resentment causes them to overlook opportunities for joy. In a workshop for married couples, a husband and wife were discussing their sexual problem and how hard they were working to solve it. They were not making much progress, since they didn't realize that sex is not a problem, but an opportunity.

Individuals and groups locked in destructive kinds of conflict focus on their differences. The change agent's job is to help them discover and build on their commonalities, so that they will have a foundation of respect and trust which will permit them to use their differences as a source of creativity. The unhappy partners focus on past hurts, and continue to destroy the present and future with them. The change agent's job is to help them change the present so that they will have a new past on which to create a better future.

RULE VIII: CAPTURE THE MOMENT

A good sense of relevance and timing is often treated as though it were a "gift" or "intuition" rather than something that can be learned, something spontaneous rather than something planned. The opposite is nearer the truth. One is more likely to "capture the moment" when everything one has learned is readily available.

Some years ago my wife and I were having a very destructive fight. Our nine-year-old daughter decided to intervene. She put her arms around her mother and asked: "What does Daddy do that bugs you?" She was an attentive audience for the next few minutes while my wife told her, ending in tears. She then put her arms around me: "What does Mommy do that bugs you?", and listened attentively to my response, which also ended in tears. She then went to the record player and put on a favorite love song ("If Ever I Should Leave You"), and left us alone to make up.

The elements of my daughter's intervention had all been learned. They were available to her, and she combined them in a way that could make the moment better.

Perhaps it's our training to linear cause-and-effect thinking and the neglect of our capacities for imagery that makes us so often unable to see the multiple potential of the moment. Entering the situation "blank" is not the answer. One needs to have as many frameworks for seeing and strategies for acting available as possible. But it's not enough to involve only one's head in the situation; one's heart has to get involved too. Cornelia Otis Skinner once said that the first law of the stage is to love your audience. You can love your audience only if you love yourself. If you have relatively full access to your organized experience, to yourself and to the situation, you will capture the moment more often.

22. Coping with the Stresses of Travel as an Opportunity for Improving the Quality of Work and Family Life

SAMUEL A. CULBERT and JEAN R. RENSHAW

The boundary between the organization and the family has remained too long inaccessible. A double standard of participation has left the families open to exploitation. On the one hand their strengths are drawn upon to help make and implement critical organization decisions, which the employee cannot manage by himself. On the other hand, they are denied formal channels of participation and, therefore, can neither initiate discussions nor react to proposals that affect them. Denying families the rights of formal members while drawing on their resources creates conditions leading to feelings of weakness and insecurity. Management exploits the myth of the weak and insecure housewife as a means of coopting her resistance to nonoptimal policies and practices. Husbands then run the risk of being considered poor organization managers if they appear not to be able to "manage" or control the stresses created at home.

This paper focuses on the stresses of business travel, one area where the family's feelings, perspectives, and resources obviously affect the organization. It studies families coping with a problem directly affecting an organization and its management, as well as the families themselves. It describes an approach designed to fit the norms of an industrial culture even though the approach itself, direct involvement of wives, represented a considerable deviation from precedent. To work within the organizational context, it was necessary to circumvent fears that family problems would be confused with work issues or that family privacy would be invaded. Typical of the work world, the approach was problem-oriented rather than open-ended. It emphasized developing new resources for coping with the stresses incurred by the managers and their families as a result of a heavy travel schedule.

We begin with some general characteristics of the population involved in this study. Included is a perspective on the approach used in coping with the stresses experienced and a description of therapeutic technique, a workshop where couples worked together to develop new resources. Next is a description of the results of research undertaken to evaluate the general effects of this approach on the organization and the travelers' families, as well as its specific impact on travel stresses. The paper concludes with a section that summarizes the findings and raises issues for further study.

Reprinted from *Family Process.* Vol. 11, No. 3, September 1972, pp. 321–337.

THE ORGANIZATION SIDE OF THINGS

This study took place in a large, diversified organization whose members travel frequently on business. Management recognized that travel placed pressures on personnel and had developed practices to ease the strain. At the corporate level policies automatically entitled personnel to an extra round-trip ticket on travel assignments lasting four weeks. Personnel could use these tickets either to visit home for a weekend or to have their wives visit the work location. Management encouraged overseas travelers to rest a day before resuming business activity. Streamlined accounting procedures minimized the toil of expense statements. In principle, management encouraged personnel to consider personal needs, as well as their jobs, when scheduling travel. Individual managers were expected to monitor travel pressures and facilitate transfers in cases where pressures became too intense.

However, several forces subverted the human considerations of corporate policy. The organization's criteria encouraged personnel to exercise individual prerogatives only under extreme stress. Following the "management way" meant accepting new assignments with a positive attitude. Thus, in many cases where travel was commensurate with new responsibilities or evolved naturally as a new part of established job, staff suppressed personal considerations. For example, they usually felt obliged to travel to overseas locations on weekends so that they would not waste a work day. If something had to give, it usually gave at home, not at work. Staff rationalized this by telling themselves that their families would eventually gain as a result of their job advancements.

THE PROBLEM AND THE CLIENT GROUP

The subjects of this study are members of a research unit that develops new agricultural products and improves established ones. Many of its members have managerial responsibilities. All of them do research, traveling a great deal during the summer to test their products under field conditions. They expect to spend 70 per cent of their time away from home from the beginning of May to the middle of September and less than a third of their time away from home during the rest of the year. Most of them expected heavy travel schedules when they accepted assignments to this unit, but the complex problems of heavy travel surprised them all. Organization problems included project coordination, supervisory relationships, and the need for collaboration in one another's projects. Family problems stemmed from disconnected relationships, lack of social life, shifts in responsibilities during absences, and needs for emotional support. Travel made members feel tired, lonely, and guilty—to the point of depression about being away from home.

Seven married men ranging in age between 26 and 38 and a single woman, 26, comprised the professional staff. All but two held university degrees; three including the woman, held advanced degrees. Six of the seven married men were highly committed to their wives and families. One man had ambivalent feelings about his marriage. All of them considered travel essential to their jobs and to the organization.

The wives ranged in age from 23 to 35. All but one had children, and all but one had university degrees. The seven families followed conventional role patterns: the husband working and the wife staying home with the children. Each couple valued marriage and religion highly and derived considerable satisfaction from their identification with the company. These people were younger, more liberal members of a conservative, established organization.

Members of this research unit used the available company policies to ease travel pressures. They sometimes condensed their schedules to finish travel assignments by the weekend and return home for a few days before starting another trip. In a couple of instances staff dealt with prolonged assignments by bringing their wives along and renting family accommodations. But wives then waited long hours without the benefits of their own routines and friends, and the family incurred extra expenses. The unit's manager tried hiring university students as summer help. However, students could not acquire sufficient research skills to replace more highly trained staff.

The unit's manager sought a better solution but did not know exactly what such a solution might entail. Occasionally at staff meetings he devoted time to the subject of travel and asked his staff to consult their wives. These discussions vented frustrations but produced little substantive change. Some suggestions led to minor improvements, such as burying the charges for phone calls home in the annual budget. Most suggestions, however, were built on paternalistic assumptions about the corporation; they looked for changes in either corporate policy or managerial practices as avenues for improving the quality of their lives.

This unit had recently begun an organization development project that emphasized, among other things, involvement and team action.[1] Its staff managed more of their own work and improved their analytic and problem-solving skills. Teams took over many tasks that formerly were the exclusive responsibilities of individual managers. The teams were seeking to replace "fire fighting" with long-lasting solutions to what had heretofore been recurrent problems. But despite their satisfaction with this new approach, the staff hesitated to apply it to the stresses of business travel. To do so they would have to involve their wives who represented key resources for dealing with the problem. Furthermore, the wives would be essential to the implementation of any solution agreed upon by the unit.

The manager in charge of this unit and the consultant helping with the organization development project took up the issue of how to apply this team

---

[1]For an overview of the philosophy and practice of organization development, cf. Beckhard (1969), Bennis (1969), Bennis, Benne & Chin (1969), and Culbert and Reisel (1971).

approach to the stresses of business travel. The constraints they agreed would apply to the discussions were:

a. Family problems must remain private.

b. Staff and wives would participate in the discussions only by their own choice, after being informed of the plan.

c. The program would focus on the stresses of travel, not on the entire marriage.

d. People should not feel pressured to talk about things they didn't want to talk about.

e. Problem-solving techniques should emphasize the strengthening of current problem-solving capacities, not the criticizing of deficiencies.

With these constraints in mind the unit manager and the consultant formulated a sequence of guiding hypotheses for a seminar designed to address the problems of travel:

a. Participation in the seminar would improve problem-solving resources of the husband and wife team.

b. Focusing these resources on the couple's problems with business travel would strengthen each person's capacity to cope with separation.

c. New and strengthened resources for coping would be generalized to apply to other organizational issues and problems.

The format they agreed upon consisted of a two-day seminar in which couples would engage in activities designed to strengthen their analytic and problem-solving skills. Couples would use adaptations of many of the organization development techniques to which the staff had been exposed. The seminar would take place during regular work days, off-site, to demonstrate the company's commitment to the program and free couples from responsibilities at home. The manager and consultant described the program to the staff, who discussed it with their wives before deciding to participate. All but one of seven married couples agreed, the declining couple being the one in which the husband had expressed ambivalence about his marriage.

RESEARCH

The experimental nature of this project led management to include pilot research both to evaluate this activity and to consolidate the findings it might produce. The consultant and a researcher[2] interviewed each couple prior to the off-site seminar. The interviews served the dual purpose of enabling the consultant to establish rapport and the researcher to collect data necessary for assessing the effects of the seminar. The consultant asked about participants' expectations for the seminar and discussed their anxieties with them. The researcher administered questionnaires and interviewed husband and wife separately. Later she submitted the same questionnaires to a control group of travelers from other units of the company, and their wives.

Interviews revealed that, despite similar briefings, couples had different expectations. The staff who felt least secure in their jobs, and with their

---

[2]The consultant is the first author of this paper; the researcher, the second.

wives, expected to discuss the ways in which the organization might make travel easier for the families. The seminar, in their opinion, would produce no dramatic improvements. The staff members who felt most secure in their jobs hoped, too, to find ways to make business travel less of a strain on their families, but they, and their wives, viewed the seminar also as an opportunity for improving their marital relationships, which they presented as quite good already.

SEMINAR FORMAT

A description of the seminar format should help the reader picture how organization technology can be applied to family problem-solving, as well as provide a basis for understanding the changes it produced. The seminar used the following techniques from organization development to improve the process of problem-solving: gathering information, defining problems, identifying contributing forces, generating new alternatives, facilitating collaborative action, and reflecting current practices against longer-term objectives. Each of these techniques applies generally to both managerial and marital problem-solving.

The program took place in a motel. It began with the consultant reviewing expectations and discussing hoped-for outcomes. He told participants they'd be taking part in exercises to teach them new ways of coping with stresses of business travel rather than proceeding as if all stresses might be eliminated. Each couple had a room to which they could invite the consultant when they needed him. When called to a room the consultant did not "psychologize" but assumed that momentary blocks resulted from insufficient data or lack of integration. He asked questions to elicit more data or provided better concepts for what people "already" knew.

Establishing Individual Differences. The first exercise helped each person place his life in its unique perspective and share that perspective with his (or her) spouse. On a piece of paper each person drew a line representing the path of his life from birth to death and then placed a mark indicating his present position on that line. After each person had showed his "life-line" to his spouse, they joined the other couples to share their reactions.

Developing Awareness of One's Position and Empathy. The next exercise was directed at developing awareness of how one's spouse views himself and empathy for his position. It also continued the process of articulating intra-couple differences, a necessary prelude to formulating specific plans for coping with the stresses of travel. Each person spent ten minutes reflecting on his most distinguishing characteristics. He then wrote a single word or phrase on each of ten small pieces of paper naming one of these characteristics. He could name a role or a personal characteristic or write any words of personal significance. Next he rank-ordered the papers from their most essential aspect to their least. The couples returned to their rooms with instructions to share their self-descriptions, one person at a time, with their spouse. The listening spouse was instructed to ask questions to understand better what was being shared but try not to change it.

Lunch Break. The couples reassembled to share reactions or insights from which others might profit. This took about twenty minutes. Then they split up into groups of threes for lunch, two groups of women and two of men. This lunch break provided some relief from the intensity of the morning's work and gave each person a chance to gain perspective by being with others who had had a similar role in the program.

Recognizing Forces on the Marriage. The afternoon session began with a demonstration of the "force-field analysis," a method of analyzing complex situations and problems. The couples returned to their rooms with large sheets of newsprint and felt tip pens. Working independently each person portrayed the forces pushing them towards a more satisfying relationship with their spouse and the forces pushing them away from one. After each spouse had depicted the forces on their marriage to his satisfaction, they looked at each other's "force-field" and discussed it. This exercise re-emphasized *understanding* how one's spouse viewed the forces on their relationship and de-emphasized changing the other's viewpoint. It taught them to see differences in perception as opportunities for learning. On the newsprint the couples had tangible products to take home for updating and/or charting changes in their situation.

Time for Reflection. Each person spent at least an hour alone before dinner to reflect and to integrate the events of the day.

Keeping Perspective. The evening provided an opportunity for husbands and wives to have a dinner date. Much material had been covered during the day, and evening was seen as a chance to support the fun aspects of the relationship.

Using Feelings as Data. The couples began the second day with an exercise in fantasy, focusing on separation. It provided an indirect way of expressing feelings difficult to articulate in face-to-face discussion. It also demonstrated that husbands encounter as many difficulties as wives during separation. In this exercise each couple was asked to imagine that the husband had just left on a business trip. They were asked to reflect on their feelings when separated from one another. After a period of reflection, each wrote his spouse a letter describing the emotional experiences he was having. Then the couples returned to their rooms and read aloud the letters they had written to each other.

Exchanging Empathy. The next exercise helped participants demonstrate empathy for their spouses. It also provided a structure for receiving empathy. The consultant described and demonstrated the managerial technique of brain-storming. Each person used this technique to list all the stresses he expected to experience during the upcoming period of summer travel. On a sheet of paper divided into three columns the stresses were listed in the first column. After listing the stresses each person went back through his list and, using the second column, rated the intensity of each stress on a ten-point scale. When each had rated the intensity of his stresses, he exchanged lists with his spouse. Each person read his spouse's list of stresses and considered how each stress manifested itself in his spouse's behavior. He then wrote a brief description of how his spouse expressed that stress in the third column. Afterward the couples returned to their rooms. Each couple discussed the accuracy of their perceptions and their feelings about being understood.

Relaxation. Lunch, like breakfast, found couples eating together with couples of their choosing.

Building Support. The next exercise made participants reflect on the resources they already had for supporting their husbands or wives and helped them recognize their own preferred ways of giving support, separate from the spouse's preferences for receiving. A man traveling on business often feels so guilty about being absent from home that he neglects his own needs for support. This exercise legitimized and reinforced giving and receiving support on the part of both partners.

The participants pondered ways to help their spouses cope with stresses of travel—roles they might take, action they might initiate, or feelings they might express. The lists of stresses developed in the preceding exercise provided cues for this one. Participants reflected on which actions they would actually *like* to take and wrote each action on small single sheets of paper. They then exchanged lists with their spouses and ordered the papers they received to indicate the supportive actions they would value most to help them cope with their own stresses. Next each participant discussed what his spouse had offered, explained his own preferences in receiving support, and negotiated "trades."

Consolidation. The couples reconvened as a group to share their reactions to the "seminar" and to discuss the effectiveness of the format. At this time couples could also recommend organizational changes for helping with their stresses.

RESULTS OF THE RESEARCH

These summarized descriptions don't begin to cover the spectrum of human issues dealt with by individual couples. Statistical data is presented to indicate measurable changes, but the range of impact seemed at times to strain the credibility of our research. One couple uncovered core resistances, set up by their interaction patterns, to the husband's desire for a child. Two months later, the wife was pregnant, and now they're both delighted with their baby daughter. Another's struggles spilled over from their lack of sexual activity to their mutual desire for more excitement in their lives. The wife planned to resume, on a part-time basis, her former career, allowing her to express a part of herself that she had been suppressing, and which her husband finds exciting.

Important issues in the family lives of the participants, such as their sex lives and implicit and explicit agreements around it, were not appropriate for our investigation in the organizational setting. It is known that such issues were present, but our research contract placed constraints on the issues considered appropriate for direct inquiry.

The pilot scale of the project, six couples attending a two-day seminar, makes data analysis an inconclusive procedure. The data were inspected for systematic differences between husbands and wives, but in this small sample differences were not extreme enough to reach statistical significance. Changes were induced from comparisons between the seminar group and the control group of travelers.[3] The analyses which follow treat data as if they came from two groups of twelve participants each, rather than two groups of six couples each. Thus the analyses can only provide preliminary indicators for future hypotheses and research.

The analyses follow the three guiding hypotheses used in planning the seminar: a) participation in the seminar would improve problem-solving resources of the husband and wife team; b) focusing these resources on couples' problems with business travel would strengthen each person's capacity to cope with separations; c) new and strengthened coping resources would be generalized to apply to other organizational issues and problems.

A. Improving Problem-Solving Resources

The first part of the seminar format developed appreciation for differences between husband and wife. Couples frequently err in automatically assuming that both feel the same way on a given issue. If this part of the seminar succeeded, participants would emerge with renewed appreciation for their differences and therefore changed perceptions of themselves and their marriage.

A questionnaire[4] measuring attitudes was given to the group participating in the seminar and to the control group of "travelers" and their wives. The self-attitudes held by these two groups were comparable at time 1. After the seminar (time 2) the self-attitudes held by the participants changed significantly on two of the three attitude factors measured by the questionnaire.

---

[3]The control group consisted of six men and their wives from other parts of the company whose work causes them to travel a comparable amount to the group which is the focus of this study. These couples filled out many of the same questionnaires at time intervals similar to the seminar group.

[4]The semantic differential questionnaire measures attitudes along three relatively independent factors: evaluation, potency, and activity. This instrument is described in C. E. Osgood, G. J. Suci, and P. H. Tannenbaum, *The Measurement of Meaning* (Champaign, Ill.: Univer. of Illinois Press, 1967). The targets for attitudes measured in the present study include "myself," "business travel," and "my company."

Participants changed in how they evaluated themselves and in how potent they felt ($t = 2.48$, df $= 70$, p <.05; and $t = 2.57$, d.f. $= 70$, $p <.05$, respectively).

The researcher collected data on each participant's view of the norms operating in his marriage, prior to the seminar (time 1), just after the seminar (time 2), and three months later, at the conclusion of the peak travel season (time 3). Participants responded to 24 statements representing 12 norms hypothesized to characterize successful problem-solving relationships.[5] Each person estimated the percent of time he behaved in accordance with a standard statement and the percent of time he behaved differently. The analysis counted changes of 25 percent or more for each person. The number of changes in participants between times 1 and 2 (the period of the seminar) was compared with the number of like changes registered by the control group. The group taking part in the seminar did register significantly more changes than the control group ($t = 3.62$, d.f. $= 22$, and $p <.05$).

Further analysis of the changes showed that the group taking part in the seminar made the majority of their (≥ 25 per cent) changes in the direction opposite from that hypothesized to relate to problem-solving effectiveness. The control group registered an equal number of changes in both directions. Interpretation of these "opposite direction" changes made by the seminar group is open to various lines of reasoning. On one hand, it might be inferred that participation in the seminar actually decreased a couple's problem-solving effectiveness. Alternatively, it might be inferred that participation introduced a more realistic perspective. The latter is deemed more likely inasmuch as there is a sharp contrast between the idealized descriptions of relationships recorded prior to the seminar and the more balanced descriptions obtained three months later.

Comparisons were made between the number of changes registered by the two groups between times 2 and 3. Again, the group participating in the seminar registered significantly more changes than the control group ($t = 2.52$, d.f. $= 22$, $p <.05$). This time the seminar group made two-thirds of its changes in the direction of problem-solving effectiveness. The control group changed about the same number of times in each direction. Again, one might ask whether these results represented an increase in the seminar group's problem-solving effectiveness or a return to former "misperceptions." Data reveal that those participating in the study felt better able to cope with travel stresses after participating in the seminar.

---

[5] These norms are: awareness, authenticity, trust, inquiry, objectivity, collaboration, changefulness, altruistic concern, consensual decision-making, competence based power, emotionality as data, and individuality. The present research is adapted from a questionnaire and procedure found in D. M. Callahan, *Conformity, Deviation, and Morale Among Educators in School Systems,* unpublished doctoral dissertation, Columbia University, 1968.

Recall that during the seminar participants individually listed the stresses they attributed to travel and then estimated the intensity of each stress. The participants handed these lists in during the seminar and got them back with their intensity ratings omitted at time 3. At time 3 they added new stresses and rated them all for intensity. Total intensity scores for nine of the twelve participants decreased substantially (an average decrease of 31 per cent). Two of the remaining three participants' intensity scores did not change, and one man's increased 25 per cent. The last individual had stated in the pre-seminar interview that he experienced "no problems in particular" due to the stress of travel. Examination of the data showed that the stresses that changed were in areas of personal control such as "loneliness" and "concern for spouse." Situational stresses such as "fear of airplanes" did not change.

The seminar format was built on the assumption that information sharing and personal re-examination would increase understanding between spouses and thus increase their ability to cope with stresses. Many examples of this took place. One that aptly illustrates this effect involved a husband who doubted his wife's ability to manage the family during his absence; the wife openly complained of physical reactions. During the seminar they noted that he always called while she was putting the children to bed. The timing of this call was a symptom of their lack of communication. For his part, he chose this time intentionally, feeling that she could not make it through this period of stress without his support. The calls upset him and aggravated her problems. She also wanted to support him and felt guilt when sensing his concern. The conference format brought out her desire to give support and function autonomously, leading them to decide that he would call at a calmer moment. They learned that each felt best when he could give, as well as receive. At the conscious level, they decided to reschedule their phone calls; at the implicit level they learned to communicate directly when expressing caring and giving support, with each gaining confidence in the other's ability to handle stress. Later the wife reported a substantial reduction in her tensions and physical symptoms.

B. Focusing Problem-Solving Resources on the Problem
of Business Travel

We have already noted that the intensity of travel stresses decreased for most participants. Travel logs, which seminar participants filled out after each trip, provide additional data. The participants had recorded the length of each trip, significant events, and their predominant moods during separation.

Data from travel logs, validated by company expense vouchers, reveal that the members of the research unit spent approximately the same time traveling during the season immediately following the seminar as they had in the previous year (year prior to the seminar, 658 days; year subsequent to the seminar, 648 days). The number of days was nearly equal but even this figure represented change, for the unit had 40 per cent more personnel and increased business substantially during the second year. The pattern of travel also indicated change. The number of days traveled by those not taking part in the seminar increased. Seminar participants took fewer long trips, more "one night" trips, and only three trips over a weekend. Husbands and wives reported themselves in substantially higher spirits. Ninety percent of their responses in the "predominant mood" column were either slightly or very good. Only one response indicated continued depressed feelings during separation. No comparable data were collected from the control group. But the seminar group's high morale during the travel season contrasted with the previous year when stress and managerial concern were sufficiently high to produce this seminar.

Post-travel interviews confirmed these positive ratings of moods. Most participants cited changes they had made that improved their morale, based on their planning during the seminar. Wives generally began to see themselves able to function more autonomously and to reach outside the home. One began tennis lessons to make new acquaintances, and to continue her tennis game during her husband's absence. Another family joined the YMCA to provide an activity the family could enjoy without the husband. One of the women had an extra phone installed upstairs in her sewing room to provide a feeling of security when working alone at night after her children had gone to bed. One woman who had complained about her social life during her husband's trips now plans lunches with friends that she otherwise would not see and tries out dishes that her husband wouldn't like. Another woman with fears about her car breaking down listed with her husband the things she could do to repair it and people to call, if she had no success.

The men generally felt freer to enjoy themselves when separated from the family. Two independently decided to plan their business trips far enough ahead to invite co-workers and business associates to dinner, avoiding dreary meals alone. Overall, both men and women felt better about themselves and their ability to function when apart.

Couples' living styles also changed. One couple initially reported high stress when separated; neither spouse could have a good time without the other. During the seminar they recognized their pattern of living for the future and not taking enough from the present. Both decided to find ways of enjoying periods of separation. He now plans his trips ahead to avoid dull evenings of TV in the motel. She makes plans to get out of the house, taking the baby if necessary. Together they decided to buy a new car on time, something they resisted doing despite the ease with which they could make payments. At the explicit level, they each planned specific ways to make the periods of separation more enjoyable. On the implicit level, this couple learned to take more enjoyment from the present, and to worry less about the future. As a result, they report better times while apart and more to share when back together.

At first glance these changes seem to require little effort. But they did make important differences to the people involved. These changes take on more significance when seen as the consequences of an improved problem-solving process. In this case more open discussion and collaborative planning produced conscious change and participants can use this same process to solve new problems when these arise.

The questionnaire measuring attitudes toward travel revealed inconclusive differences between the seminar and control groups. Despite the increased ability of seminar participants to cope with the stresses of travel, they did not change their attitudes about travel.

C. Increased Effectiveness in the Organization

The project nypothesized that focusing couples' problem-solving resources on an organization problem, the stresses of travel, would increase the effectiveness of the organizational team. This hypothesis gained some support in the research.

The questionnaire measuring attitudes toward the organization turned up no differences between the seminar group and the control group and no changes over time. The questionnaire measuring perceptions of the norms operating in the organization turned up some changes over time but no significant differences between the number of changes made by the seminar group and the number made by the control group (time 1 to time 3). However, the *ad hoc* analysis of the types of changes made showed the seminar participants viewing the organization as changing in the direction of problem-solving effectiveness significantly more often than the control group viewed changes in this direction ($t = 2.03$; d.f. $= 22$; $p < .05$).

Interviews conducted at the end of the travel season indicated the seminar had a positive effect on organizational functioning. Some problem-solving approaches learned during the seminar carried over directly to problems in the work setting. Some changes in decision-making and problem-solving styles were used at work. Finally, the easing of family pressures on some organization members released more energy for dealing with work issues.

One example of direct carryover from the seminar to work involved the man who learned that he could schedule his phone calls to his wife at more productive times. His colleagues report him increasingly able to schedule his work to deal with pressures more effectively. They say he's a much easier person to work with. One man's over-organization irritated his wife, as well as his colleagues. He stopped trying to change her and his colleagues benefited. He learned to organize around their differences. Another man learned during the seminar that he didn't need to withhold feelings for fear of hurting his wife. He now reports freedom to criticize the work of other members of his group. His colleagues say they like the openness of his new style. They always felt the implicit criticisms but could not respond directly; now they can deal with them.

Changes in problem-solving styles among some couples were used at work. One husband, whose wife had voiced *his* complaints when asked about travel stresses and other aspects of the job, began doing his own griping. His work style improved—to his boss' satisfaction. One husband with managerial responsibilities discovered that he made too many family decisions. He and his wife redistributed their responsibilities in this area. He made no conscious connection between his treatment of his wife and his treatment of his subordinates, but the latter subsequently commented on his less paternalistic style.

In one dramatic example, reduction of family pressures brought greater freedom to the work organization. One couple had become so troubled by the husband's business travel that they had considered his looking for another job. During the seminar they discovered ways of experiencing love and security while separated. By the end of the travel season he not only decided to stay on but accepted a promotion which would involve even more travel.

The examples above do not include one of the six couples. They felt fairly neutral about their seminar experiences, although they appreciated the change to have two days of talking together, away from their children.

Somewhat involved in the planning and sponsoring of this seminar was a higher level manager. Interviewed after the period of heavy travel, he stated: "I don't know what happened in the seminar, but it must have been good since I haven't heard anything like the complaints I had to listen to last year."

SUMMARY

While interesting, the results obtained in this pilot study must be considered suggestive. Further work is being carried out to determine the applicability of these findings to other groups. The findings in this study support each of the hypotheses guiding the seminar format:

a. The seminar seemed to increase the problem-solving resources of husbands and wives. Those participating reported changes in self-attitudes, changes (for the better) in their perceptions of the problem-solving norms of their marriage, and anecdotes indicating increased problem-solving effectiveness.
b. The seminar seemed to increase couples' abilities to cope with travel stresses. The couples developed and expressed empathy for one another's pressures, jointly engaged in personal planning which reduced travel stresses and led to more positive experiences when separated.
c. The seminar seemed to produce changes that applied to other areas of organizational effectiveness. This occurred because newly acquired problem-solving approaches carried over to work, personal changes benefited colleagues, and some

found that the easing of family pressures released more energy for dealing with work issues. In addition, husbands traveled less often, for shorter periods of time, and almost eliminated weekend travel, illustrating the extent of the control they did have over their work lives.

The format producing these findings need not be considered prototypal. Its utility lies in demonstrating the interdependence of the family and organization and showing that progress can result from meeting issues at that interface head on. There are countless other areas of non-technical problem-solving where management's success depends on conditions at home, and the result of this study would predict organizational gains from more direct involvement of family. This study's format illustrates a rather "controlled" way to include wives in improving the organization. However, societal trends are raising consciousness so that future handling of issues at the boundary between organization and family will not necessarily happen with such control, nor only at the organization's initiative.

REFERENCES

Beckhard, R. *Organization Development: Strategies and Models.* Reading, Mass.: Addison–Wesley Publishing Co., 1969.

Bennis, W. G. *Organization Development: Its Nature, Origins and Prospects.* Reading, Mass.: Addison–Wesley Publishing Co., 1969.

Bennis, W. G., Benne, K. D. and Chin, R. *The Planning of Change.* New York, N.Y.: Holt, Rinehart and Winston, Inc., 1969.

Culbert, S. A. and Reisel, J. Organization Development: An Applied Philosophy for Managers of Public Enterprise. *Public Adminstration Review* (March/April 1971).

23. Reality Teaching: The Self-Analysis Classroom

RORY O'DAY

The purpose of education is to make people intelligent in their conduct, and this kind of intelligence requires that a person learn how to observe the objective reality of his own behavior as well as that of others. The classroom as a learning situation can be structured to help students become more conscious and skillful as participant observers in their own lives. Educational

Reprinted from *Interchange*, Vol. 5, No. 1, 1974, pp. 36-45.

techniques can produce people who are effectively self-conscious and who are able to monitor not only the nature of their actions but also the social and personal context (antecedents and consequences) of those actions. In order to do so, however, students must learn to recognize inconsistencies between the level of self-belief about action and the level of action itself. This view of education requires, of course, that the teachers orient themselves toward crystallizing the contradictions between one's self-image and one's performance, one's knowledge and one's practice. Such an orientation is independent of whether one is teaching at the school, college, or university level.

People know about the realm of social science not just because they have done a lot of conceptual reading but because, as humans, their behavior is guided by the personal and social context in which they find themselves. However, it is true that, for the most part, people are not particularly aware of the various forces that shape the nature of their conduct. As one teacher remarked to his colleagues,

We forget that our students, and we ourselves for that matter, for most of our lives have been systematically trained to perceive selectively, and that there are strong defenses against recognizing many social processes, particularly as they relate to our own behavior. (Dunphy, 1967, p. 202)

We human beings, for the most part, function in two very distinct realities: one is how we are behaving and the other is how we think we are behaving—what we are doing as distinct from what we think we are doing. Leary (1957) made reference to a similar distinction in his concept of "interpersonal reflex," and Bem and Bem (1970) argued that the contradictions between self-image and actual behavior frequently result from the fact that people are nonconscious about their conduct. An analogy can be drawn with young children first learning to read. Teachers can assist this learning by endeavoring to dispel the illusion of magic that children might attribute to the phenomenon called reading. An effective way to do so is to show children that they already know how to read because they can recognize and read popular advertisements and trade names. Young children read, but they do not understand what reading is. Similarly, people are living psychology, sociology, and anthropology, but they do not understand what these disciplines are.

Teachers in the social sciences can use the classroom situation to help students discover the nature of their own selective perceptions and to recognize the defensive maneuvers they engage in to avoid examining not only the personal but also the social forces that guide and shape their own behavior. The classroom can be a valuable medium through which people can discover directly from their own experience those principles and concepts that the social sciences attempt to clarify and understand. Unfortunately, the classroom situation typically has been utilized in such a narrow, constricted manner that most students and teachers despair of its being anything more than an uneasy truce zone.

The all-too-familiar lecture procedure requires an extremely constraining type of social structure that permits virtually no opportunity for the many latent social and personal forces operating in the classroom to become manifest and observable. It therefore becomes necessary to create a situation in the classroom where these social and personal forces can be experienced in a direct, conscious fashion by the students.

THE SELF-ANALYSIS CLASSROOM

If a teacher is willing to break the lock-step of lecturing and note-taking, it becomes possible to structure the classroom situation so that the students are able to engage in direct self-analysis of their own behavior. Each classroom is rich in the personal and social realities of human existence, and it is these realities that are the particular concern of the social sciences and the humanities. Therefore, in these areas of study the classroom situation, when used appropriately, can bring to the attention of the students in direct and unavoidable ways the complexities of human relationships.

The dynamics of the classroom make it a valuable microcosm of the larger society. Many of the elements are there: the emphasis on individual performance, competition for scarce resources in the form of grades, the hierarchy of command, the relative inflexibility of the curriculum as part of the bureaucratic master plan. Other elements include the importance of delay of gratification, the present as a means to a future end, and stratification on the basis of talent, as well as systems of differential reward.

Not only can students come to realize important dimensions of their own socialization processes but they can also become aware of universal dilemmas of human existence. These universals include the problems of arriving at appropriate and effective balances between individuality and collective commitment, affection and hostility among peers, and dependency and independence in authority relations.

The self-analysis classroom is in most respects similar to other classrooms. There is a teacher. There are students. The class meets regularly and is part of a recognized curriculum. The students are assigned readings and write term papers and are examined on the material covered during the course. Usually the teacher is solely responsible for assigning a grade to each student on the basis of the quality of his performance on the examinations and term papers.

The self-analysis classroom is not a group counseling situation. It is not a sensitivity or encounter group experience designed to teach the students effective patterns of human conduct and interpersonal relationships. The teacher in a self-analysis classroom is not a therapist or a counselor. His role is much more didactic and analytical as he tries to help the students to understand the complex behavioral events occurring in the group.

Most sensitivity group experiences advocate some particular one best way for getting to know yourself and others, for proper human communication and effective interaction. The experience in these groups generally involves the training of the members in the prescribed relationship manner. As a result, these groups are basically totalitarian because they seek to cope with the difficulties of human relationships by reducing the variety of actions and reactions to a prescribed few, which everyone must use. These kinds of groups train the members "to listen with the third ear"; "to be empathic"; "to be understanding"; "to be objective and nonevaluative"; etc. Of course, eventually this type of sensitivity training reduces and in some cases completely eliminates conflict and discord in the group. However, it does so at the expense of human variety. As a consequence, these group experiences become excruciatingly boring for everyone except those few who are particularly desperate for any sort of human contact. Most sensitivity training exercises eliminate the exciting possibilities offered by that uncertainty in interpersonal relationships that arises directly from the many possible combinations of interpersonal coping styles.

Most teaching styles range from autocratic authority to benevolent authority, and as a result they do not directly confront the issues involved in the teacher-student relationship. Lecturers can be either demanding or lenient, e.g., holding extra classes to finish the course material or excusing the students from being responsible for material not covered in lectures. On the other hand, the "Sesame Street" format, while intriguing and obviously stimulating interest in the content being presented, still involves adult authorities doing interesting things for subordinate children and does not encourage much self-initiative. In many ways, the shift to classroom demonstrations and gimmicks (games and simulations) is really an attempt by benevolent authority to rekindle interest and enthusiasm in a largely bored, dissatisfied, and cynical constituency without focusing on the reasons for that boredom, that dissatisfaction, and that cynicism.

Most teachers adopt classroom styles that prevent, in particular, the exploration of the hostility component of their relationship with their students. The lecture method is only the most usual way. When teachers engage in developing interesting class formats that are novel and stimulating, they prevent the students' latent feelings of anger and resentment at being in a subordinate position from becoming manifest. However, by preventing the direct expression of the hostility, teachers are undercutting the process by which their students can achieve some degree of independence in relation to them and a sense of intimacy with each other.

Teaching can be approached in ways that permit exploration of the reality of the teacher-student relationship, its roots in previous experience, and its consequences for such aspects of the situation as authentic intimacy among peers, a sense of personal independence, and collaborative interdependence. In a self-analysis class, for example, students are encouraged to explore openly the hostile feelings they have toward the teacher as a particular authority figure. In this way they come to identify with some parts of the teacher's style, primarily the analytic-interpretive aspect in which psychological and sociological concepts are used to illustrate what is happening in the class. As students become more observant about the dynamics of the classroom and as they read more, they too begin to offer their descriptive and explanatory comments to the proceedings.

Recent research on a variety of self-analytic group experiences (Mann, 1966, 1967; Mills, 1964a; O'Day, 1973, 1974; Slater, 1966) suggests that leader tolerance for the direct expression of member hostility is an important part of the process by which the members become independent of the leader, develop a sense of self-reliance, and begin to create a colleague-type relationship with the group leader and with other members of the group. Experiments by Mills (1964b) and Ogilvie (1965) have clearly demonstrated the incorporative and identification-producing properties of verbal aggression.

Education should literally be an expansion of consciousness where people can come into contact with a wider range of ideas, people, and perspectives than they have experienced before. Self-analysis classrooms help people get beyond the limitations of academic major, prior friendships, roommate, hometown, neighborhood, and socioeconomic group. This last one is easier to overcome at the school level than at college or university. People do make friends and enemies of each other in classes of this kind, and some of these relationships are short-lived while others are more enduring. One result of a self-analysis classroom experience is that the members begin to acknowledge each other's existence and to some degree understand each other's behavior.

The self-analysis class really does offer the students an invaluable opportunity to see themselves as others see them. However, this kind of class is quite unlike most sensitivity or encounter group types of classes. It is different primarily because it encourages the members to examine common personal and interpersonal dilemmas from within the variety of perspectives and behavioral styles represented in the group itself rather than advocating some one best way for people to relate to each other. The comparative approach frees the members from the constraints of habitual thinking and opens up to them the wide range of patterns possible in human interaction.

Traditional teaching methods in the social sciences deal primarily with *verbal reality* and as such allow students to learn a psychology, sociology, and anthropology of the other. The self-analysis method, on the other hand, focuses as well on *behavioral reality* and as a result permits students the opportunity to learn how to be effectively self-conscious about the antecedents and consequences of their own behavior and that of others.

THE ROLE OF THE SELF-ANALYTIC TEACHER

In the self-analysis classroom the teacher does play an important role, which is linked to the accomplishment of particular goals. These goals are student self-direction, independence, thoughtful observation of one's own behavior and the behavior of others, and the ability to engage in effective collaborative group action to resolve common dilemmas and accomplish collective learning goals. These goals are not represented by some final end-state reached by all successful self-analysis classes. The members of the class learn over time to more easily and confidently assert independence and self-direction in the face of such recurring interpersonal issues as authority and intimacy.

Basically, the instructor should talk as little as possible. This stance places a great deal of pressure on the students themselves to initiate and maintain classroom discussion. The instructor in a self-analysis class has to refuse to assume the normal duties of the teacher role: begin and end each class; present lectures or, in some discussion-leader fashion, be responsible for the communication of content and pattern; be the universal evaluator of what is true and what is not true; determine for the class members what is important and what is unimportant; or tell them what they should remember and what they should forget.

Many of the usual teacher functions (e.g., lecturing, setting assignments, and issuing grades) have the consequence, if not the intention, of impressing and intimidating students. The message that emanates from this vast array of teacher power is: "See how smart I am." As a result, students are perpetually involved in a situation that continually reminds them of their inferiority. So, of course, currying favor with the superior becomes the primary strategy of personal survival in this one-down position.

In the typical classroom situation there is no viable avenue by which the students can explore reality free from the external constraints provided by the teacher. As a result, students are never free to create for themselves a more satisfying, intricate, and exciting definition of the situation. However, the classroom teacher is in a unique position to provide his students with the opportunity to take that kind of freedom. It should be noted, of course, that freedom and independence can be experienced only when they are seized. They cannot be bestowed on a person by someone else. Therefore, it must be understood that the self-analytic teacher does not *give* his students freedom and independence. All the teacher can do is provide the circumstances that make it possible for the students to take control over the situation for themselves.

The task of the instructor is to work "toward encouraging the student to achieve a synthesis between the concepts he acquires in the readings, the behavior he observes in his own group, and his own emotional reactions, cognitions and experiences of life" (Dunphy, 1967, p. 203). The instructor tries to help the class develop some kind of dynamic balance between thought and spontaneous action. It is important that the students come to realize that it is possible to be thoughtful about actions and that thought and action do not nullify each other. The teacher tries to help the students move from a position of contradiction to one of synthesis and balance so that they can become more aware of the richness and complexity of the situation. The self-analysis teacher does this not through lectures but through periodic comments on and interpretations of the ongoing behavior he observes in the class.

THE REACTIONS OF STUDENTS

The dynamics involved in the authority relation between teacher and student is the central focus of a self-analysis class because the teacher–student relationship is the fundamental reality in the educational system. Furthermore, since this relationship is also representative of all authority relations in the society it becomes possible for the students to generalize from their relationship with the teacher-as-authority and gain insight into relations with parents, other teachers, bosses, supervisors, and husbands or wives.

The teacher–student relationship becomes the central issue when the instructor stops talking on the first day of a self-analysis class after introducing himself, indicating the title of the course, checking enrollment, handing out the reading list and outlines for various assignments, and finally stating that he does not intend to take responsibility for what transpires during the class sessions. During the subsequent silence, which can extend anywhere from 5 to 40 minutes, everyone feels anxious and confused.

It is of course true that for some students this initial silence can extend throughout the entire life of the class. The largest faction in a self-analysis classroom situation is the silent students (Rosenwein, 1970). They are usually silent because they have no definite convictions about the class. Typically they fear rejection, especially by the teacher but also by their peers. Most silent members suffer from a "damned if I do, damned if I don't" dilemma. They want to please everyone or at least not offend anyone. They desire total harmony, and because they are afraid it cannot be achieved they resign themselves to anonymity.

However, this neutered stance becomes increasingly difficult as the various vocal factions quarrel with each other as to which of their positions is the way or the only path to important learning. As the verbal members compete for the support of the silent members, the latter are pressured to confront their dilemma. They are forced by their peers to make up their minds, to choose sides. But that is exactly what is threatening to them because they might make the wrong choice, both in some mystical sense of losing out entirely in the acquisition of knowledge and in the more immediate sense of earning the enmity of or facing ridicule from their peers or from the teacher. Under this kind of pressure most of the silent ones withdraw even more, some to the point of dropping the course entirely. Most, however, alternate between attending and not attending depending upon the intensity of the pressure being placed on them.

Those who are unwilling to confront the class situation and so leave the field raise important issues for the self-analysis teacher. The success of any educational procedure depends upon the presence of the learner as a minimal requirement. A common solution to ensure some reasonably systematic attendance is to make one of the required assignments on analysis of the class experience over the term using, as data, a session-by-session observational log for which each student is responsible. As an aid to the students in writing the log, the instructor may distribute an outline of general issues and themes they might consider examining. However, no constraint is foolproof and many students do not attend any sessions.

In large self-analysis classes (numbering 100 students or more) it is very likely that the majority of students will leave the class situation before they ever get to the point of asserting themselves in the room. This is especially true if there is no reason for them to stay in terms of getting a mark (where attendance is not compulsory either in the sense of it being part of the grade or where the assignments are not directly based on material covered in class sessions).

It is, of course, a debatable issue as to whether students should be compelled to stay in class. On the one hand, they will learn a lot if they stay. So, of course, they should stay. On the other hand, if the instructor encourages them to stay because he thinks it is important, then he is making up their minds for them and setting up the old "authority knows best—trust me" pattern. What a self-analysis instructor can do when people start to leave is ask them why they are leaving. Many will take this question as an order not to leave and will obediently sit down thankful that authority has taken control for them. Others will feel embarrassed that attention was called to them during their otherwise noiseless, unobtrusive exit. A few of these students will then dash for the door. However, often someone will stand in front of the class, coat on and clutching books, and expound on his feelings (usually negative) about the class. Frequently, another student will subsequently ask him to come back and join the class.

While a self-analysis instructor does not have any right to demand attendance or to interfere with his students' right to leave when they want, he can require, as a minimal definition of their commitment to each other, that a student clarify as much as possible his reasons for leaving. For some people, this requirement is all it takes for them to continue to stay.

It is also difficult in a self-analysis class to prevent a few talkative members from completely dominating the air-time. Therefore, it is important for the teacher to help the reticent ones be more expressive since the primary aim of the class is to explore the personal and interpersonal reality of the situation. The fact that no one person or subgroup owns reality can be demonstrated only if everyone contributes his particular variety of experience to the unfolding mosaic. The instructor should not try to act as a discussion leader who silences the most verbal and encourages the silent ones to speak. Instead the instructor should try to wait out the silent ones until their level of tolerance has been exceeded and they themselves silence the talkative members. In this way, they begin to own the situation by becoming an active part of it and their initiative serves to discourage them from looking to the instructor to make an opening for them.

Among the talkative members of the class, there are four distinct patterns of response to the self-analysis classroom format involving the two dimensions of assertiveness and personal intimacy. For purposes of discussion, I differentiate between active and passive personals and active and passive counterpersonals. Also, for purposes of discussion, the assumption is made that all members of the self-analysis class are initially to some degree or other dependent upon the instructor.

The *personals* are those students who welcome this relinquishing by the teacher of some of his prerogatives. They typically want to pursue learning goals that are very different from those of traditional education and that revolve around the themes of intimacy, trust, and the public sharing of thoughts and feelings usually considered private and personal especially in the classroom. The motto of the personals is: "The teacher has given us the freedom to experience something different so let us really have an experience." The personals believe that important human truths will be revealed during intense emotional experiences with each other and with the instructor.

The *active personals* are of the persuasion that they can make these emotional experiences happen by directly controlling the events that will take place during the class sessions. So they encourage and initiate talking about personal experiences and emotional reactions that have occurred and are occurring both outside and inside the class. The *passive personals,* on the other hand, espouse a "Che sera sera" philosophy. They believe that enduring truths will be revealed and authentic intimacy will develop only if they are already latently present in the situation. They also believe that this revelation and development will be spontaneous and will require no effort at all on anyone's part. In fact, the passive personals often argue that any active attempt to discover the truths or to develop authentic intimacy will have precisely the opposite effect.

The *counterpersonals* recite the formal course description as if it were some ordained litany. They wish to remain with prescribed content and familiar teaching procedures. The active counterpersonals are different from their more passive brethren in that they suggest alternative structures such as student lectures to replace teacher lectures. The motto of the *passive counterpersonals* is: "If the teacher is not going to teach us then we won't learn anything." The motto of the *active counterpersonals* is: "If the teacher won't teach us, we'll have to teach ourselves."

The personals tend to be anti-intellectual. They deride the value of learning from books and praise direct emotional involvement. The counterpersonals, on the other hand, stress the necessity of "knowing what you're talking about" and "not just sitting around talking off the top of your head."

The personals tend to see themselves as siding with the instructor against the need for structure and against the traditionalism and the cautiousness of their peers. They frequently act as self-ordained bodyguards who shield the instructor from what they believe to be misguided verbal attacks by other students. The personals see their major obstacle to important learning as being the counterpersonals and the silent members. The counterpersonals typically see their major conflict as being with the instructor and they frequently become concerned with how to replace him if they cannot get him to assume the traditional role as teacher. The counterpersonals act as bodyguards for each other and for the silent members in order to protect themselves from what they believe is emotional harassment from the personals, allowed to go unchecked by the instructor.

SELF-ANALYTIC GROUP DEVELOPMENT

The self-analysis classroom can be described metaphorically as a crucible in which the participants come to experience themselves not only as separate individuals but also as an identifiable collective when they confront their common personal and interpersonal dilemmas. The self-analysis group experience is the periodic realization by the members that they are collectively experiencing common and universal dilemmas and are developing group solutions to those dilemmas. Individual concerns and group concerns ebb and flow throughout the designated life of the group. Each person alternates and vacillates in his own particular rhythm between relating to the self-analysis experience as a separate individual and relating to it as a group member. When a significant number of individuals simultaneously relate to the experience as group members, there is a felt sensation of togetherness, of cohesiveness. At that instant, the group becomes, however briefly, a directly experienced reality.

The course of evolution of the self-analysis class from its beginning to its termination can be depicted in terms of the points of conflict and solidarity that occur among the five subgroups of participants. For purposes of clarification, I discuss the developmental issues in terms of the early, middle, and final phases of the group's life.

Early Phases

The initial silence is usually broken by the most anxious member of the passive counterpersonals asking a structural or procedural question. "Is the class over?" "What are we supposed to do in here?" "How many assignments are we required to do, sir?" "When are the assignments due?" "What readings are we required to do and when?"

Initially, the instructor answers such questions with a question such as, "What do you want to do?" When met with such a response the counterpersonals express their frustration by directing more barbed questions at the instructor. "Well, if you're not going to lecture, do we have to come to class?" "What are you being paid for anyhow?" Other people express a more plaintive note: "We're just not used to anything this different and so we can't handle it." "It's not fair to expect us to change overnight because we've had 12 or 13 years of conditioning. You just can't perform miracles." "We can't do anything without your help." Then come more hostile comments: "I didn't pay good money to waste my time." "I'm paying $1.50 per lecture and I want my money's worth." After the initial mobilizing anxiety, the counterpersonals alternate between tactics of ridicule and shame as well as displays of ingratiation in their attempts to shape up the instructor, to get him to assume overt control and prevent what appears to be impending chaos—a situation where, in truth, the "center cannot hold."

In response to this show of blatant dependency and conservatism, the personals express solidarity with the instructor and move against the counterpersonals. Their solidarity with the instructor is often demonstrated by the fact that members of the personals subgroups (particularly the active personals) move their seating positions so that they are physically close to the instructor. This physical closeness represents both a desire to protect the instructor from possible harm from the counterpersonals and a desire to have an exclusive personal relationship with him.

The orientation of the personals toward the counterpersonals ranges from initial appeals to give this new kind of class experience a fair chance, to ultimatums to stop complaining or drop the course, to sarcasm and ridicule for being so timid and tradition-bound. The passive counterpersonals, for the most part, react to the accusation of being unimaginative cowards with an air of superior cynicism and are heard to mutter comments about true believers and disciples. The same accusation usually spurs the active counterpersonals to try to take control of the class because they feel that their position represents the views of the majority of the class and the will of the majority should determine the pattern and content of class sessions.

The active counterpersonals attempt to institute student lectures, systematically required reading assignments, and shared student responsibility for sections of the formal course content since the instructor is obviously not doing his job. They attempt this imposition of structure by calling for a vote, which is, in many ways, a symbolic show of democratic opposition to what they perceive as the unilateral stance of the instructor.

However, most of the students look first to the instructor to see how he is going to vote, and since he remains stubbornly neutral and does not cast a vote, no one votes for the proposals. The attempt by the active counterpersonals to seize control over the situation fizzles. At this moment in time, the active counterpersonals feel deceived by their passive counterparts and by the silent members and for a time retreat into disillusioned silence leaving the center stage to the personals.

Initially the personals are united in joy at seeing the forces of tradition so easily defeated. But it is precisely at this time that the coalition between the active and passive personals becomes less stable as their common enemy retreats into brooding silence and it appears as if they have the experience and the instructor all to themselves. While the active and passive personals agree in some abstract sense about the relations between enduring truths and authentic intimacy, they begin to quarrel about the best way to proceed.

The active personals now direct their affection and attention toward the instructor, thinking that he should be pleased that they got rid of all those annoying uptight students for him. But the instructor is still as noncommittal and questioning with them as he was originally with the counterpersonals.

The passive personals interpret the instructor's lack of positive responsiveness to the demonstrations of allegiance and reverence by the active personals to mean that the latter are destroying any chance that truth and intimacy will be revealed in the class. In response to being accused of "ego-tripping" or "being on a power trip," the active personals accuse the passive personals of being lazy, of being pseudo-Siddharthas and false mystics who think that all goodness will fall magically from the sky as long as they do not do anything, especially any work. This falling out among the personals sets the stage for the active counterpersonals to come out of retirement.

Middle Phases

During this period of the group's life, the passive personals and the passive counterpersonals often withdraw from the class, some permanently and others temporarily, because they feel the class is an exercise in futility. The passive personals withdraw because they despair of ever getting the other members of the class to understand that they cannot make truth appear or intimacy happen. The passive counterpersonals leave because they have given up hope of ever getting the instructor to do his job.

Members of the passive subgroups may periodically reappear to sit on the edge of the class as silent and bemused observers just to see whether or not the class has changed to their liking. In general, though, the passive personals and the passive counterpersonals never again involve themselves directly in the class proceedings. The overt contribution of the passive members is short-lived because they feel that the present and future events in the class are beyond their control. The passive personals also believe these events are beyond anyone's control, while the passive counterpersonals are convinced that the events are under the complete control of the instructor. For differing reasons, then, the passive personals and passive counter-personals do not engage in any sustained effort to get their points of view across.

The middle phases belong to the active personals and the active counter-personals, who spend much of this period bickering at each other with the instructor as the primary audience. Frequently the two factions try to enlist the allegiance of the silent ones who have continued to stay only because they cannot make up their minds to do anything else. The silent ones come to class because that was the activity first assigned to that time period in the day and they feel that, other things being equal, attendance is thereby an under-stood requirement. The active subgroups soon find themselves in a bind: the more they pressure the silent ones to make up their minds, the more likely the silent ones are to stop coming to the class. Eventually the silent ones are left alone by the active members except as periodic objects of ridicule, a situation that is easier for the silent ones to endure than being forced to choose up sides.

The active personals, also discouraged by the lack of success of their direct demonstrations of loyalty to the instructor, shift gears a bit in order to capture his attention and affection. The active personals become the instigators and managers of intense emotional experiences in the class, and these range from the sacred to the profane. They alone decide that the class is to be held outside on warm sunny days. They bring food and drink and have communal feasts by candlelight. They turn the class into a carnival by wearing costumes and playing musical instruments. They recount their religious and sexual experiences. They bring unannounced guests whose purpose is to observe, mystify, or enlighten the rest of the class members. Throughout all this, the instructor is the primary audience. The active personals hope that their provocative behavior will so impress the instructor that he will bestow his favors upon them and them alone.

While the active personals continue to express solidarity with the instruc-tor throughout the group, their earlier quarrels with the passive personals and their bickering with the active counterpersonals are often an expression of their displaced feelings of unrecognized anger toward the instructor for not reciprocating their affection and loyalty—in effect, for not providing them with an exclusive personal relationship. It is important that the instructor focus the attention of the active personals onto the suppressed hostile feelings they have toward him. To the extent that the active personals are able to explore these negative feelings openly and direct them toward the instructor, they come to recognize that there is more to the group experience and the instructor than simply a devotional relationship with a charismatic leader.

Having already gone through their rebellion and their period of self-imposed banishment, the active counterpersonals, during the latter part of this period, begin to praise the instructor for his imagination and his curious attempt at innovative education. However, this praise is coupled with the argument that the experiment failed because the classroom and the particular population of participants did not provide a favorable environment for such an experience. The instructor must be careful at this point not to respond positively to the praise in order to make himself feel good. He must understand that the active counterpersonals are attempting to separate the class experience from him and themselves as if it were something out there, non-human, unrelated to their behavior, and beyond their control. He must turn the attention of these members to the issue that the group experience is what all the participants have made of it. The important learning for the active counterpersonals is to recognize and accept the subtle and complicated interplay of the subjective and objective realities of human conduct.

Final Phases

An ideal conclusion to the self-analytic class experience would be for the two dominant subgroups (the active personals and the active counterpersonals) to recognize and accept their ambivalent feelings toward each other as well as their ambivalent feelings toward the instructor, the passive members, and the silent members. In short, an ideal self-analytic learning experience would occur when everyone in the class was able to see a part of themselves in everyone else. The acceptance of ambivalence in interpersonal relationships and the awareness of the complicated mix of competing and complementary needs and impulses in any single human personality are necessary preconditions for the members to arrive at an understanding of the nature of the class experience as a human phenomenon and of the role each person and each subgroup played in it.

More typically the self-analysis class ends up with a more fragmentary and incomplete picture of human personality and social interaction. During the final phases, the class alternates between expressions of internal harmony and satisfaction with the experience and continuing civil war between the active subgroups. Frequently, the internal harmony results simply from the fact that the active members have temporarily joined forces to scapegoat the silent members and the passive members. It is important that the instructor again focus the attention of the active members onto their attempts to avoid responsibility for the experiences by using the mechanisms of denial and scapegoating. In general, though, the final session is a melancholy time during which the members express a desire for reunion.

It is important to keep in mind that for most students the initial confusion created by the teacher's passivity does not lead to aggression against or support for the teacher. On the contrary, this confusion frequently produces feelings of inadequacy, guilt, and self-recrimination for not having behaved correctly or appropriately. Students hold themselves personally responsible by believing that their passivity, anxiety, and "unthinkingness" are direct results of their own shortcomings. This is precisely why the instructor has to point out that since everyone is, at least initially, withdrawn and frightened the concepts of personality differences and deficiencies do not seem to provide appropriate or adequate explanations of the phenomenon. It is also important for the instructor to introduce, through readings and his infrequent comments, social system concepts such as roles, distribution of power, social hierarchies, privilege, and group membership in order to illustrate and explain the behavior occurring in the class. Instructors should avoid personal concepts because it is too easy for students to drift into a series of discussions about their "hang-ups" and the impossibility of any meaningful change in their lifetimes.

APPLICATIONS OF THE SELF-ANALYSIS METHOD

While this particular educational format has been used primarily at the college and university levels (Bales, 1970; Dunphy, 1967, 1968; Mann, 1966, 1967; McLeish, Matheson, & Park, 1973; Mills, 1964a; Slater, 1966), it is by no means inappropriate for younger students particularly at the secondary levels. The self-analysis classroom situation can be a valuable part of the school curriculum provided it is not seen as a special or auxiliary function designed to rehabilitate problem students or as a panacea for the problems of adolescence. This type of classroom technique, to be effective, must be an integrated aspect of a coordinated curriculum that, in its practice as well as its rhetoric, recognizes the importance of learning about the varieties of human nature.

Educators should be wary of various sensitivity techniques purporting to teach students how to be independent individuals and effective group members. What people can be taught is how to learn about interpersonal relationships. Once they have learned how to learn about interpersonal relationships they are in a better position to judge for themselves which interpersonal styles are more or less effective for the realization of important human goals (authentic intimacy, personal independence, and collaborative interdependence).

The self-analysis class situation in a secondary school curriculum provides the students with the opportunity to examine and understand adolescent interpersonal relationships not as manifestations of personal problems but as more effective or less effective ways of coping with universal dilemmas in human relationships. In such a noncounseling-oriented environment, the students can begin to discover experientially as well as intellectually how they relate to authority figures and their peers. Since the instructor does not systematically encourage or discourage any particular interpersonal style as being better or worse than any other, the students are free to change in ways they feel are more effective for realizing important personal, interpersonal, and group concerns. What the teacher does try to encourage is that the students engage in some honest reflection on the nature and circumstance of the behavior occurring in the group.

Since the self-analysis class has a didactic focus rather than a therapeutic or rehabilitative focus, it serves to reinforce important processes of learning in general and therefore support the ongoing educational goals of the school. The ongoing dynamics of the self-analysis situation require that the members think about and try to understand the present behavior occurring in the group within the larger context of prior socialization and their expectations, positive and negative, about the future. Being able to integrate the past, present and future of a phenomenon one is interested in understanding is a crucial part of effective knowledge-gathering.

More specifically, the self-analysis class is "a strong situation of deep consequence to the participants" (Milgram, 1965, p. 57) and as such is an important medium through which the study of personality, human interaction, and social order can be introduced into the secondary school curriculum. In this sense, the self-analysis class is a "strategic site" (Merton, Broom, & Cottrell, 1959) for the understanding of human behavior that goes beyond the usual social studies, social etiquette, and personal hygiene courses that secondary school students are required to endure.

However, it should be pointed out that the educational value of the self-analysis class format will be lost if it is used to counsel the "problem" students or to focus on the problems of adolescence. Its value will also be lost if it is turned into a "gripe session" designed to act as a safety valve for the periodic cathartic release of the students' pent-up anger at being ruled and regulated. Of course, to ensure that this does not happen, the education of teachers and school administrators will have to include training in the theory and practice of the self-analytic group method as a teaching technique.

CONCLUDING REMARKS

The value of the self-analysis class lies not in its curative properties, so carelessly attributed to various sensitivity and encounter group experiences.

The real value derives from the fact that the self-analysis classroom affords an all too rare opportunity to its members to examine the degree of consistency between their self-images and their actual behavior. As a result, the students learn how to be effectively self-examining about others' conduct as well as their own. This kind of learning has been so neglected in our society that people's self-images are dangerously at odds with their actual behavior. Witness, for example, the research by Milgram (1965) on obedience to authority and by Darley and Latane (1968) on helping others in distress.

It is crucial for the emergence of democratic functioning in our society that people not be trained to believe that they are independent, tolerant, and democratic (at the level of self-perception) while the very process of that training makes them obedient, passive, and increasingly dependent on "those who know more." There is already too much of a situation where "authority is freedom and freedom is authority." Teachers must avoid participating in and thereby maintaining pseudo-democratic proceedings where the students and the teachers collude (knowingly and unknowingly) in pretend egalitarianism—where the students are permitted to address the teacher on a first-name basis, and play at discussing and considering each other's ideas but pay particular attention to the teacher's comments, which after some "serious" deliberation are accepted as being the most valid.

Critics of the self-analysis style of teaching argue that it sacrifices content for process and that it has quasi-therapeutic aims. These criticisms have validity only from a perspective that separates content and process and distinguishes between education and personal awareness and change. This practice of subdividing reality actually produces false distinctions. For example, what is really being learned in a political science class where the students are lectured at on the 10 points of democracy? Or in a social psychology class where the lecturer holds forth on the research and theory of cooperation while each student is isolated from and in competition with his peers? In most of our classes, students are learning a "social science of the other," where other people—but not they—are gullible, obedient, prejudiced, and, in general, victims of social and personal forces. We must here ask "whether the illusion of knowledge . . . is not potentially more misleading than unpretentious ignorance" (Dunphy, 1967, p. 202).

The "therapy" criticism is most perplexing because it can stem only from a perspective that separates the classroom situation from the rest of the students' educational experiences. At the typical North American university, for example, there is an extensive formal counseling apparatus with, among other things, individual counseling sessions, sensitivity training groups, rap rooms, crisis centers, and peer counselors. The major complaints of the students who come to these facilities are of loneliness and boredom. The point that must be raised in classes, especially the large ones, is the contradiction between the high incidence of loneliness on campus and the fact that students spend so much of their time in rooms full of other people of similar age and interests. It seems a strange goal for education to be training people to remain silent and alone in the company of others.

It should be noted that most of the reactions from the students in the early sessions of a self-analysis class stem from an overwhelming sense of power-lessness. This feeling was clearly illustrated at one point by a student who lamented: "What do you want from us? Do we have to beg you?"

It is important that students wrestle with this felt sense of powerlessness not abstractly but in concrete terms in the class with the instructor as an immediate figure of authority. Control over one's life begins at home and home for students is the classroom. Until students can achieve some degree of power in the classrooms, until they see that influencing and controlling the process of learning on that level on a day-to-day basis is crucial, then all the talk of student parity on university and school committees will be hollow because these actions will have no basis of support in the daily process of the institution.

It must also be understood that, in order to devise classroom situations that can permit students to see themselves as they function within a complex of psychological and sociological forces, it is not necessary to espouse a "noble savage" model of the student. The majority of students, like the majority of teachers, are willing captives of traditional educational proce-dures. Most students are not overwhelmingly enthusiastic about radical (to use their phrase) styles of teaching. A colleague recently remarked that as his teaching style departed increasingly from the straight lecture procedure, the student ratings for the course dropped. At least initially, in a classroom situation that differs from the lecture format, most students are as reluctant to relinquish the security provided by the role of student-as-human-xerox-machine as most teachers are to surrender the immense privilege provided by the role of teacher-as-master-copy. It is definitely a privileged position, not unlike that of magistrate, where people tend to believe what you say whether you know what you are talking about or not.

The teaching orientation that has been described here has been used in classes numbering 12, 20, 30, and 150 in courses on general social psychol-ogy, interpersonal relations, small-group processes, introductory psychology, and educational psychology, and similar themes and issues have arisen in all these classes. While the size and explicit analytical orientation of the course (as spelled out in the course description) affect the rate and range of analysis that can occur in any given time period, it is the variety of interpersonal styles manifested by the students that is the most important factor. The more variety of styles, the greater the number of issues that become explicit. If the overwhelming number of students happen to favor the same general inter-personal coping strategy, the subsequent learning tends to be narrow and shallow because the class has no real opportunity to experience various definitions of social and personal reality in the situation.

The active confrontative students (personal and counterpersonal) can learn from each other, as well as acting as models for their more passive peers by illustrating the various ways to assume responsibility for the conduct of the classes when the teacher deliberately refuses to do so. The trick is to effectively develop intimate relationships with other people, to be personal and counterpersonal, to be active and passive, as is required by the pursuit of individual and social goals. To be able to stand alone and at the same time live and work effectively with others is not a mutually exclusive proposition. It represents a healthy paradox about the realities of human life, which can be vitalized and revitalized by a learning environment such as is provided by the self-analysis classroom.

Finally, as educators must continually remind themselves,

most important in questions of technique is variation itself—that a given approach not be maintained after it has become style and ossified . . . any educational innovation almost always generates excitement and enthusiasm for a few years and then becomes a dead hand throttling the learning process. At this point another innovation is required, and even if it is nothing more than a sharp reversion to traditional techniques it will tend to generate some of the same responsiveness for a period of time . . . no change is of permanent value. A leader who never alters his technique has ceased to learn, and he who has ceased to learn can hardly help others to learn. (Slater, 1966, p. 258)

REFERENCES

Bales, R. F. *Personality and interpersonal behavior.* New York: Holt, Rinehart & Winston, 1970.

Bem, S. L., & Bem, D. J. We're all nonconscious sexists. *Psychology Today,* 1970, *4* (6), 22.

Bennis, W. G., & Shepard, H. A. A theory of group development. *Human Relations,* 1956, *9,* 415–437.

Darley, J. M., & Latane, B. Bystander intervention in emergencies: Diffusion of responsibility. *Journal of Personality and Social Psychology,* 1968, *8,* 377–383.

Dunphy, D. C. Planned environments for learning in the social sciences: Two innovative courses at Harvard. *The American Sociologist,* 1967, *2,* 202–206.

Dunphy, D. C. Phases, roles and myths in self-analytic groups. *Journal of Applied Behavioral Science,* 1968, *4,* 195–225.

Leary, T. The level of public communication: The interpersonal reflex. In T. Leary, *Interpersonal diagnosis of personality.* New York: Ronald, 1957. pp. 91–131.

Mann, R. D. The development of the member-trainer relationship in self-analytic groups. *Human Relations,* 1966, *19,* 85–115.

Mann, R. D. *Interpersonal styles and group development.* New York: Wiley, 1967.

McLeish, J., Matheson, W., & Park, J. *The psychology of the learning group.* London: Hutchinson, 1973.

Merton, R. K., Broom, L., & Cottrell, L. S., Jr. (Eds.) *Sociology today.* New York: Basic Books, 1959.

Milgram, S. Some conditions of obedience and disobedience to authority. *Human Relations,* 1965, *18,* 57–75.

Mills, T. M. *Group transformation: An analysis of a learning group.* Englewood Cliffs, N.J.: Prentice-Hall, 1964. (a)

Mills, T. M. Authority and group emotion. In W. G. Bennis, E. H. Schein, D. E. Berlew, & F. I. Steele (Eds.), *Interpersonal dynamics: Essays and readings on human interaction.* Homewood, Ill.: Dorsey, 1964. Pp. 94–108. (b)

O'Day, R. Training style: A content-analytic assessment. *Human Relations,* 1973, *26,* 599–637.

O'Day, R. The sensitivity group trainer: A study of conflict in the exercise of authority. In G. S. Gibbard, J. J. Hartman, & R. D. Mann (Eds.), *Analysis of groups: Contributions to theory, research and practice.* San Francisco: Jossey-Bass, 1974.

Ogilvie, D. M. Aggression and identification. *Journal of Personality and Social Psychology,* 1965, *1,* 168–172.

Rosenwein, R. E. Determinants of low verbal activity rates in small groups: A study of the silent person. Unpublished doctoral dissertation, University of Michigan, 1970.

Slater, P. E. *Microcosm: Structural, psychological and religious evolution in groups.* New York: Wiley, 1966.

24. An Equal Employment Opportunity Sensitivity Workshop

THOMAS H. PATTEN, JR. and LESTER E. DOREY

Training and manpower specialists have recently been asking in this *Journal* whether training and development can be made relevant to the racial crisis.[1] We not only believe that it can but also have some relevant evidence which we

Reproduced by special permission from the January, 1972 *Training and Development Journal,* pp. 42, 44, 46-53. Copyright 1972 by the American Society for Training and Development, Inc.

[1]Robert Moore, "Can Training and Development Be Relevant to the Racial Crisis?" *Training and Development Journal,* January, 1970, pp. 26–27.

wish to share in this article. Our focus of attention is a new kind of sensitivity laboratory experience which adds yet another dimension to the types of programs,[2] and kinds of thinking[3] which the Personnel Management Program Service of the School of Labor and Industrial Relations, Michigan State University, has been trying out in recent years to assist employers in solving some of the problems blocking implementation of the equal employment opportunity concept in their organizations.

Black-white sensitivity training laboratories are, of course, not new[4] but until the late 1960's we heard little about them. Perhaps the unique aspect of our laboratory was that it included blacks and whites, men and women, all employed in the same organization, all working in the personnel office or as equal employment opportunity representatives, and all part of an initial organizational development effort designed to bring about change.

In this article we proceed by explaining: the basis for the interest in equal employment opportunity at the U.S. Army Tank-Automotive Command (hereinafter referred to as TACOM); the establishment of an experimental training program and the ground rules for participation; the design of the black-white change-agent sensitivity workshop; various pre- and post-measures of the training, included an overview of how the participants perceived the workshop experience; and, lastly, the conclusions and implications of this training for further organizational development (OD) programs at TACOM as well as for organizations of all kinds concerned with the racial crisis.

EQUAL EMPLOYMENT OPPORTUNITY AT TACOM

The black-white change-agent sensitivity workshop discussed in this article was developed as a consequence of Executive Order No. 11478, "Equal Employment Opportunity in the Federal Government," which was promulgated by President Richard M. Nixon on August 8, 1969. This Executive Order superseded and strengthened earlier federal policies on providing equal opportunity in federal employment on the basis of merit and fitness and without discrimination because of race, color, sex, religion or national origin. The order applied to almost all federal employees; and as in this article, to military departments of the federal government.

In 1970 Major General Shelton E. Lollis, Commander of TACOM, which employs 5,900 people (about 25 per cent black), developed a plan to imple-

---

[2]Virginia W. Baird, "Employing the Disadvantaged Fraught with Challenges," *Training and Development Journal,* July, 1969, pp. 44–46.

[3]John F. Sullivan, "Assimilating the Newly Employed Hard-Core," *Training and Development Journal,* September, 1970, pp. 44–48.

[4]For example, Esalen Institute has been conducting interracial confrontation weekends for several years co-led by one white and one black. Some of the learning obtained from these encounters is reported in Price M. Cobbs and William Grier, *Black Rage* (New York: Basic Books, Inc., Publishers, 1968).

ment equal employment opportunity and re-emphasized President Nixon's Executive Order. This plan identified actual and potential problems and defined specific goals, projects, responsibilities and measures for evaluating progress in implementing equal employment opportunity.[5] The plan pinpointed responsibility together with target dates for the accomplishment of objectives. In addition, the plan included considerable statistical information documenting the employment categories, grade level distribution, salary group and similar information for blacks and whites and males and females at TACOM. A Department of the Army pamphlet, *Equal Employment Opportunity in Action, An Evaluation Guide,*[6] was made available to supervisors.

The carefully-prepared plan and the pamphlet represented tangible efforts to cope with anti-discrimination and take action to remove bias. However, to translate these plans into behavioral change within TACOM, it was thought desirable to make an initial administrative start by enabling key personnel office employees and other employees who handle equal employment opportunity complaints to become more sensitive to the issues of interest to higher management. As a consequence, an employee development officer contacted the Personnel Management Program Service at Michigan State University to see what relevant education and training could be designed.

SETTING TRAINING OBJECTIVES

In struggling with the question of "how to make it happen," the designers of the laboratory had to tighten up their own thinking in a relatively new area and decide upon a design which would be practicable and relevant to the TACOM problems.

Early, it was decided to use "sensitivity training," which is a catch-all term that needs to be made specific if program designers are to set clear objectives, measures and eventually obtain results.

We decided that the specific goals should be to improve certain aspects of the program participants' performances by: (*a*) insuring that their values concerning equal employment opportunity were identified and understood, and (*b*) increasing their inter-personal awareness and skills.

The results to be expected were as follows. We hoped that TACOM management at a future date (after the training had been completed) would observe that equal opportunity as a value was better understood by the participants. Furthermore, it was expected that management would observe that the program participants had greater skill in communicating the equal

---

[5]See United States Army Tank-Automotive Command, "Equal Employment Opportunity Plan of Action, FY 71," (Warren, Mich.:) 37 pp. (processed).

[6]Headquarters, Department of the Army, *"Equal Employment Opportunity in Action, An Evaluation Guide,"* Pamphlet No. 690–25 (Washington, D.C.: U.S. Government Printing Office, February 26, 1970).

opportunity concept and in assisting line and staff supervisors in understanding it. The program designers hoped that these understandings would be reflected in changes in behavior on the job, however, it was cautioned that this behavior would need reinforcement by top management in the process of day-to-day operations if it was to become a way of life.

DAY 1

8-12:00 Noon
- Administer Questionnaire on attitudes toward race.
- Micro-lab on learning in dyads, quartets, octets, and total community.
- Decision on learning goals for lab.

1-4:00 P.M.
- Political power exercise.
- Debriefing of the exercise and the day's accomplishments.

DAY 2

8-12:00 Noon
- Film, "In the Company of Men."
- Blacks and whites work separately to state prejudices and then confront one another on them.

1-4:00 P.M.
- Blacks and whites mix in quartets and work on roleplays of issues in prejudice on the job and in the self.
- Role plays are repeated with remedial courses of action acted out.

4-5:00 P.M.
- Period of rest and relaxation.

5-7:00 P.M.
- Debriefing of entire lab to date using a relatively unstructured T-group geared to "do-your-own-thing."

7-9:00 P.M.
- Dinner for the learning community.

DAY 3

8-12:00 Noon
- Learning community develops symbolic pastels of concepts of presently perceived and ideal occupational roles.
- Public sharing and interpreting of the pastels.

1-4:00 P.M.
- Continuation of the morning exercise.
- Administer questionnaire on attitudes toward race.
- Administer overall workshop evaluation questionnaire.
- Award certificates of completion and terminate program.
- Have books and literature available on further reading laboratory education, planned change, and locally available laboratories.

Figure 5.8. Equal Employment Opportunity Sensitivity Workshop Design

Note: All participants read Elliot Liebow's *Tally's Corner* (Boston: Little, Brown and Company, 1967), before program participation.

PARTICIPANT SELECTION

Having set the goals and identified the results expected, it was necessary to decide who should attend the laboratory and what ground rules would apply in choosing them. Although this was to be a "sensitivity training" approach the program was called a "workshop" and was built around the idea of enabling the participants to become change agents with TACOM.

It was also determined that between 16 and 20 voluntary participants would be needed, chosen among men and women and blacks and whites, to have a group sufficiently large and diversified for the conduct of exercises and laboratory learning experiences.

The program was to last three days and be held off-site. Participation would be voluntary, but anyone who attended the first day was committed to all three days. A certificate of completion from MSU would be awarded those who attended all sessions. This was not a "live in" learning situation and the participants returned home each evening.

The program was conducted by three trainers, one on the staff of Michigan State University, one at the University of Michigan and the third a counselor-at-law in private practice. All three trainers had known one another for several years and had had varied training experiences.[7] One was a professional member of NTL-IABS.

DESIGNING THE WORKSHOP

Figure 5.8 shows the design of the laboratory as it was conducted. The design was kept flexible and some planned activities were changed as the group behavior evolved and required appropriate responses in design. Yet the fundamental concept, i.e., to provide some initial change-agent skills to the participants within an organizational context that related to equal employment opportunity served as a unifying focus.

As is the case in much sensitivity training, social-emotional issues concerned with self-awareness were of interest to the trainers and were thought to be appropriate educational issues to be raised in the laboratory. There was also a desire to instrument the laboratory, and pre- and post-measures were taken on an *ad hoc* questionnaire concerned with attitudes toward race.

As one common experience to be shared by the trainers and participants, everyone was asked to read *Tally's Corner,*[8] a popularly-written social anthropological study of a black ghetto in Washington, D.C. (although no exercises were built around this book).

A subjective "testimonial-type" questionnaire was utilized after the laboratory to provide the trainers with feedback as to the participants' perceptions of the laboratory.

---

[7]Acknowledgement is given to Dr. Marilyn E. Harris and William F. Dannemiller, who assisted in the design and conduct of the workshop together with the senior author.

[8]See Elliot Liebow, *Tally's Corner* (Boston: Little Brown and Company, 1967).

The reader can discern there were three days of activity. Following the terminology of Schein and Bennis,[9] one might say that Day 1 was used for "unfreezing," Day 2 for "changing" or at least "moving" toward change; and Day 3 for "refreezing." In terms of the philosophical issues, where one might view change as being categorized as either evolution, revolution or planned change, our approach was to involve the group in self-education, hoping that greater self-awareness and feedback with supportive re-emphasis by the trainers on using skills "back home" would help get the participants started as change agents.

FIRST DAY MICRO-LAB

Turning to the specific days, on the first day the participants were involved in a "micro-lab" where they started to learn in dyads and small groups by introducing themselves to one another in terms of their strengths and weaknesses. This served to inventory the group resources and provide a basis for deciding upon individual learning goals in the workshop later in the morning. These goals were made public to all participants.

In follow up to the morning session, the trainers utilized a political power exercise.[10] The exercise essentially allows individuals to experience differential degrees of power and to try to influence one another through written and oral communications. It is also useful in unfreezing a group by building new organizational structures in the laboratory that may not accord with backhome culture. This exercise was debriefed later in the afternoon, and the accomplishments of the day were reviewed.

FILM STARTS SECOND DAY

On the second day, a film, "In the Company of Men," was used as a starter. This film was developed by *Newsweek* magazine and focused upon training using psychodrama with disadvantaged blacks and white foremen in an automotive plant in a southern state. The film had a great deal of verisimilitude for the TACOM participants and served as a meaningful springboard for the remainder of the second day. For example, it enabled us to deal openly with white prejudice and black resentment, and we made effective use of the film in formulating small-group task exercises.

Specifically, we asked all whites to go in one room and reduce to newsprint their answers to the query: "What bugs me about blacks?" Similarly, blacks were asked to go in a separate room and address themselves to the question:

---

[9] Edgar H. Schein and Warren G. Bennis, *Personal and Organizational Change through Group Methods: The Laboratory Approach* (New York: John Wiley and Sons, Inc., 1965), pp. 277–310.

NOTE: All participants read Elliot Liebow's *Tally's Corner* (Boston: Little Brown and Company, 1967), before program participation.

[10] The originator of the exercise and a source of reference to it are not known, although many laboratory and OD trainers are familiar with the exercise.

"What bugs me about whites?" Their comments were also reduced to news-print.

Subsequently, the two groups came together and posted their comments side by side. This confrontation enabled the trainers to match the blacks and whites in the afternoon in task groups for learning and to ask them to work on role plays of issues that were bugging them as determined in the morning exercise.

These role plays were used for self-education and provided much insight into issues of concern and ways in which changes could be brought about in dealing with the issues. The participants were asked not only to role-play the issues but also to repeat the role plays with recommended courses of remedial action to deal with the issues that were bugging them. In essence, these repeated role plays provided valuable self-education and experimental opportunities in the laboratory for demonstrating change techniques as well as a chance for mutual feedback.

EVENING T-GROUP

Later in the afternoon there was a period of rest and relaxation; and in the evening, a debriefing of the entire workshop experience up to that time, using a relatively unstructured T-Group. This session did not utilize the conventional T-Group of individuals sitting in a circle dealing with one another at the intragroup or intra-personal level, although there was some of this. Our design was even less structured and encouraged persons to "do their own thing."

The design allowed some people to engage in role playing, role reversals, role soliloquy, sharing of feelings, theoretical discussions of categories of black militancy and quite a range of issues of group interest. Using the T-Group was a spontaneous outgrowth of what had happened in the lab and in no way seemed to be an artificial exercise engrafted on the workshop simply to provide a T-Group experience.

SYMBOLIC PASTELS

On the third day, we decided that the participants would be interested in and probably should once again deal directly with self-awareness and back-home application of the training. As a consequence, we asked each participant to take two sheets of newsprint and various pastel pencils and marking crayons and to draw a picture, cartoon, representation, symbol or any other representation he desired, indicating how he thought he was presently perceived in the conduct of his organizational role at TACOM (on one sheet of paper) and on the other sheet the same kind of indication or representation as to how he would like to be perceived in carrying out his organizational role. Participation in this exercise was voluntary but the symbolic pastels developed should be publicly shared and interpreted. All

TABLE 5.3
CHARACTERISTICS OF PARTICIPANTS

	White	*Black*	*Total*
No. of Males	4	4	8
Average Age (yrs.)	49.5	43.7	46.6
Range	38-62	39-45	38-62
Average Education (yrs.)	13.7	14.0	13.8
Range	12-17	12-16	12-17
No. of Females	5	4	9
Average Age (yrs.)	47.2	45.4	46.2
Range	28-54	25-61	25-61
Average Education (yrs.)	13.7	13.0	13.3
Range	12-16	10-16	10-16
Totals	9	8	17
Average Age (yrs.)	48.3	44.6	46.6
Range	28-62	25-61	25-62
Average Education (yrs.)	13.7	13.4	13.5
Range	12-17	10-16	10-17

participants agreed to work on their symbolic pastels, and almost the entire day was spent on sharing and interpreting them from the standpoint of how they related to organizational effectiveness in implementing equal opportunity back on the job at TACOM.

In addition to the elements of the design previously discussed, the points at which the various questionnaires were introduced are shown in Figure 5.8.

After the lab had terminated, some books and literature were made available for those who wished to know more about laboratory education planned change and locally available laboratories considered by the trainers to be of acceptable quality.

PRE- AND POST-MEASURES

Undoubtedly, the most "sticky wicket" in running a sensitivity training workshop is the evaluation of results. We do not claim to have developed a very sophisticated evaluation design and indeed wish that we had better tools for measuring the results. However, in distinction to many laboratories we did make various attempts at evaluation.[11]

In this laboratory there were nine whites (four males, five females) and eight blacks (evenly divided by sex). Table 5.3 indicates other characteristics

[11]Acknowledgement is given to Mr. John F. Sullivan of Michigan State University who developed and has previously used the attitudinal and evaluation instruments referred to in this article.

TABLE 5.4
ANALYSIS OF RESULTS

	White			Black		
	Before	After	Difference	Before	After	Difference

I. Personal/Stereotyped Beliefs

	Before	After	Difference	Before	After	Difference
When it comes to politics, blacks band together as a race in pursuit of their own selfish interests rather than considering what's good for America as a whole.	2.9	1.9	-1.0	1.4	1.6	.2
Today the majority of blacks are overly aggressive and prone to violence.	2.6	1.8	- .8	2.0	1.6	-.4
If black executives are not "spoon-fed" they have a higher chance of failure than whites.	2.6	1.8	- .8	1.9	1.5	-.4
Blacks tend to lack self-discipline; they tend to give in to every impulse.	2.4	1.7	- .7	1.6	1.6	-
Most blacks go too far in trying to be white; they should not try to disguise their racial identity.	2.8	2.2	- .6	3.0	2.9	-.1
To maintain a nice residential neighborhood, it is best to prevent blacks from moving in.	2.2	1.7	- .5	1.0	1.0	-
Most blacks are extravagant and foolhardy when it comes to handling money.	2.5	2.0	- .5	1.5	1.8	.3
Blacks seem to prefer a much more sensual way of living than do whites.	3.3	2.8	- .5	2.3	1.8	-.5

Table 5.4—*Continued*

Statement						
It is doubtful that integration will turn out to be the final solution to Americans' race relations problems—separate but equal treatment for blacks may well be the answer	2.6	2.2	-.4	2.8	3.0	.2
A major problem in race relations today is the white person's attitude toward blacks	3.8	3.4	-.4	3.9	4.0	.1
I am probably about as much of a "racist" as is any other American adult	2.4	2.1	-.3	3.0	3.4	.4
A step toward solving the race problems would be to prevent blacks from getting into superior positions in society until they learn how to act	2.2	1.9	-.3	1.2	1.7	.5
Blacks smell different from whites	2.7	2.4	-.3	1.6	1.8	.2
As a group, blacks tend to be shiftless and lazy	1.9	1.6	-.3	1.9	1.0	-.9
Most middle-class whites believe in full integration, including intermarriage	2.0	1.7	-.3	1.9	1.4	-.5
It is wrong for blacks and whites to intermarry	2.3	2.1	-.2	2.0	.9	-1.1
Black power and the establishment of black institutions are out of line in the American democracy	3.2	3.0	-.2	2.3	2.4	.1
Today, blacks must be considered a negative influence on the American culture	1.9	1.7	-.2	1.0	1.0	-
Most blacks like to live in beat-up houses and rundown parts of a city	1.8	1.7	-.2	1.0	1.6	.6
A major problem in race relations today is the increasing prevalence of an anti-American attitude among young blacks	3.2	3.0	-.2	3.0	3.3	.3

Table 5.4—*Continued*
ANALYSIS OF RESULTS

	Before	White After	Difference	Before	Black After	Difference
I. Personal/Stereotyped Beliefs—Continued						
Black people drop out of school mainly because they are not too bright to begin with	1.8	1.7	- .1	1.1	1.4	.3
On the whole, blacks have probably contributed less to American life than any other group	2.0	1.9	- .1	1.8	1.1	-.7
One trouble with blacks is that they stick together and connive, so that whites who offer help are shut out	2.2	2.1	- .1	2.3	1.9	-.4
It is best that blacks should mix only with each other socially since they have their own interests, just as whites get along with other whites	2.1	2.1	-	1.8	1.8	-
I find the natural hairdos or "Afros" offensive	2.0	2.0	-	1.3	1.4	.1
"Afro" hairdos are definitely out-of-place in a business setting	2.2	2.3	- .1	1.4	1.4	-
Colleges should adopt a quota system for admissions by which they increase the proportion of blacks that attend colleges and universities	2.4	2.6	.2	3.4	2.8	.6
The growing crop of unemployed blacks is just a side effect of the country's economic progress	2.0	2.2	.2	2.1	2.8	.7
There is a much lower level of morals among blacks than there is among whites	1.7	2.0	.3	2.1	1.3	.8

Table 5.4—*Continued*

Blacks should be more concerned about their personal appearance, and not be so dirty, smelly and slovenly	1.8	2.3	.5	2.1	2.0	-1
Most white adults are deeply concerned about the state of race relations in this country	2.4	2.9	.5	1.6	1.6	-

II. Work-Related Beliefs

It would hurt the business of a large concern if it had too many black employees.	3.1	2.3	.8	1.8	1.8	-
A double standard for evaluating employee progress should be employed for blacks, at least during their first six months of employment.	1.9	1.6	.3	1.9	2.6	.7
It is not right for an organization to require its regular employees to work side-by-side with blacks if they strongly object to doing so	2.2	2.0	.2	2.1	2.6	.5
Companies should actively recruit blacks to fill jobs in every category and develop outstanding prospects for top jobs.	3.9	3.9	-	4.4	3.6	-.8
Given the way things are, it would certainly be ill-advised to place a black supervisor over an all-white work group.	2.0	2.1	.1	1.5	1.9	.4
I would much rather be supervised by someone of my own race.	2.3	2.6	.3	2.5	2.0	.5
A company with 10 openings in middle management positions should place the 10 best-qualified people, even if all happen to be black.	3.7	4.3	.6	3.8	3.8	-

Table 5.4—*Continued*
ANALYSIS OF RESULTS

	White			Black		
	Before	After	Difference	Before	After	Difference
II. Work-Related Beliefs—Continued						
Because they were severely discriminated against in the past, blacks should be given more than an even break today when it comes to jobs, education and opportunity..........	2.4	3.0	.6	4.1	3.3	-.8
III. Governmental Intervention Beliefs						
Government officials tend to be overly concerned with the problem of the blacks...........	2.9	2.2	-.7	1.1	1.1	-
There are too many blacks in the various federal agencies and bureaus in Washington D.C....	2.3	2.1	-.2	1.6	1.6	-
The government should generally go slower in its efforts to increase the number of blacks employed in industry....	2.1	2.0	-.1	1.5	1.5	-
The government should not be allowed to set guides specifying the number of minority group employees that an employee must have.	3.0	3.3	.3	2.8	3.3	.5
The race problem in the United States today is so general and so deep that one often doubts that democratic methods can ever solve it....	2.2	2.5	.3	3.2	3.9	.7
You cannot legislate integration; it must be done voluntarily........	3.2	3.6	.4	3.8	4.0	.2

of our participants. The most striking demographic fact about them is probably their similarity. The ranges in age and education are also shown. There was a mixture among the participants in race, sex, age and education.

In Table 5.4 we display data derived from the questionnaire on attitude toward race administered before and after the laboratory. The instrument which we used was tested once before in a study at MSU, but it is still in need of further refinement. It was a Likert-type summated scale of favorableness-unfavorableness.[12] The main weakness of the instrument was that it was designed to measure whites' attitudes towards blacks.

In general, any changes of less than ± .5 for these data will be arbitrarily omitted from the discussion which follows. It should be borne in mind that the data in Table 5.4 are group means where the strongest degree of agreement would be 5.0 and the strongest degree of disagreement, 1.0.

The 45 items can be grouped under personal/stereotyped beliefs, work-related beliefs and governmental intervention beliefs. The items are arranged for analysis under these three groupings in order of the magnitude of differences pre- and post-training for the whites, a choice made simply because the evaluative instrument made it possible.

For some of the items the greater the strength of disagreement on the part of the respondent (such as the first item in Table 5.4) contrasting pre- and post-workshop scores, the more intense the measure of change in belief. The directionality of white responses did not necessarily suggest that those of the blacks should logically run opposite to them. For example, in the second and third items in Table 5.4 we need not expect both whites and blacks to move toward disagreement with each item, although they did to a slightly different degree. On the other hand, in the case of the fourth item shown, whites changed and blacks remained unchanged. The seventh item is one where the directionality shown could be logically expected, given the nature of the item.

The reader can inspect the remaining items in the table and draw his own conclusions regarding the changes in scores shown.

PERSONAL BELIEFS

Turning to personal stereotyped beliefs, it can be seen that 10 out of 31 beliefs changed for the whites (+.5) whereas nine of the blacks' beliefs changed in the same magnitude. The pattern of these changes is notable because in only one item did the whites and blacks share a change of .5 or more—and for this case, in the same direction. It may be obviously interpreted that the changes reported vary between whites and blacks. The whites'

[12]See Claire Selltiz et al., Research Methods in Social Relations (rev. 1-vol. ed.; New York: Holt, Rinehart & Winston, Inc., 1959), pp. 366–70 for a discussion of these scales. Many of the scale items are adaptations of items which originally appeared on the Levinson and Sanford Anti-Semitism Scale. See D. J. Levinson and R. N. Sanford, "A Scale for the Measurement of Anti-Semitism," Journal of Psychology, April, 1944, pp. 339–70.

changes reflect hypothetically a demolition of certain stereotyped beliefs as they interacted with blacks during the workshop. The blacks' changes reflect hypothetically a strengthening of their self-concepts as they get to know white co-workers and associates better through close contact. As a consequence of this interaction, blacks see that many of the foibles attributed racially to blacks also apply to individual whites. With their perception sharpened in this manner, blacks start to take on an improved concept of themselves, freeing themselves of having to explain away stereotypes or taking refuge in rationalizations such as race pride. If these hypotheses are correct, it may be concluded that the equal employment opportunity workshop did accomplish some unfreezing among the participants and provided an opportunity for them to see their shared common humanity and its potential for both a work organization and everyday life when unobstructed by biased beliefs.

WORK-RELATED BELIEFS

The changes in work-related beliefs are perhaps most interesting of all. First, it should be noted that the whites' pre-and post-scores indicate a strong acceptance of equal employment opportunity concepts. This finding could probably have been expected from personnel specialists and employment opportunity representatives. Most notable perhaps in this connection is the increased rejection pre- and post-workshop of the first item: it would hurt the business of a large concern if it had too many black employees.

At the same time, in five out of eight items the blacks score ± .5 in respect to work-related beliefs. If there is a common thread that ties together these five changes, it would appear to be an improvement in self-concept. For example, the reduced intensity of belief in a need for a double standard of performance evaluation based upon race, for active black recruitment, for a black supervisor, and for opportunity restitution in the form of more than an even break suggest that the blacks started to look more toward their own resources than to external actions needed for implementation of the full equal employment opportunity concept.

GOVERNMENT-INTERVENTION BELIEFS

Lastly, governmental-intervention beliefs changed slightly. The whites were less prone to agree with the idea that governmental officials tend to be overly concerned with the problems of the blacks. The blacks tended to increase their belief that the depth of the race problem in the United States may not admit of democratic solution. Yet they also wondered if the government should set guides specifying the number of minority group employees an employer must have. The blacks' firmness pre- and post-workshop on other aspects of government intervention suggest strong endorsement by them of governmental endeavors in the equal employment opportunity sphere. It is possible also to interpret the whites' responses to mean they

TABLE 5.5
TACOM PROGRAM EVALUATION

1. Overall, I thought that the program was:

POOR	FAIR	GOOD	VERY GOOD	EXCELLENT	UNMARKED
1			7	8	1

2. In terms of their knowledge and presentation, I thought that the trainers were:

POOR	FAIR	GOOD	VERY GOOD	EXCELLENT
		1	4	12

GROUP COMMENTS –
— I was surprised, compared to most courses I have had in government.
— Emotional experience that should carry over into the work situation and perhaps effect some of the needed changes.
— Could have geared us to a higher key.
— Method of approach forced one to explore and examine one's own mind, thoughts and weaknesses.
— A little reserved in pursuing certain areas.
— They seemed to know people.
— They did not "force" when a person did not wish to take part.

3. The physical facilities and conference arrangements were:

POOR	FAIR	GOOD	VERY GOOD	EXCELLENT
		3	9	5

4. In order to improve such workshops as these in the future, I suggest

GROUP COMMENTS –
— Employee-supervised confrontations.
— People in policy-making positions attend.
— Live-in situation: Management-employees workshop together.
— More films. Reduce group size.
— Expose top management, middle management and supervisors to this type training on a mandatory basis.

5. Some problems or areas of interest that the trainers might want to build future workshops around are:

— Management receive this training.
— Take whole employee into account (home, work, play).
— Individual thoughts and experiences in relation to racial discussions.
— Control non-related discussions.
— Techniques to isolate potential problem areas, to prevent problems from occurring.
— Reasons for lack of training and self-development for lower graded employees.
— Why aren't more blacks in higher paying positions?

believed the government should do more, although their feelings on this matter were less intensively felt than were the blacks'. A word of caution is warranted in considering these data. The evaluative instrument is in the earliest stages of development, and this sample size is too small to reach global conclusions. Yet these data when examined together with other evidence obtained during and after the workshop are persuasive that the modest goals of the workshop in respect to self-awareness and understanding of the equal employment opportunity concept were attained.

Given the concentrated design of the sensitivity workshop, the goals worked on in the laboratory, and the degree of factor control exercised, it is plausible that the workshop had an effect on the participants in the desired direction. Only time will tell whether there will be obvious and durable behavior changes back on the job at TACOM.

It is difficult to single out exactly what might have had the most potent effect. In Table 5.5 we reproduce the results of the overall program evaluation which suggests that the novel nature of the program and the favorable reaction to it and the trainers were important variables.

LATER ANECDOTAL EVIDENCE

Another rough measure of the effectiveness of the workshop is anecdotal evidence gathered two months after the training. The workshop participants were given additional information back at TACOM about one month after the workshop was completed in two training sessions on fhe personnel classification and salary administration system used in the Command. The need for this technical personnel training was made obvious in the workshop. This training, reported changes of behavior on-the-job, and expressions by a number of participants that their heightened sense of awareness in respect to their occupational roles in implementing equal employment opportunity comprise additional evidence not only of the effectiveness of the workshop but also responsiveness of the employing organization to making the concept a living reality.

CONCLUSIONS

The equal employment opportunity sensitivity workshop seems to be a useful training device for getting an organization started on developing black and white change agents. There is sufficient information presently available about self-awareness and change agentry so that organizations which desire to translate well-conceived plans into effect should consider the value of this kind of workshop as a step in the direction of implementation. Obviously, the evidence is limited and needs to be buttressed by other studies. However, from the standpoint of action needed to respond to social problems in American society, we feel that training and development specialists can make progress toward changing their organizations in the direction of installing a larger degree of equal employment opportunity through the use of sensitivity workshops such as ours.

IMPLICATIONS FOR THE FUTURE

The kind of workshop discussed in this article may be viewed as a "seeding operation." By this we mean entry into an organization at the level of the personnel office can be potentially useful but is not necessarily the most desirable point of entry for maximum moving effect upon an organization over the long run. The advantage of entering through the personnel department is that trainers are likely to find there some people who are familiar with applied behavioral science concepts and are willing to try them out. People in personnel departments also often have interface contacts in the organization and can "spread the word" about new programs, plans and policies. Yet in many organizations the personnel department is somewhat removed from operations and line activities and it is in the line organization that entry is needed for an OD program to have maximal organizational and personnel affect.

As the next step in organizational development, we could, of course, run a similar workshop for those in the personnel office who did not attend the first workshop. This would have some valuable effects but would be less potent than starting anew from the top down with the commanding officer and his immediate staff. These laboratories could also be oriented towards equal employment opportunity but might be more generally geared to basic human relations and the identification of behavior which needs to be unfrozen in order to identify change issues.

Once an organizational development effort has begun at the top it can then fan down and throughout the organization. This might lead to a period of what Schein has called "process consulting"[13] using an external change agent(s). Eventually the long-run goal should be the development of internal change agents to keep the organizational development effort alive and on-target. The ultimate result would be to develop managerial personnel in the organization, transmitting to them the skills possessed by the external change agents. This would have the effect of building within the organization internal change agent skills so that, once started, the momentum for change would not be dissipated. In other words, people will be left on the scene who themselves can then cope with change and bring about cumulative changes in the organizational culture in line with directions set by management.

---

[13]See Edgar H. Schein, *Process Consultation: Its Role in Organization Development* (Reading, Mass.: Addison-Wesley Publishing Co., Inc., 1969); and William G. Dyer *et al.,* "A Laboratory Consultation Model for Organization Change," *Journal of Applied Behavioral Science,* April-May-June, 1970, pp. 211–27.

25. A Multi-District Organizational Development Effort

FRED C. FEITLER and LAWRENCE L. LIPPITT

INTRODUCTION

This article describes some of the thinking and implementation which went into development of a fourteen-school change project that has come to be known as the "Consortium of Schools."

The Southern Tier Office for Educational Planning[1] began this endeavor in the Spring of 1970. The purpose of the project was to provide training input through Organizational Development to a number of schools in a five-county region which would allow specific schools to determine for themselves the nature and kinds of organizational and program changes that were appropriate and critically needed. Through training in planning, interpersonal skills and small group leadership skills, schools have begun to move proactively toward self-determined goals and objectives. This is in marked contrast to our previous experience with innovative programs in schools, which indicated that typically they were reactive. That is, they tended to react to symptoms and try to come up with cures for problems that could have been avoided. Frequently these innovations are either neutralized by the system or produce unanticipated outcomes which call for additional remedial action.

WHY BOTHER WITH OD?

Schools are under increased pressure for change, both from within the educational establishment and from the communities and society which they serve. Increased demands for accountability, for more relevant programs, the decreased availability of funds for education, and teacher militancy are examples of the external press for change. At the same time, personalized learning, open education, affective education, etc., are programmatic thrusts which have placed teachers and administrators in new and largely uncomfortable situations calling for dramatically different and untried modes of behavior. Generally speaking, these internal and external forces have created an impasse, because both teachers and administrators tend to be deficient in the skills of planning, organizing, and problem-solving which these changes require in order to have a real chance for success.

The Consortium of Schools was seen as a way to provide the necessary skill training to teachers and administrators so that they could increase their

Reprinted from *Educational Technology*. Vol. 12, No. 10, October, 1972, pp. 34–38.
[1]The Southern Tier Regional Office for Educational Planning, Elmira, New York.

ability to develop solutions to their own problems, marshal resources more effectively and redirect energy in modes which were consistent with their basic concern to make schools better places for children. An additional value of OD involvement for participating schools was that of developing the capacity of planning in a fashion which integrates programs into a unity that reflects the goals and desired outcomes specified.

WHY A CONSORTIUM EFFORT?

There were three reasons for a regionally focused effort rather than concentrating on one school. First was the issue of cost. OD is expensive, particularly because it usually makes use of outside consultants. Thus, by involving a number of schools, the cost per school was considerably reduced. Second, a major concept behind the Consortium was that of developing norms of sharing between and among schools. Finally, it was conceived that the Consortium would develop ways to become self-sustaining, if and when the resources of the Planning Office staff ceased to be available.

WHAT HAPPENED?

First, Central Office administrators and principals in the region were invited to explanatory meetings. The Consortium concept and goals were proposed, explained and discussed. The goals were:

1. To assist local school systems in diagnosing their existing ability to manage a productive process of planned change.
2. To develop strategies for improving the system's capacity for self-renewal.
3. To improve procedures and structures for the management of educational change.
4. To mobilize a large resource base for the planning and implementation of activities supporting the local school's progress toward self-renewal through cooperative effort.

Those principals who wanted to explore the concept further were invited to bring a team of five to ten volunteer teachers to a two-day introductory workshop in April, 1970. The goal of the workshop was to provide a clearer picture of what involvement in the Consortium might mean. Subsequent to the workshop, twelve of the sixteen teams in attendance opted to commit both human and financial resources, thereby forming the Consortium.

Training Was Provided

The first total Consortium event was a five-day workshop during the month of August, 1970. It was planned and executed by the consultant staff of the Regional Planning Center. Each member school sent a team of principal and teachers. The goals were: (1) to provide instruction and experiences which would help the individuals from each school develop a cohesive team; (2) to acquire interpersonal group leadership and planning skills; (3)

to help teams focus on change strategies which would involve other school staff; and (4) to form a Consortium Council to assume responsibility for Consortium-wide activities.

The initial day and a half of the workshop focused on team building. This helped members get to know each other better by sharing personal feelings, perceptions and ideas about the task with which they were confronted. Activities which provided training in inter-personal and group leader-member skills were also included. The second and third days of training focused on problem-solving skills and concepts relating to organizational change. Techniques for identifying problems and making them operational were introduced. Time was given to providing general information about organizational climates and behaviors, as well as focusing on ways of identifying areas of needed change in each team's own school organization.

The fourth day's activities were planned to develop strategies for inducing change in each team's school. There was discussion of effective and less effective approaches to change. The teams planned together and tested their plans with other teams.

The final day of the workshop dealt with regional development of a working Consortium. An assessment of resources was made in each school district as well as the Consortium as a total sharing unit. The Consortium Council was formed. It included one member from each school.

The activities of the week were planned to develop a sequential flow. Conceptually the workshop participants moved from individual and team development to considering the team in the larger school organization and, finally, the school within a larger regional structure. These elements were couched in the context of improved education in school organizations through conscious planning and implementation.

Participants evaluated the workshop as providing many extensive and useful learnings and felt quite positive about the experience. All team members perceived their decision-making/problem-solving ability to be markedly improved and were optimistic about the future influence and effectiveness of their teams and the Consortium.

Follow-through

Three months after the workshop, many Consortium-related activities had transpired in member schools. For example, school "A" had gained permission from the central office to waive their participation in the city-wide orientation program so that their change team could put on one of their own. A total faculty meeting, which was planned during the five-day workshop, was held. The faculty orientation time was spent working in a large group and then in small groups, identifying, defining and analyzing a communication problem of interest to the faculty. Some unification of the faculty also took place. Subsequently, work was begun on clarifying principal and teacher role definitions (including work on the ideal role). Brainstorming as a useful technique had been adopted by many teachers. Decisions by consensus and improved decision-making skills were reported. It was also felt that more training was necessary. Some frustration had been voiced about having to "make haste slowly."

A less successful attempt to apply consortium training took place at School "B." An orientation meeting was held for twenty-five percent of the faculty who had expressed interest in the Consortium. Little else had been attempted by change team members. In the Council meeting they expressed a feeling of "infancy," including a need for further external help. Meetings were then held with the consultant staff and the team members working together to plan next steps.

In the other ten schools first steps had been taken by administrators and teachers to identify and define problems which needed to be solved as prerequisites for improved education. Techniques such as brainstorming, small groups, decisions by consensus, setting agendas prior to meetings and widening the base of decision-making were observed in use where they had previously been absent. There had already been an increase in use of group leadership skills by team members, and these had occasionally been picked up and used by colleagues. A majority of the teams had conducted workshops for their faculties to improve group leadership skills and/or problem-solving skills. Several faculties were helped to develop more collaborative work relationships and to build more cohesive total faculty teams.

Simultaneous to this flurry of activity and new behaviors, the team members discovered that the role of a change agent was difficult, and feelings of stress were reported. Many team members voiced a need for time to meet together to receive and give support. In addition, there were feelings of frustration because time was needed to help others understand and to include them in planning and decision-making. There were also requests from teams for further training and planning help from the consultants.

It was of vital importance during this time that the consultant staff be readily available. At times, teams needed to recount their efforts and receive support and help in recognizing their successes and planning next steps. Meetings occurred where "at-the-elbow" help was provided to teams in planning and executing change attempts. Occasionally teams were helped to focus on and increase their own ability to work together. The nature of this project, as a new approach, raised the same issue for both school personnel and consultants: Where do we go from here? A one-day workshop was held in November for all teams so that this problem could be dealt with.

During January, 1971, the consultant team systematically collected diagnostic information in preparation for a series of additional one-day workshops tailored to each team's own needs. Interviews were held with team and non-team personnel in each school. Many teams were feeling neutralized by forces in their organization, some were feeling guilty due to their lack of continued effort, and others were feeling hopeful and needing continued support. All the teams needed to review and further their training.

In the spring each team was asked to evaluate its progress and explore future goals and needs. Subsequent to this activity and before the end of the year, meetings were held with each team to determine whether continued membership in the Consortium was desired and to make commitments for the following year.

The Consortium Council

During the first year the Council grew and developed into a strong self-renewing force within the Consortium. The first meeting in September dealt largely with procedural matters. Decisions and discussions focused on questions such as: What rules will we follow in our meetings? What is the purpose of our meeting together? What is the Council's overall goal? What is the role of the Council? Decisions for operation include the following:

1. There would be no chairman.
2. When ideas were being explored, brainstorming would be used.
3. Decisions would be arrived at by consensus whenever possible.
4. Members would each be responsible for keeping the group "on task."
5. Process (or how we are working together) would be attended to as needed and at the close of each meeting.

The major objective was expressed as the creation of a "self-renewing and sustaining and expanding Council for the improvement of education." This was to be achieved: (1) through interschool communication; (2) through development of more effective process skills; (3) through sharing and evaluating ideas; and (4) by becoming self-operative, i.e., the Consortium would become less dependent on outside help.

The role of the Council was defined to include: (1) sharing ideas between schools; (2) helping member schools in change projects; (3) providing a leadership body for the Consortium, including making the Consortium autonomous; (4) increasing the resources of the Consortium, possibly by adding schools and sharing between schools and school systems; (5) testing possible change strategies; and (6) serving as a clearing house for ideas and resources. Other decisions in relation to the role of the Council focused on the planning role, communication and dissemination, and evaluation.

Progress reports and giving help to several schools which requested aid were the major concerns for the second meeting, held in October. Those teams which appeared least certain about the appropriateness of their new roles as catalysts for change seemed most reluctant to ask for help from the consultants. The Council urged these teams to move ahead and get help where needed. Experiences judged to be successful and less than successful were shared. This made identification of common problems possible, provided support for new team behaviors and was judged quite valuable.

Process observers, requested by the Council, were impressed with the high level of both group problem-solving and interpersonal skills in evidence.

The Council continued to meet throughout the year and to provide this kind of sharing and support. In addition, exchanges of curriculum and teaching ideas took place, and the Council served as an important communication link between the Regional Center consultant team and the school teams.

The Documentarians

In addition to the training workshops, the follow-through activities and the Council, an evaluation thrust was initiated by the Regional Center staff. The use of faculty change agent teams is a relatively new approach to OD. Emphasis was placed on determining the appropriateness of this means of introducing organizational change into schools. With the exception of research and development emanating from the Center for the Advanced Study of Educational Administration (CASEA) at Eugene, Oregon, organizational development activities typically have been initiated and implemented by outside change agents working with school personnel. Specifically desired were data which provided evidence of behavioral change as well as perceptual and attitudinal change. To achieve this end, the concept and role of a documentarian was developed. The Consortium Council approved the idea and served as a vehicle for appointing a faculty team member as documentarian in each school. The role was essentially that of a participant observer in the school.

A documentarian training day was held. At this meeting the role and function of the documentarian were defined, some personal ownership for this new role was developed, and the documentarians were trained in skills needed for their role. Documentarians committed themselves to utilizing a standard report form for all regular faculty meetings and other school meetings they would normally attend. The report form was designed to gather information relevant to the content of topics discussed and observations of behavior employed by each group in its operation. Specific variables for which data were collected included decision-making processes, problem-solving processes, the nature of interpersonal interactions and the quality of communication exhibited. Unexpectedly, this became an additional training intervention. Documentarians found that repeated use of the form greatly increased their sensitivity to group processes.

WHAT SORT OF MULTI-DISTRICT DEVELOPMENT OCCURRED?

During the first year the teams spent most of their time developing change attempts in their own schools and growing as teams. Toward the end of the first year and during the second year, Consortium schools with similar interests, such as individualized instruction or reading, joined together across districts to share planning efforts and costs of outside specialists. One such school faculty was to soon take up residence in a new facility designed to allow much more flexibility than traditional buildings. The faculty was anxious and fragmented. The team helped their total faculty to begin stating their concerns openly and unifying their goals. This resulted in a total school decision to implement an individualized program. Another Consortium school had similar desires and through the resource provided by the Consortium these two schools held joint training workshops for their faculties. Costs were shared and many ideas were exchanged.

Other programs in the region have been supported by the presence of the Consortium-trained teachers. The director of a new preservice teacher training project, which depended on the cooperation of schools in various districts and nearby colleges, indicated that the first-year success of the project might have been doubtful without the skills present in Consortium teachers who were participants.

In one district a Consortium member teacher became involved with affective education. This teacher has, largely through her own initiative and with the help of the Planning Office, offered several three-day workshops in affective education to teachers in her district. The first workshop was held with fifty teachers volunteering to attend, on their own time. Because of the demand this was repeated a second time. Then came a third workshop, and there is still demand for a fourth. More than half the teachers in this city district will have participated voluntarily in this training. And it is having significant effects on the classrooms of many teachers. While this might have happened without the Consortium, it is likely that the Consortium training served to facilitate it.

Furthermore, the Consortium Council has become a vehicle for dissemination of new ideas and multi-district development. For example, it has asked that the affective education workshop be conducted for Consortium School teachers and administrators. This makes possible region-wide exploration of affective education as a new practice.

HAS THERE BEEN ANY DIRECT EFFECT ON CHILDREN IN THE CLASSROOM?

There are many teachers who have started adding new behaviors to their teaching styles. They have begun to use such techniques as brainstorming and consensus decision-making in their own classrooms. They have also started to use the training techniques in their classes to help children establish priorities and engage in responsible decision-making and resource-sharing. One such teacher of English has involved her classes in many activities focused on trust, openness and group leadership. This same teacher, when directing the school musical, began by employing team-building activities similar to those learned in the Consortium training. Two other teachers solicited the help of the planning center to design and implement a one-week workshop for their two most resistant and least motivated classes. Their objectives were to establish better rapport with the students and try something new, because the present methods were wasting everyone's time. Both the students and teachers involved were enthusiastic and perceived the effort as a success.

HAS THERE BEEN ANY EVALUATION OF THE PROJECT?

The results of the first years of the Consortium of Schools can be looked at in two ways. An extensive evaluation design was developed and implemented. This provides hard data which will form the basis of an ongoing evaluation of the effects of the Consortium effort. Data were collected from teachers and administrators involved actively in the Consortium, from teachers not actively involved and from students. A second area of evaluation is more subjective, but nevertheless reveals a great deal about the perceived success of the OD involvement.

Some information in the latter category, anecdotal data, has already been reported as it pertains to results of the training which occurred. Some additional comments are in order. Of the twelve schools which began the project, one dropped out at the end of the first year. However, the reasons for dropping out were more related to problems inherent in the system, distance from the Regional Planning office, and a change in regional boundaries than with disenchantment with the Consortium, per se. Two additional schools opted to join the Consortium at the end of the first year—at a time when districts were trimming budgets and cutting back on new programs.

Another piece of data is relevant. Plans for the week-long workshop for new teams were made. When the plan was presented to the teams, there was an across-the-board request that they be allowed to send new people from their schools to the week-long workshop for new teams. This was agreed to, and as a result some of the involved schools sent larger groups of teachers than had attended the original week-long workshops, and one school included students on its team. In most instances teachers attended on their own time and without receiving compensation from the school district.

The School as an Organization

On the hunch that changes in consortium school program efforts would be accompanied by changes in their organizational character, data were collected from each school concerning its organizational processes. The instrument used was the Profile of a School (Form T).[2] The Profile is designed to provide information about the relative participativeness of a

---

[2]Adopted by Fred C. Feitler and based on the work of Rensis Likert, *The Human Organization: Its Management and Value* (New York: McGraw-Hill, 1967).

school along such dimensions as leadership, teamwork, communications patterns and motivation processes. Of twelve schools involved in the first year of the Consortium, eleven moved in the direction desired and developed through OD training. The data were analyzed both for team members actively involved in the training and for non-team members. Where differences between team and non-team members occurred, this was the basis for survey feedback and discussion.

Schools have used these data to plan for the coming year and have voluntarily requested that the Profile be given again. The use of data by the schools to further their own planning and development is unusual and gives further indication of the degree of commitment of these schools to develop the kind of organization that is both productive for students and satisfying for teachers.

In many respects the results of the Consortium program are peculiar to an individual school. In some instances, teachers are working together to solve and deal with numerous kinds of problems that would not have been attempted in the past. Teachers work together with their principals in a more open and trusting manner. Some schools have used the training as a means to implement new programs, such as individualized instruction. Still others are exploring alternative programs, such as open education.

WHAT ARE THE IMPLICATIONS FOR OTHER SCHOOLS?

The total effects of this effort will not be felt for several years in this region, but there are some things we can say:

1. The organizational development technology and methods developed in this project are transferable to most school settings, for several reasons. The schools presently involved and working together represent urban, suburban, and rural elementary and secondary schools. They also vary widely in size. Furthermore, these are schools not known for being open and progressive.

2. The type of training employed in this OD attempt has been successfully employed with many different populations of educators (administrators, college professors, teachers, etc.) in all parts of the country. This means that the training components of this project are readily transferable to other regions and school systems. This suggests that total efforts such as the one described here would be successful in other school systems and regions.

3. When school personnel were provided with interpersonal group leadership and planning skills through training in workshops and "at-the-elbow" help, they were able to manage change productively and take steps to build self-renewing school organizations as well as a self-renewing support system, the Consortium. They were also able to build bridges across school systems, suggesting the feasibility of regional educational planning.

4. It is possible for several schools to share the services and costs of outside

OD consultants, and to do so in a way that enhances their resources much beyond the efforts and abilities of those consultants.

5. It is being demonstrated that change can be productively managed and implemented in schools in spite of the tremendous pressures from without and within.

26. Durability of Organizational Change[1]

STANLEY E. SEASHORE and DAVID G. BOWERS

The aim of this article is to add a modest footnote to the growing literature concerning planned change in the structure and function of formal organizations. The question asked is whether changes that have been planned, successfully introduced, and confirmed by measurements, over but a relatively short span of time, can survive as permanent features of the organization. Will such a changed organization become stabilized in its new state, or will it continue the direction and pace of change, or perhaps revert to its earlier state?

This report will include a brief review of an earlier effort to change an organization, a presentation of some new data about the present state of the organization, and some first speculations about the meaning of the data for the understanding of psychological and social phenomena in formal organizations.

BACKGROUND

The earlier events against which our new data are to be set are reported rather fully elsewhere (Marrow, Bowers, & Seashore, 1967). A brief review of the essential facts will set the stage.

In late 1961 the Harwood company purchased its major competitor, the Weldon company. This brought under common ownership and general management two organizations remarkably similar in certain features and remarkably different in others. Both made and marketed similar products using equipment and manufacturing processes of a like kind; were of similar

Reprinted from *The American Psychologist*, Vol. 25, No. 3, May 1970, pp. 227–233. Copyright 1970 by the American Psychological Association. Reprinted by permission.

[1] Presidential Address by Stanley E. Seashore presented to the Division of Industrial Psychology (Division 14) at the annual meeting of the American Psychological Association, Washington, D.C., September 1969.

size in terms of business volume and number of employees; served similar and partially overlapping markets; were family-owned and owner-managed firms; and had similar histories of growth and enjoyed high reputation in the trade.

The differences between the two organizations are of particular interest. The Harwood company had earned some prominence and respect for their efforts over many years to operate the organization as a participative system with high value given to individual and organizational development, as well as to effective performance. The Weldon company had for years been managed in a fashion that prevails in the garment industry, with a highly centralized, authoritarian philosophy and with secondary concern for individual development and organizational maintenance. The two organizations were, in 1962, rather extreme examples from the continuum vaguely defined by the terms authoritarian versus participative. Measurements in both firms in 1962 confirmed that the difference was not merely impressionistic, but was represented in quantitative assessments of the organizational processes for planning, coordination, communication, motivation, and work performance, and was represented as well in member attitudes. The two firms were also sharply contrasting in their performance in 1962, even though over a longer span of years their business accomplishments had been similar. In 1962 Weldon, in sharp contrast to Harwood, was losing money, experiencing high costs, generating many errors of strategy and work performance, suffering from member disaffection with consequent high absenteeism and high turnover. Weldon, despite its technical, fiscal, and market strengths, was near the point of disaster.

The new owners set out on a program to rebuild the Weldon enterprise according to the model of the Harwood company. The ultimate aim was to make the Weldon firm a viable and profitable economic unit within a short period of time. A rather strenuous and costly program was envisioned, including some modernization of the plant, improved layout and flow of work, improvements in records and production control methods, and product simplification, as well as changes in the human organization. The renewal program concerning the organization itself concerns us here.

The approach to organizational change can be characterized briefly in three respects: (*a*) the conception of the organizational characteristics to be sought; (*b*) the conception of processes for changing persons and organizational systems; and (*c*) the linking of the social system to the work system.

The guiding assumptions or "philosophy" on which the change program was based included elements such as the following:

1. It was assumed that employees would have to gain a realistic sense of security in their jobs and that this security would have to arise basically out of

their own successful efforts to improve their organization and their performance, not out of some bargained assurances.

2. The introduction of substantial change in the work environment requires that employees have confidence in the technical competence and humane values of the managers and supervisors; this confidence can be earned only if it is reciprocated by placing confidence in the employees.

3. In a situation of rapid change it is particularly necessary to use procedures of participation in the planning and control of the work and of the changes; such procedures are needed at all levels of the organization.

4. The rebuilding of an organization may require an input of technical resources and capital on a substantial scale—not unlike the investments required to rework a technology or control system of a factory.

5. Management involves skills and attitudes that can be defined, taught, and learned, and these skills and attitudes need not be confined to high rank staff; each member of the organization, at least in some limited degree, must learn to help manage his own work and that of others related to him.

6. Guidelines such as these are not readily understood and accepted unless they can be linked to concrete events and to the rational requirements of the work to be done and the problems to be solved.

The conception of change processes incorporated in the rebuilding of the Weldon organization emphasized the application of multiple and compatible change forces. The physical improvements in work resources and conditions were to be accompanied by informational clarity, enhanced motivation through rewards, and ample skill training and practice. That is, change was to be introduced simultaneously at the situational, cognitive, motivational, and behavioral levels so that each would support the others.

The linking of the social organization to the work system was to be accomplished through efforts, however limited, to design work places, work flows, information flows, and the like in a manner not merely compatible with but integral with the associated social organization and organizational processes.

The program of rebuilding the organization was carried out by the local management with substantial assistance and stimulation from the new owners and from a variety of consultants, including psychologists. The general planning and guidance of the program were influenced primarily by Alfred Marrow, Board Chairman of the Harwood Corporation and Fellow of Division 14. The role of the Institute for Social Research was not that of change agent, but rather that of observing, recording, measuring, and analyzing the course of events and the change that resulted.

The change program was successful in important respects. Within two years there occurred improvements in employee satisfactions, motivations, and work performance. The organization took on characteristics of an adaptive, self-controlling, participative system. The firm as a business unit moved from a position of loss to one of profit. At the end of 1964, after two years of change effort, the factory was abandoned as a research site, the rate of input of capital and external manpower into the change program diminished substantially, and the factory and its organization were expected to settle down to something like a "normal" state.

EXPECTATIONS ABOUT CHANGE

From the start of this organizational change program there was a concern about the long-run consequences of the program, and there was uncertainty about the permanence of change. The following quotations from our earlier report illustrate the intentions, hopes, and doubts (Marrow et al., 1967):

the whole organization, from the plant manager down to the production workers, were taken into an exercise in joint problem-solving through participative methods in groups, with a view toward making such procedures a normal part of the management system of the plant [p. 69].

The refreezing of Weldon in a new and more effective state is not regarded as a permanent thing, but as another stage in the evolution and continuous adaptation of the organization. Some features of the conversion plan explicitly include the provision of built-in capacities for easier change in the future [p. 232].

Will the changes at Weldon last? The only evidence we have at the present time is that the change from a predominantly "authoritative" to a dominantly "consultative" type of management organization persisted for at least two years in the view of the managers and supervisors involved. Surely there exist forces toward a reversion to the old Weldon form of organizational life; it remains an uncertainty whether they will or will not win out over the new forces toward consolidation of change and further change of the intended kinds [p. 244].

In mid-1969, four and one-half years after the termination of the intensive change program, Dr. Bowers and I invited ourselves back to the Weldon plant for a follow-up measurement of the state of the organization. This remeasurement consisted of a one-day visit to the plant by a research assistant who administered questionnaires to managers, supervisors, and a sample

TABLE 5.6
CHANGES IN JOB ATTITUDES

Item	1962 Percent	1964 Percent	1969 Percent
Company better than most	22	28	36
Own work satisfying	77	84	91
Satisfied with pay system	22	27	28
Company tries to maintain earnings	26	44	41
Satisfied with supervisor	64	54	54
Like fellow employees	85	86	85
Group cohesiveness	25	25	30
Plan to stay indefinitely	72	87	66
Expect future improvement in situation	23	31	43

of the employees.[2] In addition, certain information was abstracted from the firm's records, and the views of the plant manager were solicited as to changes that had taken place and possible reasons for change. We can turn directly to a few tables and figures representing the changes and the situation as of 1969.

RESULTS

First, we present some data from the production employees. Table 5.6 shows selected items from our questionnaire survey bearing on the issue of whether there has occurred a decline, a rise, or a stabilization of the attitudes, satisfactions, and optimism of the employees. The table shows the percentage of employees giving the two most favorable responses, of five offered, to each question. The columns represent the results in 1962 before the change program began, in 1964 at the conclusion of the formal change effort, and in 1969.

The general picture is one of the maintenance of earlier gains in the favorability of employee attitudes or the further improvement in attitudes. This observation holds for seven of the nine indicators. The remaining two deserve brief special comment.

Satisfaction with supervisors declined during the period of the active change program but has remained relatively high and constant since 1964. The initial decline is viewed as a consequence of the substantial change in the supervisors' role during the active change program. During that period, the supervisors acquired substantially more responsibility and authority as well as some new activities and duties that are thought to have removed the supervisors from a peerlike to a superior status relationship with the operators, which they retain now. This interpretation is, of course, speculative but made before the 1969 data were in hand.

The decline in the proportion of employees planning to stay on indefinitely is rather difficult to assess. The rise between 1962 and 1964 can be attributed to the improvement in pay and working conditions in that period. The subsequent decline is to be accounted for, partly, by the fact of recent production expansion and the presence on the payroll of a relatively larger number of turnover-prone short-service employees. One might also speculate that rising prosperity during the period might have increased the attractiveness of marriage, child bearing, or retirement for these female employees. In any case, the decline in the percentage committed to long job tenure appears to be at odds with the general rise in job satisfactions and in the marked rise in optimism about the future improvement in the Weldon situation. We should add that the decline in percentage committed to long tenure is confirmed by the fact of a moderate rise in actual turnover rates in recent months.

---

[2]The assistance of Edith Wessner is acknowledged.

TABLE 5.7
CHANGE IN TASK-ORIENTATION INDICATORS

Item	1962 Percent	1964 Percent	1969 Percent
Company quick to improve methods	18	24	31
Company good at planning	22	26	35
Not delayed by poor services	76	79	90
Produce what rates call for	44	67	53
Expect own productivity to improve	63	55	62
Peers approve of high producers	58	58	66
Closeness of task supervision	38	27	47
Desired closeness of supervision	57	52	64
Mean productivity (percent of standard)	87	114	?

Table 5.7 shows a few selected items bearing on the question whether the rise in satisfactions and expectations is accompanied by some loss in productivity concerns and task orientation. The data, again, are from employee questionnaire responses (except for the last line) and show changes from 1962 to 1964, and then to 1969.

Five of the indicators reflect a rise in level of task orientation and production concern since the end of the formal change program. The remaining items are not negative, but merely indeterminate. There is clearly a rise in recent years in the percentage of employees who say the firm is quick to improve work methods, good at planning, provides efficient services (maintenance, supplies, scheduling), who report that their peers approve of high producers, and who themselves desire frequent and ready access to supervisory help. Two sets of data require special comment.

The data on productivity, three lines in the table, should be considered as a set. The numbers show that the self-report of "Nearly always producing what the rates call for" rose substantially during the active change program, and this is confirmed by the actual productivity records of the firm as shown in the last line "Mean productivity against standard." During the same period, the percentage of employees expecting a further gain in their own productivity declined, as it should have considering that more employees were approaching the firm's hoped-for level of high productivity and earnings. By 1969 there was some decline in the percentage reporting high productivity and a corresponding rise in the percentage expecting a future rise in their productivity; this pair of related changes appears to reflect the presence on the staff of an increasing number of relatively new employees not yet up to the level of skill and performance they may reasonably expect to attain. There is a crucial item of missing data in the last line of the table; for technical reasons, we have not been able to calculate the current actual productivity rate in a form that allows confident comparisons with the earlier figures. Our best estimate is that productivity has been stable with a slight decline in recent months arising from the recent introduction of additional inexperienced employees.

Attention is also suggested to the pair of lines in Table 5.7 concerning closeness of supervision. At all three times of measurement, these production workers desired more close supervision than they actually experienced; these employees, unlike those in some other organizations, see their supervisors to be potentially helpful in improving productivity and increasing piece-rate earnings. The decline in experienced closeness of supervision during the period 1962–64 matches other evidence to be presented later that during this period there was a substantial change in the supervisors' role that diverted the supervisors from immediate floor supervision and left a temporary partial shortage of this service to production workers. The figures show that by 1969 this supervisory deficit had been recouped and more. This sustains our general view that during the years following the Weldon change program there has been not a decline in concern for task performance among employees and in the organizational system generally but rather a further gain in task orientation.

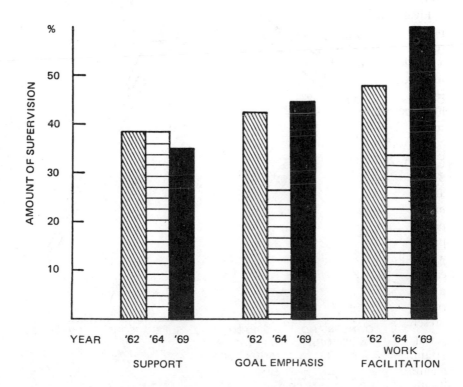

Figure 5.9. Change in Three Dimensions of Supervisory Leadership Behavior

The change in supervisory behavior mentioned earlier is shown in Figure 5.9. We attempted at the three points in time to measure the extent to which supervisors, in the view of employees, engaged in behaviors we categorize as "supportive," "goal emphasizing," and "work facilitating." (Two additional dimensions of leader behavior that we now use in describing organizations are not represented here because they were not yet identified in 1962; we chose to continue use of the initial measurement methods rather than to update them.)

Figure 5.9 shows that the amount of supervisory supportiveness experienced by employees remained constant during the 1962–64 period and has risen slightly since then. Goal emphasis and work facilitation both dropped during the active change program, for reasons mentioned earlier, and have since risen above their 1962 levels. These data sustain our belief that the Weldon organization since 1964 has increased its expression of concern for

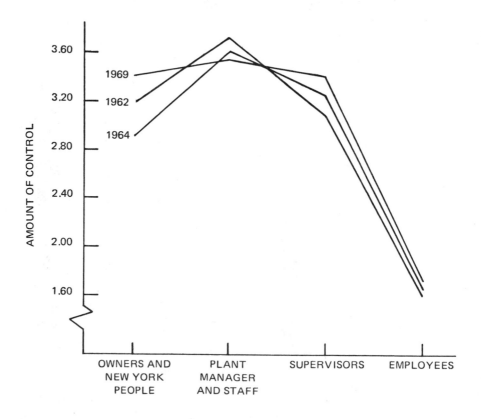

Figure 5.10. Change in Amount and Hierarchical Distribution of Control

production goals and its provision of conditions for effective work performance, and at no cost of declining concern for employee attitudes and satisfactions.

One more set of data from the employees is pertinent here, namely, their description of the amount and hierarchical distribution of control in the Weldon organization. One of the explicit aims of the change program was that of increasing the total amount of control and of altering the distribution of control so that lower rank people—supervisors and operators—would have some added degree of control. This was accomplished during the change program period to a very limited and nonsignificant degree. Subsequent changes have been in the direction intended and more substantial in degree. The data are shown in Figure 5.10. In 1969, compared with the earlier periods, there is more control being exercised in total, with a notable increment in the case of the headquarters staff, a further small decline for the local plant management, and increments for the supervisors and for the employees. There appears to have been a change of modest degree, more or less as hoped for, and there has clearly not been a reversion to the original condition of concentrated control in the hands of the plant manager.

We turn now to some indicators of the state of the Weldon organization from the views of the supervisors and managers. The data presented in Figure 5.11 are derived from Likert's assessment instrument "Profile of Organizational and Performance Characteristics" (Likert, 1961, 1967). Most readers will have some acquaintance with this instrument and the theory and research data that it expresses, but a brief characterization might be helpful. The instrument used is a 43-item graphic-scale rating form that allows the respondent to describe his own organization as it presently functions and as

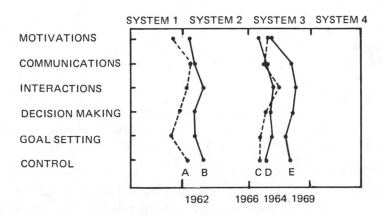

Figure 5.11. Change in Profile of Organizational Characteristics

he ideally would like it to function. The items are so chosen and arranged that the respondent may report a syndrome of organizational characteristics that locates the organization on a scale ranging from "authoritative" to "participative." Likert discerns four regions of this scale, named Systems 1, 2, 3, and 4, with word labels ranging from "Authoritarian" through "Benevolent Authoritarian" and "Consultative" to "Participative." The conception is analogous to McGregor's "Theory X" and "Theory Y" scale, and also to Blake's two-dimensioned matrix. To put it somewhat disrespectfully, the bad guys are thought to have and to prefer System 1 organizations while good guys aspire to and approach the System 4 state. The results for Weldon, 1962, 1964, and 1969 are presented in Figure 5.11.

At the left of the field are two graph lines showing the state of the Weldon organization in 1962, first as rated by the Institute for Social Research research team from interview protocols and observations, and next and somewhat more favorably as rated by the supervisors and managers on the scene. Weldon at that time was described to be autocratic—in some respects rather harshly autocratic and in some respects more benevolently autocratic. The state of the organization in 1964 and in 1966 is represented in the next two lines. These data are from supervisors and managers; they indicate a pattern of change that is substantial in magnitude and wholly compatible with the intentions embodied in the Weldon change program. There was no regression toward the earlier state during the 1964–66 period. The right-hand line represents the results of our 1969 assessment; it shows that in the view of the managers and supervisors at Weldon, the organization has progressed still further toward their ideal of a participative organizational system.

A final remark should be made about measured changes in Weldon before we turn to a consideration of the meaning of these data. Some readers will be interested in business outcomes as well as in the attitudes and behavior of the members of the organization. Briefly, Weldon moved from a position of substantial capital loss in 1962 to substantial return on investment in 1964; this direction of change in profitability has continued through 1968, the last year of record. Employee earnings which rose substantially between 1962 and 1964 have been sustained at a relatively high level. During the period since 1964 there have been substantial gains in efficiency and volume for the factory as a whole. New products and work methods have been introduced. By such business indicators, Weldon is a successful organization.

DURABLE CHANGE

The evidence we must weigh, although somewhat mixed and with a few contrary elements, appears to sustain the conclusion that the Weldon organization, far from reverting to its prior condition, has during recent years made additional progress toward the organizational goals envisioned by the owners and managers in 1962, and envisioned as well by supervisors and production employees at a somewhat later time. This outcome invites speculations about the psychological and social forces that are at work.

We confess a brief regret that there was not an opposite outcome, for we are rather better equipped with ideas about organizational stability and regression than we are with ideas about organizational change and continuing development. For example, before the data became available, we were prepared to make some remarks about the "Hawthorne effect"—about the superficiality and transient quality of organizational and behavioral changes induced under conditions of external attention and pressure; but it boggles the mind to think of a "Hawthorne effect" persisting for over eight years among people half of whom were not on the scene at the time of the original change. Similarly, we were prepared to make wise remarks about cultural forces, habits, and the natural predilection of managers for nonparticipative methods; these we thought would help explain a reversion to the prevailing conditions in organizations. We were prepared to assert that in the absence of contrary environmental forces, external influences, and purposive continuing change efforts of a vigorous kind, an organization would migrate back to some more primitive form of organizational life.

Clearly we need to appeal to other ideas than these. We are, all of us, ill prepared to do so. Two recent and fairly comprehensive reviews of organizational change strategies (Leavitt, 1965; Shepard, 1965) say nothing about the permanence or continuation of change processes except for a remark by Shepard that "change in the direction of collaboration-consensus patterns [participative patterns] . . . facilitates growth, change and adaptation to new environmental challenges and opportunities [p. 1141]."

A first explanatory idea rests on the possibility that the heavy investment of external talent, money, and effort that characterized the original change period at Weldon has been continued during the subsequent years. We are assured that this is not the case. There has indeed been some additional use of external consultants, but at a modest rate that is considered normal and permanent. There has indeed been further improvement and change in the work system and the production facilities, but at no more than a permanently sustainable rate. There has indeed been a continuation of certain organizational activities introduced as part of the original change program, but these are regarded as normal operating procedure and not as special change efforts. Economic conditions have been favorable to the firm, but they were also favorable at the distressed time preceding the change of ownership in 1962.

We believe that there are three other lines of explanation that do bear scrutiny. These thoughts about the Weldon experience are not offered with any sense of great insight or of conceptual innovation. They are offered only as suggestions for lines of inquiry and emphasis in future organizational research. The first concerns the provision of "lock-in" devices that make difficult the reversal of the original change.

It was mentioned earlier that the original change program contained some notions of seeking mutually reinforcing change actions across the psychological, organizational, and technological domains. A central idea was to make structural changes in the organization that matched the work system and that did not violate reasonable assumptions about the values and motives of individual members. For example, the revitalized piece-rate pay system was viewed to be viable only if sustained by the provision of assured services that allowed high earnings, a revision of the record and information flow system that assured instant supervisory response to low earnings, and a moderating of the prior job assignment system so that a production employee could become skilled in the work assigned. The idea of systemic consistency is surely an elementary one, no more than common sense—a habit of thought for those who have learned to view the factory as a total system in which all elements are interdependent. The interdependence of elements tends to preserve, to enhance, and to "lock-in" the central characteristics of the system and thus to prevent retrogression.

A second factor in Weldon's continuation of intended change might lie in the earlier legitimation of concern about organizational processes. This is speculative, for we have no ready way to assess the extent to which there was implanted the habit of deliberate and self-conscious examination of the potential side effects of the many policy and operating decisions, usually technical or economic in origin, that arise daily. One of the fragmenting features of many organizations is the tendency to isolate problems, to treat them as if they could be optimally resolved without reference to their broader context. An organization habituated at all levels to think about, discuss openly, and to weigh properly the full range of elements in the organizational system might well have unusual capacities for self-maintenance and self-development.

A third possible explanation of the maintenance of the changes at Weldon and their further development under conditions of limited continuing external influence might lie in the inherent merit of the participative organizational model. Could it be that people who have experienced a taste of it get hooked, know what they want, and lend their effort to maintaining it? A glance at the newspaper headlines on almost any day will suggest that some of our fellow citizens do not like what they are experiencing in formal organizations and have thoughts of having something better, by force if necessary.

REFERENCES

Leavitt, H. J. Applied organizational change in industry. In J. G. March (Ed.), *Handbook of organizations*. Chicago: Rand–McNally, 1965.

Likert, R. *New patterns of management.* New York: McGraw–Hill, 1961.

Likert, R. *The human organization.* New York: McGraw–Hill, 1967.

Marrow, A. J., Bowers, D. G., & Seashore, S. E. *Management by participation.* New York: Harper & Row, 1967.

Shepard, H. A. Changing interpersonal and intergroup relationships in organizations. In J. G. March (Ed.), *Handbook of organizations.* Chicago: Rand–McNally, 1965.

27. Integrating Disrupted Work Relationships: An Action Design for a Critical Intervention

ROBERT T. GOLEMBIEWSKI, STOKES B. CARRIGAN, WALTER R. MEAD, ROBERT MUNZENRIDER, and ARTHUR BLUMBERG

This study has two central themes, both of which are relevant to applications of the behavioral sciences in "real-life situations." First, considerable psychological trauma can be generated by events such as the demotions reported on here. Second, substantial evidence suggests that a learning design based on the laboratory approach can significantly moderate such trauma. Methodological problems inhibit assigning all observed effects to the learning design. But the presumptive evidence is strong that this action design is one way to apply in organizations the massive forces often observed in sensitivity training groups, one way to apply *in vivo* the values that commonly guide the development of the miniature societies that are T-Groups.

This study details one example of a broad family of critical interventions at work. The focus is on the demotion of 13 field sales managers, many of whom were senior employees. The basic intent of the intervention was to help ease the inevitable stresses on the demotees. These stresses inhered in diverse

Initially prepared for the NTL Conference on New Technology in Organization Development, New York, October 8–9, 1971. Sponsored by NTL Institute of Applied Behavioral Science and OD Network.

Reproduced by special permission from *The Journal of Applied Behavioral Science,* Vol. 8, No. 2, "Toward Building New Work Relationships: An Active Design for Critical Intervention," Robert T. Golembiewski, Stokes B. Carrigan, Walter R. Mead, Robert Munzenrider, & Arthur Blumberg, pp. 135–148, 1972, NTL Institute of Applied Behavioral Science.

Equation A:

Imaginings triggered by demotion	Relative +aloneness	Relative + helplessness	Initial = increases in	anxiety depression hostility

Equation B:

Imaginings triggered by demotion	+ Community	+ Mastery	Effective = coping, or reductions in initial	anxiety depression hostility

personal adaptations required of demotees as they changed jobs, schedules, and routines, and as they modified levels of aspiration of perhaps self-concepts. Stresses also inhered in the need to develop viable work relations between the demotee and his new manager, who formerly had been a peer.

The intervention had both personal and organizational aspects. For the demoted men themselves, the intent was to ease what was probably a major and even painful emotional experience for all of the men, and one that was economically costly for most demotees. For the organization, the intent was to preserve its valued human resources. Although they were demoted, that is to say, the men's past efforts and their anticipated future contribution were perceived as significant enough to warrant risking a difficult transition.

The intent of the intervention also can be suggested by two crude equations.[1] Equation A sketches the grim consequences to be avoided. It proposes that the imaginings or speculations induced by the demotions, given the aloneness of the field situation and the helplessness to do anything but resign, would generate immediate increases in anxiety, depression, and hostility. Such effects probably would not serve the individual nor would they help in making necessary adjustments at work. In contrast, Equation B proposes to confront the imaginings induced by the demotions with the sharing of resources in a community setting that hopefully will increase a demotee's sense of mastery over the consequences of his demotion.

LABORATORY APPROACH AS *GENUS*

The action design for this critical intervention is based on the laboratory approach.[2] Perhaps the term "action design" is dramatic, but we wish to distinguish the design from sensitivity training in several major senses. To illustrate these differences only, the design in this case deals with a "very real" problem; the target-concerns are rooted firmly in specific organiza-

---

[1] Richard M. Jones, *Fantasy and Feeling in Education* (New York: New York University Press, 1968), p. 77.

[2] Robert T. Golembiewski and Arthur Blumberg (Eds.), *Sensitivity Training and the Laboratory Approach* (Itasca, Ill.: F. E. Peacock Publishers, Inc., 1970).

tional relationships, although the focus may extend beyond the worksite; and the thrust is toward a working resolution of major concerns that have long-run implications rather than toward dealing with reactions and feelings in a temporary group. Although they differ in important particulars, however, this action design and sensitivity training are viewed as *species* within the *genus* laboratory approach. The "laboratory approach" is, in brief,

an educational strategy which is based primarily on the experiences generated in various social encounters *by the learners themselves,* and which aims to influence attitudes and develop competencies toward learning about human interactions. Essentially, therefore, laboratory training attempts to induce changes with regard to the learning process itself and to communicate a particular method of learning and inquiry. It has to do "with learning how to learn."[3]

THE DEMOTED POPULATION

As part of a broader reduction-in-force, 13 regional managers from the marketing department of a major firm were given two choices, of accepting demotion to senior salesmen, or terminating. The demotees were a heterogeneous lot. Table 5.8 presents some descriptive data about the men and

TABLE 5.8
SELECTED DATA ABOUT DEMOTEES

Demotee	Age	Years with Company	Years as Regional Sales Mgr.	Decision to Accept Demotion
1.................	36	12	1	No
2.................	35	10	5	No
3.................	40	7	6 mos.	Yes
4.................	39	9	7 mos.	Yes
5.................	51	23	16	Yes
6.................	33	5	10 mos.	Yes
7.................	43	12	5	Yes
8.................	44	17	7	Yes
9.................	43	12	5	Yes
10.................	35	11	8 mos.	Yes
11.................	55	24	17	Yes
12.................	35	10	2 yrs. 6 mos.	Yes
13.................	50	13	10	Yes

their eventual choices. Relatedly, although most of the demotees would suffer a major reduction in salary, reductions would range from less than $1,000 to approximately four times that amount for the demotees with most seniority.

---

[3]Edgar H. Schein and Warren G. Bennis, *Personal and Organizational Change through Group Methods* (New York: John Wiley & Sons, Inc., 1965), p. 4.

TABLE 5.9
THE TIMING OF THE ACTION DESIGN

Day 1	Day 2	Day 6	Day 7	Day 45
13 managers informed of choices:	Decision required	Three major activites:	Two major activities	Demotees and superiors respond to MAACL:
—demotion to salesman —termination	—11 managers accept demotion	—demotees and superiors respond to MAACL: pre-test	—demotees meet individually with their new superiors	test of persistence of changes
If demotion accepted, an early work assignment would involve reporting to a midwestern city for an "integrative experience" along with their new superiors		—demotees spend balance of day in discussion —superiors have briefing meeting	—demotees and superiors respond to MAACL: post-test	

Several forces-in-tension influenced the decisions of the 13 men. In favor of choosing termination were such factors as the generous separation allowances available to those with seniority affected by reductions-in-force. To suggest the countervailing forces, the job market was tight, the company was considered a good employer, and market conditions required cutting as deeply as the 13 managers, all of whom were satisfactory performers.

All but two of the managers accepted the demotion and, as Table 5.9 shows, were given an early work assignment intended to facilitate their making the required adaptations as effectively and quickly as possible. The demotees knew that the "integrative experience" had been discussed with, and approved by, several managerial levels in the marketing department. In addition, almost all of the demotees and all of their superiors had long-standing relations of trust with four of the authors of this paper, who variously participated in the development and implementation of this action design.

BROAD PURPOSES

Five broad goals of the critical intervention may be distinguished. First, the action design was intended to build on the values of the laboratory approach. The company had invested in a major way in a program of Organization Development, in which an offsite sensitivity training experience was a major early learning vehicle.[4] Eighteen of the 22 participants—the 11 demotees and their immediate supervisors—had such an learning experience earlier. The other four men had their sensitivity training postponed only by the major reduction-in-force at issue here. Moreover, 19 of the men had been involved in various "team development" activities that attempted to extend the initial offsite training directly into organization activities.

The thrust of the initial sensitivity training experience is to help organization members in two ways: to build a specific set of norms or values into their workaday relations; and to aid in the development of attitudes and behavioral skills appropriate to those norms. Table 5.10 sketches three sets of such norms, or values, and suggests some of the appropriate behaviors. The norms are meant in the sense of ideals-to-be-strived-for, as individuals become increasingly convinced that it is safe to do so, and as they learn by experience whether they can meet their own needs by following the norms.

The challenge posed by the demotions was simply to apply the norms of the laboratory approach in a specific case that was personally and organizationally meaningful. Significantly, the specific case is a complex matter. Demotions involve difficult and subtle adjustments, in emotions, in work routines, and in relations. In the case of most of the present demotees, as was

---

[4]For the basic design, see Robert T. Golembiewski and Arthur Blumberg, "Sensitivity Training in Cousin Groups: A Confrontation Design," *Training and Development Journal,* Vol. 23 (August, 1969), pp. 18–23.

TABLE 5.10
FOUR VALUE-LOADED DIMENSIONS RELEVANT IN LABORATORY
APPROACH TO ORGANIZATION CHANGE AND DEVELOPMENT

A *Meta-Values** *of Lab Approach*	B *Proximate Goals* *of Lab Approach*	C *Organization Values Con-* *sistent with Lab Approach*†
1. An attitude of inquiry reflecting (among others): *a)* a hypothetical spirit; and *b)* experimentalism	1. Increased insight, self-knowledge	1. Full and free communication
2. Expanded consciousness and sense of choice	2. Sharpened diagnostic skills at (ideally) all levels, that is, on the levels of the *a)* individual; *b)* group; *c)* organization; and *d)* society	2. Reliance on open consensus in managing conflict, as opposed to using coercion or compromise
3. The value system of democracy, having as two core elements: *a)* a spirit of collaboration; and *b)* open resolution of conflict via a problem-solving orientation	3. Awareness of, and skill-practice in creating, conditions of effective functioning at (ideally) all levels	3. Influence based on competence rather than on personal whim or formal power
4. An emphasis on mutual helping relationships as the best way to express man's interdependency with man	4. Testing self-concepts and skills in interpersonal situations	4. Expression of emotional as well as task-oriented behavior
	5. Increased capacity to be open, to accept feelings of self and others, to risk interpersonally in rewarding ways	5. Acceptance of conflict between the individual and his organization, to be coped with willingly, openly, and rationally

*Adapted from Edgar H. Schein and Warren G. Bennis, *Personal and Organizational Change through Group Methods* (New York: Wiley, 1965), pp. 30–35; and Leland P. Bradford, Jack R. Gibb, and Kenneth D. Benne (Eds.), *T-Group Theory and Laboratory Method* (New York: Wiley, 1964), pp. 10, 12.

†Philip E. Slater and Warren G. Bennis, "Democracy Is Inevitable," *Harvard Business Review,* Vol. 42 (1964), pp. 51–55.

noted, major salary cuts also could require economic adjustments for many of the men.

Second, the purpose was to begin developing integrative linkages at the earliest possible time after the demotion announcements. The focus of the derivative two-day design was on common personal or interpersonal data. On the first day, these data included the reactions of the demotee, his concerns about attending regional sales meetings as a peer rather than as the superior of the salesmen, etc. On the second day, the focus was on supervisory relations between the 11 pairs of men who had been peers, the demoted one of whom would sometimes have substantially more seniority than his new superior.

Third, the intent was to provide a specific action arena in which feelings could be expressed *and* worked through, if possible. The working symbolism was the cauterization of a wound, not pleasant but preferable to the possible or probable alternatives. The anti-goals were obsessiveness, and the postponement of a required facing-up to new work demands that would probably loom larger with the passage of time.

Fourth, the goal was to provide diverse support to the demotees at a critical time. This support was to come from demoted peers, superiors, and the employing organization. The common theme was: "We want this to work for you as much as possible, and not against you." At the most elemental level, most managers perceived that the expense of the integrative experience itself was a signal measure of "the organization's" concern and support.

The vicious cycle to be avoided can be sketched. Depression was an expected result of the demotions, for example, especially for the more senior men. Unless carefully managed, depression can work against the man. The consequences of believing "the organization is against me" can be both subtle and profound, especially for the field salesman. Incoming cues and messages might be misinterpreted, and outgoing projections of self might trigger unintended consequences. More broadly, Kiev traces an unattractive catalog of the "manifestations of depressions," which include "diminished incentive, interest, morale, and ability to concentrate, feelings of alienation, inability to assume responsibility or to follow a routine, diminished ability of self-expression, self-assertiveness and decreased pride, irritation with interference, feelings of being unappreciated or worthlessness. . . . [The] psychophysiological concomitants of early depression . . . include insomnia, loss of appetite, excessive worrying, indigestion, and decline in energy."[5]

CHARACTERISTICS OF THE ACTION DESIGN

A simple learning design was developed to meet these multiple goals. The constant target was adaptation to the new status, which implied the development of new work relations. In terms of time, roughly 50 percent was spent with the demotees working together, and 50 percent with the demotees individually attempting to work through issues of concern with their new supervisors.

The first design component brought the demotees together for discussion of their concerns, problems, and needs. Approximately four hours were devoted to this exploration, with two resource persons available. The formal afternoon session was kept deliberately short, although it provided the model for several informal sessions in the evening. The announced design intent was

[5]Ari Kiev, "Crisis Intervention in Industry," p. 2. Paper delivered at Annual Meeting, New York State Society of Industrial Medicine, Occupational Psychiatry Group, December 10, 1969.

to help prepare the demotees for the next day's sessions with their individual managers concerning work relations. This action-thrust sought to harness emotional energies to organization purposes rather than to diffuse them through ventilation.

The role of the resource persons in this initial phase to harness emotional energies rather than to diffuse them was a mixed one. In capsule, the resource persons sought to direct attention to "content" as well as to "process," whereas the trainer's role in sensitivity training emphasizes "process." The distinction is not an easy one to make briefly, but the notions refer to an emphasis on *what is done* and on the *way things are done,* respectively.[6]

Specifically, the first design component began with personal reactions to the demotions and then trended toward an emphasis on the problems that demotees perceived as relevant in developing the required new work relations. In the later phases, the reactions of the men to the problems expected in their new roles were stressed, as were their concerns about facing these problems. Whenever possible, alternative ways of coping with problems were explored. The following list provides some flavor of the main themes dealt with, beginning with personal reactions and trending toward issues that were more work-related:

1. Comparing experiences, especially about the diverse ways in which various relevant organization policies were applied to their individual cases;
2. Encouraging expression of anxiety or hostility about the demotions themselves or about the associated processes or their style, timing, etc.;
3. Surfacing and testing suspicion of management, as in the concern that another personnel purge was imminent;
4. Isolating and, as possible, working through demotees' concerns about authority/dependence, as in the complaint that the demotees did not see themselves being treated as adults, or that they were men enough to take the demotions without the integrative experience;
5. Dealing with a variety of topics—e.g., explaining the demotions to clients or other salesmen—so as to develop norms that would reduce the probability of either avoiding the topics or awkwardly handling them in the field; and
6. Identifying relevant others with whom interaction had been stressful, or with whom it might prove to be so, the emphasis being on strategies for handling such interaction.

Surely success varied from case to case, but the intention of the resource persons was constant. That intention, in sum, was to: facilitate expression of

---

[6]Edgar H. Schein, *Process Consultation* (Reading, Mass.: Addison–Wesley Publishing Co., Inc., 1969), p. 13-75.

feelings and reactions; to help reveal the diversity of the demotees' experiences and coping strategies; and to work toward a successful adaptation to the demands of the new job. More specifically the model for interventions was an insight-action model, with the emphasis clearly on the action. To illustrate, assume that individual A was sending signals of fear and anger concerning some technical aspect of his new job. The resource persons sought to intervene at a process level as in a T-Group, with the goals of making A aware of those signals and of putting him in touch with the inducing emotions, if possible. The seven old T-Group hands among the demotees were very active in this regard, also. The capstone intervention here tended to be associated with the readiness of individual A to raise the concern and the associated feelings with his new manager, with whom he would meet the next day. The action-thrust is patent. Moreover, the technical content at issue also would be explored. Sometimes the resolution was easy, as in clarifying a misunderstanding or a misinterpretation. When the resolution was difficult, interventions by the resource persons tended to be questions with an action-thrust. What does individual A prefer? What are the other alternative strategies? What role can or should his new manager play in the matter, especially in the meeting between the two that was scheduled for the next day?

More broadly, resource persons were not advocates of management actions; nor were they neuters without emotional response to the sometimes tragicomic dynamics of the demotions. But they were committed to helping the demotees face their demotions as clearly and realistically as possible. Hence the resource persons considered it an open option that some demotees might decide to accept the termination after the integrative experience. None of the men did so.

It is not possible to convey the diversity of the products of this first design component, but two themes provide a useful substantive summary. First, almost all demotees emphasized the positive meaning of the integrative experience, whatever its specific outcomes. The design implied to them their value to the organization, and also reflected a continuing effort to provide resources which would help them do the job. From this perspective, the design had substantial value as a sign that efforts to act on the norms sketched in Table 5.10 would be made even under conditions of substantial stress, which no doubt provide the best test of managerial intentions. This positive evaluation was variously shared by all the supervisors. One of the demotees took a different approach. He resented the integrative experience as "hand-holding" and "coddling."

Second, the first component of the learning design emphasized some common elements among the demotees, as well as some differentiating factors. The training staff saw both the commonality and differentiation as being reality-based, and their conscious strategy was to avoid at all costs a strained display of ardent but feigned homogeneity or good fellowship among the demotees.

The elements of commonality that emerged in discussion among the demotees were expected ones. They include: the impact of the demotion on the self; experiences with important referents such as wives, colleagues, or salesmen from other firms; and concerns about taking on the salesman's job, about "picking up the bag again" to cover a sales territory, about participating in sales meetings, and so on.

The differentiating elements were harder for the men to openly identify, but they were no less clearly reality-based. For example, the demotees included both long-service employees, as well as recent managerial appointees. Reasonably, on balance, the younger men could be expected to feel more optimism about being re-promoted. The future for the longer service men was far less bright, realistically, and they generally if sometimes grudgingly acknowledged the point. Relatedly, some men professed shock at being confronted with the choice of demotion or termination. Others maintained they more or less expected some action, because of falling demand in the industry, or performance problems, or both. A few even expressed pleasure that the action was not so severe for them as it had been for many others affected by the major reduction-in-force.

The second component of the integrative experience took two approaches to extending demotee concerns into action, via the development of new working relations between the managers and their new subordinates. First, the managers met for some two hours to discuss the design for the next day and their role in it. The meeting's initial tone was a kind of gallows humor, which the training staff interpreted as understandable anxiety among the managers about their role. This initial tone quickly dissipated into the theme of making the transitions as easy as possible for all concerned. The basic thrust was to empathize with how the demotees were feeling, and to channel those feelings toward making the most successful adaptation possible.

Second, the demotees spent approximately three hours with their managers in one-to-one situations. The resource persons sat in on some of the dyads, as time permitted, and especially the dyads with senior demotees. The major concern involving these dyads were:

1. The building of early supervisory relations, as in mutual pledges to work harmoniously together, which was easy enough in some cases because some of the demotees were able to choose their new managers;
2. Technical problems such as going over sales territories, etc.;
3. Developing strategies by which the manager and man could be mutually helpful, as in discussing ways to moderate the formation of cliques that the demotions could encourage; and

4. Isolating likely problems and cementing a contract to agree to meet any such problems mutually and early.

Some dyads concentrated on one of these concerns, while others gave attention to several themes.

MEASURING INSTRUMENT

The effects of the action design for helping integrate disrupted work relationships were judged by changes in the Multiple Affect Adjective Check List (MAACL) developed by Zuckerman and Lubin. MAACL is a brief instrument for tapping the psychological aspects of emotion, which conceives of affect not as a trait but as a state. That is, a time referrent is specified for the respondent, who reacts as he feels "today" or "now" as opposed to how he feels "generally" or "occasionally." The researchers explain that MAACL[7]

was designed to fill the need for a self-administered test which would provide valid measures of three of the clinically relevant negative affects: anxiety, depression, and hostility. No attempt was made to measure positive affects but some of the evidence indicates that the scales are bipolar, and that low scores on the full scales will indicate states of positive affect.

Its authors place MAACL "in a research phase and . . . not yet recommended for routine applied use," but accumulating evidence suggests its value.[8] In an initial study, the validity of the test was suggested by changes in the Anxiety scale administered just prior to an examination showed significant increases from an established base, as expected. Similar changes in the Depression and Hostility scales were induced by administering a classroom examination a week earlier than announced. An extensive bibliography provides detailed reinforcement of the illustrations of validity.[9]

The expectations in this case were direct. The demotees were expected to have high initial scores on Anxiety, Depression, and Hostility, which a successful intervention would reduce significantly in a post-treatment administration of MAACL. Lower initial scores were expected for the managers, and the post-treatment administration was not expected to reveal any major shifts in scores, except perhaps on Anxiety. This expectation is based on the assumption that the managers, who had to develop new relations with their former peers, might be somewhat anxious initially about their role in the

---

[7]Marvin Zuckerman and Bernard Lubin, *Manual for the Multiple Affect Adjective Check List* (San Diego, Calif.: Educational and Industrial Testing Service, 1965), p. 3.

[8]*Ibid.*, pp. 6–16.

[9]Marvin Zuckerman and Bernard Lubin, *Bibliography for the Multiple Affect Adjective Check List* (San Diego, Calif.: Educational and Industrial Testing Service, 1970), 8 pp.

TABLE 5.11
OVERALL EFFECTS OF INTERVENTION ON THREE
MAACL ADMINISTRATIONS

	Mean Scale Scores, by Administrations			t = Test Values for Paired Administrations		
	1	2	3	1 v. 2	1 v. 3	2 v. 3
Demotees						
Anxiety.............	9.8	7.5	6.5	2.59*	2.74*	2.14†
Depression.........	17.8	14.8	13.6	2.88‡	2.65*	1.09
Hostility...........	9.5	7.2	7.2	2.90‡	1.98*	0.15
Managers						
Anxiety.............	6.3	5.3	4.6	1.24†	1.83†	0.83
Depression.........	9.8	9.5	9.5	0.23	0.38	0
Hostility...........	5.1	5.3	5.7	− .30	− .87	− .62

* Indicates .025 level of statistical significance.
† Indicates .05 level of statistical significance.
‡ Indicates .01 level of statistical significance.

learning design. This anxiety was expected to fall as the design unfolded and especially as it proved useful.

A third follow-up administration of MAACL was administered by mail approximately a month after the planned intervention. The purpose was to develop data about the persistence of any before/after changes. A potent training intervention was expected to preserve over time any reductions in anxiety, depression, and hostility induced by the demotions, in the face of the relative isolation and threat of the field situation.

Respondents were given code numbers that permitted comparing the before/after responses of specific individuals.[10] One of the 22 subjects did not respond to the third administration. Hence the N in the several statistical tests reported on below varies.

SOME MAJOR RESULTS

Five themes emerging from the results deserve spotlighting. First, as expected, the demotees initially generated high scores on all three MAACL scales. That the demotions were traumatic can be demonstrated in several ways. For example, the demotees initially scored higher than the managers on all three MAACL scales, the differences being statistically significant far beyond the .005 level. To a similar point, Lubin and Zuckerman tell us that a transformed "score of 70 is generally accepted as the point beyond which scores on a psychometric instrument are considered to be unusually high, as that point represents a score higher than that achieved by 98 per cent of the

---

[10]Note that on the third administration, researchers made an assignment decision in one questionable case. Statistically, it turns out, the assignment affects the results in trifling ways only.

standardization sample."[11] Only 2 of the 33 transformed scores for demotees on the three scales reach that level on the initial administration, but an additional 8 men have transformed scores of 60 or above on the pre-test. In sum, the demotees reacted strongly to the demotion, but their scores were not "unusually high."

Second, the data meet all expectations concerning changes attributable to the training intervention. Specifically, as Table 5.11 shows, demotees reported statistically-significant decreases on all three scales on the second administration of the MAACL, and these sharp and sudden reductions were at least maintained through the third administration. As Table 5.11 also shows, indeed, a comparison of the Anxiety scores on administrations 2 versus 3 shows a statistically significant reduction following the earlier and major reductions.

The major and sudden reductions in MAACL scores between the first two administrations imply the potency of the brief training intervention. The conclusion is reinforced by the lack of evidence that respondents became adapted to the MAACL items in responding to successive administration. What is not known is how long this initially-high level would have been maintained in the absence of the training intervention.

Third, the scores of the managers showed a significant change only for Anxiety. That reduction is most easily attributed to a successful intervention, a building-down from a realistic prior concern about what the integrative experience would demand of the supervisor. Interestingly, scores on the Hostility scale increased for the managers, although not significantly so. This may reflect a reasonable reaction against the action design, or against the training staff, whose focus was clearly more to help the demoted men than the managers. The moderate increase in Hostility scores suggests a neglect of supervisory needs, in sum, which subsequent design variations should recognize.

Fourth, a variety of analytical approaches establishes that the design had quite uniform effects for all demotees, regardless of their other differences. For example, correlation analysis revealed insignificant associations between changes on MAACL scores and four variables describing individual demoted managers: age; years with company; years as regional manager; and loss of salary involved in the demotion. The four individual variables were highly and positively intercorrelated. The intercorrelation matrix contains these five values: .7309, .7430, .8317, .8593, and .9545, all of which attain at least the .01 level of statistical significance. However, in only 1 case in 72 does one of these four variables correlate significantly with any of 18 measures of outcomes: the 9 absolute scores on Anxiety, Depression, and Hostility in each of the three administrations; and the 9 measures of relative change on

[11]Bernard Lubin and Marvin Zuckerman, "Levels of Emotional Arousal in Laboratory Training," *Journal of Applied Behavioral Science,* Vol. 5 (October, 1969), p. 488.

the three MAACL scales which compare scores on the three administrations, taken by pairs. Consider "salary loss," for example. Not one of its 18 correlation coefficients with the various outcome variables attains the .05 level of statistical significance, :.60 by two-tailed test. In fact, only 3 of the 18 coefficients reach :.40, while 9 coefficients fall in the interval $+.199$ through $-.199$.

Such data support the dominance of treatment effects. No attempt was made to deal with partials in the correlation analysis, however, given the small N.

Fifth, the effects on individuals also establish the efficacy of the design. Three perspectives on the data provide evidence. First, consider a crude comparison of the first and second MAACL administrations. Of the 33 comparisons—11 demotees three MAACL scales—26 were reductions and 3 were no-changes in scores. No demotee had an increased score on more than one scale, in addition. Looked at from another point of view, second, the data show only a single demotee who has even one score significantly greater than the mean of any scale on the first administration, and whose scores were not significantly lower in later administrations. Using a more demanding convention, third, the demotees can be divided as:

1. 3 men all of whose scores on the third MAACL administration were "major decreases," that is, they were at least one standard deviation less than the means on each of the three scales on the first administration;
2. 3 men who had major decreases on two MAACL scales and a more modest reduction on the third scale;
3. 1 man who had a major decrease on one MAACL scale and more modest reductions on the other scales;
4. 2 men who experienced no reduction of greater than a standard deviation on any scale; and
5. 1 man who had a "major increase" on the third administration of one standard deviation greater than the initial mean on one MAACL scale and who was at or near the initial means on all three scales; and
6. 1 man who had a major increase on one MAACL scale plus a major reduction on another, and who was substantially above the initial means.

Sixth, post-experience interviews with the demotees and several levels of their managers underscore the value of the design. Many of the details cannot be revealed since they might identify individuals. But the overall thrust of the interviews is clear. The integrative experience was considered valuable in smoothing what had been predicted to be a very stormy and costly transition. Significantly but not conclusively, all 11 demotees are still on the job some six months later, and 10 are considered to have made the transition "in great shape" and "more than adequately" on a 20-point scale running through "adequate," "somewhat inadequate," and "critically inadequate."

CONCLUSION

The application of a learning design based on the laboratory approach, then, seems to have induced the intended consequences. Conservatively, the intervention seems to have quickly reversed emotional states that can generate consequences troublesome for the individual and the organization. Specifically, scores on Anxiety, Depression, and Hostility scales were reduced significantly for a small population of demoted field supervisors, following the learning experience. These reductions were maintained or augmented in a third administration of the measuring instrument, spaced in time far enough after the intervention to test persistence.

Note also that it seems likely that the present learning design profited from earlier work in the host organization to develop norms, attitudes, and behaviors consistent with the laboratory approach. No concrete proof exists, but the training staff feels strongly that the observed effects derive in some substantial part from the earlier work in sensitivity training groups, as that training influenced individual behavior and as it helped develop appropriate attitudes and norms in the host organization. At least in the absence of very compelling (and presently unavailable) evidence, this design may not be applicable in organizations as a first-generation effort.

Methodological inelegancies prohibit uniquely attributing the effects to the learning design, but the presumptive evidence is strong. For example, the initial reductions cannot easily be attributed to the passage of time. The interval between the first and second MAACL administrations was a brief one, and the demotees had patently developed and sustained high scores on the three marker variables in the five or six days intervening between the demotion notices and the integrative experience. It is of course possible that the observed changes were artifacts of the design. But it does not seem likely that, for example, the announcement of the integrative experience alone triggered the high MAACL scores, which naturally dropped when that experience proved benign. Post-interviews with the demotees largely scotch this explanation, although some minor "anticipation effect" no doubt existed.

In other senses, however, more substantial reservations must hedge attributing the observed results to the learning design. For example, was the real magic in this case in the "process analysis" and the values of the laboratory approach? Or did some or all of the potency derive from the very act of bringing the men together, a kind of Hawthorne token that management really cared, and no matter about the specific learning design? Similarly, it is not known how long the initial levels of anxiety, depression, and hostility would have persisted if nature had been allowed to run its course.

Only a fool or a very wise man could definitely answer the latter questions. The issues are incredibly complex. This pilot study at least suggests one promising extension of the laboratory approach into large organizations, and urges the comparative analysis of other designs that can safely be added to the kit of the change-agent.

28. Community Action Groups Come to the Classroom

JOSEPH M. PETULLA

As a teaching clergyman assigned to a large central city parish for 10 years, I had the opportunity to work with a variety of small community action groups. The groups were primarily directed toward social action projects, rather than toward the development of knowledge or feelings, and took their inspiration from a socially oriented Belgian priest who helped workers organize themselves after World War II. His method was simple, if slightly crude. Before a group could change any social situation, it had to *observe* all sides of the problem, make *judgments* about the actual or potential benefits or harm involved and *act* to change the undesirable aspects of the situation.

The 30-odd groups—students, married couples, professional and working people—with whom I worked, utilized the *observe, judge, act method;* and I noticed that regardless of the age or occupation of the group members, each group usually passed through similar stages. It took a period of time for group members to get enough information to act on a problem and also to fully trust or feel comfortable with one another. Eventually, though, we did seem to change a few things for the better, we learned a lot about previously opaque urban structures, and we became a bit more sensitive as people.

OBSERVE, JUDGE, ACT METHOD

It occurred to me that this simple method of dealing with neighborhood or community problems was indeed a powerful *educational device.* The approach demands a knowledge of governmental structures, of bureaucratic procedures, of technical data about particular problems. It also demands that the group learn collective problem solving and sharing. Furthermore,

Reprinted from *Social Change,* Vol. 2, No. 4, 1972, pp. 1–3.

the reward for the achievement of a group goal is an energizing hope, which spurs the group on to more difficult tasks. Even failure has proved to be a strong incentive.

Graduate school took me away from action groups for a few years, but during that time I was able to reflect on the process and to some extent sharpen its method. The following report sketches a number of what I call *Urban Action Groups*, which I recently developed out of the urban studies departments of two San Francisco Bay Area colleges. One is a large community college, two-thirds of whose students are from minority groups; the other is a small private college with a totally white student population.

I usually begin the projects by asking the students to read articles on issues detailed in the local press. As stimulus material I keep files of clippings from five or six local papers (establishment, investigative, and underground) under 12 headings: population growth, transportation, poverty agencies, housing, education, health, welfare, public finance, municipal and regional government, crime and violence, air and noise pollution, and planning problems (the last category, my substitute for a "miscellaneous" file). Students "get into" a project or join a group by reading through folders I make from these clipping files and discussing the issue with me.

I act as a facilitator for each group until I can train one of its members in the fundamentals of group process. In any case, I stay in close contact with the group throughout the duration of the project. There is no established way for an "expert," of either group or urban skills, to relate to a group. The cardinal rule is to try *not* to run things. The groups do preliminary research based on information from the folders, then set goals for themselves, research the questions more thoroughly, clarify tactics, and finally act.

Of course, many detours and blind alleys impede the simple solution. Sometimes there is the weak link(s)—individuals not carrying their weight. Personality conflicts and fundamentally opposing viewpoints also block smooth group interaction. Yet all of these difficulties enhance the educational value of action groups, provided that an effort is made to understand what is short-circuiting the group system.

A TYPICAL GROUP

On the other hand, a group can quickly gather momentum and accomplish amazing achievements in a relatively short time. Such was the case with a group of minority students who became aware that the local Traffic Department planned to route truck traffic through their neighborhood. The students obtained a copy of the proposal and noted that white neighborhoods were not to be touched by truck traffic. At first they wanted to storm City Hall. They decided instead to write a report showing the harmful effects of the Traffic Department proposal, offer an alternative plan, and then fight for their own proposal.

We first brainstormed the question of trucks running through the neighborhood. Trucks have always been part of the ghetto scene, and people just learned to accept them. Now it was different. New low-income housing was being built. People were trying to improve their neighborhoods. It was as though the city wanted to reslumify the area all over again. The students began to become aware of all the harmful effects of traffic, specifically, truck traffic.

On the basis of these discussions, group members researched what they considered the main sides of the issue: the population density of the area and the construction of new low-income housing, the effects of truck pollution—noise and diesel fuel fumes, health hazards, incidence of accidents, street maintenance costs, and probable decline in property values—and took a survey of neighborhood opinion. Students gave regular progress reports at meetings and put together a final draft of their report, "The Reslumification of West Oakland." They next lobbied City Council members, persons in the Traffic Department itself, Model Cities' staff, citizens groups, the Redevelopment Agency, even local church members. Although the question has not yet been voted on in City Council session at this writing, there is good reason to believe that the group effectively blocked enactment of the Traffic Department proposal. And the students know it.

Social change can also come about through legislative processes; but unfortunately, lawmakers are slow to act if their political future seems in jeopardy. Consequently, groups large and small have chosen the initiative process to get needed legislation on the books. The experience is a rewarding, if long and painful, one. To pass an initiative, a group must understand the legal procedures involved in putting a question on the ballot. Group members must thoroughly understand why they want it on the ballot because they will be called on to defend their position hundreds of times. People advocating an initiative have to deal with citizens who are potential signers of it, with groups which are potential allies and co-workers, with the media, with governmental officials, and an ever-present opposition. If the advocates don't know what they are talking about, they're dead.

I have assisted two student groups which chose to work on state-wide initiatives—one calling for a full income tax on capital gains and another establishing regional planning committees to protect the coastline—and one group which supported a local initiative setting up a rent control board. Although our groups were only small parts of much larger campaigns, in each case the members did much research on tax questions and loopholes, on land-use problems, and on local housing needs, respectively, and assisted in the organizational, financing, and publicity aspects of the projects, as well.

Other Urban Action Groups have worked on such issues as discrimination in a suburban community; a housing lobby for tenants in the state capital; welfare problems; a co-op grocery store in a minority community; a report on the conduct of probation officers (three out of six in this group were actually on probation); elections for a Model Cities board; a citizens' group concerned with integration in the local school system.

"TURNING ON" STUDENTS

It seems to me that a major educational value of the groups has been their "turn-on" effect. Students who had previously lacked focus in their lives suddenly began to believe in themselves, to enlarge their visions, and to understand that they could make some contribution. Group projects led some students into subject areas that influenced a choice of careers. In fact, this happened with over half of the students involved in Urban Action Group projects. What is most important, members of these groups proved to themselves and others that with persistent and collective action, some changes can be effected by small groups, either alone or in concert with other groups. The Traffic Department *was* influenced to propose an alternative route for truck traffic. Probation officers *were* confronted and forced to re-think their behavior. A large group of welfare mothers *did* get technical assistance at a critical time in their lives. An ongoing housing discrimination committee *was* set up. Rent control *was* passed by the voters. And so on. In some cases the accomplishments of these inexperienced groups were insignificant; in other cases they had considerable impact on their urban environment.

IMPACT ON THE INDIVIDUAL

But it is easier to measure the impact which the group activity had on individual members. Beyond the "turn-on" effect, beyond the information mastered by many on a variety of subjects, students learned to explore libraries for all kinds of technical data, such as block statistics on population density; to examine Public Health Department records, or to spend entire days in Planning Departments. Then there was the experience gained in spending evenings with the city councils, extended periods of time in municipal, county, and private agencies, and even occasional appearances in court. For the most part, an individual's interest was born with his involvement in an Urban Action Group and flourished because he felt a personal stake in some issue on which the group was working.

The commonality of the projects is no doubt in large measure responsible for the "turn-on" effect. The fact that other people are depending on you to perform some function, that you are needed and need the support of others in the group, that in a way *you* are the expert on some aspect of the project, that for the first time others really seem to be listening to you when you talk, that you know you will succeed or fail together—all of these personal feelings play an important role in the emergence of a unique group spirit and commitment.

In fact, there are hundreds of variables which affect group process. Simple things can impede, like individuals who are consciously or unconsciously left out of the action, or those who withdraw without explanation, or those who are destined from the beginning to clash in a group. Yet I find that norms simply stated and made clear from the beginning can become the biggest aids to effective group process: come to the meeting prepared, keep to the agenda, no competing, no status seeking, no dominating, no cliques.

DISCIPLINE AND SENSITIVITY

Successful collective problem solving requires a great deal of discipline —the discipline of accepting responsibility and carrying out tasks, of cultivating an awareness and relatedness during meetings. From the discipline of this exercise is derived the feeling of commonality.

Many students in our urban studies programs have preferred to work on their own, learning about the city through individual projects or internship placements. These teach a certain resourcefulness, an ability to find one's way around the city's "labyrinthine ways," but they also tend to further privatise the student, already locked into his own individualistic world of thinking and acting by an educational system which has rewarded him for just that. Although internships can have great practical value and good ones are becoming more and more scarce, they are actually only an extension of old educational models. In Urban Action Groups students learn as much from one another as from the project—because of diverse backgrounds, the nonelitist, egalitarian nature of the model, and each member's unique motivation and commitment.

One of the unexpected side effects of this blending of theory and practice has been an increase of sensitivity not only among group members themselves but even toward others outside the group. In many cases, perhaps in more than I was able to notice, students seemed to radically change viewpoints and behavior within as brief a period as five months. During nearly every project someone whose approach had been authoritarian or legalistic began to look on people and problems in a much more compassionate and empathic manner. Of course, some are undoubtedly influenced by their more mature fellow students, but I firmly believe (it is not wishful thinking) that it is the group process and activity that tends to increase sensitivity.

In this connection it is interesting to note the research of Lawrence Kohlberg of Harvard University, who maintains that cognitive structures include moral structures and develop in stages of organizational wholes through *action* and *interaction* between people and their environment. (See his "Stage and sequence: The cognitive-developmental approach" in *Handbook of socialization, theory and research,* edited by D. Goslin, 1969, Rand.) That is, a person whose cognitive faculties and structures become enriched through interaction with his environment develops at the same time his "moral" structure, outlook, and behavior. Kohlberg's Piagetian model is far too sophisticated to describe here in a few lines, but I have found enough corroboration for it in my own experience in working with Urban Action Groups to wish to pursue other possible connections.

Some groups don't jell, don't last, don't "make it" together. But many do. And they come up with enough exciting achievement, in all shapes, to keep you coming back for more.

29. Working with Hostile Groups: A Reexamination

JAMES E. CROWFOOT and MARK A. CHESLER

In a recent (Vol. 4, No. 1, 1974) *Social Change* article, "Working with Hostile Groups," Cyril Mill examines problems of group resistance and hostility encountered by trainers and organizational consultants. The author details several sources or reasons for "hostile groups," and discusses some ways of overcoming hostility and building "positive" group climates. In our view Mill's focus upon group hostility reflects a general concern for harmonious and well-controlled group processes rather than the specific ends of group learning or social change. His perceptions of the sources of group hostility to consultants and trainers are inadequate because they do not take into account the politics of the social unit involved and the politics of the training enterprise. What results is a classic case of "victim blame." Finally, Mill's suggestions for action represent an attempt to "cool out" the hostility, rather than meet and work with the underlying organizational and social change issues involved. In this article, we seek to reanalyze some of the explanations Mill offers, and to place them in an appropriate ideological and political context. Then we offer alternative suggestions for dealing with the same phenomena, actions we think are more in tune with concerns for fundamental social and organizational change.

RESISTANCE IS RELATIVE—FROM A POLITICAL PERSPECTIVE

Mill's article is important because it represents a significant historical trend in the field of change-agentry. Well within the paradigms of analyzing

Reprinted from *Social Change,* Vol. 5, No. 3, 1975, pp. 3–6.

resistance established by Watson (1967) and others, Mill essentially sees hostility as inappropriate or unfortunate—even basically irrational—in the well-ordered world of scientifically oriented planned social change (Bennis, Benne, & Chin, 1969).

In a recent article (1974), we located views such as Mill's within a professional-technical perspective on planned social change.[1] We suggested that at the root of the value position of the professional-technical change agent lies a commitment to gradual change in the social order and a belief that progress always lies ahead, to be achieved through incremental and continuous adaptation. The recognition of partisanship and the legitimation of group goal conflicts is distasteful to practitioners and theorists of this persuasion. From this perspective, authorities are viewed as people of good will who for the most part seek the common goal of all members of the systems for which they are responsible. Thus, resistance usually is seen as arising from inadequacy, fear, lack of information, or some other individual inability to adjust responsibly and rationally to the good and better future.

A political perspective on change, on the other hand, treats conflict and resistance as natural and normal elements of the everyday contest of interests and values in a differentiated society. From this perspective authorities are recognized as protecting and advancing particular interests that are not necessarily synonymous with the interests of the different groups and parts of systems for which they are responsible. Resistance usually is seen as protection of one's interests in the face of reallocation of resources or encroachment on preferred values.

Mill fails to acknowledge the relativity of his analysis or resistance and the importance of perspectives different from his own. This is but one illustration of what has been the monolithic ideological character of publications such as *Social Change.* Our hope is that the "profession" of change-agentry can speak with more clarity and honesty about value differences and their important implications. As a step in this direction we propose to reexamine Mill's article in light of what other approaches—particularly the political perspective—seem to say about the phenomena of group resistance and hostility.

Mill identifies the following sources of group hostility often directed at organizational trainers and consultants: 1) involuntary attendance at sessions wherein "others have decided that the training program would be a 'good' thing"; 2) prejudice against experiential learning per se; 3) the laboratory effort seen as just one more in a series of oversold events which have produced little in terms of significant change; and 4) the predictable resistance met whenever the training is part of a larger organizational change

---

[1]Crowfoot and Chesler (1974) argue that the field of planned social change can be understood in terms of three distinct ideological perspectives: professional-technical, political, and counter cultural-redemptive. Each perspective has its own assumptions, value priorities, preferred strategies, clusters of practitioners, and explanations for resistance to change.

effort: people are unwilling to accept changes that may disrupt their customary ways of thinking, feeling, and behaving.

INVOLUNTARY ATTENDANCE VERSUS PATERNALISTIC REASSURANCE

Faced with the first source of hostility, the captive "subject," one might suggest "overcoming" it by mounting an offensive against the organizations or supervisors who so oppress their staff as to subject them to training without options. Certainly such action would be consistent with the rhetoric of free choice and democratic participation in training programs. But Mill neither elects nor mentions such an option; rather, he recommends a series of tactics for overcoming the hostility in the trainees. One tactic referred to is "contract building"—where participants share their fears and hopes with the trainers, who in turn, tell them how these will be taken care of. If this is really a "contract," it is clearly not a reciprocal one. Trainers don't share their fears and hopes; there is no bargaining or negotiating. Why not call this paternalistic reassurance or professional supportiveness, in which the authority conceals vulnerability while requesting clients to share or confess vulnerability and dependence, following which, the authority can respond, at his/her discretion, with reassurance.

Mill does discuss cancellation of training as a last resort, but he claims that he knows of no instance where training programs once begun have been cancelled. We cannot "buy" this "if all else fails" stance. Many problems of poor planning or manipulated recruitment call precisely for the termination of training on principle alone, perhaps after an initial session at which these problems and inadequacies are surfaced. The fact that the author knows of no such instances clearly tells us that in his view it is not in the consultants' interest to do this. If the training were cancelled, what would happen to the trainers' fees? Trainers and consultants in the service of organizational elites apparently feel they cannot afford to alienate these clients—nor to risk the loss of their own remuneration. This is collusion—whether the consultant realizes it or not.

RESENTMENT, PREJUDICE VERSUS COOLING-OUT AND DIVERSIONARY TACTICS

Mill's second source of hostility is "resentment amounting to a prejudice against experiential learning." We personally favor experiential learning: most of the time, although not all of the time, it has worked best for us. But it does not work well for everyone, for every cultural group, or for every situation. Sometimes, an experiential focus may emphasize individual subjective issues in ways that fail to clarify objective interests and "realpolitik." Such training can operate cooptively—and discouragingly—anchoring people further to status quo objective conditions while encouraging exciting subjective explorations. For Mill to label "resentment amounting to a prejudice" without including, even by implication, the possibility that different goals and different values about styles of learning also legitimately may be at stake, is almost to label all resistance irrational.

CLIENT EXPECTATIONS VERSUS TRAINER CONTROL OF RESOURCES

The third source of resistance to specific training events is in part traceable to the tactics utilized by the broader social movement of human relations and OD training, which has sought to capture the market with extravagant claims. The consultant often feeds into these expectations by virtue of his/her own needs for recognition, acceptance, and employment. Mill's analysis is one-sided again, discussing only participant aberrance rather than trainer collusion as well. Frequently, professional trainers fail to identify and confront the inappropriateness of training due to their having been manipulated, their own carelessness, or their own pecuniary or status self-interests. After all, management's desires to "retrain" employees may suit their change objectives yet not advance those of their employees. Several exposures to these dominant biases in OD programs should generate in participants (employees especially) the feeling that nothing new is happening: basic power arrangements are not being altered, goals of top-level authorities are still being pursued, and so on.

Mill's diagnoses and suggestions for "overcoming" hostility and resistance are rife with the maintenance of trainer and professional authority and control. We review this later, but its presence is enough to convince the sensitive participant that the training workshop or OD program subtly represents the same power dynamics of the large organization—but in this case, the special power of the helping professions.

PLURALISM, COMPETING VALUES VERSUS DELEGITIMATION

Any organizational change effort should be expected to meet resistance —resistance in the form of other persons or organizational units who hold values and interests that differ from those favored by groups (usually managing elites) who call in trainers and consultants. But rather than seeing such resistance as symptomatic of natural conflict within a pluralistic system, Mill seems to view the hostility engendered by it as stemming from an unwillingness or inability to accept the need for change. Maybe from the client's status and viewpoint, there is no need for change.[2]

---

[2] The reduction of an organizational conflict into personal terms and variables, whether intentional or not, further delegitimizes the politics of interest group conflict in organizations and encourages overpsychologizing and "victim blaming."

Trainers and consultants in the pay of organizational elites often come to adopt their employers' views as the only legitimate ones. Of course this is even more likely when the trainers and consultants themselves are white, male, and of the same status, background, and value orientations as are the governing elites. The net result is that differences are seen as illegitimate, as resistance to the legitimate and rational goals for change stressed by managers and consultants.

We believe that social change is always a political process. It involves the alteration of organizational norms, styles, policies, structures, and resource distributions; it also involves the pursuit of cherished values or interests. In the pursuit of one's own priorities and the influence or alteration of others', various technologies and tools are used. When some of the tools of change (money, status and power of "professional" change agents, scientific information or knowledge) are captured by one competing party, they become weapons in that party's defense and advancement of its own interests. (One example of this is when professionals create articles, training designs, analyses of hostility, and myths about conflict that delegitimize resistance to managerial and consultant goals.)

Of course the profession of change-agentry has its own politics and power issues. The commitment to maintain professional control is clear in Mill's recommendations of ways trainers may overcome hostility. For instance, he recommends a quick exposure to exciting, unusual, and perhaps competitive tasks to dispel participants' fantasies about what will occur. He does not say that such techniques can divert attention from basic conflicts in the trainer-trainee relationship. Another technique he recommends is open staff planning (in reality a canned substitute of actual staff planning), but even there he warns that this is a technique only for a "well-integrated, professionally secure staff." What happens if the staff is not well integrated? One assumes that in Mill's view, differences among themselves and uncertainties should not be shared with participants. Why not? Or at least why not be open that the reason they should not be shared is fear of surfacing staff conflict and thus making the staff more vulnerable in the staff-participant contest?

TOKENS AND EUPHEMISMS: NO POWER PARITY

As a contingent strategy to be used only if the trainers' initial effort at establishing a positive climate is unsuccessful, "a contract openly arrived at" is suggested by Mill. He describes it equivocally: "Trainers may find it desirable to open the planning procedures and share some of the leadership function . . ." with participants. One wonders why this would not be desirable all of the time; why share only some of the leadership functions? And why should not trainees decide that? The entire line of argument here poses alternative strategies for maintaining trainer control with token target participation in "leadership." A "positive climate" here means one in which learners will comply with professional direction, and thus becomes a euphemism for trainer control.

In the vast majority of instances, trainers do exercise control over whether or not the training event goes on, what will be covered, and how. The kind of control the participants have is to be absent from sessions, late to sessions, present in sessions and participating in obstructive ways, and so on. That is, the only forms of power and control participants in general have available to them may center on the options of resisting or being "hostile." To set participant hostility within the paradigm of power and control over the workshop or change design requires consultants to see themselves as responsible parties in a power relationship, not as bystanders watching the irrational hostility of participants. Mill's suggestions maintain the power differential between consultants and trainees in the workshop: he elects corrective action at the level of communication and interpersonal relations rather than power parity between trainers and participants or renovation of program goals and structures.

Another technique Mill recommends is prepared questions directed at the staff. A staff panel "may then respond to the questions or indicate that a question will not be answered. . . . Depending on the type of program, the staff may choose not to answer the questions about a few issues, such as salary and sexual behavior." Why shouldn't all questions be answered? After all the salary of trainers is important data in disclosing who they are, what their priorities are, to whom they are accountable. Likewise, in a situation where participants anticipate vulnerability, risk-taking, experimentation— what the laboratory method calls for—staff members' sexual preference and outlooks (like their race, age, and class) may be exceedingly important information in determining the reality of potential trust relations and the probability of one's being taken advantage of.

DEMOCRATIZING THE PROFESSIONS

Mill's recommendations emphasize trainers' needs for techniques for overcoming resistance instead of exploring new structures, roles, decision-making processes, and distributions of power in a training situation. Further, the underlying theme in these recommendations is that trainers establish and preserve control through distraction, pretended openness, increased interpersonal communication, i.e., a united trainer front.

Change traditions other than the professional-technical now seek to democratize the professions and to create situations where clients/targets control their consultants rather than the reverse.[3] Mill's gentle and decent

---

[3]One might argue, accurately we presume, that Mill's clients are not really the lab participants but the managers who send them there and contract for the consultant or trainer. In the situation, the consultant or trainer is being controlled by or accountable to his/her client, but the client is the manager, not the participant. Under such circumstances, the distinction between client and target should be clear, and target (employee) resistance to manipulation or control by managers and manager's representatives (consultant) should be natural and expected.

recontrolling efforts would be inappropriate in such a scenario, wherein change agents are expected to provide partisan advice, support, and expertise to clients who control them and determine how to use them. In target groups committed to social-justice objectives Mill's suggestions perpetuate concealment of the real effects of racial, class, and sexual power—impotence of the oppressed and rage at continual oppression by the elite. For such groups and perhaps for us all, getting in touch with that rage is an essential element of our personal liberation and a key source of energy for social change.

HOSTILITY AS A SOURCE OF ENERGY AND GROWTH

Apart from the seriousness of Mill's failure to understand and articulate his own political bias, and perhaps even to propose alternative perspectives, he demonstrates a limited understanding of the role played by hostility and negative feelings in individual and system change. While Mill judges that hostility should be eliminated from the change situation, we feel that hostility can be a major source of energy and personal growth (Fanon, 1963; Laing, 1967). Such hostility can indicate investment in a situation, and when legitimated can be manifest in engagement and encounter. With this expressed energy is the potential for discovery of related feelings, revised perceptions, altered behaviors, and deepened passion and commitment to cherished values. Hostility—latent or actualized—in intergroup conflicts can be a vehicle for achieving new systemic boundaries, revision of goals, and clarified, renewed, or terminated group and individual commitment.

Deutsch (1969, p. 35), certainly no advocate of escalated personal or social conflict, indicates: "Harnessed rage or outrage can be a powerful energizer for determined action, and if this action is directed toward building one's own power rather than destroying the other's power, the outrage may have a socially useful, constructive outcome." And he notes that both rage and fear "are rooted in a sense of helplessness and powerlessness." Constructive responses to them will require renovation of existing personal and social power arrangements—in the society, in small-group role relations, and in organizational training programs.

REFERENCES

Bennis, W., Benne, K., & Chin, R. *The planning of change.* New York: Holt, Rinehart & Winston, 1969.

Crowfoot, J., & Chesler, M. Contemporary perspectives on planned social change: A comparison. *Journal of Applied Behavioral Science,* 1974, 10, 278–303.

Deutsch, M. Conflicts: Productive and destructive. *Journal of Social Issues,* 1969, 25 (*1*), 7–41.

Fanon, F. *The wretched of the earth.* New York: Grove Press, 1963.

Laing, R. D. *The politics of experience.* New York: Ballantine Books, 1967.

Mill, C. R. Working with hostile groups. *Social Change,* 1974, 4 (*1*), 1–4.
Watson, G. Resistance to change. In G. Watson (Ed.), *Concepts for social change.* Washington, D.C.: National Training Laboratories, National Education Association, 1967. Pp. 10–25.

VI. HOW CAN T-GROUP DYNAMICS BE STUDIED?

Conceiving and Executing Research

INTRODUCTION

Research has been a major concern of laboratory training since its inception, although the focus of that research has decidedly swung from "pure science" to an increasing concern with "applied science." The distinction between "pure" and "applied" science has to be a rough one, but it is meaningful in this case, in the sense of "more or less." The proof of both points is vividly clear in the crucial role that the T-Group has played in the development of an applied behavioral science approach to individual, group, and organizational problems.

A "pure science" bias is clear in the earliest research, using T-Groups which focused on the processes of group development, as they interacted with the characteristics of group members. Hence the earliest major compendium of T-Group research—published under the editorship of Dorothy Stock and

Herbert Thelen—was entitled *Emotional Dynamics and Group Culture*.[1] The least dominant theme was "outcomes," the payoffs associated with specific internal group processes such as attitudinal or behavioral change. The typical focus was on "pure science," on isolating relations of various group and individual properties, such as: High cohesiveness is associated with a high degree of agreement about norms.

Developments in T-Group research have shifted the research focus to "applied" concerns, while elaborating the basic interest in phenomena at several levels of organization. That is, recent studies have been less concerned with internal T-Group dynamics than they have with the results of training, with the diverse factors that affect these results, and with applications of the T-Group model in various contexts. Not everything is known about the internal dynamics of T-Group dynamics, of course. Much remains to be tested and learned. However, at least at this juncture in time, emphasis is on the applied issue of how to achieve certain desired outcomes.

In a highly developed science, pure and applied work will be hard to distinguish. But there is unlikely to be an easy and early resolution of their differential emphases in the case of T-Groups, for at least two reasons. First, there is a strong humanistic and existential bias in sensitivity training, and this bias for human uplifts fits but imperfectly with the intendedly objective procedures of the scientific method. For example, some observers have pointed up the conflict between such values of the laboratory approach as trust and openness, and the deception that may be appropriate in setting up "controls" or "comparisons" that are so central in much of the scientific approach. Second, all research on T-Groups is complicated by peculiar methodological and interpretation difficulties.

In an early paper, Harrison[2] incisively confronted a number of these difficulties. He recognized three classes of training designs—normative, individual growth, and general improvement of participant capabilities—and research designs related to them. Harrison's major point was that research should gear into training design. As this is done methodological problems arise involving controls, temporal change in training outcomes, dimensions and directions of anticipated change, the variability of training experiences, the timing of data collection, and the effects on research efforts of the experimentor's common involvement in the laboratory setting.

Given these problems of design and subsequent interpretation, applied research on the T-Group has an outcome bias which provides some (but not

[1] Stock, D. and Thelen, H. *Emotional Dynamics and Group Culture*, Washington, D.C.: National Training Laboratories, 1958.

[2] Roger Harrison, "Problems of Design and Interpretation of Research on Human Relations Training." *Explorations in Human Relations Training and Research*. Washington, D.C.: NTL Institute for Applied Behavioral Science, 1967, pp. 1-9.

unqualified) support that encourages practitioners to use T-Groups. Consider the early set of generalizations provided by Bob Luke and Charles Seashore.[3] They tease out, among others, the following generalizations from research that may be applied to laboratory training. The outcome bias of these generalizations is patent.

- Evidence indicates that an inverse relationship exists between the congruency of the trainee's behavioral style with the laboratory milieu and his relative level of learning as judged by peers and trainers.
- Laboratory training does induce change in participants, but there is conflicting evidence about the permanence and application of new attitudes and behavioral styles.
- Involvement in the training process, more than personality factors, appears to be the critical determining factor which influences learning and change.
- The trainer can manipulate the group climate which produces differential trainee performance and learnings.

The generalizations above contain several points worthy of discussion. For example, people whose behavioral styles are at some variance with the culture that develops in a laboratory seem to attain a higher level of learning than those whose initial styles are relatively congruent with the culture. Where significant but not overwhelming incongruity exists, apparently, the trainee is confronted with more of a dilemma than where it does not. Reasonably, the greater dilemma motivates the person involved to seek a wider range of alternative behaviors than fellow group members whose dilemma is less severe. Many learning approaches, in contrast, tend to affect those whose behavior is already most like that which the approach intends to induce.[4] This implies a major advantage of the laboratory method.

The generalizations above also contain their measure of pessimism about the viability of applied behavioral science. Consider, for example, the conflicting evidence about transfer of laboratory learnings to the back-home setting. Whether the problem is research methodology, measuring instruments, or the researchers' inability thus far to discover the critical variables is not clear. The fact is, to repeat, that "hard data" does not unequivocally support the efficacy of sensitivity training, as measured by transfer of learning to back-home situations.

The generalizations above also suggest that pure science approaches to T-Groups often barked up the wrong tree. Consider the interaction between learning and personality or T-Group characteristics, a concern near and dear

---

[3] "Generalizations on Research and Speculations from Experience Related to Laboratory Training Design," a National Training Laboratories Memorandum, pp. 1–5. Copyright 1966 by NTL Institute for Applied Behavioral Science.

[4] Analysis of attempts to influence behavior and attitudes in election campaigns shows this to be a significant, if not the major, result of partisan publicity. See the line of research beginning with Paul F. Lazarsfeld, Bernard Berelson, and Hazel Gaudet, *The People's Choice* (New York: Columbia University Press, 1948).

to the pure science approach. However, learning in a T-Group seems to be more related to the extent that a person involves himself in the process rather than to any particular personality variable or group property. People not actively involved can learn in a vicarious sort of way, but their learning will tend not to include the crucial testing of behaviors that encourages feedback from others.

The last generalization above highlights a major difference between pure and applied approaches—the latter requires some agent to help make the desired things happen. That agent—the trainer—must be a major concern of an applied behavioral approach. Though the role of the trainer is not that of the controlling leader, he is a very powerful person in a T-Group. He is the one, in a very ambiguous situation (from the point of view of the group member) who really "knows what is happening." The dynamics of his influence seem to be, then, that participants cue in on his behavior and the messages he sends. If his orientation is more toward the group than the individual, focal learnings will move in that direction. If he is very much concerned with control, T-Group members probably will center a good bit of attention on their own control needs.

These generalizations do not tell the detailed story concerning research about T-Groups, but fortunately a growing literature[5] is becoming available that provides kaleidoscopic evidence of the difficulties sketched by Harrison. There is no need to reproduce that literature here, but some sense of its thrust can be provided economically. Consider the essentials of the comprehensive review by John P. Campbell and Marvin D. Dunnette.[6] Overall, Campbell and Dunnette adopt the perspective of the pure scientist, and they are quite critical of what they see in the T-Group literature. They make two essential points. Much evidence establishes that T-Group experiences have major impact on participants. However, existing research does not often permit high confidence in statements of what specific changes may be anticipated under the specific conditions. The failure to respect normal canons of scientific method in much T-Group research, Campbell and Dunnette argue, requires such a judgment.

---

[5] Illustratively, see Dorothy Stock, "A Survey of Research on T-Groups," in Leland P. Bradford, Jack R. Gibb, and Kenneth D. Benne (eds.), *T-Group Theory and Laboratory Method* (New York: John Wiley & Sons, 1964), pp. 393–441; Cary L. Cooper and Iain L. Mangham, "T-Group Training Before and After," *Journal of Management Studies* Vol. 7 (May, 1970), pp. 224–39; Jack R. Gibb, "The Effects of Human Relations Training," in A. E. Bergin and S. L. Garfield (eds.), *Handbook of Psychotherapy and Behavior Change* (New York: John Wiley & Sons, 1971); and Martin Lakin, *Interpersonal Encounter* (New York: McGraw-Hill Book Co., 1972), pp. 181–207. Robert T. Golembiewski, *Renewing Organizations* (Itasca, Ill.: F. E. Peacock Publishers, Inc., 1972), esp. pp. 227–71; and Morton A. Lieberman, Irwin D. Yalom, and Matthew B. Miles, *Encounter Groups: First Facts* (New York: Basic Books, 1973).

[6] "Effectiveness of T-Group Experiences in Managerial Training and Development," *Psychological Bulletin,* Vol. 70 (August, 1968), pp. 73–104.

Campbell and Dunnette's survey has three motivations. Tremendous resources are being invested in T-Group training; psychological damage to participants has been allegedly induced by sensitivity training; and serious ethical questions have been raised about sensitivity training particularly in regard to its effects on human relations and management behavior in organizations.

A similar if earlier survey of T-Group research was undertaken by Robert J. House, and he proposed a set of guidelines for any managements considering the use of T-Group training in their organizations. He recommends:[7]

- Careful study of the organizational needs to see if they are congruent with T-Group goals;
- Careful preselection of participants;
- Careful explanation of T-Group goals to the participants in order to allow for voluntary withdrawals of a person prior to the training experience;
- Careful selection of the trainer;
- Continued research in the program in order to refine methods; and
- Precautionary backup measures should the T-Group program not meet expectations, or should the well-being of the participants become threatened.

SOME INTEGRATIONS OF PURE AND APPLIED CONCERNS

There is substantial hope for a far brighter tomorrow, however, as far as research on sensitivity training and the laboratory approach is concerned. The purpose here is to highlight several recent research efforts, whose basic virtue is that they at once deal with basic research questions in approved ways while they also relate to important applied concerns of the practitioner using T-Groups and the laboratory approach.

In "Sensitivity Training and Self-Actualization" John F. Gilligan's research focussed directly in on the personal learning dimension of a T-Group experience. Gilligan's data revealed significant changes in measures of self-actualization on both a post-test and a six-month, follow-up test on the part of a volunteer experimental group when compared with a non-volunteer group. Despite these encouraging results, Gilligan urges more refined research designs that pay particular attention to the way experimental and control groups are composed.

"Some Effects of Trainers on Their Groups: A Partial Replication" by Lee Bolman sheds light on a thrust of research on trainer behavior. The concern is, what do trainers do that seems to produce a productive learning climate for group members? The results of both studies that Bolman recounts seem to indicate that trainer behavior that communicates congruence-empathy is significantly related both to liking for the trainer and perceptions of having

---

[7] Robert J. House, "T-Group Education and Leadership Effectiveness: A Review of the Empiric Literature and a Critical Evaluation," *Personnel Psychology*, Vol. 20, No. 1 (Spring, 1967), pp. 26–28.

learned from the group. Trainer affection is related to liking of the trainer but not to learning. Love, seemingly, is not enough.

In "Encounter Groups: Their Effect on Rigidity" Richard T. Hoerl hypothesized that participation in an encounter group would result in increased scores on measures of tolerance for ambiguity and flexibility. Neither hypothesis was confirmed. A comparison of flexibility scores indicated that the population of the experiment was significantly different and higher than the national norm. These findings led Hoerl to comment on the emergence of "the Grouper," the type of person who, on a somewhat regular basis, attends group sessions. They may, indeed, bias research samples. Based on his findings, Hoerl also suggests the possibility that people who could most profit from a group experience are precisely those who do not attend.

The question of the systematic effects of variations of group composition on learning and change seems to have been first posed by Roger Harrison and Bernard Lubin.[8] They postulated that individual learning would be most apt to occur in those T-Groups in which the composition would somehow provide both support and confrontation for its members. Peter B. Smith and Michael J. Linton deal with this problem directly in an experimental study, "Group Composition and Changes in Self-Actualization in T-Groups." The individual variable that was manipulated was the extent to which the T-Groups in the experiment were composed of people who had homogeneous or heterogeneous control and/or affection needs, using Schutz's FIRO-B measure.[9] The findings of the study support the Harrison and Lubin contention, "the effects of composition appear to be that a particular composition enhances certain changes and depresses others, rather than that different compositions generate radically different outcomes." Thus, for example, though changes in outcome measures occurred in all experimental conditions, most change was observed in the groups that had the most heterogeneous compositions.

The final selection in this section is a pertinent piece of applied research, as it deals with the effects of experiential group learning on the relationships between teachers and students. In "The Impact of Marathon Encounters on Teacher-Student Relationships," Cary L. Cooper explores the changes that can occur when teacher and students participate together in an intensive encounter group experience. The experimental group took part in a 24-hour marathon encounter. There were significant changes in the student perceptions of regard and congruence,[10] by the teachers as measured by *The Relationship Inventory* compared with the perceptions of students in a

---

[8] Roger Harrison and Bernard Lubin, "Personal Style, Group Composition and Learning," *Journal of Applied Behavioral Science*, Vol. 1 (1965), pp. 276–301.

[9] William C. Schutz, *FIRO: A Three Dimensional Theory of Interpersonal Behavior* (New York: Rinehart, 1958).

[10] G. T. Barrett-Lennard, "Dimensions of Therapist Response as Causal Factors in Therapeutic Change," *Psychological Monographs*, Vol. 76, No. 43, 1962.

control group. Though the sample size in this study raises questions about the generalizability of the results, the implications hold interesting possibilities for dealing with problems of public school education.

30. Sensitivity Training and Self-Actualization

JOHN F. GILLIGAN

Proponents of sensitivity training have assumed that T-Groups will be composed of well-functioning individuals who will function even better as a result of training (Broedel, 1969; Golembiewski & Blumberg, 1970). Gilligan (1973) used the Omnibus Personality Inventory and the Personal Orientation Inventory in a test of the first part of the above assumption. T-Groups were composed of well-functioning students according to the Omnibus social-emotional adjustment scales. Not only were these groups composed of well-functioning participants, but the inventory scale of Inner Directedness showed that volunteers for sensitivity training were significantly more self-actualized than the nonvolunteer group. Other studies by Cooper (1971), Culbert, Clark, and Bobele (1968), Foulds (1970), Guinan and Foulds (1970), and Young and Jacobson (1970) have demonstrated increases in self-actualization as a function of sensitivity training. Their groups were composed of students who responded to the Personal Orientation Inventory (Shostrom, 1963), a purported measure of self-actualization, in a pre- and posttesting design. From the available research it appears that sensitivity-training groups for the most part are primarily composed of well-functioning individuals, college students, who function even better, i.e., more self-actualized, as a result of their group experiences.

It is possible, however, to identify at least four weaknesses in the research on self-actualization and T-Groups. (a) The control and experimental groups were relatively small ranging from 7 (Young & Jacobson, 1970) to 20 participants (Foulds, 1970), while other designs used no control groups (Cooper, 1971; Culbert, et al., 1968). (b) Statistical analyses did not account for initial differences between experimental and control groups (Foulds, 1970; Guinan & Foulds, 1970; Young & Jacobson, 1970). (c) There was no evidence of any follow-up to evaluate the enduring effectiveness of training (Cooper, 1971; Culbert, et al., 1968; Foulds, 1970; Guinan & Foulds, 1970;

Reprinted from *Psychological Reports*, Vol. 34, 1974, pp. 319–325.

Young & Jacobson, 1970). (d) The research groups were led by highly trained and talented group leaders (Culbert, *et al.*, 1968; Guinan & Foulds, 1970; Young & Jacobson, 1970). Although this is not a weakness, one may ask whether the more available but less skillful trainer can achieve similar significant results.

The present study considers these four points. Control and experimental groups were composed of 50 or more participants. Paraprofessionals, college, and graduate students enrolled in a group dynamics course, were employed as trainers. In addition to the post-test, there was a 6-week follow-up to determine the continuing effectiveness of training. Finally, an analysis of covariance was the statistical technique used to account for the initial group differences.

METHOD

Subjects

Ss were selected from a group of 527 students enrolled in a first semester introduction to psychology course at the University of Idaho during the 1971 academic year (Gilligan, 1973). They each received an abridged copy of the *NTL News Letter* entitled "Commonly Asked Questions about Sensitivity Training" (Seashore, 1968). A form was attached to the news letter with a Likert scale from 1 to 7 on which each student could indicate his level of desire to participate in a weekend sensitivity experience.

Students who circled numbers 1, 2, or 3 on the scale were considered to be nonvolunteers, i.e., they did not want sensitivity training. Those who circled numbers 5, 6, or 7 and also registered for a 24-hour weekend sensitivity experience were identified as the volunteers for this study.

Out of a total group of 527 students: 250 were nonvolunteers; 140 were volunteers; 137 students indicated a desire to participate in a T-Group but were not able to attend the actual training session and were by definition excluded from the experiment. Sixty students were randomly chosen from the volunteer group and 60 were likewise chosen from the nonvolunteer group to form the two groups under consideration.

Trainers for the groups were enrolled in a graduate group dynamics course and had previously experienced a common 40-hour sensitivity training program in addition to common theoretical training models described by Schein and Bennis (1965). The director of Psychological Services at the University of Idaho and two of his assistants under whom the training program was conducted were available during and after the session for consultation and help requested by trainers and participants.

Instrument

The Personal Orientation Inventory was developed by Everett Shostrom (1963) to meet the need for a comprehensive measure of values and behavior

TABLE 6.1
PRE-TEST PERSONAL ORIENTATION INVENTORY SCALES: MEANS,
STANDARD DEVIATIONS, AND t-RATIOS FOR NONVOLUNTEERS
$(N=55)$ AND VOLUNTEERS $(N=50)$

Personal Orientation Inventory Scales	Nonvolunteers		Volunteers		t
	M	SD	M	SD	$(df=103)$
Time Competence (TC)	15.45	2.69	15.78	2.96	.60
Inner-directedness (I)	76.53	9.16	82.60	10.90	3.10[2]
Self-actualizing Value (SAV)	18.95	2.52	19.82	2.22	1.88[1]
Existentiality (Ex)	18.07	3.68	21.04	4.25	3.99[3]
Feeling Reactivity (FR)	14.36	3.23	15.50	3.10	1.84[1]
Spontaneity (S)	11.11	2.84	12.58	2.30	2.90[3]
Self-regard (SR)	11.20	2.32	11.26	2.39	.13
Self-acceptance (SA)	13.67	2.83	14.74	4.01	1.57
Nature of Man (NC)	11.31	1.74	11.86	1.71	1.63
Synergy (Sy)	6.66	1.11	7.08	1.26	1.84[1]
Acceptance of Aggression (A)	15.02	3.06	15.84	3.52	1.28
Capacity for Intimate Contact (C)	15.86	2.88	17.32	3.68	2.28[1]

[1]$p<.05$, one-tail test.   [2]$p<.005$, one-tail test.   [3]$p<.001$, one-tail test.

believed to be important in studying self-actualization. Conceptually this inventory relates well to the overriding goal of sensitivity training as presented by its proponents (Schein & Bennis, 1965), namely, to increase the individual's personal growth level and self-actualization. Because of its conceptual relevance and applicability to sensitivity training it was chosen as a criterion for this study. Previous research (Cooper, 1971; Culbert, *et al.*, 1968; Foulds, 1970; Guinan & Foulds, 1970; Young & Jacobson, 1970) has demonstrated its ability to detect movement within a group receiving a self-actualization treatment such as sensitivity training.

The inventory has 150 two-choice paired-opposite statements of personal values, concepts and self percepts. Scores are reported for 12 scales (see Table 6.1) which assess personality characteristics commonly associated with positive development. However, the scale of Inner-directedness includes 123 of the 150 items and makes it the single most representative over-all measure of self-actualization (Knapp, 1965).

Procedure

In this study the inventory was administered to the volunteer and nonvolunteer groups 1 week prior to the training weekend, the Tuesday following the weekend, and again 6 weeks after the experimental treatment. All inventory responses were kept anonymous by using a code known only to the student.

A 24-hour sensitivity training weekend was designed for the 60 volunteers on the University campus. Six groups were formed by randomly assigning 5 males and 5 females to each group. Each group had two co-leaders, one male and one female, also randomly assigned to the group. All groups met separately following a common schedule for a period of 24 hours. After a

TABLE 6.2
POST-TEST PERSONAL ORIENTATION INVENTORY SCALES WITH ADJUSTED
MEANS, STANDARD DEVIATIONS, AND ANALYSIS OF COVARIANCE FOR
NONVOLUNTEERS ($N = 55$) AND VOLUNTEERS ($N = 50$)

Personal Orientation Inventory Scales	Nonvolunteers		Volunteers		t
	M	SD	M	SD	($df = 102$)
Time Competence (TC)	15.94	2.55	16.79	2.55	1.70[1]
Inner-directedness (I)	72.62	7.38	83.62	7.38	2.65[3]
Self-actualizing Value (SAV)	19.49	2.30	19.48	2.30	0.00
Existentiality (Ex)	19.61	2.84	20.13	2.84	0.79
Feeling Reactivity (FR)	14.49	2.23	15.58	2.23	2.48[2]
Spontaneity (S)	11.51	3.75	12.94	3.75	1.87[1]
Self-regard (SR)	11.72	2.04	11.94	2.04	.55
Self-acceptance (SA)	14.62	2.93	15.62	2.83	1.72[1]
Nature of Man (NC)	12.06	1.57	12.27	1.57	.69
Synergy (Sy)	6.70	1.14	6.81	1.14	.50
Acceptance of Aggression (A)	15.35	2.63	16.16	2.63	1.57
Capacity for Intimate Contact (C)	16.48	2.42	17.42	2.42	1.94[1]

[1]$p < .05$, one-tail test.   [2]$p < .01$, one-tail test.   [3]$p < .005$, one-tail test.

TABLE 6.3
FOLLOW-UP PERSONAL ORIENTATION INVENTORY SCALES WITH ADJUSTED
MEANS, STANDARD DEVIATIONS, AND ANALYSIS OF COVARIANCE FOR
NONVOLUNTEERS ($N = 53$) AND VOLUNTEERS ($N = 47$)

Personal Orientation Inventory Scales	Nonvolunteers		Volunteers		t
	M	SD	M	SD	($df = 102$)
Time Competence (TC)	16.22	2.43	16.30	2.43	.05
Inner-directedness (I)	82.16	7.79	85.36	7.79	1.95[1]
Self-actualizing Value (SAV)	19.94	2.26	20.22	2.26	.62
Existentiality (Ex)	19.97	3.65	21.24	3.65	1.62
Feeling Reactivity (FR)	14.85	2.45	15.62	2.45	1.53
Spontaneity (S)	12.21	2.18	12.58	2.18	.81
Self-regard (SR)	11.47	1.97	12.52	1.97	2.66[3]
Self-acceptance (SA)	15.25	3.16	16.18	3.16	1.45
Nature of Man (NC)	12.85	6.47	12.06	6.47	.59
Synergy (Sy)	6.87	1.17	7.20	1.17	1.37
Acceptance of Aggression (A)	15.64	2.60	16.72	2.60	2.04[2]
Capacity for Intimate Contact (C)	17.16	2.90	18.10	2.90	1.58

[1]$p < .05$, one-tail test.   [2]$p < .025$, one-tail test.   [3]$p < .01$, one-tail test.

brief introduction and assignment to groups the schedule was as follows·
Friday evening from 7:00 P.M. to 1:00 A.M.; Saturday from 9:00 A.M. to
12:30 P.M., in the afternoon from 1:30 P.M. to 5:00 P.M., and in the
evening from 7:00 P.M. to 1:00 A.M.; and Sunday from 1:00 P.M to 6:00
P.M.

Analysis of the Data

Loss of data (about 35 respondents) occurred due to incomplete
responses, improper identification, and absenteeism on the post· and follow-

up inventories. The results are based on the responses of an average of 31 male and 24 female nonvolunteers and 29 male and 21 female volunteers. Data were computer analyzed by the least squares analysis of covariance method (Harvey, 1960),[1] with the pretest as the covariate. It was hypothesized that volunteers would be more self-actualized prior to and as a function of sensitivity training in comparison to nonvolunteers who experienced no training. Given this directional hypothesis, a one-tail test with the significance level of .05 was used.

RESULTS

Initial differences in scores on Personal Orientation Inventory for nonvolunteers and volunteers for pretest were established by comparing the two groups. One-tail t tests indicated the appropriateness of a covariance analysis, since the volunteers had a significantly ($p<.005$) higher mean on the Inner-directedness scale. There were also differences ($p<.05$) on 6 of the 10 supporting sub-scales (Table 6.1).

Analysis of covariance disclosed significant changes ($p<.05$) in the predicted direction on 6 of the 12 scales for the post-test (Table 6.2), and on 3 of the 12 scales for the 6-week follow-up test (Table 6.3). One-tail t tests were obtained by taking the square root of the original F value (McNemar, 1969) and locating its appropriate significance level on a distribution of t table.

Volunteers appeared to change significantly ($p<.005$) in a positive direction on the post-test scale of Inner-directedness. The inventory's over-all scale of self-actualization is Inner-directedness (Knapp, 1965). This scale assesses one's level of self-support and tendencies to be more guided by internal motivations rather than external influences.

The significant complementary scales support the basic self-actualizing tendencies of the volunteer group. Time Competence refers to an individual's ability to live more fully in the present by integrating past experiences and future goals. Volunteers reported a greater sensitivity to their own needs and feelings (Fr); an increased freedom to react spontaneously with greater access to and expression of their feelings (S); greater self-acceptance in spite of weaknesses or deficiencies (Sa); an ability to develop intimate relationships with other human beings unencumbered by expectations and obligations (C).

The continuing effects of sensitivity training are shown in Table 6.3. Inner-directedness, the most comprehensive measure of self-actualization, was the only major scale significant ($p<.05$) after 6 weeks. Although other scales were not significant on the follow-up, two new complementary scales of self-acceptance and acceptance of aggression lend some support to the relatively

---

[1] A complete record of all analyses conducted in this study has been deposited with the American Society for Information Science. Order Document NAPS–02279 from Microfiche Publications, 305 East 46 Street, New York, N.Y. 10017. Remit $1.50 for microfiche or $13.10 for photocopy.

enduring effectiveness of the training group. Self-regard ($p < .025$) measures an individual's affirmation of personal worth or strength. Acceptance of Aggression ($p < .01$) assesses one's ability to accept one's natural aggressiveness as opposed to defensiveness, denial, and repression of aggression.

DISCUSSION

It appears from scores on the Inner-directedness scale that trainees develop somewhat increased self-support and rely less on environmental factors in giving meaning and direction to their lives. Training apparently helps its participants to say they are more guided by their own internal feelings, values and goals and less controlled by external influences. Their T-Group experience has perhaps given them better access to their feelings, increased self-acceptance and self-regard. Sensitivity training not only increased self-actualization, but its effects lasted at least 6 weeks.

The results are especially encouraging when one considers the number of participants and the limited theoretical and experiential background of the trainers. Control for trainer variables was limited to their course work and 40 hours of sensitivity training. An examination of trainer-trainee personality variables and training outcomes is also needed in order to construct groups that will be beneficial to each member.

The 24-hour weekend design seems to be an economical investment of an individual's time, but other designs must be explored. One wonders if a more structured or focused training design with "skillful" leaders would not greatly improve a participant's learning.

There are some differences between the post- and follow-up tests that should not be overlooked. The comparison of scores on the scale of Inner-directedness reached a lower significance level ($p < .05$) on follow-up than on post-test ($p < .005$). In addition, the four post-test scales of Feeling Reactivity, Spontaneity, Self-acceptance, and Capacity for Intimate Contact were not significant at follow-up. Finally, the appearance of Self-regard ($p < .01$) and Acceptance of Aggression ($p < .025$) on the follow-up raises the question as to what dynamics are at play if one were to rule out chance.

One possible explanation for such differences can be found in a study of the post- and follow-up means for both groups. There seems to be a marked increase in nonvolunteer group means from post-test to follow-up while the volunteer group means remained relatively constant or had some slight increases. Perhaps this sudden "improvement" by the nonvolunteer group can be attributed to an overfamiliarity or greater verbal acquiescence and insight into the nature of the testing instrument. This might result in a tendency to make their responses look good. Of course, it can be argued that the same thing is true for the volunteers, but individuals with high Self-regard ($p < .01$) just might not have a need to look good on a testing instrument. Whatever the explanation for the rise in nonvolunteers' scores, future designs should involve a control group who are initially comparable to the training group. It would be worthwhile to compare a group of students who volunteered for sensitivity training by randomly assigning them to a control or experimental setting.

REFERENCES

Broedel, J. W. Sensitivity training: what's it about? *Northwest Association of Secondary and Higher Schools Newsletter,* 1969, 2, 7-16.

Cooper, C. L. T-Group training and self-actualization. *Psychological Reports,* 1971, 26, 391-394.

Culbert, S. A., Clark, J. V., & Bobele, H. K. Measures of change toward self-actualization in two sensitivity training groups. *Journal of Counseling Psychology,* 1968, 15, 53-57.

Foulds, M. L. Effects of personal growth group on a measure of self-actualization. *Journal of Humanistic Psychology,* 1970, 10, 33-38.

Gilligan, J. F. Personality characteristics of selectors and nonselectors of sensitivity training. *Journal of Counseling Psychology,* 1973, 20, 265-268.

Golembiewski, R. T., & Blumberg, A. *Sensitivity training and the laboratory approach.* Itasca, Ill.: F. E. Peacock Publ., 1970.

Guinan, J. F., & Foulds, M. L. Marathon group: facilitator of personal growth. *Journal of Counseling Psychology,* 1970, 17, 145-149.

Harvey, W. Least-squares analyses of data with unequal subclass frequencies. *USDA Agricultural Research Service,* ARS 20-8, 1960.

Knapp, R. R. Relationship of a measure of self-actualization to neuroticism and extroversion. *Journal of Consulting Psychology,* 1965, 29, 168-172.

McNemar, Q. *Psychological statistics.* New York: Wiley, 1969.

Schein, E. H., & Bennis, W. G. *Personal and organizational change through group methods.* New York: Wiley, 1965.

Seashore, C. What is sensitivity training? *NTL Institute News and Reports,* 1968, 2.

Shostrom, E. *Manual, Personal Orientation Inventory.* San Diego: Educational & Industrial Testing Service, 1963.

Young, E. R., & Jacobson, L. I. Effects of time-extended marathon group experiences on personality characteristics. *Journal of Counseling Psychology,* 1970, 17, 249-251.

31. Some Effects of Trainers on Their Groups: A Partial Replication*

LEE BOLMAN

A previous study (Bolman, 1971a) reported relationships among a number of dimensions of trainer behavior, members' reaction to the trainer, group climate, and participant learning. Those data were obtained from 10 T-Groups, each with two trainers, in a basic human relations laboratory held at Bethel, Maine, in 1966. A major conclusion of that report was that congruence and empathy are the aspects of a trainer's behavior most critical to his effectiveness.

Hurley (1971) criticized the study on several methodological and substantive grounds, and this report provides additional data relevant to some of those criticisms. One criticism raised the possibility that the results were attributable to chance. This report indicates that most of the results do generalize to another sample. A second criticism suggested that Bolman overemphasized the trainer's congruence–empathy and underemphasized the extent to which the results were undergirded by the dimensions of self-acceptance and other-acceptance. This report shows that certain specific findings occur in both studies that could not be predicted from Hurley's view.

This report compares the results from Bolman's (1971a) study, referred to as *Study A,* with the results of a second study of trainer behavior, referred to as *Study B.* Study B was methodologically almost identical with Study A, and provides a check on the generality of the results reported earlier.

METHODOLOGY

Subjects and Setting

Study A obtained data from 109 participants in a two-week basic human relations laboratory program held at Bethel, Maine, in the summer of 1966. Study B obtained data from 59 participants in a one-week laboratory for business executives, also held in 1966. Further information on the characteristics of the Study A population can be found in Bolman (1971a); Bolman (1970) provides additional information on the participation in Study B.

* The author deeply appreciates the cooperation and help of participants and staff members in the two laboratories which provided the data for this report. John Hurley's suggestions and criticisms were of considerable help. The charming unpredictability of the time-sharing system at Carnegie-Mellon University made the data analysis considerably more challenging, and is gratefully acknowledged.

Reproduced by special permission from *Journal of Applied Behavioral Science,* Vol. 9, No. 4, "Some Effects of Trainers on Their Groups: A Partial Replication," Lee Bolman, pp. 534–539, 1973, NTL Institute for Applied Behavioral Science.

In both studies, the participants were divided into T-Groups consisting of approximately 12 members each. In Study A, each group had two trainers, a "senior" trainer who was a Fellow or associate of the NTL Institute for Applied Behavioral Science, and a "junior" trainer who was completing the

TABLE 6.4
VARIABLES USED IN STUDIES A AND B[1]

Trainer Behavior	Members' Reaction to Trainer	Group Climate	Member Learning
Affection Conceptual Input Conditionality Congruence-empathy Dominance Openness (Perceptiveness)	Discomfort with trainer (Identification with trainer) Liking for trainer	Tension Withdrawal	Own learning Others' learning (Peer-rated learning)

[1] Variables in parentheses were measured only in Study A. All other variables were measured in both studies.

TABLE 6.5
TRAINER BEHAVIOR AND MEMBERS' REACTION TO TRAINER

	Liking for Trainer		Discomfort with Trainer	
	Study A	Study B	Study A	Study B
Affection	.49[1]	.55[1]	—.10	—.32[1]
Conceptual Input	.06	.27	.02	—.06
Conditionality	.06	—.16	.33[1]	.59[1]
Congruence-Empathy	.47[1]	.58[1]	—.10	—.31[1]
Dominance	—.08	—.10	.18	.17
Openness	.01 [2]	.35[1]	—.20	.01

[1] Significant at .05 by two-tailed test.
[2] The difference between the correlations is significant at the .05 level.

TABLE 6.6
TRAINER BEHAVIOR, MEMBERS' REACTIONS TO
TRAINER, AND GROUP CLIMATE

	Tension		Withdrawal	
	Study A	Study B	Study A	Study B
Affection	.09 [2]	—.23	—.20	—.18
Conceptual Input	—.21[1]	—.16	—.17	.02
Conditionality	.24[1]	.35[1]	—.08 [2]	.26[1]
Congruence-Empathy	—.04 [2]	—.43[1]	—.18	—.26[1]
Dominance	.07	.16	—.17	—.03
Openness	—.22[1]	—.22	—.15	—.21
Identification with Trainer	—.01	——	.02	——
Discomfort with Trainer	.28[1]	.54[1]	—.04	.24
Liking for Trainer	.07 [2]	—.32[1]	—.29[1]	—.09

[1] Significant at .05 by two-tailed test.
[2] The difference between the correlations is significant at the .05 level.

NTL Applied Behavioral Science Intern Program. In Study B, each group had one trainer, an NTL Fellow with a national reputation.

Variables and Measures

The variables used in the two studies are listed in Table 6.4 (the conceptual meaning of each variable is discussed in Bolman, 1971a). All the measures were obtained from questionnaires filled out by participants: three times during the two-week Study A program; twice, during the one-week Study B program. Because of certain differences in the questionnaires, a few variables in Study A were not measured in Study B. In Study A, all variables were measured using factor scores. In Study B, variables analogous to the Study A factors were obtained by using items that had high loadings on the Study A factors.

Bolman's (1971a) report analyzed separately the within-group and between-group components of variance. The small number of groups in Study B made this impractical. In the current report, T-Group membership is ignored, and individuals are taken as the unit of analysis.

RESULTS

Tables 6.5, 6.6, and 6.7 present the major results, and indicate substantial consistency in the results of the two studies. In both studies the trainer behavior represented by the congruence–empathy measure (which combines trainer empathy, congruence, and personal security) are significantly related to liking for the trainer and perceptions of having learned from the experience. In both studies, trainer affection is related to liking for the trainer, but not to measures of learning. The fact that congruence–empathy is consistently related to learning, while trainer affection is not, contradicts Hurley's contention that both are simply

TABLE 6.7
TRAINER BEHAVIOR, MEMBERS' REACTION TO TRAINER,
AND MEMBER LEARNING

	Others' Learning		Own Learning	
	Study A	Study B	Study A	Study B
Affection	.15	.07	.05	.02
Conceptual Input	.18	.09	.15	.07
Conditionality	.09	—.09	.11	—.00
Congruence-Empathy	.35[1]	.28[1]	.29[1]	.27[1]
Dominance	.04 [2]	—.28[1]	—.05	—.16
Openness	—.09	.18	—.01	.01
Identification with Trainer	.21[1]	——	.23	——
Discomfort with Trainer	.12	—.14	.09	—.03
Liking for Trainer	.42[1] [2]	.02	.31[1] [2]	—.08

[1] Significant at .05 by two-tailed test.
[2] The difference between the correlations is significant at the .05 level.

manifestations of the trainer's acceptance of others. The results suggest that love is not enough, unless combined with empathy and congruence.

In both Study A and Study B, trainer conditionality (tendency to reward and punish group members) is related to discomfort with the trainer and to group tension, but it is *not* significantly related to learning measures. In both studies, trainer openness fails to show a hypothesized relationship with participant learning. A few hypothesized relationships which received scant support (or none at all) in Study A were more strongly supported in Study B, including: (a) a negative relationship between congruence–empathy and group tension; (b) a negative relationship between trainer openness and tension; (c) a positive relationship between trainer openness and liking for the trainer. On the other hand, Study B fails to confirm a positive relationship found in Study A between liking for the trainer and learning.

Most of the results accord with available theory and data, but one is controversial. In both of the studies reported here, no direct relationship was found between trainer openness (a measure of trainer self-disclosure) and participant learning. Culbert (1968) reported that higher openness produced greater learning in the early phases of a T-Group. Culbert's study has an advantage in that his measures were much more thoroughly validated than those reported here, but his study included only two T-Groups. Culbert attempted to make the groups as equivalent as possible, but it is still entirely possible that observed differences between the groups resulted from variables other than trainer self-disclosure (e.g., differences in group composition, unique events in one or the other group, interaction between trainer personality and the effort to be more or less self-disclosing, and so on).

Hurley and Force (1971) report a correlation between participant ratings of trainer effectiveness and a measure of trainer self-disclosure, but their self-disclosure measure has a distinctly evaluative tone and includes many aspects of personality or behavior (e.g., rigidity, inhibition, defensiveness, concern for others' feelings) which are conceptually distinct from self-disclosure. Bolman (1971b) hypothesized an interaction between self-disclosure and

TABLE 6.8

MEAN LEVELS OF SELF-RATED LEARNING UNDER CONDITIONS OF HIGH OR LOW CONGRUENCE-EMPATHY AND OPENNESS[1]

		Congruence-Empathy	
		Low	High
Openness	Low	115 (N = 3)	116 (N = 2)
	High	113 (N = 2)	126 (N = 3)

[1] Study A T-Groups were dichotomized into high and low groups along the dimensions of congruence-empathy and openness. The N in each cell refers to the number of groups. No statistical analysis was undertaken because of the very small sample size.

empathy, such that greater self-disclosure facilitates participant learning only when the trainer is also in touch with his impact on participants. Data presented in Table 6.8 provide some support to this hypothesis, although they are inadequate for a real test because of the small sample size. Those data suggest that the level of trainer congruence–empathy makes little difference in participant learning when trainer openness is low, but makes a substantial difference when openness is high. The two groups which saw their trainers as high on openness but low on congruence–empathy reported lower levels of learning than groups in any other condition, whereas the groups which saw their trainers as high on both these dimensions reported higher levels of learning. The reliability of that result is unknown, but it is consistent with Anderson's (1968) study of psychotherapists. He found that "confrontation" by therapists who provided high levels of "facilitating conditions" (empathy, unconditional positive regard, genuineness, self-disclosure) usually resulted in increased patient self-exploration, whereas confrontation by therapists who provided low levels of facilitating conditions never produced increased self-exploration. (In his sample, Anderson found that the therapists who provided high levels of facilitating conditions also did most of the confronting.)

SUMMARY

A partial replication of Bolman's (1971a) study of the effects of trainers on T-Groups shows that the major results of that study generalize to a distinctly different laboratory setting and population. Since the validity of many of the measures is not well established, further research using alternative methodologies is needed to determine the extent to which the results reported here are method-specific.

REFERENCES

Anderson, S. C. Effects of confrontation by high- and low-functioning therapists. *Journal of Counseling Psychology,* 1968, *15,* 411–416.

Bolman, L. Laboratory vs. lecture in training executives. *Journal of Applied Behavioral Science,* 1970, *6,* 323–335.

Bolman, L. Some effects of trainers on their T-Groups. *Journal of Applied Behavioral Science,* 1971, *7,* 309–325 (a).

Bolman, L. Point by point: Reply to Hurley. *Journal of Applied Behavioral Science,* 1971, *7,* 649–651 (b).

Culbert, S. A. Trainer self-disclosure and member growth in two T-Groups. *Journal of Applied Behavioral Science,* 1968, *4,* 47–73.

Hurley, J. R. The neglected effects of trainers on T-Groups. *Journal of Applied Behavioral Science,* 1971, *7,* 647–649.

Hurley, J. R., & Force, E. J. Interpersonal competence in T-Groups: A multiobserver-multimethod assessment. Unpublished manuscript, Department of Psychology, Michigan State University, 1971.

32. Encounter Groups: Their Effect on Rigidity

RICHARD T. HOERL

INTRODUCTION

The problem of rigidity has been the focus of much research. Adorno (1950) speaks of the authoritarian personality, while Rokeach (1960) writes about the open and closed mind. Gough (1964) states that individuals who are rigid in their behavioral patterns, that is, inflexibly fixed or set in their opinions and conduct, often seem trapped in their own rigidity, and also sometimes tend to be intolerant and judgmental of any opinions or behavioral patterns other than their own.

The question could then be asked: Is there some possible way for individuals who tend to be rigid, to become more flexible and tolerant of others? Otto and Mann (1968) found that there is a growing interest in designing methods that will aid in the movement towards flexibility. Bennis (1962) mentions that individuals need practice and positive reinforcement for such behaviors; he suggests that an encounter group may be an excellent crucible for attempting new behaviors. Rogers (1967) describes an encounter group as a place where an atmosphere is set which encourages one to drop his defenses and facades and deal more openly with others. He further states that the climate of openness, trust and acceptance in an encounter group, allows a person to express his beliefs knowing he won't be judged. Through the group experience the rigid individual is then freed from fear and distrust, and feels comfortable in opening himself to new learning. In a climate of trust, an individual can not only receive feedback from others concerning the impact he has on them, but group members can also aid one another in testing basic assumptions.

One other aspect of encounter groups that may help to optimize the rigid individual's learning is the ambiguity of the encounter group situation itself. When the leader does not "lead" there is an absence of stable criteria for judging the rightness of transactions. As alternative belief systems emerge, the rigid individual may experience the group giving positive reinforcement for tolerance of differing belief systems. The rigid individual may himself be reinforced in the group for attempting to understand other belief systems and ways of behavior.

Brochures describing encounter groups often indicate that movements toward greater personal freedom, flexibility, and tolerance of others, are

Reprinted from *Human Relations*, Vol. 27, No. 5, pp. 431–438.

inherent in the group encounter. It was this hypothesis which was tested. Is the encounter group a useful vehicle for aiding individuals in a movement from rigidity toward flexibility and greater tolerance of ambiguity?

METHOD

The hypothesis is stated: The mean scores on the Flexibility and Tolerance of Ambiguity scales of the California Psychological Inventory (CPI) will increase significantly following encounter group training.

Setting

The setting was a three week encounter group session sponsored by the Center for the Studies of the Person (CSP), on the campus of the University of California, San Diego.

Population

The population consisted of 162 persons who applied for encounter sessions sponsored by the CSP. Since first preference for admission to the program is given to those in the "helping" professions, the population generally consisted of teachers, psychologists, guidance counselors, clergymen, and social workers. All had a college education.

From this population, encounter groups consisting of 12 persons in a group, are established on the basis of maximum heterogeneity. Therefore each encounter group has, as closely as possible, an equal distribution of men and women, and an equal mean age and educational level.

Of the 162 persons involved in the encounter training, 112 volunteered to participate in the study. Of the 112 volunteers, 62 attended the encounter sessions from June 24-July 14, 1969. The remaining 50 attended encounter sessions from July 22-August 11.

For experimental purposes, a typical classroom group of professional people, not attending encounter groups, was added to the study. They were taking a course at the University of California, San Diego, entitled 'The Education and Guidance of Children with Learning Difficulties.' The class was composed of 26 active teachers and guidance counselors, all doing post BA work, and ranging in age from 22 to 52 years old.

Design

The basic design for this study was the Solomon Four-Group Design. The classroom group was added for research purposes. The design is as follows:

Group	Pre-Test	Independent Variable	Post-Test
A	41	encounter group	41
B	30	no encounter group	30
C		encounter group	21
D		no encounter group	20
E	26	lecture	22

Group A was composed of the first 41 participants to arrive for the opening session on June 24, 1969. They took the pre-test before any of the sessions began, received three weeks of encounter group training, and took a post-test on July 14, 1969.

Group B, a control group, was composed of 30 subjects who attended the second session. They were mailed a pre-test on June 19, and were asked to return it as close to June 24 as possible. They received no training, since they were at home during this period, but received a post-test when they arrived for the opening of the second session on July 22.

Group C, a control group, was composed of the remaining 21 participants in session one who either did not take the pre-test at the opening session on June 24, or refused to become involved in the testing. They received training, and agreed to take the post-test on July 14.

Group D, a control group, was composed of 29 persons who were not mailed a pre-test, received no training, but received a post-test when they arrived on July 22 for the second session.

Group E, the class group, took a pre-test on June 25. On July 7 they received a lecture on the value of being flexible, and on July 16 they took a post-test.

Instrument

The full CPI was administered on both pre- and post-tests, but only the Flexibility and the Tolerance of Ambiguity scales were scored. The purpose of the flexibility scale is to indicate the degree of flexibility and adaptability of a person's thinking and social behavior. The purpose of the tolerance scale is to identify persons with permissive, accepting, and non-judgmental social beliefs and attitudes.

RESULTS AND DISCUSSION

The two scales were analyzed separately.

Tolerance of Ambiguity

The data from groups A, B, C, D were analyzed using a 2 x 2 analysis of variance for unequal N's. There was no statistically significant difference due to either pre-test ($F = 1.29$) or the treatment effect ($F = 1.62$).

However, when the three pre-test groups were considered (A, the encounter group; B, the no encounter group; E, the classroom lecture group) analysis of covariance showed a statistically significant treatment effect at the .01 level ($F = 8.55$, $df = 2$). The comparison test, as given by Winer (1962, p. 100) showed that there was a statistical difference at the .01 level between groups A and E, and groups B and E. There was no statistical difference between groups A and B. Since groups A and B had volunteered for encounter group training, and group E did not, it can be demonstrated statistically, that the treatment effect is probably due to the volunteering factor (difference between A, B vs. E) rather than the effect of the encounter group (difference between A and B).

For those that volunteer (groups A and B) it seems to make little difference whether they receive encounter group training or not. It can be seen then, that the significance of the treatment effect depends more on who goes (volunteers vs. non-volunteers) rather than what happens (lecture vs. encounter group). This can be seen in even greater contrast when investigating flexibility scores.

Flexibility

Groups A, B, C, D were likewise analyzed using a 2 x 2 analysis of variance for unequal N's. There was no statistical difference due to the pre-test. There was a significant treatment effect at the .05 level ($F = 4.94$, $df = 1$). There was a significant interaction effect at the .01 level ($F = 8.80$, $df = 1$).

Analysis of covariance for groups A and B was used to investigate the interaction effect. Results showed there was no significant difference in treatment effect ($F = .018$, $df = 1$). There was likewise no significant treatment effect when groups A, B, E were investigated using analysis of covariance ($F = 2.40$, $df = 2$).

The significance of the interaction effect was further investigated using the mean scores on the flexibility scale.

The significance of the interaction effect listed above can be directly attributed to the difference between the post-test mean scores of control group B (13.40) and control group C (16.33). The difference between the post-test means for these two control groups was found to be statistically significant at the .05 level of confidence (t test). The post-test for group A as compared with group B approached significance. One might therefore be tempted to say that those with encounter group experience (groups A and C) are more flexible; however, group D, having no encounter group experience and having similar post-test scores to groups A and C, would not support this proposition.

Two reasons may account for group C's higher post-test as compared with group A. The first reason may be the effect of the pre-test; this has been ruled out. The second reason may be that those who arrived early for the testing, were given the pre-test and they by that process, became group A. Their coming early may show that they are more methodical and bound to the tradition of being on time. Those in group C were the individuals who came later or refused to take the pre-test; this may show that they are more assertive and less deferential toward authority. It can be seen, then, that there may be a bias in the way groups A and C were made up. This could have caused the significant difference in post-test scores between groups A and C,

TABLE 6.9
MEAN SCORES ON FLEXIBILITY SCALE

Group	Pre-Test	Treatment	Post-Test
A	14.92	encounter group	15.34
B	14.33	no encounter group	13.40
C		encounter group	16.33
D		no encounter group	15.25
E	11.12	lecture	10.14
National norm			9.00

and thus could be the reason for the significance of the interaction effect mentioned earlier.

One other aspect of this research is of significance. Upon investigating mean scores shown in Table 6.9, it can be seen by using the comparison test given by Winer (1962, p. 100) that there is a significant difference at the .01 level between all those involved in encounter groups (all volunteers) and both the class group and the national norm (non encounter group volunteers.) This seems to point to the fact that people entering encounter groups may be self-selective; that is, people who are already more flexible are the people likely to come to an encounter group. This then, seems to account for the significant difference between: (1) those signed up for encounter groups and (2) both the class group and the national norm, thus verifying the findings of Sutton (1968).

As mentioned above, there is a significant difference between the national norm on the one hand, and any of the encounter groups on the other hand, on both the pre- and the post-test scores. Therefore another reason why there may not have been significant changes between the pre- and post-test scores may be due to the relatively high initial mean scores, and the fact that there are only 22 items on the Flexibility scale, thus making it more difficult to obtain a significant change.

SUMMARY

The mean scores of the Flexibility and Tolerance of Ambiguity scales of the CPI did not increase significantly following encounter group training.

Two reasons may account for this lack of change. First, because of the relatively high initial scores of the encounter group people, it was more difficult to effect significant statistical change. This fact bears directly on the second and most important reason for the lack of change. All those volunteering for encounter group sessions, because of their high scores, seemed to be a self-selected sampling; that is, statistically they were already more flexible (at the .01 level) than either the class group or the national norm, thus pointing to the fact that people who are already more flexible seem to be the people who choose to come to encounter groups.

Although little has been written on this topic, group workers are beginning to speak about the emergence of "The Grouper." This is a person who attends encounter groups on a somewhat regular basis. In this study, all those who enrolled for encounter sessions were tested, including those who had participated in groups before. A suggestion for further research is to test only those who have had no previous encounter group experience.

In answering the question: "Is there some way for individuals who tend to be rigid, to become more flexible?" it must be said that although the encounter group showed no statistical change, nevertheless the encounter group is still not to be ruled out. This study shows that people who are already more flexible seem to be attending encounter groups (and are, perhaps, getting reinforced for their flexibility). Perhaps the people who could profit most from encounter groups, are the individuals who are not attending them.

REFERENCES

Adorno, T., *et al. The authoritarian personality.* New York: Harper & Brothers, 1950.

Bennis, W. Goals and meta-goals of laboratory training. *Human relations training news,* 1962, *6* (3), 1–4.

Gough, H. *California psychological inventory manual.* Palo Alto: Consulting Psychologists Press, 1964.

Otto, H. & Mann, J. *Ways of growth: approaches to expanding awareness.* New York: Grossman, 1968.

Rogers, C. A Plan for Self-Directed Change in an Educational System. Draft manuscript, Western Behavioral Sciences Institute, La Jolla, California, 1967.

Rokeach, M. *The open and closed mind.* New York: Basic Books Inc., 1960.

Sutton, R. Relationship between change in student perceptions of teachers and sensitivity training of teachers. Unpublished doctoral dissertation, USIU, 1968.

Winer, B. *Statistical principles in experimental design.* New York: McGraw-Hill, 1962.

33. Group Composition and Changes in Self-Actualization in T-Groups

PETER B. SMITH and MICHAEL J. LINTON

INTRODUCTION

Attempts to assess the outcomes of T-Group training are beginning to move beyond the use of open-ended descriptive measures (Campbell & Dunnette, 1968; Cooper & Mangham, 1971; Smith, in press). The use of more precisely delimited instruments, measuring attributes related to the goals of the T-Group, offers much greater potentiality of clarifying the change processes at work in such groups. One instrument widely used in recent years has been Shostrom's (1966) Personal Orientation Inventory (POI), which purports to measure self-actualization. Increased scores on some of its scales following sensitivity training have been reported among university students (Foulds, 1970, 1971; Guinan & Foulds, 1970), high school students (Alperson et al., 1971) and educators (Khanna, 1971). In each case control subjects did not show equivalent increases. A number of further studies have detected increases on POI scales after group experience, but these have occurred equally among untrained controls (Sherrill, 1973; Jeffers, 1972; Treppa & Fricke, 1972). The research to date using POI suggests that increased scores are a fairly dependable effect of sensitivity training, but limitations in the research designs employed leaves open the possibility that such effects may be due to test-sensitization or other extraneous causes.

One method for testing the linkage of increased self-actualization to the T-Group experience is to explore the relation between increased scores and group composition. If significant relations are found between group composition and increased POI scores, this raises the likelihood that such increases are a genuine effect of the experience. This approach has been utilized by Reddy (1972a, b) who examined the effect of variations in group composition. Group composition was assessed through the use of Schutz's (1958) FIRO-B. This questionnaire yields for each of a number of need areas, an originator score and an interchange score. The originator score reflects the subject's wish to initiate rather than to receive behavior in a given need area. The interchange score reflects the degree to which the subject prefers his relations with others to be focussed on a given need area. In his first study Reddy found that, among naturally occurring T-Groups,

Reprinted by permission from *Human Relations*, Vol. 28, No. 9, pp. 811–823.

members whose affection interchange scores differed from the rest of their group showed most change on POI. In his second study, he showed that two T-Groups deliberately composed with a wide range of affection interchange scores achieved more change than did two other groups homogeneously composed.

The present paper provides a further test of the relationship between FIRO-B composition and increase in POI. Three T-Groups were composed optimally for control scores and non-optimally for affection scores; three T-Groups were composed optimally for affection scores and non-optimally for control scores; and the remaining four groups were composed optimally for both criteria. The notion of optimal composition was derived from the work of Harrison & Lubin (1965). Harrison & Lubin postulated that the optimal T-Group composition would be one in which members experienced both some support and some confrontation. The support is seen as providing the security necessary for the participant to express himself freely, while the confrontation provides impetus for change. Reddy's data provide some evidence in favor of the Harrison & Lubin model, as do the studies by Pollack (1971) and Smith (1974) which used different criteria of change. In the present study it was anticipated that control behaviors in the T-Group had a potential equal to affection behaviors for generating support and confrontation.

Optimal composition was defined as that encouraging both support and confrontation in the group. On the affection scale, Reddy's use of interchange scores was adopted. Groups composed optimally on affection were defined as those in which all members' scores were equally distributed from high to low. Non-optimally composed groups were defined as those in which all members' scores fell in the median third. One would expect that the non-optimal groups would score high on support but not on confrontation, since everyone in these groups is relatively similar to one another. On the other hand, the optimal groups should score high on both support and on confrontation, since there are some members within each group who are similar and others who are dissimilar.

Control originator scores are among the most successful predictors of behavior from the FIRO-B (Schutz, 1958; Borg, 1960; Smith, 1974). Whereas with affection behavior the reciprocity of an interchange is often crucial, in the control area the issue of who initiates behavior is frequently more salient. On the control scale the use of originator scores was therefore preferred. Optimally composed groups on control were defined as those on which members' scores were equally distributed from high to low. Non-optimally composed groups were those on which all members' scores fell in the median third. As with affection scales it was expected that the non-optimal groups would achieve support but no confrontation, while the optimal groups should achieve both support and confrontation.

METHOD

The study was conducted on a five-day ten group sensitivity training laboratory which formed part of the M.B.A. program at Cranfield Institute of Technology. Participation in the laboratory was voluntary, but the laboratory had been held annually for a number of years, and it was customary for most if not all students to attend. All but two of the 88 participants were men. The laboratory was held on the college campus, which is in a rural setting, and took place in January 1972, three months after the students commenced their program. Copies of FIRO-B were completed by participants and trainers several weeks before the laboratory. Proposed group compositions were presented to the trainers at their planning meetings and accepted by them. Trainers were assigned to groups in such a manner as to satisfy as far as possible the criteria which had been used in assigning participants. Neither participants nor trainers were aware of the basis of group composition or the hypotheses until data collection was complete. The trainer group adhered to a wide variety of training styles, ranging from some who worked within the Tavistock tradition to others who fell within the NTL tradition (Klein & Astrachan, 1971). The Tavistock-style leader tends to remain separate from the group and to interpret what he sees, while the NTL-style leader tends to adopt a much more member-like position. Partly because of the range of trainer orientations and partly because of the sheer size of the trainer group some difficulty was experienced in finalizing a design for the week's program. Ultimately a design was agreed by the trainers which included some emphasis on both interpersonal and intergroup phenomena. Total training time during the laboratory was about 35 hours. The POI was completed by participants on the first day of the

TABLE 6.10

DISTRIBUTION OF FIRO-B SCORES IN GROUPS OF EACH COMPOSITIONAL TYPE

Group No.	Compositional type	Control scale scores			Affection scale scores			No. in group
		H	M	L	H	M	L	
	Optimal for control:							
2		3[1]	3	4	0	10[1]	0	10
7		4[1]	2	4	0	10[1]	0	10
9		3	2	5[1]	0	9	1[1]	10
	Optimal for affection:							
4		0	10[1]	0	3	2[1]	5	10
5		0	9	1[1]	3	3[1]	4	10
8		0	10[1]	0	3	2[1]	5	10
	Optimal for both scales:							
1		4	3[1]	4[1]	4[1]	3[1]	4	11
3		4	2	4[1]	4[1]	2	4	10
6		6[1]	1	3	4	1	5[1]	10
10		4	3[1]	3	3	3[1]	4	10

[1] Indicates subtotals in which trainer's score is included. Group 1 had two trainers.

laboratory and again on the final day. Participants also completed ratings describing themselves and others at the close of the laboratory.

In order to determine cut-off points for use in composing the groups, all FIRO-B scores were arrayed and divided into equal thirds. This procedure indicated that on the control originator scale, scores of +3 to +9 were high, −1 to +2 were medium, and −2 to −9 were low. On the affection interchange scale scores of 9 to 18 were high, 3 to 8 were medium and 0 to 2 were low. The actual distribution of FIRO-B scores in each of the groups is given in Table 6.10.

RESULTS

Seventy-seven complete sets of data were obtained due to non-completion of forms by a few subjects at each testing. Overall changes in the mean scores on the POI are shown in Table 6.11. It can be seen that significant changes were obtained in this sample on five of the twelve POI scales. The magnitude of the changes is somewhat smaller than that reported in other studies. The most closely comparable data to have been published are those of Cooper (1971) who studied English managers in one week T-Groups. Both samples agree in finding significant increases on "Inner directedness," "Existentiality," and "Feeling reactivity." Cooper also found changes on "Acceptance of Aggression" and "Spontaneity" whereas the present sample did not change on these dimensions, but did increase on "Nature of Man" and on "Self Acceptance."

Before comparing the incidence of POI change in the groups of various compositions one needs to check on the degree to which the different groups' scores on POI diverged from one another at the beginning of the week. Table

TABLE 6.11
OVERALL CHANGES IN THE POI

Scale	Mean pre-score	Mean post-score	Significance of change[1]
Time competence	16.3	16.7	ns
Inner directedness	82.4	86.0	.001
Self-actualizing values	19.3	19.2	ns
Existentiality	20.9	22.4	.001
Feeling reactivity	15.3	15.9	.05
Spontaneity	11.5	12.1	ns
Self-regard	11.9	11.9	ns
Self acceptance	15.9	16.7	.05
Nature of man	11.1	11.7	.01
Synergy	6.9	7.1	ns
Acceptance of aggression	16.5	16.3	ns
Capacity for intimate contact	17.1	17.7	ns

[1] Significances are 2-tailed values of P based on t tests.

TABLE 6.12
INITIAL POI SCORES AND CHANGES DURING THE WEEK

Scale	Groups optimal for control		Groups optimal for affection		Groups optimal for both	
	Initial score	change	Initial score	change	Initial score	change
Time competence	16.8	+0.2	16.1	+0.7	16.1	+0.4
Inner directedness	84.7	+1.9	82.2	+5.3[2]	81.3	+3.3[2]
Self-actualizing values	19.5	−0.5	19.3	−0.1	19.1	+0.1
Existentiality	21.3	+1.4[2]	21.2	+1.2	20.5	+1.6[3]
Feeling reactivity	16.1	−0.7	15.6	+1.0[3]	14.6	+1.0[3]
Spontaneity	12.2	+0.3	10.6	+0.8	11.7	+0.5
Self regard	12.4	−0.7	10.9	+0.8	12.3	−0.1
Self acceptance	17.0	−0.1	16.2	+1.6	14.9	+0.8
Nature of man	10.7	+0.6[3]	11.7	+0.3	11.0	+0.8[1]
Synergy	6.8	+0.4	7.1	−0.1	6.8	+0.3
Acceptance of aggression	17.9	−0.7	15.7	+0.9	16.1	−0.5
Capacity for intimate contact	17.9	0.0	17.3	+1.0	16.5	+0.7

[1]$p<0.01$; [2]$p<0.02$; [3]$p<0.05$; 2-tailed probabilities
Values of N: Control—20; Affection—23; Both—34

6.12 indicates that the initial POI scores of the different experimental conditions mostly did not differ greatly from one another. This is an important point to clarify since if initial differences in POI scores were found, any subsequent differences in amount of change found in the different experimental conditions might be attributable to regression effects. Three of the possible thirty-six comparisons between initial POI scores do in fact show significant differences. The groups composed optimally for control behaviors were higher than those optimal for affection on spontaneity ($P<.0.05$) and on acceptance of aggression ($P< 0.02$); they were also higher than groups optimal for both FIRO-B scales on self-acceptance. Thus the initial POI scores of the three experimental conditions do not differ significantly from one another on nine scales. On the remaining three scales differences do occur and any changes found on these three scales during the week would need to be examined for evidence as to whether or not they were due to regression effects.

There are a number of problems in determining the appropriate procedure for testing for change in POI. In Table 6.11 the procedure adopted was the same as that used by previous researchers, namely the use of a separate "t" test for each of the twelve POI scales. Strictly speaking this procedure is not legitimate, insofar as many of the items on the POI are scored on more than one of the scales. This means that the scores obtained by a subject on each of the subscales are not independent. If an increase is obtained on one scale the probability of obtaining changes on other scales also is enhanced. POI has two major scales, Time Competence and Inner directedness, which together comprise all of the items. The remaining ten subscales also together comprise all of the items. This one valid procedure would be to test for change only on the two major scales. This has the disadvantage that the inner directedness scale comprises items of considerable diversity. Much information is discarded by treating it as a single scale. A second alternative is to test for changes only the ten subscales. For the reader's convenience in comparing the results with those of other workers, significance tests are in fact presented for all twelve scales, but it should be born in mind that this procedure tends to exaggerate the significance of the changes found.

Table 6.12 shows the amount of change occurring on each of the POI scales in groups of each type of composition. It will be seen that groups composed optimally for the control scale showed significant increases on the "existentiality" and the "nature of man" subscales of POI. Groups composed optimally for the affection scale showed significant increases on "inner-directedness" and "feeling reactivity." Groups composed optimally for both scales showed significant increase on "inner-directedness," "existentiality," "feeling reactivity" and "nature of man." These results suggest a simple additive effect of composition on each of the FIRO-B scales. Optimal composition on either scale yielded two significant changes, while groups optimal for both scales yielded four significant changes. These four changes were on the same POI subscales which changed in the other conditions. None of the four subscales on which changes were found was the same as the subscales on which pretest differences between conditions occurred. The changes obtained are therefore not explicable as regression effects.

Examination of the change scores shown in Table 6.12 indicates that in addition to the significant changes detected there was a general tendency for scores in the affection groups to rise. This was less marked in the groups composed optimally for control, which showed a tendency toward decreased scores on three of the subscales. Tests of the significance of the difference in changes between experimental conditions showed most differences to be nonsignificant. However, the groups composed optimally for control did show significantly less increase on feeling reactivity than affection groups ($P < 0.01$) or "both" groups ($P < 0.02$). They also showed less increase on self-regard than the affection groups ($P < 0.05$).

DISCUSSION

The differences in changes on POI found between groups differently composed are thus somewhat modest. The effects of composition appear to be that a particular composition enhances certain changes and depresses others, rather than that different compositions generate radically different outcomes.

The changes found in the different types of group may be expected to reflect their differing compositional basis. Groups optimal for control showed most increase on the "existentiality" and "nature of man" scales. These changes imply that trainees became more willing to respond to the needs of a situation flexibly rather than in a stereotyped manner and that they took a more constructive view of the nature of man. It will be recalled that groups optimal for control were composed in a manner intended to provide some confrontation on control issues. The changes found suggest that whatever conflict arose in these groups had a satisfactory outcome rather than a frustrating one. The changes found in groups composed optimally for affection have a somewhat different flavor. The principal increases were in "inner directedness" and "feeling reactivity" and there was also more increase in self-regard than in the other groups. In the affection groups it appears that members became more reactive to their own feelings, felt more favorably about themselves and were likely to take their own decisions rather than following the lead of others. The groups composed optimally for affection contained members with a wide range of needs for affection. The changes found nonetheless suggest that these groups attained a warmer more accepting climate than did the control-oriented groups. No systematic data is available on what did occur in each of the types of groups, but this examination of the differences found in POI changes suggests that the effect of the compositional manipulation may be to focus the attention of each group on the area which initially causes it problems.

The findings of this study provide additional support for the view that group composition does have a measurable effect on T-Group outcomes and that this effect may be controlled by the trainer if he so wishes. The amount of effect of group composition is likely to be underestimated by the present study since it included no condition in which the groups were poorly composed on both criteria. The conditions under which it should be most fruitful for trainers to attempt to control group composition will be those where there are large, heterogeneous, populations of trainees who are initially strangers. Where prior organizational linkages exist, the effect of long standing role expectations and organizational history is very likely to outweigh the effect of the personality predispositions assessed by FIRO-B. Where populations are small or homogeneous it is likely to be impossible to create groups of a specified composition simply because there will be an insufficient number of participants scoring at one or other point on the scales.

Group composition did affect group outcome despite the wide diversity of trainers working on this program. Some people would argue that one of the essential skills of a group trainer lies in his ability to adapt his approach to the particular needs and composition of his group and this clearly does occur to some extent. But the author's impression is that there remain large and consistent differences between trainers working within different training traditions (see also Lieberman et al., 1973). There are two possible reasons why one might nonetheless successfully predict group outcome regardless of trainer orientation. One possibility is that whether a particular trainer worked within the Tavistock tradition or within the NTL tradition had little effect on the way his group developed. The second possibility is that trainer style did have an effect, but that this effect augmented rather than obliterated the effects of differing composition. Since trainers were assigned to T-Groups on the basis of their FIRO-B scores, this could easily have occurred if there was a correlation between a trainer's FIRO-B score and his training style. It will not become possible to clarify the interplay between trainer behavior and group composition more fully until studies become available in which both variables are varied independently.

It was suggested in the introduction to this paper that some uncertainty surrounds the use of POI as a criterion measure of change after sensitivity training. Some results have suggested that changed POI responses may be due to test-sensitization effects rather than to genuine training effects. The present results do not support this criticism of the validity of POI. Since different effects were obtained within groups of different composition, the changes found must be attributed to composition rather than to sensitization effects which should be equally operative in all conditions. Further use of POI as a criterion of change should explore its sensitivity to variations in training design and the persistence of the effects detected by it.

REFERENCES

Alperson, B. L., Alperson, E. D. & Levine, R. (1971). Growth effects of high school marathons. *Experimental publication system, American Psychological Association (Feb.), 10.*

Borg, W. R. (1960). The prediction of role behavior in small groups from personality variables. *J. Abnorm. Soc. Psychol., 60:* 112–117.

Campbell, J. P. & Dunnette, M. D. (1968). The effectiveness of T-Group experiences in managerial training and development. *Psychol. Bull. 70:* 73–104.

Cooper, C. L. (1971). T-Group training and self-actualization. *Psychol. Reports, 28:* 391–394.

Cooper, C. L. & Mangham, I. L. (eds.) (1971). *T-Groups: a survey of research.* Chichester, England: Wiley.

Foulds, M. L. (1970). The effects of a personal growth group on a measure of self-actualization. *J. Humanistic Psychol., 10:* 33–38.

Foulds, M. L. (1971). Measured changes in self-actualization as a result of a growth group experience. *Psychotherapy, 8:* 338–341.

Guinan, J. F. & Foulds, M. L. (1970). Marathon group: facilitator of personal growth? *J. Couns. Psychol., 17:* 145–149.

Harrison, R. & Lubin, B. (1965). Personal style, group composition and learning. *J. Appl. Beh. Sci., 1:* 286–301.

Jeffers, J. J. L. (1972). The effects of marathon encounter groups on personality characteristics of group members and group facilitators. *Dissertation Abstracts, 32:* 7A, 4153.

Khanna, J. L. (1971). Training of educators for hard-core areas—a success? Paper presented at the 17th Congress, International Association of Applied Psychology, Liege.

Klein, E. B. & Astrachan, B. M. (1971). Learning in groups: a comparison of study groups and T-Groups. *J. Appl. Beh. Sci., 7:* 659-683.

Lieberman, M. A., Yalom, I. D. & Miles, M. B. (1973). *Encounter groups: First Facts.* New York: Basic Books.

Pollack, H. B. (1971). Change in homogeneous and heterogeneous sensitivity training groups. *J. Cons. & Clin. Psychol., 37:* 60-66.

Reddy, W. B. (1972a). On affection, group composition and self-actualization in sensitivity training. *J. Cons. & Clin. Psychol., 38:* 211-214.

Reddy, W. B. (1972b). Interpersonal compatibility and self-actualization in sensitivity training. *J. Appl. Beh. Sci., 8:* 237-240.

Schutz, W. C. (1958). FIRO: *a three dimensional theory of interpersonal behavior.* New York: Rinehart.

Sherrill, J. D. (1973). The effects of group experience on the personal-vocational development of vocationally undecided college students. *Dissertation Abstracts, 34:* 2A, 573.

Shostrom, E. L. (1966). *The Personal Orientation Inventory: an Inventory for the measurement of self-actualization.* San Diego: Educational and Industrial Testing Service.

Smith P. B. (1974). Group composition as a determinant of Kelman's social influence modes. *Europ. J. Soc. Psychol., 4.*

Smith, P. B. (in press). Controlled studies of the outcome of sensitivity training. *Psychol. Bull.*

Treppa, J. A. & Fricke, L. (1972). Effects of a marathon group experience. *J. Couns. Psychol., 19:* 466-467.

34. The Impact of Marathon Encounters on Teacher-Student Relationships

CARY L. COOPER

Increasingly various participation-based methods of small group training (i.e., T-Group, encounter groups, etc.) are being used in industry, the civil service, hospitals, the social services, and in schools and universities (*Cooper, 1973*). The initial thrust of these developments was aimed at providing *individuals* within these settings the opportunity of enhancing their own self-awareness and potential. More recently there have been attempts to adapt these techniques to improve the *institutional environment* within

Reprinted by permission from *Interpersonal Development,* Vol. 5, 1974-75, pp. 71-77.

which these individuals function, on the assumption that this will, in addition to promoting organizational development, provide in the longer run, greater opportunities for individual personal growth (*Appley and Winter,* 1973). In higher education, in particular, there has been a significant movement in this direction. *Levine* (1973), for example, suggested that there should be more involvement and interdependency in the learning process within educational institutions, and strongly advocated the expanded use of experiential group techniques in these contexts. *Rogers* (1970) in his book "Encounter Groups" summed up the position for further innovation in the use of encounter groups and related methods in enhancing the teacher—student relationship: "in our schools, colleges, and universities, there is a most desperate need for more participation on the part of learners in the whole program, and for better communication between faculty and students, administrators and faculty, administrators and students. There have been enough experiments along this line so that we know it is perfectly feasible to improve communication in all these relationships, and it is nothing short of tragic that education has been so slow to make use of this new social invention."

Although the number of group work innovations in educational institutions is on the increase, very little empirical evidence is available to support these methods in these contexts. The research questions which need to be answered are: do encounter groups run for teachers and students improve communication and help develop a meaningful relationship between them? And if so, does this improved relationship create a better and more effective learning environment? It is the purpose of this study to attempt to provide some tentative answers to these questions.

METHODS

Subjects and Procedure

The subjects (Ss) were 60 university undergraduates. They were social science students, aged between 19 and 22. All Ss were enrolled in a course in social and organizational psychology, 36 in course A and 24 in course B. Both courses were taught by the same faculty member and contained the same content material. In A, the beginning of the course was organized so that the students and teacher spent a 24-hour period together in a marathon encounter group while course B had no such experience. In order to provide the teacher and his students with an intensive group experience, which it was hoped would enable them to develop a closer working relationship, it was decided that the training should be *massed* as opposed to *spaced*. That is, that the group experience should be held over a short but intensive period of time (i.e., 24 h) as opposed to 1-hour weekly meetings, since research (*Mitchell,* 1970; *Simmons,* 1972) seems to indicate that massed sessions are more effective than spaced. In addition, it was felt that the encounter group would then not be seen as just another course but an effort at team-relationship building. Course B was extended in class contact time to include additional group seminars, to compensate for the increased teacher-student time of course A due to the marathon encounter group. The teacher and students of both courses therefore had roughly an equal amount of actual contact time.

The encounter group employed in course A emphasized the development and improvement of interpersonal communication and relationship between the teacher and students through experiential processes, i.e., by using planned exercises to focus on helping and improving relationships, by emphasizing a here-and-now interpersonal process, by creating a climate of behavioral experimentation, and by sharing personal perceptions and experiences (*Rogers,* 1970). It should be noted that the encounter group was run by the teacher himself who was a trained group counsellor.

The Relationship Inventory

The Relationship Inventory (RI) (*Barrett-Lennard,* 1962) was selected as the instrument for securing study data on the nature of the relationship between the teacher and student. The Inventory is comprised of 64 items broken down into four scales; level of regard, empathy, unconditionality and congruence. The RI was given to course A and B students to assess their perception of their relationship with their teacher at the beginning and the end of the term of lectures. The RI was given to all students at the end of the third week of term and the encounter group was run several days later. In addition, the RI was adapted (third-person-plural form) to obtain the teacher's perception of his students.

The *level of regard* scale measures the degree to which the students experience the teacher as expressing a warm, positive and acceptant attitude toward him, e.g., "he respects me as a person," "I feel appreciated by him," "he cares for me." The *empathy* scale measures the extent to which the students perceive the teacher as sensing the feelings and personal meanings which the student himself is experiencing and trying to communicate, e.g., "he nearly always knows what I mean," "he realizes what I mean even when I have difficulty saying it," "he understands me." The *unconditionality* scale measures the degree to which the teacher not only accepts the student but does so without reservations, without evaluations, that is, the degree of unconditional positive regard, e.g., "I don't think that anything I say or do really changes the way he feels towards me," "how much he likes or dislikes me is not altered by anything that I tell him about myself," "his feeling toward me doesn't depend on how I feel toward him." And finally, the *congruence* scale assesses the degree to which the student perceives the teacher as genuine and without facade in his relationship to him/her, e.g., "I feel he is real and genuine with me," "he is willing to express whatever is actually in his mind with me, including any feelings about himself or about me," "I have not felt that he tried to hide anything from himself that he feels with me." Each scale contains 16 items, half of which are expressed positively and the other half expressed negatively in order to minimize acquiescence response set. A six-point Likert-type rating scale is used for each item. Theoretically, negative items are reversed and summated with positive ones and each S is assigned a single score for each scale. A constant of 48 was added to change the theoretical scoring limits from -48 to $+48$ to 0 to 96. Split-half and test-retest reliabilities for the RI scales are very high (*Barrett-Lennard,* 1962) and the RI has been extensively validated in a wide range of differing contexts (*Blumberg,* 1968; *Caracena and Vicory,* 1969; *Hollenbeck,* 1965).

RESULTS

Differences between pre (beginning of academic term) and post (end of term) test scores on each scale of the RI were tested by t tests for correlated

TABLE 6.13
MEANS AND T-VALUES FOR SIGNIFICANCE OF DIFFERENCES BETWEEN
PRE- AND POST-TEST RI SCORES FOR STUDENTS

Relationship Inventory Scales	Marathon encounter group				Control group			
	M pre	M post	t	p	M pre	M post	t	p
Level of regard	71.69	80.94	2.14	<0.05	73.75	74.62	<1.00	—
Empathy	62.31	69.06	1.67	0.10	65.66	63.00	<1.00	—
Unconditionality	67.50	67.37	<1.00	—	65.30	66.22	<1.00	—
Congruence	71.56	83.94	2.44	<0.02	69.82	71.24	<1.00	—

means for the marathon encounter and control Ss. The data are represented in Table 6.13.

First, it can be seen that there is no significant pre-test difference on the RI scale scores between the marathon and control group Ss, so that any significant change observed is not a function of initial score bias between experimental and controls. Second, it can be seen that the students who attended the marathon encounter group showed significant increases in their perceptions of their teacher on the *level of regard* (LR) and *congruence* (C) scales, and a movement in the direction of significance on the *empathy* (E) scale. No change was found on the *unconditionality* (U) scale. In contrast, no change for students' perception of their teacher was found on any of the RI scales for the control Ss.

If we examine the RI scale scores for the teacher, that is, his perceptions of his students on the four RI attributes, we find the same trend as in the student results for the marathon encounter group course, his pre- and post-test RI scores, respectively, were as follows: LR scale 64 and 85; E scale 58 and 70; U scale 61 and 59; C scale 57 and 67; for the control group: LR scale 65 and 67; E scale 60 and 61; U scale 58 and 54, and C scale 60 and 63. In summary, positive changes were observed on the LR, E, and C scales for the students in the marathon encounter group, but no improvement for the teacher in his relationships with the control group students on any of the RI scales.

DISCUSSION

It seems from this evidence that there is some relationship between intensive encounter group experiences among teachers and students and an improvement in the teacher-student relationship. Obviously, shared personal experiences between staff and students are only one way in which a better relationship can be created but it seems noteworthy that the responsibility for enhancing the relational climate must go beyond the confines of traditional classroom behavior and role relationships, as the control group results suggest. These results also help us to partly answer the second question posited at the beginning of this paper "does an improved teacher-student relationship create a better learning environment." From the voluminous data accumulated on the RI over the past 12 years, there is substantial evidence that an improvement in RI attributes can help to create a measurably more effective learning climate. For example, *Scheuer* (1971) found a significant gain in academic achievement level in disturbed and maladjusted pupils who saw their teachers as possessing a high degree of RI characteristics. *Mason and Blumberg* (1969) found that high-school students, who, judged by independent assessors to have *learned the most,* rated the perceived relational responses (RI) of their teachers significantly higher than those students judged to have *learned least. Emmerling* (1961) found among 600 pupils and 20 teachers that those teachers receiving high RI scores were also assessed as significantly more pupil-centered, more open to their experience, and more effective in the classroom as judged by the students themselves. These and other studies (*Van der Veen and Novak,* 1970) provide some rather convincing evidence of a link between the nature of the teacher-student relationship as measured by the RI and learning outcomes. While the results in this study are potentially useful, there are a number of points we should make about it. First, it seems fairly reasonable to expect that the more contact teachers and students have with one another the closer the relationship. We did to some extent control the gross amount of contact time between courses but it is obvious from the results that the *quality* of contact is likely to be more important. It might have been a better control, therefore, had we organized for course-B students to spend their additional teacher contact time in a "social" as distinct from a "classroom" setting. The impact of the encounter group experience could have been more clearly demonstrated. There is some evidence, however, that the relationship between frequency of "social" contact between people, and closer personal relationships, is to some extent a function of the size of the group (*Snortum and Myers,* 1971), that is, the larger the size of the group, the weaker the relationship. There is no compelling reason to expect, therefore, that additional "social" time in a group of 24 would have contributed significantly to RI attributes—it is open to investigation, however. Second, it is interesting to note that no change was found on the unconditionality scale. This might reflect the organizational reality that an "evaluative" relationship does and will continue to exist between the faculty member and particular students, which indeed is imposed on both in their respective roles within the university. *Mason and Blumberg* (1969) also found that unconditionality was the only non-predictive RI variable within their study. Third, it would have been more useful to have obtained some objective data on subsequent student performance among the subject population in this study. Within the UK context this presents some practical difficulties, for in English universities there is, in the vast majority of cases, no examination or grading system for individual courses. Students are assessed by their performance in examinations taken at the very end of their final year, which is meant to cover their whole performance during their 3 years at university. If we could have instrumented a specially designed examination of attainment test it would have presented, considering English university norms, other methodological difficulties. Since there is a great deal of evidence of the predictive validity of the RI it was felt that we should concentrate on change in relational variables.

In conclusion, higher education is undergoing a new and exciting period of experimentation and exploration of teaching techniques and methods of enhancing the learning community. Experiential group methods such as encounter and T-Groups for teachers and students is only one small development and as *Levine* (1973) suggests "a development toward a more relevant and active educational experience; and while they certainly do not constitute answers to all problems, they, nevertheless, represent a step forwards."

REFERENCES

Appley, D. G. and Winter, A. R.: T-Groups and therapy groups in a changing society (Jossey-Bass, San Francisco 1973).

Barrett-Lennard, G. T.: Dimensions of therapist response as causal factors in therapeutic change. Psycholog. Monogr. *76* (43) (1962).

Blumberg, A.: Supervisor behavior and interpersonal relations. Educat. Administr. Quart. pp. 34-45, Spring, 1968.

Caracena, P. F. and Vicory, J. R.: Correlates of phenomenological and judged empathy. J. couns. Psychol. *16:* 510-515 (1969).

Cooper, C. L.: Group training for individual and organizational development, pp. 40–67 (Karger, Basel 1973).

Emmerling, F. A.: A study of the relationship between personality characteristics of classroom teachers and pupil perceptions of these teachers. Unpublished PhD dissertation, Auburn University, 1961 (available University Microfilms, Ann Arbor, Mich.).

Hollenbeck, G. P.: Conditions and outcomes in the student-parent relationship. J. cons. Psychol. *29:* 237-241 (1965).

Levine, N.: Group training for students in higher education; in *Cooper* Group training for individual and organizational development, pp. 40- 67 (Karger, Basel 1973).

Mason, J. and Blumberg, A.: Perceived educational value of the classroom and teacher-pupil interpersonal relationships. J. second. Educat. *44:* 135-139 (1969).

Mitchell, R. R.: An evaluation of the relative effectiveness of spaced, massed, and combined sensitivity training groups in promoting positive behavior change. Dissert. Abstr. *29:* 4834 (1970).

Rogers, C.: Encounter groups (Allen Lane, London 1970).

Scheuer, A. L.: The relationship between personal attributes and effectiveness in teachers of the emotionally disturbed. Exceptional Children 723-731 (1971).

Simmons, R. C.: Intensity as a variable in programmed group interaction: the marathon. Dissertat. Abstr. *31:* 2494 (1972).

Snortum, J. R. and Myers, H. F.: Intensity of T-Group relationships as a function of interaction. Internat. J. Group Psychother. *21:* 190-201 (1971).

Van der Veen, F. and Novak, A. L.: Perceived parental attitudes and family concepts of disturbed adolescents, normal siblings, and normal controls. Inst. juv. res. J. *7*(3) (1970).

NAME INDEX

SUBJECT INDEX

THE BOOK MANUFACTURE

Sensitivity Training and the Laboratory Approach: Readings about Concepts and Applications, Third Edition, was set by Fox Valley Typesetting, Menasha, Wisconsin. Printing and binding were by George Banta. Cover design was by Charles Kling & Associates. The type is Times Roman with Helvetica display.